# Learning to Teach

**BILLIE J. ENZ**
ARIZONA STATE UNIVERSITY

**BETTE S. BERGERON**
ARIZONA STATE UNIVERSITY

**MICHAEL WOLFE**
KAPPA DELTA PI

KENDALL/HUNT PUBLISHING COMPANY
4050 Westmark Drive Dubuque, Iowa 52002

Book Team

Chairman and Chief Executive Officer   Mark C. Falb
Senior Vice President, College Division   Thomas W. Gantz
Director of National Book Program   Paul B. Carty
Editorial Development Manager   Georgia Botsford
Developmental Editor   Tina Bower
Vice President, Production and Manufacturing   Alfred C. Grisanti
Assistant Vice President, Production Services   Christine E. O'Brien
Project Coordinator   Angela Puls
Permissions Editor   Colleen Zelinsky
Designer   Jodi Splinter

Cover images courtesy Adobe and Getty Images.

Interior images © 2007 by JupiterImages, PhotoDisc, Stockbyte,
Creatas, Comstock, Eyewire and Banana Stock.

The authors would like to dedicate
this text to our parents,
our first and best teachers!

# Contents

## SECTION FIVE
# Teacher as Advocate   243

## CHAPTER NINE
# Advocacy in the Profession   245

## CHAPTER TEN
# Advocacy in the Classroom   269

# SECTION SIX
# Teacher as Artist   293

## CHAPTER ELEVEN
## How Do Teachers Grow Professionally?   295

## CHAPTER TWELVE
## Enhancing the "Art" of Teaching   313

# Preface

As we have discovered in our own classroom experiences, teaching is an exciting, rewarding, challenging, and complex career. It is also a career that we as authors feel personally and professionally passionate about, and therefore it is one that we are excited to share with our readers! In this text, we hope to capture the myriad facets of teaching, while offering our readers a "slice" of what this career holds both in and out of the classroom. We also hope to guide our readers in exploring the influences of history and society on teaching, learning, and schooling, and how these influences impact what we do in classrooms today. By understanding the people and events that have shaped our nation's history, we hope that our readers can better understand how to make decisions that will positively impact the learning experiences of all of their future students.

## Goal of the Book

This text is intended for courses that are exploring teaching as a career, or as part of introductory coursework in a teacher preparation program. It is divided into six sections, each with two chapters, to enable instructors to utilize the text over a one-semester period. We have designed the textbook to provide slices or glimpses into a variety of aspects of teaching, to promote discussion and encourage self-exploration. It is suggested that course experiences include opportunities for actual classroom observations, through designed field experiences or service learning, in order to fully engage the readers in the concepts presented and in their professional self-exploration. The concepts introduced in this text are intended to provide a foundation that will be enhanced through experiences and coursework that will be later embedded across a teacher preparation program.

It is our intent that each of the chapters in this text provide a descriptive "slice," upon which the readers and their instructors can continue to explore and dialogue together. Our goal is not to provide answers, but to challenge readers with questions and new ways of considering the profession. Through this exploration, we hope that our readers will learn more about what it takes to become an effective teacher, and how their own beliefs and experiences will guide and shape their own development.

## Section One: Teaching as a Multifaceted Career

In Section One, we introduce the reader to the multi-dimensional nature of the profession, and how teaching fits into the wider context and culture of schooling.

*Chapter One, The Role of Teaching within the Classroom,* introduces the reader to the complexities of teaching and offers a variety of definitions regarding teachers' multiple roles. Also included in this chapter is a brief exploration of our nation's history, with a focus on how people and events have shaped what we know today as schooling.

*Chapter Two, The Role of Teaching in the Educational Community,* takes a look at education in today's classrooms, and suggests elements of effective teaching and schools. Also described in this chapter are descriptions of roles reflective of a variety of school personnel, including those of paraprofessionals, department chairs, school administrators, and school boards, and how they interact with the role of the classroom teacher.

## Section Two: Teacher as Scientist and Scholar

This section looks at a very specific aspect of a teacher's role, as both a scientist and a scholar who understands how learning theory and philosophies impact instructional decisions within the classroom.

*Chapter Three, Understanding Learning Theories,* provides foundational knowledge into the Behaviorist, Cognitive, Constructivist, and Biological theories and the theorists who influenced their development. While understanding how these theories differ is addressed, also offered is how the theories shape our practices with students.

*Chapter Four, Understanding Educational Philosophy and Your Professional Beliefs,* provides an in-depth look into the classical educational philosophies and most prevalent teaching styles and their impact on learning. This chapter concludes by inviting the reader to explore a variety of careers in education, from early childhood education to special education, and how both science and scholarly knowledge have shaped these careers today.

## Section Three: Teacher as Craftsman

The focus of this section is on the definition and development of the "craft" of effective instruction.

*Chapter Five, What Makes a TeacherEffective* describes the characteristics and skills of effective teachers.

*Chapter Six, Examining Effective Teaching,* further develops these concepts by providing the reader with concrete examples of effective proactive management, lesson planning, and closures. Intertwined throughout this section is information regarding the knowledge, skills, and dispositions that effective teachers possess, and how these are identified in classroom practice.

## Section Four: Teacher as Politician

Section Four turns to the more current—and often controversial—aspects of the role of teachers in today's society.

*Chapter Seven, Politics in the School* introduces the reader to the critical role of teacher as politician. This chapter explores current "hot-button" issues, such as accountability, standards, standardized testing, and school funding, and encourages future teachers to consider how their own politics will affect their roles as teachers and leaders within the community.

*Chapter Eight, Politics in Your Community* delves into issues of religion, school choice, racial and gender equity, and home schooling. While teachers often hold very different views on these issues, the readers are asked to consider many facets of a community's politics, and how to best advocate for all students in their future classrooms.

## Section Five: Teacher as Advocate

This section considers how effective teachers can support and advocate for the needs of students and their families.

*Chapter Nine, Advocacy in the Profession* explores an additional aspect of advocacy, understanding one's own professional obligations. Issues such as teacher testing, professional associations, merit pay, and a teacher's legal obligations and liability are discussed.

*Chapter Ten, Advocacy in the Classroom* focuses on how understanding professional advocacy allows teachers to more effectively advocate for students and families. This chapter encourages dialogue on such topics as inclusion, bilingual education, ability grouping, and retention, and the impact of related policies on the success—or potential failure—of students.

# Section Six: Teacher as Artist

As we wrap up our look at the myriad "slices" of the teaching profession, we focus here on how teachers progress professionally from novice to veteran . . . and to artist.

*Chapter Eleven, How Do Teachers Grow Professionally?* This question is explored through a discussion on the phases of a teacher's growth cycle and induction programs that guide a novice into the professional career.

*Chapter Twelve, Enhancing the "Art" of Teaching,* takes a look at the National Board's Professional Teaching Standards, professional development, and organizations. Each of these provides teachers with the opportunity to continue to enhance their effectiveness and artistry, as they and their students grow and learn together.

# Pedagogy

In order to provide readers and instructors with a context for exploration, we have provided throughout this text a variety of "tools" to facilitate dialogue and interaction.

- A **Definition Box** begins each chapter, and contains definitions of terms that will be used in the chapter, in order to familiarize readers with some of the most common "jargon" of our profession.
- **Charts and figures** throughout the chapters enable readers to understand the content, compare and contrast ideas, and facilitate discussion.
- **Special Features,** written by leading educators and practitioners and related to chapter topics, offer different perspectives and "lenses" on the materials presented.
- **Classroom Glimpse** are vignettes that provide a glimpse into a variety of classrooms that span grade levels and content, and make the information more concrete for the reader.
- **Group Talk** suggestions, along with in- and out-of class activities, engage the readers with the material and with their peers.
- Many **activities** take the reader out into classrooms, where they observe and interview teachers, in order to reflect on best practices within their own communities.
- **Learn More About** . . . boxes provide in-depth information on important people in education.
- **Talking to Teachers** are insightful comments from real teachers about their motivation to teach. This insight can help readers realize what their true motivation is in joining the teaching profession.
- **Think About It** are questions posed to readers to aid them in personalizing the topics covered throughout each chapter.

Our goal is accessibility—both in terms of the material in this text, as well as within the individual reader who is questioning and learning along with all of us!

As authors, we are excited to share our text with you, and invite your comments and feedback as we engage in a dialogue together on those conditions and skills that define effective teaching in today's classroom. As teachers, we hope to share our passion and vision for our profession, and to guide the next generation of educators to understand the artistry, scholarship, and craftsmanship that lies within the heart of every teacher!

# Acknowledgments

We gratefully acknowledge the constructive criticism of the colleagues who provided reviews for individual chapters of this text. They include:

Harriet Arnold
University of the Pacific

John Bertalan
Hillsborough Community College

Jeanne Blevins
Chowan College

John Bruno
Florida State University

C. L. Bunton
Lake Land College

Darrol Bussler
Minnesota State University

Christy Carroll
Athens State University

Diane Craft
State University of New York – Cortland

Bola Delnao-Oriaran
St. Norbert College

Constance Golden
Marietta College

Dale Henze
University of Wisconsin – Platteville

Glenda Hernandez
Montgomery College

Dwight Holliday
Murray State University

Donna Irwin
Campbellsville University

Hal Jenkins, II
Mississippi University for Women

Gwen Traylor
Southeastern Louisiana University

Harold Waters
Southern Wesleyan University

# About the Authors

## Billie Enz

(Ph.D. Elementary Education) is the Associate Director of the Division of Curriculum and Instruction in the Mary Lou Fulton College of Education at Arizona State University. She is responsible for establishing professional development programs with local school districts. Dr. Enz is the author and co-author for several books on new teacher development and mentor training, including: *Trade Secrets for Primary and Elementary Teachers, Trade Secrets for Middle and Secondary Teachers; Ready, Set, Teach: A Blueprint for a Successful First Year, How To Win the Job You Want,* and *Life Cycle of the Career Teacher.*

Dr. Enz is a member of the Early Childhood faculty and teaches language and literacy courses. She has co-authored two textbooks in this area, *Teaching Language and Literacy: From Preschool to the Elementary Grades* and *Helping Young Children Learn Language and Literacy: From Birth through Preschool.*

## Bette S. Bergeron

(Ph.D. Language & Literacy) is currently the Associate Dean and Director of the School of Educational Innovation and Teacher Preparation at Arizona State University's Polytechnic campus. Dr. Bergeron's research interests include early literacy instruction, teacher preparation, and program assessment. Her research is applied in its focus, and seeks to address solutions to current issues in PreK-12 education.

Prior to joining the ASU faculty, Dr. Bergeron was a Professor of Education and Chair of Teacher Education at Purdue University Calumet in Hammond, IN. Dr. Bergeron earned her Master's and Doctorate degrees at Purdue University, and completed her undergraduate studies at the University of Maine. Dr. Bergeron entered the education profession as a second grade teacher in Veazie, Maine.

## Michael P. Wolfe

Dr. Michael P. Wolfe is Executive Director of Kappa Delta Pi, the 60,000+–member International Honor Society in Education. He is the fourth Executive Director of KDP and has served in that capacity since 1990.

Dr. Wolfe has been a public school teacher and program coordinator and has served as a professor of teacher education and administrator at Central Michigan University, Texas Christian University, and SUNY-Plattsburgh. He received a B.A. at Beloit College, an M.S. at the University of Wisconsin, and an Ed.D. at Arizona State University.

He has co-authored a book entitled *Critical Incidents in School Administration,* and he has co-authored book chapters entitled *The Future of Teacher Education and Models of Mentoring Practices in Teacher Education.* He is co-editor of the *Life Cycle of the Career Teacher, The Life Cycle of the Career Teacher in Practice, The Mission of the Scholar,* and *The Life Cycle of the Career Teacher in Practice* books.

# Teaching as a Multifaceted Career

You are considering teacher as a career? As former classroom teachers ourselves, we applaud you! We have found teaching—whether it is in a classroom of twenty-five second graders or forty college seniors—to be an outstanding and rewarding career path. It can also be the most frustrating and challenging profession that an individual could choose. So how do you decide? How do *you* know that you have what it takes to make a difference in the lives of K through 12 students?

In this book, we will "slice the apple," and explore the many complex roles of teaching, including the tools it takes to be successful with classroom planning (Section 1), how your own theories of education make a difference in what you teach and how you create your instruction (Section 2), characteristics of effective teachers and maximizing management and learning (Section 3), how current policies and politics might influence your decisions and tasks within your classroom (Section 4), how to best advocate for your students and your profession (Section 5), and how to grow both personally and professionally (Section 6). As these sections are "pared," we hope to show you that teaching is much more than imparting knowledge on willing and eager minds. *Effective* teaching requires a skillful balance of artistry and science, and the compassion of one who advocates for every child.

In this introductory section, we will explore the career of teaching as one that is multifaceted and multidimensional, and how this profession fits within the wider educational community. This section will include:

**Chapter One: The Role of Teaching within the Classroom**
- The Multifaceted Dimensions of Teaching: Looking Inside the Classroom
- Defining the Roles of a Classroom Teacher
- Teaching at the Turn of the Century
- History's Influence on the Role of Teaching
- Societal Changes and the Role of Teaching

**Chapter Two: The Role of Teaching in the Educational Community**
- Effective Teachers Today
- Parents and Schools
- What Makes Schools Effective?
- What about Schools at Risk?
- Keys to Effective Schools: School Personnel

# The Role of Teaching within the Classroom

# 1

While teaching in today's society is rich in its complexity, teaching has always been a multidimensional profession. Those dimensions, however, have changed over time as society and the role of education have transformed. But how significantly have the times altered the roles of teachers?

Take a moment to think about some of your previous classroom teachers. Which teachers were effective? Which were not? Why? What kinds of *roles* did the effective teachers assume that were different from those teachers that you felt were less effective? Was it simply a matter of personality and smarts—or something much more?

Also think about the different *tasks* that your teachers completed during the day. Perhaps you saw them collect and grade papers, lecture to the class about a new topic you were learning, circulate around the room while you were making chapter notes, or provide instructions as small groups of students collaborated on a special project. These instructional tasks are those that usually come to mind when we think of the "typical" role of a teacher. We've often heard that *teachers teach, and students learn.* If only it was as simple as that!

The process of getting to the point of learning requires a much more complex set of tasks or roles that occur "behind the scenes," out of view of the students. Let's take a look at what may be a typical day in the life of a classroom teacher. As you read through the following description, taken from our own experiences as teachers, think about the roles that a teacher plays throughout the day. Notice that little is included here regarding the actual instruction in the classroom—we'll be taking a very deep look at instruction throughout the remaining sections in this book. Instead, use this "slice" to focus on the *other* tasks that are expected from teachers throughout the day.

**Definitions**

**Certification**   typically issued by the state, this is the documentation that an individual has passed all of the state's requirements so that he/she can legally teach in a public K through 12 classroom. Certification rules usually include requirements for the completion of a degree, specific content that is to be included in the degree program, a practicum such as student teaching, and a state exam.

**Collective bargaining**   the process of negotiation between the representatives of organized workers, such as a union, and their employers to determine wages, hours, and working conditions. Collective bargaining is used in some states to draw up teachers' contracts.

**Content standards**   the material that is covered in subjects such as math, science, history, and language arts. Each state has established its own standards for each content area and each grade level, which guide what teachers are expected to teach in their curriculum. These standards are often assessed using state-wide exams.

**Corporal punishment**   the use of physical force, such as spanking, to punish students. The use of corporal punishment is considered by many educators to be inappropriate. However, many states still persist in allowing its use in schools under the supervision of school personnel.

**Endorsement**   a state certificate in a specialty area such as reading, bilingual education, special education, or gifted education. Endorsements are typically added onto a regular teaching certificate, and require additional coursework beyond the teacher's original certification area.

**Reading inventory**   an informal assessment tool used by teachers to determine the reading level of students. This typically involves reading short passages of increasing difficulty, and observing students' fluency and comprehension.

**Resource room**   a term most often associated with special education programs. Students are placed in resource rooms to receive specialized instruction, often with students with similar abilities. Resource rooms are not as common today, as most students with special needs are placed with their peers in regular education classrooms.

**Segregation**   the practice of separating students based on race, which led to the practice of establishing all-white and all-black schools. Segregation is now illegal in the United States, but was a critical issue in the emergence of civil rights during the 1950s.

## As you read, think about...

★ The period of education during which your grandparents and great-grandparents went to school. What stories have they told you about their high school years?

★ The life of an apprentice. What might it have felt like to leave your home as a young child to live and work with a tradesman?

## Focus Questions

★ What historical events had the greatest impact on present-day education?

★ Who are the philosophers, legislators, and educators that had the greatest impact on your schooling?

★ How did schooling differ by student gender and ethnic background?

## The Multifaceted Dimensions of Teaching: Looking Inside the Classroom

*Before school begins*–While your contract may determine the minimum time you are required to report at school, your day will typically begin much earlier if you are to prepare the lessons and activities to keep your students engaged all day. This is particularly true for novice teachers, who are often at school at least an hour before the students arrive. During this time, you may find yourself involved in many different tasks:

- You take the time to answer a few phone messages from parents who have called about homework assignments or who have questions about upcoming school events. One parent is irate about how a discipline issue was handled the previous day. You describe the incident to the parent, but also refer her to the principal for any further questions about the school's disciplinary policy.

- You check the Internet quickly to see if a requested article has been forwarded to you from the community library. The article has arrived! However, in scanning the text you note that it is probably above the comprehension level of your students. You highlight areas that are appropriate to share with students that most apply to your unit.

- You quickly scan your room, to make sure all of the day's supplies are out and ready.

- It is your turn for bus duty, and you watch to make sure that the students disembark safely. Some students go to the cafeteria for breakfast, while you must supervise others as they take a few minutes to play or socialize before the morning bell rings.

*During the morning*–As students file in for the day, you notice an unfamiliar face amongst your students. A call from the office confirms it–you have a new student. You pull a desk from the writing center into one of your student groups, and quickly assign a peer to give the new student a tour of the classroom. Other students have assumed their roles of taking attendance and lunch count. You collect and tally money for an upcoming field trip. It is time to begin your morning's instruction, which includes the following distractions and tasks:

- A student from the university arrives to observe your class; you invite him to read a book to the students while you give the new student a reading inventory so that you can get a quick check on her reading level.

- You keep track of the specialists' schedules, which this morning include sending John to speech, and Maria and Manuel to the bilingual teacher.

- You note that Stan is especially uncommunicative this morning. You suspect that he again has not eaten, and set aside some peanut butter and crackers for him to eat during break.

- It's your morning to use the technology lab, and you assist students in reviewing a new software program that they're learning as part of an ongoing activity to create a monthly newsletter. The paper will go home to parents and be shared with members of the school board.

- Two students begin fighting over a digital camera, which is being used to document class activities for the newsletter. You remind students to check the sign-out list for the camera, which successfully ends the dispute.

*During lunch*–While today you do not have cafeteria duty, and you actually have time to eat lunch, you have promised to meet with the special education lead teacher to discuss the progress of two of your students. You also use this lunch period to organize lessons for the afternoon. You are also involved in other organizational tasks:

- You write a note home to parents regarding the district's upcoming testing; you need to complete this at least a week in advance, to allow time for the school's community volunteer to translate the note into Spanish.

- You call the science museum to double-check that your upcoming field trip reservation has been received at their office.

**Classroom Glimpse**

**Classroom Glimpse**

- You set up the pendulum stands that you made the prior weekend in preparation of the afternoon's science lesson.

- As required in your school's improvement plan, you review the state content standards for math in preparation for a new unit on division.

- Ben comes in from lunch recess early, because he has scraped his knee. After a quick survey, you send him up to the office for an adhesive bandage.

*During the afternoon*–Your class grows in the afternoon, because the three students who are assigned to the resource room for the morning's reading lessons are included with their peers in the afternoon. The resource aide is in your classroom this afternoon to assist these students and to insure that they are on task. You have provided her with your lessons ahead of time, so that both of you are consistent in what you are instructing the children. Also occurring this afternoon:

- As students are completing their review assignment for math, you observe that Timon is having a great deal of difficulty with these concepts, but that Alison and Truda finish well before the rest of the class. You make a note to pull out some reinforcement activities for Timon to take home, and to speak to the school's math lead teacher to find some more challenging activities for the two girls.

- You also observe that Dennis has once again fallen asleep in class. You make a note to call home to see if something has occurred that has contributed to his fatigue at school.

- You monitor the children's experiments with the pendulum, after the class has made predictions based on the string length and pendulum weights.

- At the end of the day, you fill out a note to Ben's grandmother, who requested daily communication regarding his classroom behavior.

*After school*–Your day does not end when the final bells rings. Your responsibilities after school are varied; for example:

- You visit the school library to gather resources on your next unit, space. You are sure to select both non-fiction and fiction books, on a variety of reading levels. You'll review the books over the weekend to select those that will be most interesting to your students.

- You gather students' papers to review, which you will do later that evening.

- You attend a mandatory faculty meeting. As the curriculum chair, it's your responsibility to share your committee's recommendations regarding an upcoming textbook adoption with the rest of the faculty.

- After a very brief stop at home, you drive to the district office for your graduate curriculum course, where you are learning strategies for better adjusting your instruction to meet the needs of your students who are classified with learning disabilities. As part of your master's program, you will be earning an endorsement in special education. ■

# Defining the Roles of a Classroom Teacher

How many different roles did you identify in the vignette above? Perhaps you noted some of the following:

- Nurse
- Counselor
- Scientist
- Negotiator
- Collaborator
- Leader
- Student
- Mentor
- Advocate

Teachers assume many different roles throughout the school day.

In order to be effective, teaching requires an individual to play many different roles concurrently throughout the day.

- You need at times to *nurse* or *counsel* your students, so that they can have their basic needs met. If children are hungry or tired, for example, it will be very difficult from them to engage in learning.

- Regardless of the content that you teach, you are a *scientist* in that you are the knowledge expert and resource for your class. You are also a scientist in that you use research-based methods and strategies in your instruction, and learn how to use a variety of assessment data to continually adjust and improve your teaching.

- There are many ways in which you perform the role of *negotiator,* including settling disputes with students, dealing with irate or frustrated parents, and mediating between your own teaching peers.

- You also need to be a team player, and be a *collaborator* with a variety of professionals in your school so that children's needs are met.

- You also have a responsibility to your profession as a *leader* and *mentor,* to insure that new teachers are well prepared for the classroom and have access to the most appropriate curriculum materials and instructional strategies.

- You need to *advocate* for children, and adjust your lessons so that they are appropriate for the variety of learning styles and abilities in your class.

## Group Talk

Reread the vignette above, *Looking Inside Today's Classroom*. As you read, highlight what you see as different roles that this teacher may be playing. List these roles in the margin of your text.

In your group, create a chart to tally all of the roles that you have individually highlighted (see Figure 1.1, below).

■ Which roles are most common amongst your group members?

■ Which roles do you find the most surprising? Why?

■ Which roles do you feel *most* prepared for?

■ Which roles are you *least* prepared for?

As a group, sketch out an action plan to help you prepare for those most difficult roles.

| Figure 1.1 ↓ Role Discussion Chart | Most Common | Most Surprising | Most Prepared | Least Prepared |
|---|---|---|---|---|
| Role 1: | | | | |
| Role 2: | | | | |
| Role 3: | | | | |
| Role 4: | | | | |
| Role 5: | | | | |
| Role 6: | | | | |
| Role 7: | | | | |
| Role 8: | | | | |
| Role 9: | | | | |
| Role 10: | | | | |
| Role 11: | | | | |
| Role 12: | | | | |

**Action Plan:** Describe below how your group would address the role that you feel least prepared for in teaching.

• In order to continue to grow professionally, and to find the most effective ways to address the needs of your class, you also need to be a *student* yourself. Effective teachers are the models for "life-long learning."

## Teaching at the Turn of the Century

In the previous section, we explored some of the non-instructional roles and duties of today's classroom teachers. However, these roles and tasks have substantially changed over time. How have the roles of teachers changed? How do these changes impact teachers today?

The vignette below is taken from an interview with one of the author's great-grandmother, Helen, who grew up on an island off the coast of Maine. Much has changed in our society since the beginning of the twentieth century, and those changes have also affected the education profession. As you read the vignette, think about how the roles of the teachers at this one-room schoolhouse differed—and are similar to—the roles of teachers today.

**Classroom Glimpse**

The original schoolhouse was built by my great-grandfather as a religious meeting-house. Grandfather built it in the center of the island, so everyone would have an equal distance to travel. Before my day, they'd have school in someone's home on the island, because there were very few children. After the meeting house was built, and children kept increasing, the town asked my grandfather if he'd be willing to hold school there. When I was a child, there were 35 children on the island who went to school. Sometimes there'd be strangers of different nationalities that would come on the island. They'd set up camps, where they would chop and sell wood. The children of these laborers would also come to our school.

On the first day of school, I always rushed to the schoolhouse to get a window seat. I liked to watch the squirrels, and the birds. Once and a while a person would go by, which was quite an event out there in those woods. But usually, before the term ended, I was down a long ways from the window. The teacher would find out that I was just looking to see what was going on outside, and not paying attention. Our first desks were homemade and wooden. And then we got metal ones, similar to the desks they have today, although we had inkwells in the top. The teacher sat up on a platform beside a long bench, where sometimes she'd make the children sit.

It was pretty cold in the winter, there in the middle of the woods. We had a stove in the classroom down front, with a pipe that went to the back of the classroom. It kept us pretty warm, though on the coldest days, the teacher would let everybody sit down front. Whoever got to the schoolhouse first in the morning would build a fire. When my brothers got big enough, they would rush to school in the morning to build that fire. They made it so hot, the stove would turn red.

Our teacher would have students anywhere from subprimary to the ninth grade. There'd be two or three in each class, and she had to have the studies for all of the children. Sometimes, the teacher would have the older classes help the younger children. First thing in the morning, we'd take turns reading a verse from the Bible, and then had a prayer. Our school subjects were reading, writing, arithmetic, English, geography, and history. There seemed to be much more emphasis on our reading, spelling, and writing, because we had those subjects twice a day. While the teacher was with one class, the rest of us were doing things on the board. We didn't have music, art, or physical education, though one of our later teachers would have us do exercises.

We had our books for all of subjects. Usually, in our geography class, we would have to draw pictures of the maps of different places. I enjoyed geography, because I liked to study about the different lands, the people, and their occupations. And I usually stood at the head of my class in spelling bees. However, the only thing in our English books that interested me was learning the parts of speech, because our book would use poetry verses to learn nouns, verbs, and adverbs. That's what got me interested in poetry. But I was so frustrated—I would get one verse of a poem, and had absolutely no idea what the rest of the poem was. So I vowed to myself that, when I got older, I would hunt up the rest of those poems.

Most of our teachers were from the island. Usually, our teachers were young unmarried women, who might have had just a ninth-grade education themselves. We had some good teachers. We had one or two we didn't care for, but most of them were really awfully good. Those teachers would try very hard, and they had a lot of patience. The only thing was, I was a daydreamer. I didn't think education would do me a bit of good. Now I wish I had paid more attention. ■

**Think About It**

How much has really changed in a century of American schooling? Understanding schools and teaching today can be enhanced by understanding what occurred in our recent past. While most schools are heated by more than woodstoves, and desks no longer have functioning inkwells, what *substantial* changes have been made to teaching?

## Figure 1.2 ↓ A Century of Schooling

| | Turn of the Twentieth Century | Turn of the Twenty-First Century |
|---|---|---|
| **Facility** | • Building shared by religious and other community groups<br>• Maintenance is the responsibility of teachers and students<br>• Student desks have inkwells<br>• Teacher's desk is raised and in a prominent spot in the classroom | • Building shared by religious and other community groups<br>• Maintenance is the responsibility of specialized staff<br>• Student desks have computer ports<br>• Teacher's desk is integrated into the classroom |
| **Teachers** | • Little or no training is required<br>• Teaches are typically female and unmarried<br>• *Teachers are caring and patient* | • Extensive training and certification are required<br>• Teachers represent diverse backgrounds<br>• *Teachers are caring and patient* |
| **Students** | • *Students represent multiple abilities*<br>• *New immigrants are included in schools*<br>• *Students are grouped by age and/or ability*<br>• *Peer tutoring is encouraged*<br>• *Students work in groups and independently*<br>• Multi-age groups are often used | • *Students represent multiple abilities*<br>• *New immigrants are included in schools*<br>• *Students are grouped by age and/or ability*<br>• *Peer tutoring is encouraged*<br>• *Students work in groups and independently*<br>• Multi-age groups are sometimes used |
| **Curriculum** | • Instruction includes reading, writing, arithmetic, English, geography, and history<br>• Daily routines include Bible study and prayer<br>• *Curriculum emphasizes reading, writing,* and spelling<br>• *Textbook use is prevalent*<br>• Curriculum standards are not adopted<br>• Fine arts and PE instruction are not included | • Instruction includes reading, writing, mathematics, language arts, social studies and science<br>• Bible study and prayer are not allowed in public schools<br>• *Curriculum emphasizes reading, writing,* and mathematics<br>• *Textbook use is prevalent*<br>• Standards guide curriculum and testing<br>• Fine arts and PE instruction are included |

**Inside Classrooms: A Closer Look**   One very substantial change relates to the *preparation* of teachers. While a century ago it was acceptable to employ teachers with little or no formal training, whose educational levels were no higher than their oldest students, the profession today recognizes that substantial preparation in academic content and methods of teaching, intensive practice with a mentor teacher, and formal *certification* are required prior to entering the classroom. Figure 1.2 outlines the additional differences—and similarities—between schooling a century ago and what occurs in classrooms today (similarities are italicized). What other comparisons can you add to this chart?

## Influential Educators

Without question, many of the roles and tasks of teachers have changed throughout the history of our nation. In part, these changes are rooted in the political systems that founded public education. Some changes are directly the result of contributions made by prominent historical figures. Some individuals who have been particularly important in shaping our educational system include:

- *Benjamin Franklin (1706–1790)*   Though most known as his role in founding our nation's democracy, Franklin also conceptualized the American Academy, which focused on the utilitarian needs of a new nation. These private academies emphasized a practical curriculum, eliminated religion from instruction, and were partially funded by the public.

- *Johann Heinrich Pestalozzi (1746–1827)*   Swiss educator who supported the role of education as an agent to improve society. Pestalozzi supported the role of students' natural playfulness and curiosity in school, and recommended that teachers use concrete experiences in their instruction. He also introduced the idea of teacher training.

- *Noah Webster (1758–1843)*   The early American author of the "Blue-Backed Speller" and American Dictionary of the English Language, who believed that schools should impose order and virtue.

- *Friedrich Froebel (1782–1852)*   European educator who is regarded as the founder of kindergarten. His system of early education combined physical, moral, and intellectual training.

- *Horace Mann (1796–1859)*   Often viewed as the founder of the "common school," this nineteenth-century legislator convinced taxpayers to support a public education system. Mann viewed schools as a springboard for opportunity and an institution that could equalize differences between people. Mann also prompted the creation of "normal schools" where teachers were trained for the classroom; this support eventually led to the establishment of teaching certification. Some historians considered Mann to be the founder of our nation's public education system.

- *Alfred Binet (1857–1911)*   A French educator who assisted in the development of an intelligence test at the turn of the twentieth century. The original test was designed to predict learners' likelihood of success in the classroom. However, these tests were also used to determine what courses students were recommended to take and, in some instances, affected how teachers interacted with their students.

- *Booker T. Washington (1858–1915)*   A contemporary of Du Bois (below), Washington supported the establishment of agricultural schools for African Americans that focused on practical, hands-on learning. Washington accommodated the segregation of African Americans and whites in school, which contrasted with the views of Du Bois.

- *John Dewey (1859–1952)*   A prominent educational leader, Dewey supported teachers' use of problem-solving techniques and accommodations to children's individual differences. Dewey believed that it was more important for students to learn how to think, instead of memorizing specific items of information.

- *W. E. B. Du Bois (1868–1963)*   Du Bois has the distinction of being the first African American to earn a doctorate, and advocated for equal access to schools at every level. He also focused on the academic training of the top ten percent of African American students, who he hoped would become leaders. Du Bois helped to establish the NAACP, which paved the way for the modern civil rights movement.

Of course, the most influential educators have always been those who have had the most impact on children's learning and success—the teachers themselves. However, what these teachers do in the classroom often does echo from those who have preceded us. Figure 1.3

**Figure 1.3 ↓ Historical Contributions**

### Historical Contributions to Our Educational System

| Educator | Impact Today |
|---|---|
| Benjamin Franklin | • Public-supported education<br>• Course choices in secondary schools<br>• Vocational preparation |
| Johann Heinrich Pestalozzi | • Hands-on learning<br>• Teacher preparation programs |
| Noah Webster | • Instructional textbooks<br>• Character development |
| Friedrich Froebel | • Early childhood education<br>• Kindergarten |
| Horace Mann | • Tax-supported public education<br>• Teacher certification |
| Alfred Binet | • Standardized testing<br>• Tracking by ability |
| Booker T. Washington | • Vocational education<br>• Experiential learning |
| John Dewey | • Problem-based learning<br>• Accommodations for individual differences |
| W. E. B. Du Bois | • Desegregated schools<br>• Equal access for all students |

overviews the contributions of some of these predecessors; how else have these, and other educators, influenced what occurs in today's classrooms?

## History's Influence on the Role of Teaching

While the previous section of this chapter introduced you to a very brief overview of the evolution of public schooling, the history of education in America is actually quite complex. It intertwines the beliefs of millions of people—from many different cultures, countries, religious beliefs, and socioeconomic backgrounds—that came to this country to seek a better life. In the following section, we have provided a more complete overview of the history of education in America, which demonstrates how children and adolescents are schooled as a reflection of the social context of the time. The social context reflects the dominant cultures, religious affiliation, and the economic and practical realities of life in a particular time period. In addition to the larger social contexts, individuals have also made significant impact on educational systems by proposing (and sometimes imposing) educational reforms and legislation.

It must be remembered that this is a brief overview of American education history. Numerous research articles and books have been devoted to each educational period and to

This section has included some of the influential educators of the past. However, many individuals have made very recent and significant contributions to schooling today.

In your group, brainstorm contemporary educators that have changed schooling in America—both those who have improved it and those that your group believes have limited educational progress. On the following chart (Figure 1.4), list these individuals and how they have contributed to the roles and tasks of teachers today.

**Group Talk**

■ Who has made the most significant *positive* impact?

■ Who has made the most significant *negative* impact?

■ What changes do you anticipate will occur in education within the next decade? The next century?

**Figure 1.4 ↓ Contemporary Educators**

**Contemporary Contributions to Our Educational System**

| Educator | Impact Today |
|---|---|
| 1. | • <br> • <br> • |
| 2. | • <br> • <br> • |
| 3. | • <br> • <br> • |
| 4. | • <br> • <br> • |
| 5. | • <br> • <br> • |

the individuals who have been highlighted in this section. However, the purpose of this overview is to illustrate the evolution of the educational system and the factors that influenced these changes. This section is organized into five time periods:

• The Colonial Period (1600–1776)

• The Early National Period (1776–1840)

• Common School Period (1840–1880)

• Progressive Period (1880–1920)

• Modern Period (1920–present)

It is important to remember that education has not always been an ingrained part of the American lifestyle. When America was first being settled, the colonists brought with them whatever form of education was practiced in their homeland. This mixture of systems eventually melded together into what we now recognize as the American education system.

**Box 1.1    ↓ Hornbook**

*The Hornbook* was used by school children for several centuries, starting in the mid-fifteenth century, in Europe and America. The hornbook consisted of a wooden paddle with lessons tacked on and covered by a piece of transparent horn. The wooden paddle was about three inches by five inches with an easy-to-hold handle. A hole was put in the handle so a leather thong could be tied to it and the child could carry it on his/her belt or around his/her neck.

The lessons consisted of different combinations of the following things: the alphabet, vowel and consonant combinations, the Lord's Prayer, a form of a cross, and a praise of the Trinity. These were hand-written on a piece of parchment, then tacked to the wooden paddle. The horn was then tacked on over the lessons to keep the lessons from being soiled by the child. The horn of oxen and sheep were used to make the laminating structure. As time went on, hornbooks were also made of a variety of other materials. They were made from ivory, various metals, leather, and cardboard. They ranged from a plain, whittled type to those that were carved, tooled, embossed, and engraved.

Source: www.nd.edu/~rbarger/www7/hornbook.html

As you think back to early 1600s, where this history begins, it is important for you to remember that the simple harsh realities of life made education a luxury instead of a priority. For a long time, the majority of schooling was accomplished by teaching the basics of reading, writing, arithmetic, and religion to young children in a one-room schoolhouse. Since school attendance was not required due to the conditions of rural life in the colonies, only about one out of every 10 children actually went to school. (Mondale, 2002)

## The Colonial Period (1600–1776)

The history of American education begins with the Puritans. Leaving Europe seeking religious freedom, Puritans stripped away the traditional trappings and formalities of Christianity that had been slowly building throughout the previous 1500 years. Theirs was an attempt to "purify" the church and their lives. The Puritans believed that the Bible was God's true law, and that it provided a plan for living. The doctrine of predestination kept all Puritans constantly working to do good in this life to be chosen for the next eternal one. God had already chosen who would be in heaven or hell, and each believer had no way of knowing which group they were in.

According to the Puritans' beliefs, "those who were wealthy were obviously blessed by God and were in good standing with Him. The Protestant work ethic was the belief that hard work was an honor to God, which would lead to a prosperous reward. Any deviations from the normal way of Puritan life met with strict disapproval and discipline. Since the church elders were also political leaders, any church infraction was also a social one. There was no margin for error, as the devil was behind every evil deed. Sermons of hell fire and brimstone flowed from the mouths of eloquent ministers as they warned of the persuasiveness of the devil's power." (Barger, 2004) Children were quizzed on the material of the sermons at school and at home. Religiously motivated, Puritans had an exceptional interest in the education of their children, since reading the Bible was necessary to living a pious life. The education of the next generation was important to further "purify" the church and perfect social living. (Ornstein & Levine, 1993)

For the first time in history, free schooling was offered for all children. Puritans formed the first formal school in 1635, called the Roxbury Latin School. Four years later, the first American College, Harvard, was established in Cambridge. Children aged six to eight years old

---

**Box 1.2  ⬇ New England Primer**

*The New England Primer* (1690-1800s). Following a tradition of combining the study of the alphabet with Bible reading, the Primer introduced each alphabet letter in a religious phrase and then illustrated the phrase with a woodcut. The primer also contained a catechism of religious questions and answers. Emphasis was placed on fear of sin, God's punishment, and the fact that all people would have to face death. Here are some examples of alphabet rhymes that teach moral values as well as reading:

A  In Adam's Fall we sinned all.

B  Thy Life to Mend this Book Attend.

C  The Cat doth play and after slay.

D  A Dog will bite a Thief at night.

E  An Eagle's flight is Out of sight.

F  The Idle Fool is whipt at School.

Source: www.nd.edu/-rbarger/www7/neprimer/html

attended a "Dame school" where the teacher (usually a widow) taught children their alphabet, numbers, and prayers while she went about her daily household tasks. This instruction was typically accomplished through the use of the hornbook and, later, the New England Primer.

After young boys age 6 through 8 years completed their education at the Dame school, they were able to read, write and do sums (math). By age nine, their parents had determined their destiny—typically one of three options. Wealthier parents often considered their son's attendance at a Latin School, which had college preparatory courses, which most often led to an occupation in the ministry. As a second choice, boys could be trained at home in the occupation of their father. This had obvious benefits and required no extra cost to the family. The third option, apprenticeship, often required monthly payments to the craftsman who served as employer. Apprenticeships gave opportunity to spur on economic growth in a twofold process. The craftsman received much-needed help in his work, and children were prepared to continue the skills of business in the succeeding generation. (Haubrich & Apple, 1975)

**Apprenticeships**  Apprenticeship was a system of on-the-job training. England systematized the training and, in 1601, "The Poor Law" was transferred to the American Colonies. The Poor Law taxed the land owners in each parish, and part of these funds created an apprenticeship for children of the poor or disabled to work with skilled craftsmen (their living expenses were paid by the tax). The parish could expect to benefit from the child when they had grown up and learned a new skill. Boys were apprenticed to a master until they were twenty-four years old. If a girl could be found an apprenticeship, she would work with her mistress until she was twenty-one. "As an apprentice, a boy lived with a craftsman and was employed doing the menial tasks of the trade. Over time, the young man was to have learned all of the duties and be able to begin his own business. Along the way, his "master" was also to have educated him in the matters of faith. As the practice of apprenticeship grew, provisions began to be recorded in writing to ensure adequate living accommodations for the child. By 1647, the practice expanded to include girls, though they were given the privilege only because they were poor or orphaned." (Barger, 2004)

The system of apprenticeship, as a whole, was highly individualistic. Each parent or guardian "struck a deal" with the craftsman that then dictated the life of the child. By the mid-1770s, several laws had been enacted to help protect the rights of the child, but that did not preclude difficulties. For example, Benjamin Franklin was apprenticed to his older brother in the printing business and was promised a small salary. The idea was Benjamin's father's, but the elder son did not appreciate the help. In time, the older brother became jealous of Benjamin's literary talents, and began to beat him. Benjamin eventually abandoned his position and sought his own future in Philadelphia. (Rury, 2004)

Early colonial life did give rise to two important school reforms: Latin Grammar Schools and the Academy:

1. *Latin Grammar Schools.* In the early 1600s, Puritan communities were concerned with making sure that they would have an adequate supply of ministers for ever-expanding townships. This concern led to the establishment of Latin Grammar Schools (equivalent of today's high school). These schools were designed for the sons of property-owning citizens who believed their sons were destined for leadership positions in church, state, or courts. These schools focused on the study of Latin, Greek and religious studies. The purpose of these Grammar Schools was to prepare the boys for the entrance test for Harvard College.

2. *The Academy.* Most likely based on his experience, Benjamin Franklin developed the concept of academies in 1751. These schools were considered more practical than the Latin Grammar Schools since they focused the curriculum more on subjects that could be directly related to the students' adult lives and eliminated religion studies. Franklin also opened the Academies to young women. Prior to the academies, girls were only allowed to attend Dame schools when they were young.

**Politics in the Colonial Period**   Just as it does today, policy and legislation played a major role in shaping American education. "The earliest education laws dealt with the actual expectation that all children should receive schooling. Schooling—at least enough to read the Bible—was thought to protect the child from Satan's influence. The following two laws were critical to the evolution of the early American education system:" (Barger, 2004)

1. *Massachusetts Education Laws of 1642.* The Law stated that parents/masters were responsible for children's basic education and literacy. All children, including servants, should be able to demonstrate competency in reading and writing as outlined by the governing officials. It was believed that if all citizens could understand the written language on some basic level, all citizens would be able to understand and therefore abide by the governing laws of the land. The law also warned that if parents/masters grew lax in their responsibility, it would be the government's right to remove the child from the home and place him or her in a place where he or she could receive adequate instruction.

2. *The Law of 1647,* also known as the Old Deluder Satan Act, further evolved the 1642 law. Fearful that parents/masters would not teach children how to read the Bible—hence the children in their care would fall prey to the evils of Satan—the colonists required that towns of fifty families hire a schoolmaster who would teach children to read and write. Towns of a hundred families must have a grammar schoolmaster who could prepare children to attend Harvard College. When education became more of the community's social responsibility, as opposed to the individual family, the institution of public education was born. Teachers, or schoolmasters as they were called, were formally hired and paid for the sole purpose of teaching the townships' young people.

## The Early National Period (1776-1840)

As the Revolutionary War changed the political and social make-up of the nation, it also changed its educational system. Following the Revolutionary War, the schools of America changed through a series of events including land expansion, population growth, and a philosophical shift from religious to nationalistic curriculum. (Parkerson & Parkerson, 2001) However there were still tremendous regional differences based on social, cultural, geographical, and economic factors

- The New England Colonies focused on compulsory public education—wanting all capable children to attend school to be educated to become good citizens.

- The Middle Colonies focused on parochial education—schools were primarily for educating the children of wealth to become leaders in the church, state, or law.

- The Southern Colonies, due to the rural nature of their community, did not require compulsory education. Most education was offered through apprenticeships.

But how would this new nation pay for the education of its children? Under the Articles of Confederation, Congress did not have the power to raise revenue by direct taxation of the inhabitants of the newly founded United States. Therefore, the immediate goal of the Land Ordinance of 1785 (see below) was to raise money through the sale of land in the largely unmapped territory west of the original colonies, which were acquired from Britain at the end of the Revolutionary War. The following Land Ordinances provided both the manner to raise and collect money, it also provided for free public education.

- *The Land Ordinance of 1785* laid the foundations of land policy in the United States of America until passage of the Homestead Act in 1862. The Land Ordinance established the basis for the Public Land Survey System. Land was to be systematically surveyed into square townships, six miles on a side. Each of these townships was sub-divided into thirty-six sections of one square mile or 640 acres. These sections could then be further subdivided for sale to settlers and land speculators. The ordinance was also significant for establishing a mechanism for funding public education. The sixteenth section in each township was reserved for the maintenance of public schools. Many modern schools today still are located in section sixteen of their respective townships, although a great many of the school sections were sold to raise money for public education.

- *Northwest Ordinance of 1787.* This legislation detailed how the citizens of newly acquired land could petition for statehood. The ordinance allowed for the creation a civil government in the territory under the direct jurisdiction of the Congress. The Northwest Ordinance also established basic civil rights that foreshadowed the development of the Bill of Rights. Of particular interest is Article 3 of the ordinance, which reads in part:

 *Religion, morality, and knowledge being necessary to good government and the happiness of mankind, schools and the means of education shall forever be encouraged.*

Through these Acts, the new United States Congress had now articulated the role of public education in this new government. Schools were viewed as the mechanism for helping the population become good citizens, and good citizens were considered as necessary to build a strong government. The public school system was now part of the laws of a new country.

As settlers established homes in the new territories, the need for schooling dramatically increased. However, educating the expanding frontiers and the massing populations in the cities of the East posed logistical challenges. Dame Schools were no longer sufficient to manage the ever-growing numbers. ( Rippa, 1996; Altenbaugh, 2002) This new challenge led to the development of the Lancastrian Monitorial system (see Figure 1.5).

### Figure 1.5 ↓ Lancastrian System

*The Lancastrian Monitorial Schools* dominated the American school system from 1806 to the 1840s. Developed by Joseph Lancaster to provide an inexpensive form of public education, the system was designed to allow a single schoolmaster to teach a great number of students. The students would all be in a single large lecture hall where the teacher would give instruction to the whole group. The system was driven by an intellectual hierarchy—more advanced students had the responsibility of assisting in teaching those students below them, and so on down the line until virtually everyone within the system had a hand in the teaching process. In addition, several students would act as monitors to provide crowd control. "Though Lancaster's concept of teaching in this manner was theoretically sound, it depended on the abilities of a strong teacher—unfortunately, competent teachers were hard to find during this time. While the Lancastrian school system was able to offer an education at a quarter of the price of the private schools, given the vast number of students that were involved, monitorial teaching was not the success that Lancaster had hoped for." (Barger, 2004)

Another challenge during this period focused on the curriculum in higher education. What should the college student study? The growing concern about the question of curriculum in higher education was in large part due to the beginning industrial revolution and the increase in agriculture in the period of the nineteenth century. Advocates for change believed that college should prepare a man to make a living and believed that curriculum should be relevant to growing and changing demands of commerce, industry, and agriculture. Proponents for change suggested that the curriculum should offer vocational options. The other side of the debate was the view that traditional curriculum—philosophy, theology, history and languages—should prevail. In the Yale Report of 1828, leaders at Yale University concluded that the four disciplines of classical education would: (Barger, 2004)

1. *Act in a manner of parental control.* This discipline would enable the educated man to act in an appropriate manner in the absence of supervision.

2. *Provide a man with mental discipline* that would help a man make it through the difficult times.

3. *Vigorously exercise a man's mental faculties.* This discipline would make a man think not only about the why of the problem but also the how.

4. *Form a proper character.* This discipline would make a man a gentleman.

Advocates for traditional curriculum believed that exercising the mind and providing a general foundation common to all was more important than providing specialized education for a particular profession. Despite the strength of the leaders of Yale University, the curriculum reforms emerged by the end of the nineteenth century. (Webb, 2005) How have these debates in the 1800s influenced your college curriculum today?

**Educating Women**    Throughout the previous Colonial period, girls were not precluded from learning how to read. In fact, there was a great expectation that they would be able to read well enough to understand the Bible. However, beyond childhood there was virtually no expectation that young women would continue their education. In the mid-1700s, Benjamin Franklin's Academies did offer opportunities for young women to attend. But by the early 1800s, several societal trends contributed to a rise in demand for the education of women, including higher education. (Harper, 1970) These reasons included:

- *The expansion of the growth of the common public school system* created a desire for further learning—particularly girls who had not been able to attend the more expensive seminaries. With the growth of this system of common schools, there was a simultaneous increase in the demand for teachers. As employment opportunities in elementary and secondary schools grew, higher education for women became more acceptable. Interestingly, women were increasingly considered as better teachers and women were less expensive than men to employ; one historian writes that throughout the 1800s, "the salaries of the men teachers were quite commonly from two to four times those paid to women."

- *The proliferation of literature for women,* promoted women's literary interests and motivation to read. Moreover, the invention of the gas light and improved oil lamps were making it possible to use the evening hours for reading.

- *An increase in women's leisure time,* as the industrial revolution brought with it more domestic labor-saving devices, such as the cook stove and sewing machine, which gave women more time to read and study.

The greatest impact was the aftermath of the Civil War. The 1870 census revealed at least one woman in each of its identified 338 classified occupations, though ninety-three percent of all women workers fell into the following seven categories: domestic service, agricultural laborers, seamstresses, milliners, teachers, textile mill workers, and laundresses. So, while women were working, the range of fields in which they were employed was limited. (Pulliam & Van Patten, 2002)

The development of private secondary schools for young women, called "seminaries," began in the early 1800s. Several women's colleges were founded during the mid- to late nineteenth century in response to a need for advanced education for women at a time when they were not admitted to most institutions of higher education. Independent nonprofit women's colleges, which included Mount Holyoke and other similar institutions, were founded to provide educational opportunities to women equal to those available to men. A powerful proponent of women's higher education during the first part of the nineteenth century was Mary Lyon. (See Box 1.3)

## Box 1.3   ↓ Biographical Sketch: Mary Lyon

Mary Lyon's education began at age four in the village of Buckland, Massachusetts. When the school was moved three years later to a more distant location, she left her family and lived for the school term with relatives. She did chores to pay for her room and board. Mary Lyon was fortunate—girls could attend school year round. The school year was typically ten months long and divided into winter and summer terms. In some towns, girls could only attend during the summer, when boys were needed to do farm work. During winter, girls were forced to sit on the school steps, hoping to catch bits of the teacher's lessons.

In 1814, at age seventeen, Mary was offered her first teaching job. At the time, teachers needed no formal training—simply being an excellent student qualified one to teach. Female teachers were especially in demand due to a growth in population and large numbers of men moving west in search of better opportunities. Her job paid seventy-five cents a week, far less than the ten dollars to twelve dollars a month a man received to teach. As was the custom of the day, Lyon "boarded" in her students' homes—an arrangement that meant moving from family to family on a weekly basis.

Meanwhile, private female academies, often called seminaries, were springing up in New England. However, women of modest means, like Mary, could not afford the tuition. Further, the curricula of these schools focused on home crafts and humanities—far less challenging courses than at the men's schools where men studied geometry, science, and Latin.

As Mary's knowledge and reputation grew, she continued to teach throughout Massachusetts. Over the next twenty years, she became an authority on the education of women and gained experience in managing schools. Motivated by her own struggles to obtain an education, she was determined to open a seminary that focused on preparing women to become teachers. She crusaded tirelessly for funds and support. Writing advertisements detailing her plans for the school, Mary persuaded prominent men to back her enterprise. Though she endured ridicule, Mary never wavered in her belief that women deserved to have the same opportunities for higher education as men. (Banning, 1965) Mary Lyon's innovations included:

- Low tuition to make education affordable to students from modest backgrounds. Mount Holyoke's was sixty dollars a year.
- Rigorous entrance examinations to make sure students were adequately prepared.
- Domestic work by students to keep operating expenses and tuition low.
- Independence. Mary didn't affiliate with a religious denomination or wealthy sponsor. Instead, she formed a Board of Trustees, a group of dedicated male supporters who donated their time to help Mount Holyoke thrive and succeed.

Source: www.mtholyoke.edu/marylyon/intro.html

**The Emergence of Textbooks** In 1833, with the advent of common school, a small publishing company, Truman & Smith became interested in the idea of developing a series of potentially profitable school texts. Truman & Smith selected Rev. William Holmes McGuffey to develop the moralistic series, known popularly as "The McGuffey Readers." These widely used texts included the following readers, or books: (Barger, 2004)

- This first reader of 1841 introduced children to McGuffey's ethical code. The child modeled in this book is prompt, good, kind, honest, and truthful.
- The second reader outlined history, biology, astronomy, zoology, botany, table manners, behavior toward family, attitudes toward God and teachers, and empathy for the poor. The duties of youth were stressed.
- The third reader contained rules for oral reading. It was designed for a more mature-minded young adolescent.
- The fourth reader was an introduction to literature and contained British poetry and Bible versus among its selections. This text was addressed to today's secondary schools. It discussed Napoleon Bonaparte, Puritan fathers, women, God, education, religion, and philosophy.
- The fifth reader was designed for elocutionary exercises to increase articulation, inflection, pitch, accent, rate, emphasis, and gesture.
- In the sixth and final reader, 111 great authors such as Shakespeare, Longfellow, Dickens, and Addison were quoted. The theme of the selections included several forms of composition, description, narration, argumentation, and exposition.

These "eclectic readers"—meaning that the selections were chosen from a number of sources—were considered remarkable literary works and probably exerted a greater influence upon literary tastes in the United States than any other book, excluding the Bible.

Why were the McGuffey Readers so important? Think about your own school experiences, and the role that textbooks have played. Can you remember a grade or course that did *not* use a textbook? In particular, think about the texts that were used in your reading classes. How were they similar to the McGuffey Readers? Some similarities might include:

- The use of a "series" of books, starting with easy books that led to those that were more difficult.
- The use of a variety of authors' works in the textbook.
- The use of the textbook to teach specific reading or language skills.

Given the pervasive (and sometimes political) nature of textbooks today, the emergence of the McGuffey Reader in the 1800s demonstrates a significant way in which history directly influences our current educational practices and experiences.

The McGuffey Readers are often considered as the forerunners of today's school textbooks.

Setting the stage—Two years before Big Bill Ritchie and his band of friends hurt Jonas Lane, the school teacher, so badly he died a year later of the injuries.

It is the winter of 1866 in a small village of Malone located in northern up state New York. For several days Big Bill and his friends had been disrupting the classroom. After tolerating several outbursts from the boys, Mr. Corse, the teacher for this year's term, warned Bill Ritchie and his four friends, not to be late to class again. *If this occurs again, I shall have to punish you.*

At noon the next day a very worried Almanzo went out to play when he saw Mr. Ritchie, Bill's father, coming down the hill on his loaded bobsled. All the young boys stood where they were and watch Mr. Ritchie. He was a big, rough man, with a loud voice and a loud laugh. He was proud of Bill because Bill could thrash school teachers and break up the school. Bill and the other big boys climbed up on his load of wood. They rode, loudly talking, around the bend of the road.

Returning to class late again, Big Bill Ritchie swaggered in. The other big boys were behind him. Mr. Corse looked at them and did not say anything. Bill Ritchie laughed in his face, and still he did not speak. The big boys jostled Bill, and he jeered again at Mr. Corse. Then he led them all tramping loudly down the aisle to their seats. Mr. Corse lifted the lid of his desk and dropped his hand out of sight behind the raised lid. He said: Bill Ritchie, come up here. Big Bill jumped up and tore off his coat, yelling Come on boys! He rushed up the aisle. Almanzo felt sick inside; he didn't want to watch but he couldn't help it. Mr. Corse stepped away from his desk. His hand came from behind the desk lid, and a long, thin black streak hissed through the air. It was a blacksnake ox-whip fifteen feet long. Mr. Corse held the short handle, loaded with iron that could kill an ox. The thin, long lash coiled around Bill's legs, and Mr. Corse jerked. Bill lurched and almost fell. Quick as black lightening the lash circled and stuck and coiled again, and again Mr. Corse jerked. Come up here, Bill Ritchie, he said jerking Bill toward him. (From *Farmer Boy*, written by Laura Ingalls Wilder, 1933, pages 28-44)

## Common School Period (1840-1880)

During the 1800s, our young country quickly expanded its territories to the western coastline. As millions of immigrants settled the land, the demand for more schools and teachers exploded. However, common (public) schools were in critical need of reform. Most of the common schools in the early 1840s were still using the Lancastrian Monitorial approach. The typical school year was only four months long, due to the need to have children's help in farming. The schools were poorly attended, and usually taught by an untrained school master who offered little instruction, demanded rote memorization and recitation of the McGuffey Readers, and often practiced strict discipline. This was a time of unruly students, and teachers with hickory sticks who used *corporal punishment* for self-protection, as this vignette above from Laura Ingalls Wilder's "Farmer Boy" demonstrates.

The vignette above, based on actual events, demonstrates the critical need for qualified teachers and appropriate curriculum during this historical timeframe. Preparing teachers was perhaps the biggest challenge during the Common School period, and one that was in part addressed through the establishment of the "Normal School."

**The Emergence of Teacher Education**   The first Normal School (school devoted to teacher education and preparation) was dedicated by Horace Mann in Lexington, Massachusetts, in 1839 (see Box 1.4). At the dedication Mann declared *"I believe Normal Schools to be a new instrumentality in the advancement of the race. I believe that, without them, Free Schools themselves would be shorn of their strength and their healing power and would at length become mere charity schools and thus die out in fact and in form."* (Mondale, 2002).

The goal of the normal schools in great part was to help teachers understand and implement the methods developed by Johann Heinrich Pestalozzi, a Prussian educator (see Box 1.5). Pestalozzi described the process of teaching as directing the child in the unfolding of his/her hidden powers and emphasized the harmonious development of the individual's talents and

**Box 1.4** ↓ **Biographical Sketch: Horace Mann**

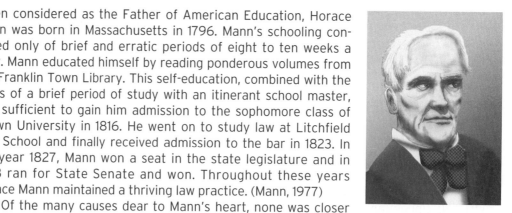

Often considered as the Father of American Education, Horace Mann was born in Massachusetts in 1796. Mann's schooling consisted only of brief and erratic periods of eight to ten weeks a year. Mann educated himself by reading ponderous volumes from the Franklin Town Library. This self-education, combined with the fruits of a brief period of study with an itinerant school master, was sufficient to gain him admission to the sophomore class of Brown University in 1816. He went on to study law at Litchfield Law School and finally received admission to the bar in 1823. In the year 1827, Mann won a seat in the state legislature and in 1833 ran for State Senate and won. Throughout these years Horace Mann maintained a thriving law practice. (Mann, 1977)

Of the many causes dear to Mann's heart, none was closer than the education of the people. He held a keen interest in school policy. April 20, 1837, Mann left his law practice and accepted the post of the newly founded Secretary of Education. During his years as Secretary of Education, Mann published twelve annual reports on aspects of his work and programs, and the integral relationship between education, freedom, and Republican government. He wanted a school that would be available and equal for all, as part of the birth-right of every American child, to be for rich and poor alike. Mann had found "social harmony" to be his primary goal of the school. Horace Mann felt that a common school would be the "great equalizer." Poverty would most assuredly disappear as a broadened popular intelligence tapped new treasures of natural and material wealth. He felt that, through education, crime would decline sharply as would a host of moral vices like violence and fraud. In sum, there was no end to the social good, which might be derived from a common school. Mann presided over the establishment of the first public normal school in the United States at Lexington in 1839. Mann also reinvigorated the 1827 law establishing high schools, and fifty high schools were created during his tenure. He also persuaded the Massachusetts legislature to establish a six-month minimum school year in 1839. Mann also led the movement to set up teacher institutions throughout the state. Mann had won his victory as the public school soon stood as one of the characteristic features of American life—"a wellspring of freedom and a ladder of opportunity for millions." (Merrell, 1972)

Source: www.nd.edu/-rbarger/www7/mann.html

abilities into a complete personality. Pestalozzi felt that children must feel secure before they could learn. He believed that children learn through their senses, not through lecturing. Thus, he would begin with "hands on" experience called the "object lesson" and gradually expand to the general concepts. This new approach fostered critical thinking and supported the social and emotional development of the child. (Harper, 1970)

Not only did high schools and colleges grow during the Common Period, schools and methods for the very youngest citizens also began to develop. Deeply influenced by the work of Pestalozzi, German citizen Friedrich Wilhelm August Froebel (1782–1852) originated the kindergarten system. He believed that the purpose of education is to encourage and guide man as a conscious, thinking and perceiving being in such a way that he becomes a pure and perfect representation of divine inner law through his own personal choice; education must show him the ways and meanings of attaining that goal (see Box 1.6).

How similar are kindergarten classrooms today, compared with those envisioned by Froebel? Considering the debates facing many states today regarding whether or not kindergarten should be mandated in public schools, Froebel's theories, and the significance of early school experiences, are particularly important to consider.

## Box 1.5 ↓ Biographical Sketch: Johann Pestalozzi

Pestalozzi's theory of education is based on the importance of a pedagogical (instructional) method that corresponds to the child's natural physical and mental development and the interactions with real-life experiences and objects. For example, his belief that education should be based on concrete experience led him to pioneer in the use of real objects, such as plants and rocks and minerals, in the teaching of science to young children.

Pestalozzi believed the individuality of each child was most important; it was something that has to be developed, over time, through educational opportunities. He deeply opposed the prevailing system of memorization and strict discipline, and was determined to replace it with a system based on love and an understanding of the child's world. (Krul, 1875)

A consistent theme in much of Pestalozzi's writing is the idea that education should be moral as well as intellectual. Deeply committed to social reform, Pestalozzi believed that society could be changed by education. His social philosophy influenced the development of his teacher preparation methods.

Although he respected the individuality of the teacher, Pestalozzi felt that education was a science that could be learned and practiced. He developed concepts like teacher training and wrote about curriculum innovations like group work, field trips, grade levels, ability grouping, and allowing for student differences.

He had a profound influence on many others in educational theory, including Friedrich Froebel, the German inventor of the kindergarten. (De Guimos, 1889)

## Box 1.6 ↓ Biographical Sketch: Friedrich Froebel

Froebel's kindergarten system emphasized learning through play. He sought to encourage the creation of educational environments that involved practical work and the direct use of materials. Through engaging with the world, understanding unfolds. Hence the significance of play—it is a creative activity through which children become aware of their place in the world. He went on to develop special materials (such as shaped wooden bricks and balls—*gifts*), a series of recommended activities (*occupations*) and movement activities, and a linking set of theories. His original concern was the teaching of young children through educational games in the family. In the later years of his life this became linked with a demand for the provision of special centers for the care and development of children outside the home. The first kindergarten was established to help children of poverty and those who had special needs. In 1872, kindergartens gained support from the National Education Association, which in 1884 established a department of kindergarten instruction. Through the efforts of many people, the kindergarten has worked its way into many schools, private and public. (Lilley, 1967)

**Politics in the Common School Period**   The 1800s not only saw the emergence of institutions specifically for teacher education and the redefinition of early childhood education, but also saw rise to new laws impacting the education of children. For example, as the government mandated student attendance in public school, the need for higher education increased. In many cases, the young citizens of the growing country were working and attending school. (Mondale, 2002) The following legislative acts secured attendance but also provided greater educational opportunities:

- *The Compulsory Attendance Act of 1852* enacted by the state of Massachusetts, this act required mandatory attendance of public school children between the ages of eight and 14. Students needed to attend either a public or private school for at least three months out of each year, and of these twelve weeks at least six had to be consecutive. "The exception to attendance was proof that the child had already learned the curriculum, the family was living in poverty and needed the child's help to provide childcare, or the child had a physical or mental impairment." (Barger, 2004)

  The penalty for not sending a child to school was a twenty dollars fine to be collected by the township. Unfortunately, the local school officials did not have the authority to enforce the law. However, the provisions in the law influenced families to send their children through greater community expectations and social pressure. By 1873 the compulsory attendance law was revised. The age limit was reduced to age twelve but the annual attendance was increased to twenty weeks per year. Additionally, a semblance of enforcement was established by forming jurisdictions for prosecution that hired truant officers to check absences.

  Simultaneously, several states enacted child labor laws that prohibited children under fifteen from being employed for more than nine months a year. Truant officers required the child to provide documentation of consistent school attendance and businesses that employed the child had to pay a fine if they did not comply with the law. It was at this time that teachers first documented student attendance through the use of attendance cards. Through this system of fines, employers as well as parents were forced to be become more socially responsible for children's education.

- *The Morrill Act of 1862* was also known as the Land Grant College Act. The grant established institutions in each state that would educate both white men and women in the disciplines of home economics, agriculture, mechanical arts, and other professions that reflected the economic and social needs of the time. "The land-grant act was introduced by a congressman from Vermont named Justin Smith Morrill. He wanted to assure that higher education would be available to citizens from all social classes. Signed by Abraham Lincoln, the grant gave states 30,000 acres of public land per congressional representation (based on the census of 1860). The land could be sold and the money from the sale of the land was put in an endowment fund, which would provide support for the colleges in each state." (Barger, 2004)

  Ultimately, the land-grant has improved the lives of millions of Americans. However, this was not the case in the early stages. At the time the grants were established, there was a separation of races. In the South, Blacks were not allowed to attend the original land-grant institutions. This Act also changed the course of higher education as the purpose of higher education clearly shifted from the classical studies, and allowed for more applied studies that would prepare the students for the world that they would face once leaving the classroom. This Act also gave higher public education direct support from the government.

Think about the impact of these two laws, enacted 150 years ago, on your own educational experiences. The fact that compulsory attendance laws still exist, and that the Land Grant institutions thrive today, demonstrates some of the many ways that political acts in our history can influence our educational experiences—and mandates—generations later. What political acts that are passed in this decade will have the most influence in the year 2150? (Rippa, 1996; Rury, 2004)

**Education of the Southern States**   In the 1840s, the growth of state-funded public educa-tion was blossoming from Connecticut to Illinois. However, many Southern states did not have a tradition of public education to build on, as the North did. In fact, it was well after the Civil War before the South passed legislation for state-supported public schools. Beyond the isolation of rural plantations and small farms, which made public education more difficult to establish, southern culture believed that education: (Barger, 2004)

- *Was a private family matter* and not a concern for the state. They were quick to point out that in all traditional societies the most important training a child receives is in the home, where he/she is inducted into the values of the society he/she is about to enter.

- *Should perpetuate their social systems and culture.* They felt a priority should be placed upon creating a small number of college-bound elite. This approach helped to sustain the sharply defined social-class structure, which existed in the South.

- *Was power.* In an attempt to keep Black slaves from having power, Southerners passed laws making it a crime to teach slaves to read and write.

Southerners justified slavery on the basis that the Black man was incapable of improve-ment, all the while denying them access to any type of formalized education. However, even in this time of great adversity, education of the Black people continued, overtly and conducted under the cover of night. The quest for knowledge could not be thwarted, although it would be another 100 years before equal rights in education would be legislated throughout the nation.

Box 1.7. provides an historical sketch of Booker T. Washington, an influential education whose life illustrated the challenges most Black people at this time faced as they struggle to receive an education.

---

**Box 1.7    ↓ Biographical Sketch: Booker T. Washington**

Booker T. Washington was born a slave in Franklin County, Virginia in 1856. Booker's family was owned by Mr. Burroughs. He went to school in Franklin County, not as a student, but to carry books for Mr. Burroughs' daughters. At that time it was illegal to educate slaves. In his memoirs Mr. Washington writes, *I had the feeling that to get into a schoolhouse and study would be about the same as getting into paradise.* In April of 1865 the Emancipation Proclamation was read to joyful slaves in front of the Burroughs home. Booker's family moved to West Virginia. The young boy took a job in a salt mine that began at four A.M. so he could attend school later in the day. Within a few years, Booker was taken in as a houseboy by a wealthy woman who further encouraged his longing to learn. At age sixteen, he walked much of the 500 miles back to Virginia to enroll in Hampton, a new school for Black students. He knew that even poor students could get an education at Hampton Institute, paying their way by working. However, the head teacher was suspicious of Booker's country ways and ragged clothes. She admitted him only after he had cleaned a room to her satisfaction. His hard work and determination led him to become a teacher at Hampton. Mr. Washington was appointed head of the Tuskegee Institute in 1881. In his memoirs he writes, *Tuskegee grew from a com-munity subsisting mainly on fat pork and corn bread to a progressive modern town.* He taught the newly freed African Americans to be teachers, craftsmen, and businessmen who had the skills to successfully make their own way in the world. (Washington & Harlan, 1986; McLoone, 1997)

Source: www.nd/edu/-rbarger/www7/african.html

> **Box 1.8    ↓ Biographical Sketch: Frederick W. Taylor**
>
>
>
> Frederick W. Taylor believed that all work could be studied, designed, and measured. Through such efforts, the most efficient work behavior for every job could be established. Such thinking had wide appeal among school administrators who were facing the problem of educating ever increasing numbers of students. It also coincided with the measurement movement in psychology that was sweeping the nation at the time. Psychologists were developing tests and other measurements that enabled them to establish a student's mental capacity and levels of achievement. (Wrege & Greenwood, 1991)
>
> The appeal of this bureaucratic model obliterated any consideration of alternate patterns of educational organization. Boards of education, superintendents, and central office administrators became the decision makers for all of the schools of their districts, just as boards of directors, presidents, and headquarter personnel became the decision makers for entire corporations. Bureaucracies, whether they were in education or private industry, were efficient and, therefore, inherently good.
>
> Individual schools of a district were also organized as small bureaucracies. Principals were hired as leaders of schools, with teachers and staff members as subordinates. It was the principal's responsibility to carry out the wishes of the central office and to guide the staff of the school as it worked with the students attending the school. (Copley, 1923)

## Progressive Period (1880-1920)

During this time in American history, opposing forces were at work. For example, a strong sense of nationalism swayed public opinion to insist that new immigrants quickly assimilate into an English-speaking nation. The public schools' mission was to assist in this American cultural accommodation. As children poured into the school, the needs of the children also emerged–issues of public health, hygiene, safety, and nutrition. On the other hand, many immigrant parents wanted to send children into the work force instead of school. These families wanted to benefit from the income they would receive if more of their family worked. As harsh as this now sounds, it then was a matter of family survival. (Haubrich & Apple, 1975)

The need to ensure an English speaking-reading citizenry and the accompanying need to protect the rights/health of young children lead to the Compulsory Attendance and the Child Labor Laws. The Compulsory Attendance laws were mandated by individual states (from 1867–1918) to ensure that children were in school receiving an education and not working in industry.

During the Progressive Period, American business and industry rapidly expanded. Along with the increase in business and industry came a dramatic increase in the number of immigrants entering the United States. The expansion of industry was driven by the "efficiency movement." This movement was basically concerned with making the factories more efficient in producing more with less cost, effort and material. The rapidly growing public school system was also greatly influenced by this efficiency movement. The school was viewed essentially as a workplace, and learning was perceived in terms of productivity. The ever-increasing numbers of students immigrating into the United States forced a rethinking of the efficiency and effectiveness of the one-room schoolhouse from the previous Common School period. (Webb, 2005; Barger, 2004)

The work of Frederick Taylor emerged as the recognized leader of the efficiency movement, or scientific management (see Box 1.8).

Consider the implications of the efficiency movement on today's public education. What specific elements exist today?

During this historical period, two changes occurred in public education: the division of schools into grades, and the rise of the modern high school. As more and more children were attending school, it became apparent that the one-room school system could no longer contain the increased population. Children by the millions, from ages five to fifteen, needed an education. Influenced by the efficiency theories prevalent in industry, businessmen began to consider how to organize the school system. Comparing education to a product—or something that could be obtained step by step—it was determined that children should be sorted and taught by age. Further, a more highly sequenced age-grade system already fit the curriculum (see McGuffey Readers for an example). The elementary school that most of us attended still reflects this model of schooling, in which schools are divided into grades based on students' ages. (Mondale, 2002)

As more children completed the elementary grades, and with the increase of mandatory attendance and child labor laws, the attendance in high schools soared during this period. However, the purpose of high schools was still unclear. In the late 1800s the question of the purpose of the American high school was divided between two academic tracks. Traditional educators saw high school as a college preparatory institution. This divided students into academic versus terminal students, whose membership was more often based on economic, social, and ethnic backgrounds than academic ability. Others believed the high school should serve more as a people's school, offering a range of practical courses. (Parkerson & Parkerson, 2001)

The National Education Association (NEA) addressed this issue by appointing a Committee of Ten in 1892 to establish a standard curriculum. This committee recommended eight years of elementary education and four years of secondary education. It defined courses that are now considered basic like foreign languages, mathematics, science, English, and history. The significance of the Committee of Ten was its contribution toward liberalizing the high school by offering alternatives to the Latin and Greek classic curricula, and the belief that the same subjects would be equally beneficial to both academic and terminal students. The goal of high school was to prepare all students to do well in life, contributing to their own well-being and society's good, and to prepare some students for college. (Ornstein & Levine, 1993) However, not all citizens were as determined to help **all** students, as demonstrated through court cases such as the infamous Plessy vs. Ferguson:

- *Plessy V. Ferguson (1896)*   After the Civil War, many Southern states were determined to try and limit the rights of former slaves. The state governments succeeded by passing *segregation* laws. Segregation required separate classrooms, bathrooms, drinking fountains, and railroads for whites and blacks. The segregation law was tested when a black man by the name of Homer Plessey volunteered to break the law. Plessey boarded a East Louisiana railroad train in New Orleans and took a seat in a white-only car. He was asked to move and refused. He was then arrested and brought before New Orleans Parish Judge John Ferguson. Plessy and his attorney argued that the separate car laws violated his civil rights. Ferguson found Plessy guilty and he was charged a fine.

    However, the case went to the Supreme Court and the law of separate cars was quickly found constitutional. The Court ruled that "separate but equal facilities" was proper under the Fourteenth Amendment. The ruling resulted in a major setback in the struggle for equality between races in the United States, and set the stage for racial segregation within the South until the overruling in 1954. This case is a constant reminder to the people of our country of the horrible damages done to society when the highest court of law in the land rules against justice and equality.

**Emergence of Professional Organizations**   In the early 1900s, teachers—especially those working in urban areas—felt they were being treated as voiceless workers rather than professionals. It was at this time that progressive education principles were being introduced which challenged some of the traditional aspects of education. Progressive educators were introducing greater freedom and activity in the classroom. Emphasis was placed on informality and

---

**Box 1.9   ↓ Biographical Sketch: John Dewey**

John Dewey (1859-1952) was an American philosopher, psychologist, and educational reformer, whose work has been hugely influential in the United States and around the world. He is recognized as one of the founders of the philosophical school of Pragmatism, a pioneer in functional psychology, and a leading representative of the progressive movement in U.S. education during the first half of the twentieth century.

John Dewey was one of the AFT'S most prominent founders and an officer of the union in the early years. At this time Dewey was very critical of the decision making process currently being used in public education. He stated that *the remedy for the evils of the control of the schools by politicians is not to have one expert dictating educational methods and subject matter to a body of passive recipient teachers, but the adoption of intellectual initiative, discussion and decision throughout the entire school corps.* Dewey encouraged cooperative social organization, association and exchange among teachers as a substitute for supervision, critic teaching, and technical training. (Martin, 2003)

---

working in groups, where discussion and activities could take place. The emphasis was moving away from learning from just one text, to gathering materials from many sources and children working at their own pace. Teachers wanted the professional freedoms to make these choices. Hence, the American Federation of Teachers was developed. (Barger, 2004)

The American Federation of Teachers (AFT) is a union associated with the American Federation of Labor and the Congress of Industrial Organization (AFL-CIO). In order to understand unionization and its role in our profession, it is necessary to examine the changes in society in the early 1900s. Industrialization and urban growth were both experiencing a period of rapid expansion. Wealth and control were in the hands of small groups of economically privileged people. Workers in the United States were becoming increasingly dissatisfied with their working conditions and lack of rights. (Hook, 1995)

Today, the AFT continues to uphold the rights of teachers to help form school policies and programs. The AFT Motto is *Democracy in Education and Education for Democracy.* The AFT continues to list as its chief objectives the promotion of professionalism in teaching as well as securing appropriate wages, better working conditions, and job security for its members. AFT members still believe that collective bargaining, along with discussion between those representing teachers and administrators, is the democratic process that allows them to achieve their goals. A more in-depth discussion of the role of unions in the profession today is offered in Chapter 11. A biographical sketch of John Dewey, one of the nation's early union leaders, is provided in Box 1.9.

**High School Reform**   Due to the increased enrollments in secondary schools and the proliferations of high schools, it became apparent that a consistent perspective of curriculum needed to be developed. The Commission on the Reorganization of Secondary Education, established in 1918, also wanted to take into account individual student differences, goals, attitudes, and abilities. (Mondale, 2002) The concept of democracy was decided on as the guide of education in America. Also prevalent in the Commission's recommendations were the following tenets: (Barger, 2004)

1. *Health.* A secondary school should encourage good health habits, give health instruction, and provide physical activities. Good health should be taken into account when schools and communities are planning activities for youth.

Herkimer High School—Class of 1915
*Courtesy*—Herkimer County Historical Society

2. ***Command Of Fundamental Processes.*** Writing, reading, oral expression, and math should be emphasized throughout the curriculum.

3. ***Worthy Home Membership.*** The development of those qualities that make the individual a worthy member of a family, both contributing to and deriving benefit from that membership were also encouraged. This principle was taught through literature, music, social studies, and art. Co-ed schools should show good relationships between males and females.

4. ***Vocation.*** Students should be exposed to a variety of careers so that they can choose the most suitable career. The student should then develop an understanding of the relationship between the vocation and the community in which one lives and works.

5. ***Civic Education.*** The goal of civic education is to develop an awareness and concern for one's own community. A student should gain knowledge of social organizations and a commitment to civic morality.

6. ***Worthy Use Of Leisure.*** Education should give the student the skills to enrich his/her body, mind, spirit and personality in his/her leisure. The school should also provide appropriate recreation.

7. ***Ethical Character.*** This principle involves instilling in the student the notion of personal responsibility and initiative.

Consider these principles, and how they continue to impact schooling nearly a century later. Which of today's guiding principles might have this longevity?

## Modern Period (1920-present)

The current Modern Period is perhaps best characterized by a focus on social issues and reform. In 1932, George Counts wrote *Dare the School Build a New Social Order?* In this work, Counts challenged teachers to lead society instead of following society. He felt that teachers were leaders and could be policy makers. While teachers should be concerned with school matters, they should also be concerned with controversial matters of economics, politics, and morality. Counts believed the school was an agency that could be actively involved in society's politics, economics, art, religion, and ethics. The school could either reflect the knowledge, beliefs, and values of the society, or it could seek to change them. The school, in order to be socially constructive, had to help solve problems. George Counts believed American schools needed to identify with such progressive forces as labor unions, farmers' organizations, and minority groups. By affiliating with groups that wanted to change society, the schools then could make social improvements. (Rippa, 1996) If school teachers were to act as statespersons, then the resolution of major issues would result in a new social order. (Barger, 2004)

One of the remaining challenges in the twentieth century was racial segregation. At the onset of the Modern Period, the nation's law was still "Separate but Equal." But as Justice Harlan, the one lone dissenting vote on the Supreme Court during the *Plessey v. Ferguson* trial, wrote:

> *The present decision . . . will not only stimulate aggressions, more or less brutal and irritating, upon the admitted rights of colored citizens, but will encourage the belief that it is possible, by means of state enactments, to defeat the beneficent purposes which the people of the United States had in view when they adopted the recent [the 13th and 14th] amendments of the Constitution.*

**Segregation Ends**   When Linda Carol Brown was seven years old, she became the center of a major court battle that would overturn the segregation laws. Linda was required to attend the Monroe School in East Topeka, Kansas, though it was twenty blocks away from her home, because it was the closest all-Black school. After Linda's father tried unsuccessfully to enroll her in the third grade in an all-White public school nearer to their home, he sought help from the National Association for the Advancement of Colored People (NAACP) to fight her unfair exclusion from the White school. The main issue was whether the Fourteenth Amendment was violated by denying education in a specific school simply due to race. The Fourteenth Amendment states, *that no person, who is a citizen of the United States, should be denied equal protections under the law or the right to life, liberty or property.* By May 17, 1954, four years after Linda Brown's rejection from the school in Topeka, the Supreme Court had reached a unanimous decision in the famous trial of *Brown vs. the Board of Education.* Chief Justice Earl Warren stated:

> *To separate [elementary and secondary school children] from others of similar age and qualifications solely because of their race generates a feeling of inferiority as to their status in the community that may affect their hearts and minds in a way unlikely ever to be undone. We conclude that in the field of public education, the doctrine of 'separate but equal' has no place. Separate educational facilities are inherently unequal."*

This public declaration against segregation in education was only the first step in making the United States school system more equal. One year later, the Supreme Court created procedures under which school boards would desegregate their schools "with all deliberate speed." This decision was not implemented easily. (Ravetch, 1983) Those school systems resisted that had been segregated since their beginning. "Three years after that ruling was made, federal troops had to escort nine Black children into a high school in Little Rock, Arkansas. Six years later, state officials were still fighting this ruling. Courts had to order and enforce the segregation ruling persistently. In 1979, Linda Brown Thompson even went to court again, to sue Topeka for allowing their schools to remain segregated." (Barger, 2004) The issue of segregation, and current concerns over "achievement gaps" between students of majority and minority ethnicities, continue to define educational reform even today.

**Federal Aid to Education**   In recent decades, American families have increasingly been concerned with the educational aspirations and opportunities of their children. As the need for unskilled and uneducated labor declines, the need for highly educated labor continues to increase. However, not everyone is able to financially afford to be better educated. Since World War II, the federal government has developed plans to help its citizens obtain a greater access to a quality early childhood education, secondary education and higher education. These plans include: (Altenbaugh, 2002)

- *The "G.I. Bill of Rights"* is a body of federal legislation, which has provided educational and other benefits for veterans of war. Since its enactment, over 11 million persons have benefited. A general aim for this legislation has been to compensate veterans for their sacrifices and services. Many historians have rated the G.I. Bill of Rights one of the most enlightened pieces of legislation ever enacted by the Congress of the United States. Some describe it as one of the most successful experiments in socioeconomic expansion undertaken by the U.S. government. Certainly, as long as U.S. citizens continue to participate in military service, this kind of legislation will remain high on the legislative priority list.

- *National Defense Education Act (NDEA)* (1958) appropriated federal funds to improve instruction in those areas considered crucial to national defense and security–mathematics, foreign language, and science. Between 1945 and 1958, there was intense debate about federal aid to elementary and secondary schools. However, in 1957 the political situation changed when the Soviet Union, the rival of the United States in the Cold War, successfully orbited a space satellite named Sputnik. The Soviet space success and well-publicized American space failures produced a climate of national crisis. Critics pointed to the deficiencies of American students in mathematics and science. The Sputnik crisis sparked national legislation to support training, equipment, and programs in fields vital to defense. The scientific community, including university scholars and curriculum specialists, were often called upon to reconstruct subject-matter content, especially on the high school level.

- *The Elementary and Secondary Education Act (ESEA) (1965).* Whereas the NDEA emphasized science and mathematics, the ESEA was a federal response to the significant social change taking place in American society. Many African American students, as well as members of other minority groups, were educationally disadvantaged because of social and economic conditions. The ESEA related to President Lyndon Johnson's program, "War on Poverty," which encouraged special programs for children of low-income families. It also created a range of early childhood educational programs for economically and culturally disadvantaged children (such as Head Start). These programs had an impact on early childhood education, not only for minority children but also for all children.

- *Educational Consolidation and Improvement Act (ECIA).* In 1992, Chapter 1 funding, aimed at low-income and economically disadvantaged schools, had been increased to nearly 7 billion dollars. Research indicates that Chapter 1 programs still do not ensure students will acquire the academic and intellectual skills necessary for obtaining good jobs in a modern economy. However, Chapter 1 students typically gain a year in reading and math achievement for each year of participation in elementary grades, and thus no longer fall further behind their advantaged peers.

In the Modern Period, the public school system faces many challenges. As students express their views, opinions, and lifestyle choices, the schools must provide a safe and equally respectful environment for all children. If a student action interferes with the educational process of others, that act may, in many cases, be suppressed. However, students' personal rights do not end at the school's property line. Two landmark cases involving Students' Rights are *Tinker Des Moines* and the *Goss v. Lopez* case. These two court cases set the foundation for our laws and policies regarding students and administrators. (Barger, 2004)

- *Tinker v. Des Moines Independent Community School District (1969),* fifteen-year-old John F. Tinker and his thirteen-year-old sister were suspended from school for wearing black armbands in protest of the Vietnam war. The principals had learned of the upcoming protest and adopted a policy stipulating that any student wearing an armband to school would have to remove it or face suspension. After the Tinkers and other students

All students, regardless of ability, have the right to a free public education.

were suspended for not complying with the policy, the Tinker parents filed suit in federal court, charging that the rule and disciplinary action taken against the young people violated their First Amendment right to freedom of speech and expression. Four years later, the U.S. Supreme Court agreed. Students do not shed their constitutional rights of freedom of speech or expression when they enter school grounds.

- *Goss v. Lopez (1975)* Dwight Lopez was a student at Columbus Central High School. In February of 1971, a number of students were involved in a disturbance in the lunchroom that resulted in property damage. Lopez denied that he was a participant in the disturbance but was suspended, before he could give his side of the story, for a ten-day period. Lopez and eight other students who received suspension filed suit in the Federal District Court claiming violation of their Fourteen Amendment Rights to due process of law. The Court handed down its decision in January of 1975, which stated that students facing suspension "must be given some kind of notice and afforded some kind of hearing" before being deprived of their education.

Another law that has made a significant impact on education and the rights of all citizens in the Modern Period is Public Law 94-142, which focuses on the rights of students with special needs.

- *Education of All Handicapped Children Act (1975)*—now called IDEA (Individuals with Disabilities Education Act). In order to receive federal funds, states must develop and implement policies that assure a free appropriate public education to all children with disabilities. This legislation improves opportunities for handicapped children and adults ages three to twenty-one be educated in the "least restrictive environment" to the maximum extent appropriate. The law allows students with special needs to be educated with typical children. Students with special needs cannot be taught in separate schools—unless the severity of the disability is such that education in regular classes cannot be achieved. Before a child can be placed in a special education program, an extensive evaluation procedure is required by PL 94-142. The school is required to receive written permission from the parent before conducting an evaluation of the child. Once the child's evaluation is complete, and it is determined that the child is indeed eligible for placement in special education, an Individual Education Plan (IEP) must be written to meet the needs of that child. Parents are provided training to enable them to participate more effectively with professionals in meeting the educational needs of their child.

**A Nation At Risk Report**    One of the most influential works of the Modern Period is the report entitled "A Nation At Risk." This landmark study was issued by the National Commission on Excellence in Education in 1983. While the report concentrated on secondary education, it found that the whole system of American education was in great distress. Some findings of this report revealed that:

*23 million American adults are functionally illiterate by the simplest test of everyday reading, writing, and comprehension. About 13 percent of all 17-year-olds in the United States can be considered functionally illiterate. (A Nation At Risk: The Imperative For Educational Reform, 1983).*

This report suggested five new basics to be added to the curriculum of America's schools. These basics included four years of English, three years of math, three years of science, three years of social studies, and half a year of computer science in America's high schools. (Barger, 2004)

This commission also suggested that teaching, teacher education, and education standards be reformed. This report cited a high demand for increased support for those who teach science, mathematics, foreign languages, and specialists in education for gifted and talented, language minority, and handicapped students. The study found that those who were interested in the field of education were often not academically qualified. The report also faulted the teacher preparation curriculum as being weighted heavily with courses in education methods instead of content knowledge. The report also encouraged the raising of teachers' salaries in order to attract and retain qualified teachers. Current initiatives, such as merit pay and incentives, are related to the concerns raised in this report.

**Goals 2000**    In late 1989, President Bush and the nation's governors met for a bipartisan Education Summit. At this summit, and building on the work of "A Nation at Risk," the groundwork was laid for Goals 2000 Education Program. The goals became the centerpiece for education reform for both the Bush and Clinton administrations. The passing of the GOALS 2000: Educate America Act on March 31, 1994 allowed the federal government a new role in its support for education. The federal government could now hold schools and teachers more accountable for student achievement. The National Education Goals include: (Barger, 2004)

1.  Every child will start school ready to learn.

2.  The high school graduation rate will increase to at least ninety percent.

3.  American students would leave grades four, eight, and twelve having demonstrated competency over challenging subject matter; and every school in America will ensure that all students learn to use their minds well, so they may be prepared for responsible citizenship, further learning, and productive employment in our nation's modern economy.

4.  The nation's teaching force will have access to programs for the continued improvement of their professional skills needed to instruct and prepare all American students for the next century.

5.  U.S. students will be first in the world in science and mathematics achievement.

6. Every adult American will be literate and will possess the knowledge and skills necessary to compete in a global economy and exercise rights and responsibilities of citizenship.

7. Every school in the United States will be free of drugs, violence, and the unauthorized presence of firearms and alcohol, and will offer a disciplined environment conducive to learning.

8. Every school will promote partnerships that will increase parental involvement and participation in promoting the social, emotional, and academic growth of children.

**The No Child Left Behind (NCLB) Act of 2001** The NCLB act revised the Elementary and Secondary Education Act, with a potent blend of new requirements, incentives, and resources. Its new requirements pose significant challenges for states and their educators.

The law sets deadlines for states to expand the scope and frequency of student testing, revamp school accountability systems, and guarantee that every teacher is qualified in their subject area. NCLB requires states to make demonstrable annual progress in raising the percentage of students' proficiency in reading and math, and in narrowing the test-score gap between advantaged and disadvantaged students. At the same time, the new law increases funding in several areas, including K through 3 reading programs and before- and after-school programs, and provides states with greater flexibility to use federal funds as they see fit. A more in-depth look at the policies and politics of NCLB is provided in Chapter 9.

## The Clash of Two Worlds: Education and Native Americans

A summary of the American educational system would not be complete without a look into the history of how Native American children were educated and assimilated as our country developed. The history of schooling for Native Americans is in great contrast to the social and educational reforms that our country accomplished. The relationship between the United States government and the original inhabitants of this country could be described as one that was disgraceful and inhumane. This brief history of Native American education will focus on the five educational time frames.

**The Colonial Period (1600–1776)** Immediately following the arrival of Europeans to the new world, Christian missionaries began "saving the souls" of the Indians whose religion was viewed as pagan and the work of the devil. By the end of the Revolutionary War, the new United States government signed the constitution in 1788, part of which gave the government power to sign treaties and regulate the commerce of the Indian tribes. During this time, the missionaries continued their religious education of the Indians. However, as more colonists began to spread into the surrounding territory, friction between the tribes and the whites began. Though the new Americans were essentially encroaching on Native American land, the settlers felt they had a greater right to the land because they erroneously viewed the Indian as uneducated, uncivilized, and primitive. Thus the new American government saw the Indians as barriers to settlers' interests. (Meriam, 1928)

**The Early National Period (1776–1840)** As floods of new settlers began moving west, the conflicts between settlers and Indians were inevitable. Indians did not believe people owned land and the settlers coming from England, Ireland, Germany, and Scotland were coming to this country for the opportunity to own land. Native American children had an education of real life apprenticeship and, as few Native American tribes had a written language, formalized schooling was not part of the Indian way of life. Each culture was alien to the other, including religious beliefs, clothing, housing, and appearance. It is little wonder that fights, often predicated on fear or the desire for cultural dominance, broke out between the two. (Reyner & Eder, 2004) Hence, the dominant governmental structure began to create laws that gave itself the right to moderate the alien civilization, including:

- *Indian Civilization Act (1819)* Prior to this congressional Act, the federal government had no official involvement with the Indians and the missionaries. However, the intent of this Act was to allow the new government to become officially involved in efforts to directly use education as a means of controlling the Indians by removing their native culture and replacing it with the "preferred and more civilized" European culture. The Act provided funding to religious affiliations to start schools to teach farming, reading and writing. Ultimately, however, the goal was for "reforming and civilizing."

- *The Office of Indian Affairs (1824)*   It is interesting to note that this Office was established under the office of the Secretary of War. In his first report, the director of the Office of Indian Affairs stated that, at that time, there were already thirty-two Indian schools in operation that served 916 students. By 1871 there were 286 schools with 6,061 Indian students. This prolific increase in Indian schools, supported by federal funding, clearly demonstrated the government's aggressive approach to using education as a tactic for addressing the "Indian problem."

- *The Indian Removal Act (1830)*   This Act uprooted the eastern tribes from their ancestral lands and moved them to the Indian Territory (parts of current-day Oklahoma, Kansas, and Nebraska). The Act was to "protect Indians from Whites," yet it is interesting to note that the Indian Removal Act was passed shortly after discovering gold in the Georgia Mountains on the Cherokee Nation's land. When the Cherokee leaders refused to leave their land, the U.S. Army forcibly marched over 11,500 Cherokees at gunpoint from Georgia to Oklahoma during the winter of 1838. About 4,000 Indians died along the way, many of which were women, children, and the elderly. This forced removal and subsequent trip became known as the Trail of Tears. After the Cherokees arrived in the new territory, they began to establish schools. The Cherokee were unique among the Indian tribes in that they had already developed a written language, which was created by Sequoyah (see Box 1.10). Their language consisted of 85 symbols representing syllables within their language. They had used this syllable-based written language since 1821 to write their tribal newspaper, the Cherokee Phoenix.

**Common School Period (1840–1880)**   In 1849, the Office of Indian Affairs was transferred from the War department to the Department of Interior. Some Indian uprisings continued to take place involving Whites that were venturing into Indian Territory. As a result, in 1867 the Peace Commission was established by Congress to investigate the problems with the hostile tribes. The Commission's report stated that almost all of the Indian uprisings were started by encroaching settlers. Further, the report declared that the U.S. government had shamefully mistreated the Indian tribes and had unlawfully broken treaties and stolen Indian land. However, the Peace Commission further declared that teaching English to the Indians was the only way to assimilate them into the White culture, thus suggesting an English-only curriculum and policy in Indian schools. One year later, the federal government signed treaties with the Sioux and Navajo, which stipulated that they would send their children to schools where they would receive an English education. (Meriam, 1928)

Simultaneously, the increased involvement of Congress in the education of Indians was a technique used to "manage" the Indians by removing them from the influences of their family and tribe and keeping them in boarding schools in order to "civilize" them. The policy was to segregate the Indian student entirely from their culture, heritage, customs, native language, and family (sometimes many states away) in order to speed up the assimilation process. To speed this cultural transition, the Indian Bureau issued an official mandate that all instruction in mission schools and government-run boarding schools was to be in English only under the threat of losing federal funding. This mandate was enforced to the fullest. Many Indian children were severely punished if they were caught speaking their native language. (Interestingly, English-only initiatives today are similarly impacting language acquisition with many children whose native language is not English; this critical issue will be explored further in Chapter 12.)

In efforts to expedite the forced assimilation of the "savage Indian" and to "save" him by removing his "bad" characteristics and replacing them with the White man's "good"

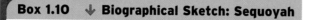

**Box 1.10** ↓ **Biographical Sketch: Sequoyah**

Sequoyah (1767-1843) was reported to have been unimpressed with the white man's ability to communicate by means of "talking leaves." He boasted that he, too, could etch symbols on stones that could have meaning.

Sequoyah conceived of a pictographic language where words or concepts are symbolized with graphics. He quickly realized that such a system would require an unmanageable number of symbols. Sequoyah soon began to experiment with a phonetic alphabet where symbols represented individual sounds (syllables) rather than concepts or things. This was much more manageable. He set to work and discovered that there are eighty-five vowel and consonant sounds in the Tsalagi language. Sequoyah assigned a character to each of these. This was the core of the Tsalagi or Cherokee alphabet.

Sequoyah's first student was his young daughter, Ahyokeh. Father and daughter gave public demonstrations, in which they would encode and decode written messages standing several hundred yards apart. When the significance of the syllabary was realized in 1821, literacy spread rapidly throughout the Cherokee Nation. In 1822, Sequoyah went to join kinsmen who were living in the Arkansas Territory. Communications between the eastern and western groups of Cherokees could now be maintained through written correspondence. (Barger, 2004)

characteristics, the U.S. government also banned native religious practices and worship customs of the Indians. (Reyner & Eder, 2004)

When Ulysses S. Grant became president, he began a peace policy with the Indians. He appointed the first Native American, a Seneca Indian named Ely S. Parker, as the commissioner of the Office of Indian Affairs in 1869. In that same year, Grant created the Board of Indian Commissioners who selected government officials that served as Indian Agents on tribal land. By 1871, Congress officially ended all treaty making with the Indians. After this, only "agreements" were formed with tribes. This change represented a shift in governmental policy from removing Indians and relocating them out West to isolating them on reservations and making them wards of the government.

**Progressive Period (1880–1920)** The focus of the progressive movement was the conviction that democracy means active participation by all citizens in social, political, and economic decisions that will affect their lives. (Ryan & Brandt, 1932) The education of engaged citizens, according to this perspective, involves two essential elements:

- *Respect for diversity,* meaning that each child should be recognized for their own abilities, interests, ideas, needs, and cultural identity; and

- *Development of critical, socially engaged intelligence,* which enables individuals to understand and participate effectively in the affairs of their community.

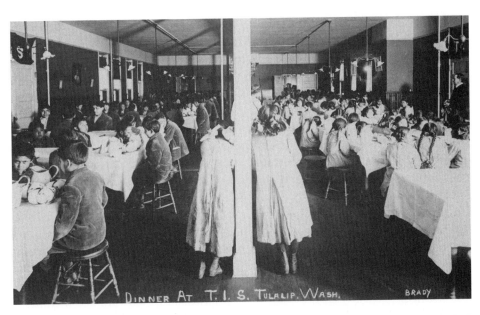

Kitchen girls, Tulalip Indian School, ca. 1900. Every student at the boarding school spent at least half of his or her day working in some part of the operation. Girls were assigned to sewing, darning, laundry, and kitchen work. The students raised most of the school's food on the grounds and prepared it in the kitchen.

© Museum of History and Industry/CORBIS

However, for the Native American, this period of American education was still one of family division, cultural assimilation, and social repression. The Dawes Act is one example of this repression:

- *General Allotment Act, or Dawes Act (1887)*   was passed in order to divide the Indians from their tribal connections. The Allotment Act gave 160 acres of tribal land to each family head, and 80 acres of tribal land to single adults. During the Allotment period, the government undermined Indian resistance by creating large geographical distances between family members. The Act promised that after twenty-five years of occupying the allotted land, the American Indian would be granted U.S. citizenship. This is a rather ironic promise, considering that the Indians were the original inhabitants of this continent.

Congress continued to use education as a tool for assimilation by passing compulsory education laws. As a way of enforcing school attendance, the government would withhold food rations and monetary annuities from Indian families who didn't send their children to school. By 1894, however, the government did start to require parental permission to send children to off-reservation boarding schools. Prior to that, no permission was required and children were typically removed by force at gunpoint. This emphasis on improving the conditions of the Indian schools led to a more sympathetic view of Indian education at the dawn of the twentieth century.

**Modern Period (1920–present)**   The Indians were not officially granted citizenship until 1924 when Congress passed the Indian Citizenship Act (this is five years after women were given the right to vote). Fortunately, influenced by the teaching of progressive philosophy, many educators began to be more concerned with Indian education. Prior to this time, students were taught to do menial, mundane vocational skills like domestic and manual labor training and farming. However, in 1902 the NEA suggested that textbooks used in Indian education needed to include references to objects and events that were familiar to the culture and daily environments of the Indian students. They proposed the "natural method" (Pestalozzi's theory of education), that was a way to teach English by using realistic and everyday objects. John Dewey's Progressive Movement also influenced the approach to teaching Indian students. Up until the beginning of the twentieth century, Indian education, like the education of other U.S. children, had involved a heavy emphasis on rote memorization and dull repetition, as well as a dominant reliance on textbook instruction. By 1915, the Indian curriculum changed to reflect that of the typical public school. This was a huge shift in the attitudes of educators, who previously and quite erroneously thought that Indians needed a different curriculum because they were unable to meet the mental demands of academically rigorous instruction. (Reyner & Eder, 2004)

A critical study emerging from this time was the Meriam Report of 1928. This study was conducted by social scientists, and revealed the deplorable living conditions for Indian peoples on reservations. The study found infant mortality rates of 190.7 per 1,000, far higher than the rate for any other ethnic group. Diseases such as measles, pneumonia, tuberculosis, and trachoma (an infectious eye disease) were rampant on the reservations. The report singled out the government's allotment policy as the greatest contributor to Indian peoples' impoverishment and called for a complete overhaul of the Bureau of Indian Affairs. Further, the study urged that Indians be given more control of managing their own affairs. On the subject of Indian education, the report further brought attention to the lack of alignment between the curriculum of the Indian schools and the realities of the reservation life of Indian students. It proclaimed that elementary age children do not belong in boarding schools, stating this approach was at variance with modern views of education and society that regard the home and family as essential institutions.

The Meriam Report further stressed the need to provide more preservice teacher training that educated new teachers about Indian customs and reservation life. It found that the food at boarding schools was "deficient in quality, quantity, and variety," and also questioned the use of Indian students as laborers, which it claimed would be prohibited in many states under child labor laws. This findings of this report led to the Indian Reorganization Act:

- *The Indian Reorganization Act (1934)* This Act ended the allotment of Indian lands and provided for religious freedom. It also mandated Indian preference in hiring Indian Service employees and encouraged a degree of tribal self-government.

The education of Indian students shifted from cultural subtraction to cultural recognition. The 1930s and 1940s utilized more humane educational practices for Native Americans. Teachers started to make deliberate efforts to begin with what was familiar to students, and avoided beginning with the outside world. That is, they started to employ the students' prior experiences and background knowledge by using concepts related to the family and home.

Congress passed a series of laws that enabled self-determination for the Indians. For instance:

- *The Indian Education Act (1972)* This piece of legislation brought about an awareness of the unique needs of Native American students who attended schools off of the reservation. The Indian Education Act provided funding for supplemental services and programs that were geared specifically to addressing the special obstacles faced by Indians. Materials and curriculum were supposed to be culturally relevant and were to provide the opportunity for bilingualism in English and their native tongue.

- *Indian Self-Determination and Education Assistance Act (1975)* This Act gave Indian people almost all power in regards to reservation activities. The BIA was required to contract its services directly to the tribes.

- *The Native American Languages Act (1990)* This Act stated that the Native American cultures and their languages are unique, and that it was the responsibility of both the U.S. government and the Indian tribes to ensure that the Native American cultures and languages are preserved. This Act made it the official policy of the federal government to promote Native language preservation and to encourage its use in educational settings.

- *National Education Goals for Indians* These ten goals were set forth in their 1991 report, with the aim of reaching them by the year 2000. The National Education Goals for

Indians emphasized readiness for school, maintaining native languages and culture, literacy, student academic achievement, high school graduation, high quality Native and non-Native school personnel, safe and alcohol-free/drug-free schools, adult education and life-long learning, restructuring schools, and parental, community, and tribal partnerships.

In order to address the problems that Native Americans have to overcome, the task force strongly recommended support of early childhood education and parent training programs, support for teacher education, and development of new and exemplary education projects designed to carry out school improvement recommendations to meet the unique cultural and academic needs of Native American students.

- *American Indian and Alaskan Native Education (1998)*   This Executive Order targeted many of the Indian Nation At Risk goals and emphasized academic accountability that continues to this present day.

The Native American experience has truly been one that involved a war of cultures. The war fostered governmental policies that blatantly sought to destroy Native culture. Most of these governmental policies were done in the effort to "help" the Indians by "civilizing" them and forcibly assimilating them into the dominant culture. The physical, spiritual, linguistic, cultural, and psychological destruction that has taken place is immeasurable.

Change has also been slowly realized. The last Indian Boarding School in Arizona, for example, didn't close its doors until 1990. Surprised? We hope that you are! We also hope that you become one of the unique educators who is acutely aware of societal and political issues that impact the lives of all of your students, and to openly accept your students for the many contributions and talents that they will bring to your classroom.

## Societal Changes and the Role of Teaching

As seen in the previous sections of this chapter, both people and events throughout history have shaped the profession of teaching and role of schooling in our society. Four specific societal changes have had an impact on the changing profession of teaching:

- a change in requirements for *professional preparation*.
- a shift in the *role of religion* in schools.
- the nation's changing *economic focus*.
- the growing *student diversity* in the classroom.

1. *Preparation of Teachers.* Through out this book, we will be emphasizing the critical role of teachers in the academic achievement and success of their students. You may already have been accepted into a teacher preparation program that includes earning a bachelor's degree or beyond, taking extensive coursework in both the content that you'll teach and the methods of teaching (often referred to as *pedagogy*). You'll also be working in classrooms for various interning or service learning experiences, and will spend at least one full semester in student teaching. More than likely, you'll also have a rigorous state exam that you will need to pass prior to earning your teaching certificate or even to enter the university's teacher preparation program. These experiences are designed so that you have the greatest chance of success once you have your own classroom. But has teacher training always been this way? Not at all.

As we have seen in this chapter, our nation's earliest school children were often taught by well-meaning, but unprepared young adults who may not have had more than an eighth grade education themselves. In some communities, these were young men who were studying for the ministry or who wanted some life experience for a year or two before they settled down and had a family. The first "normal school," or postsecondary training for teachers, didn't open until the 1830s under the leadership of Horace Mann, a noted historical figure who also introduced many of the philosophies associated with today's schools. It was also at this time that the profession of teaching shifted from an occupation suitable for young men, to one dominated by young women.

**Think About It**

What effects will these trends in certification have on the quality of teachers in tomorrow's classroom?

**Think About It**

While today we know of the importance of actively involving children in the learning process, how much has really changed inside classroom instruction?

**Think About It**

Can—and should—religion be separated from today's classroom?

The preparation of teachers has certainly evolved since the first public schools were open in this country, and since Bette's grandmother attended her one-room school. Teachers today are highly trained, certified, and experienced before they ever have their first teaching position. Interestingly, however, there is a current trend nationally toward eliminating teacher certification—or at least cutting back significantly on the pedagogical training of teachers—and focus on the content of what is taught (e.g., math, science, history).

2. *Role of Religion.* The early colonists believed that the Bible was the source of wisdom for their society. Therefore, they placed a priority on developing an educational system that would enable large numbers of people to read "God's word." Educators themselves were viewed as societal buffers against evil.

Within this educational focus on religion was the expectation that instruction was to be centered on memorization and recitation. Children were discouraged from expressing their own opinions or asking questions, because the literal interpretation of biblical passages was of most value. This focus on recitation was still evident in the schooling experiences of Bette's great-grandmother.

Although the separation of church from state is constitutionally mandated, including the separation of religion from our public institutions, current controversies still surround the role of religion in schools. Church groups often use school space to hold weekend services or after school clubs, and some schools have active prayer or religious groups that meet regularly on school grounds. Some states are struggling with the adoption of science standards that include both the theories of evolution and beliefs of creationism.

3. *Economic Focus.* Our nation has transformed from an agricultural society, to one that focused on industry and manufacturing, to today's information-based economics. The vignette of Helen reflects a society that focused on agriculture; urban industry that was flourishing in other parts of

Students today benefit from many of the societal changes that have occurred over past decades.

the country had not yet impacted small, remote rural areas. Students typically did not complete more than a middle school education, as the boys would join their fathers in field or agriculture work, and girls would be expected to learn the arts of homemaking from their mothers and grand-mothers. Interestingly, most schools today still follow an agricultural calendar, with a large chunk of time off from school in the summer that once was planned so that children could participate in agricultural tasks.

During the twentieth century, the nation transformed from an agricultural to an industrial society. School prepared students (especially boys) for blue-collar manufacturing or transportation jobs. Preparation for these careers impacted the subjects that were taught in schools. Many people today still describe schools in industrial terms. Children are sometimes viewed as products on an assembly line, receiving the same "inputs" or instruction, with the expectation that all children's skills and knowledge will be identical at the end of the schooling experience.

Today's economy, in contrast, is described as the age of information, which has been predomi-nantly impacted by a rapid expansion of technologies. As a consequence, the number of blue-collar workers is shrinking, and being replaced with a growing number of white-collar workers who make up the executive, professional, and technical workforce. The challenge for education lies in keeping up with the curriculum demands that these changes require. For example, it is no longer sufficient for students to memorize recommended lists of facts—because the "facts" and knowledge that we have access to grow exponentially every year.

4. *Student Diversity.* One of the most profound societal impacts on schooling is the changing demographics and diversity of our students. Previously, schools have been viewed as a place where children are to be "assimilated" or socialized into the dominant (i.e., White western) culture. Within this framework, the school curriculum reflected the European White perspective as being the "true" American culture, and young learners were expected to conform. This view was perhaps most dramatically represented in the "Indian Schools" that were common at the turn of the twen-tieth century, where young Native American children were taken off of their reservations, boarded in schools far from their families, and required to adopt the dress, language, and culture of White Americans.

**Think About It**

Should the existing "agricultural" school calendar be changed to better match today's informational eco-nomic focus?

**Think About It**

How are schools preparing children to be successful in a society domi-nated by technol-ogy and informa-tion access?

Schools today mirror the diversity of our American society.

**Think About It**

How is today's "cultural responsiveness" different from "multicultural education" lessons you experienced as a K through 12 student?

Fortunately, these dramatic measures were abandoned, along with race-based segregation, although these changes were slow to be adopted in many communities. *Brown v. The Board of Education,* which marked the slow end of segregation, has only observed its 50th birthday, and many of the Indian Boarding Schools operated well into the 1970s. However, the shift that is occurring in many schools today is toward *cultural responsiveness,* which stresses the heritage and contributions of a variety of ethnic groups. The goal of culturally responsive teaching is to acknowledge differences, accommodate for diversity in instruction, and to build instruction from an understanding of students' cultural experiences.

The role of gender differences has also played itself out inside our nation's schools. Until very recently, girls and boys were expected to have very different career paths, depending upon their gender. Therefore, some curriculum areas (such as business, shop, and home economics) were restricted to either boys or girls. Teachers often had different expectations for students, based on their gender. Present efforts have been made to include both male and female historical figures and their contributions into the curriculum. Girls are actively encouraged in areas often thought to be preferred by boys, such as math and science. Some advocate for specific classes or schools that separate boys from girls, with the goal of allowing all students to better focus on their own academic areas of excellence—without gender-related distractions or competition.

**Think About It**

How is diversity being celebrated—or restricted—in your communities?

The number of children who are English Language Learners (ELL) has also dramatically increased. While some states embrace the value of learning multiple languages, and emphasize bilingual instruction for all children, others (such as California and Arizona) have reverted to an assimilation view of ELL children and have banned bilingual instruction in favor of an English-only philosophy.

# Looking Forward

In this chapter, we have traced the historical foundations of education in this country, including the reforms and laws that continue to impact current educational decisions and policies. While a classroom today would superficially look very different from those of our nation's founding families, or even from our own grandparents, the fundamental elements of public education were laid when the first colony was established. Reform took time, and was influenced by a variety of cultural, social, and economic factors.

The process of change and reform in education did not equally impact all students, however. As we have seen, students of color have had to face issues of segregation and prejudice that others did not experience. The educational history of American Indians is also marked by challenge and tragedy, as these children were forcibly removed from their homes and communities in order to be assimilated into a White and English culture.

What lessons can be learn from these experiences? One lesson that history teaches us is that reforms are grounded in past events, but that we can best guide and determine future initiatives by first recognizing and understanding the consequences of past policies.

In this chapter, you have learned about many historical events and reforms that have changed education in this country. However, many of these initiatives continue to impact what occurs today in the classroom, or how teachers are prepared.

Consider the initiatives listed in Figure 1.6. As a group, answer the following questions:

- How do each of these initiatives impact education today?
- Which initiative do you think is the most influential? Why?
- What other historical factors have influenced current educational practices? How?
- What changes do you anticipate in the future?

**Figure 1.6 ↓ Historical Influences on Education**

| Historical Initiative | Impact Today |
|---|---|
| **Apprenticeships** | |
| **Old Deluder Satan Act** | |
| **McGuffey Readers** | |
| **Normal Schools** | |
| **Compulsory Education Act** | |
| **Development of Unions** | |
| *Brown v. Board of Education* | |
| **Indian Boarding Schools** | |
| **IDEA** | |

## Research Citations

Altenbaugh, R. J. (2002). *The American People and Their Education: A Social History.* Upper Saddle River, NJ: Prentice Hall.

*A Nation At Risk: The Imperative for Educational Reform.* (1983). Washington, DC: The Commission on Excellence in Education.

Banning, E. I. (1965). *Mary Lyon of Putnam's Hill: A biography.* New York, NY: Vanguard Press.

Barger, R. N. (2004). *History of American Education Web Project.* http://www.nd.edu/- rbarger/www7/ (accessed June 12, 2006).

De Guimos, R. (1889). *Pestalozzi, his aim and work.* New York, NY: C. W. Bardeen

Copley, F. B. (1923). *Frederick W. Taylor, Father of Scientific Management.* New York, NY: Augustus M Kelley Pubs.

Fröbel, F. (1826) *On the Education of Man (Die Menschenerziehung).* Keilhau/Leipzig: Wienbrach.

Harper, C. A. (1970). *A Century of Public Teacher Education.* Westport, CT: Greenwood.

Haubrich, V. F., Apple, M. W. (1975). *Schooling and the Rights of Children.* Berkeley, CA: McCutchan.

Hook, S. (1995). *John Dewey: An Intellectual Portrait.* Amherst, NY: Prometheus Books.

Indian Nations At-Risk Task Force (1991). *Indian Nations At-Risk: An Educational Strategy for Action.* Washington, DC: U.S. Department of Education.

Krul, H. (1875). *Petalozzi: His life, work, and influence.* Cincinnati, OH: Van Antwerp, Bragg.

Lilley, I. (1967). *Friedrich Froebel: A Selection from his Writings.* Cambridge, MA: Cambridge University Press.

Mann, M. P. (1977). *Life of Horace Mann.* Books for Libraries (Black Heritage Library Collection).

Martin, J. (2003). *The Education of John Dewey.* Columbia, NY: Columbia University Press.

McLoone, M. (1997). *Booker T. Washington.* Mankato, MN: Capstone Press.

Meriam, L. (1928). *The Problem of Indian Assimilation.* Baltimore, MD: Johns Hopkins University Press.

Merrell, J. (1972). *Horace Mann; A biography.* New York, NY: Alfred A. Knopf.

Mondale, S. (2002). *School: The Story of American Public Education.* Boston, MA: Beacon Press.

Ornstein, A. C., & Levine, D. U. (1993). *Foundations of Education, 5th ed.* Boston, MA: Houghton Mifflin.

Parkerson, D. & Parkerson, J. A. (2001). *Transitions in American Education: A Social History of Teaching (Studies in the History of Education).* New York, NY: Routledge-Falmer Press.

Pulliam, J. D. & Van Patten, J. J. (2002). *History of Education in America, 8th ed.* Upper Saddle River, NJ: Prentice Hall.

Reyner, J., & Eder, J. (2004). *American Indian Education: A History.* Norman, OK: University of Oklahoma Press.

Rippa, S. A. (1996). *Education in a Free Society: An American History, 8th ed.* Boston, MA: Allyn & Bacon.

Rury, J. L. (2004). *Education and Social Change: Themes in the History of American Schooling, 2nd ed.* Mahway, NJ: Lawrence Erlbaum Associates.

Ryan, W. C., & Brandt, R. K. (1932). Indian education today. *Progressive Education, 9,* 81–86.

Washington, B. T., & Harlan, L. R. (1986). *Up from Slavery: An Autobiography.* New York, NY: Penguin Classics.

Webb, L. D. (2005). *The History of American Education: A Great American Experiment.* Upper Saddle River, NJ: Prentice Hall.

Wilder, L. I. (1933). *Farmer Boy.* New York, NY: Harper-Trophy.

Wrege, C. D., & Greenwood, R. G. (1991). *Frederick W. Taylor: The Father of Scientific Management: Myth and Reality.* Chicago, IL: Irwin Professional Pub.

# The Role of Teaching in the Educational Community

## 2

In the previous chapter, we explored the multidimensional tasks of the teaching profession, and how historical influences impacted these teaching roles. In this chapter, we will introduce you to some of the basic concepts of effective teaching. Then we will focus on how teaching fits within the broader context of the community, including an exploration of the roles of parents, department chairs, administrators, and school board members and how they impact what teachers do inside their classrooms.

**Definitions**

**Achievement gap**   a recognition that substantial differences exist between advantaged and disadvantaged students in regards to how successful they are in school. The gap typically refers to differences between racial groups, and the impact of differential schooling experiences on how well students do on tests and in academic achievement.

**Direct instruction**   a way of teaching students that usually involves teaching a large group (whole-group instruction) and which focuses on directly teaching students a specific skill. The lesson usually consists of demonstrating the skill, and provides time for students to practice. In this teaching method, the teacher is in control of and the focus of the instruction.

**Manipulatives**   actual objects that are used in instruction, typically during math lessons. These might include interlocking cubes, blocks, dice, or even clay. Manipulatives give students concrete, hands-on experiences to help them learn new concepts.

**Tenure**   a term used to indicate that a professional, such as a teacher, has longevity and permanence in his/her position. Typically, a person with tenure would be very difficult to dismiss from his/her position, unless it was under extreme circumstances.

## As you read, think about...

★ Your favorite teachers, and what made them effective in the classroom.

★ The role that your parents or caregivers had in your educational experiences.

★ Roles that you have observed other educators and community members have taken that impact schools.

## Focus Questions

★ What are the characteristics of effective teachers today?

★ What makes schools effective?

★ How are schools identified as "at risk"?

# Effective Teachers Today

As a profession, we have come a long way since our grandparents were in schools, or even since we were students ourselves. As we saw in Chapter 1, individual educators across our history, as well as broader societal changes, have impacted what occurs in our classrooms, how we teach our students, and even the content that is in our instruction. Changes will continue to occur, and hopefully will make us better prepared and more effective in insuring that our students are successful.

But what makes one teacher more effective than others? The roles of teachers as craftsmen, artisans, scientists, and advocates will be explored more in depth throughout this book. However, in this introductory section, let's take a look at some of the overall multidimensional elements that make a teacher successful.

1. *Preparation.* One of the best predictors for a teacher's success in the classroom is the level and quality of his/her preparation. Effective teachers:

- Have had extensive educational coursework on pedagogy—how to teach
- Possess high verbal ability and communication skills
- Are fully knowledgeable about the content that they teach
- Are fully certified in the content and grade level that they are teaching
- Have taught in classrooms for several years; the most-experienced teachers are the most effective

2. *Students.* Another characteristic of a successful teacher is his/her connection with and focus on the students. Effective teachers:

- Set clear and high expectations for all students
- Establish a positive, interactive environment
- Engage students in their own learning
- Connect instruction with students' prior experiences in and out of the classroom
- Match instruction and materials to students' needs and abilities
- Seek and incorporate student feedback into instruction
- Stimulate and maintain students' interest and motivation
- Challenge all students to succeed to their highest potential

3. *Planning.* Quality teaching at any level requires careful and organized planning. Effective teachers:

- Focus instruction on very clear goals and objectives that are tied to district and state standards
- Align instructional goals with lesson activities and assessments
- Plan instruction so that it accommodates for different learning styles and needs
- Vary how students are grouped, and change groups often
- Integrate lessons across the curriculum

4. *Instructional Delivery.* How teachers present their material has an impact on how much students learn, and how engaged they remain in the learning tasks. Effective teachers:

- Focus classroom time on learning and teaching
- Use a variety of instructional formats, including modeling, mini-lessons, simulations, and cooperative learning
- Involve students in authentic, real-life experiences
- Include experiential, hands-on learning activities
- Create and maintain an orderly and democratic classroom

Effective teachers engage all students through a variety of activities that stimulate prior knowledge and extend learning.

- Include strong beginnings and closures in their lessons
- Have smooth and efficient transitions between activities
- Involve students actively in extended projects and investigations
- Skillfully use questioning at a variety of levels, and stimulate higher-order thinking

5. *Assessment.* Exceptional teachers continually use assessment to guide their instructional planning, and reflect on their instructional decisions to improve subsequent lessons. Effective teachers:

- Use multiple assessment systems and tools to regularly monitor students' learning
- Develop a system to continuously monitor student progress
- Provide students with immediate and specific feedback
- Expect students to keep track of their own individual progress
- Self-reflect on their efforts to improve future performance

6. *Resources.* Quality instruction also includes the decisions that teachers make about which resources to use in their classrooms. Effective teachers:

- Use a variety of resource materials, including visits from experts and field trips outside of the classroom
- Routinely use a range of technological tools, and expect students to become proficient with these tools as well
- Use ***manipulatives*** and other instructional materials to explicitly model activities and content for students
- Insure that students have hands-on access to resources

(Allington & Cunningham, 1996; Kauchak, Eggen, & Carter, 2002; Stronge, 2002; Zemelman, Daniels, & Hyde, 1998)

While there are many components of effective teaching, the keys are *preparation, flexibility,* and *variety.* And, of course, establishing an environment where all children can achieve!

# Parents and Schools

One of the most influential components of a child's success in school is the involvement of his/her parents. Parents are often referred to as a child's "first teacher," and that is certainly quite true. Children spend many more hours of the day in the care of their families, and it is from these critical caretakers that they first learn language, appropriate modes of behavior, and cultural and social values. While critical in the formative years of a child's life, the influence of parents and caregivers continues to be essential as students enter school. Some educators believe that the primary factor for children's educational success—or failure—is the level of parental interest and support (Pena, 2004).

There are many ways that parents can become involved in students' learning once they enter school. For example, defining parental or family involvement includes:

- Creating a **home environment** that encourages learning;
- Expressing **high expectations** for children's success
- **Becoming involved** in students' school activities and experiences (Wyman, 2001)

One of the most difficult tasks of a teacher is to find ways to directly involve parents and caregivers in the school experience. As a novice second-grade teacher, Bette tried many different ways to involve her students' families. Each of these activities strengthened her relationship with both students and their parents, and increased the quality of experiences for students in the classroom. The level of involvement varied, and was respectful of the differences in families' work schedules and needs. Specific ideas that Bette incorporated included the following:

- **Reading volunteers:** parents regularly volunteered to lead reading groups, using instructional plans that Bette had prepared
- **Expert guests:** during special events, such as "pioneer days," parents were invited to share their expertise in a variety of areas including weaving and quilting
- **Field trip chaperones:** Bette and her students took several field trips to local businesses or museums, which were greatly enhanced by having extra hands and eyes to ensure that the students focused on appropriate learning tasks
- **Special event assistants:** when the class planned special activities, such as cooking ethnic foods to celebrate the contributions of different cultural groups, parents were encouraged to join the class to assist in preparing special treats
- **Performance audience:** at least twice a year, Bette and her students put on an informal performance, such as reading poetry or sharing a play that the class had written, and invited parents and family members to participate
- **Project volunteers:** Recognizing that many parents and caregivers could not come to school during the day, Bette created projects that families could complete at home, including making "blank books" that were used as part of her writing curriculum; all the materials, and directions, were provided
- **Open door policy:** Bette encouraged family members to come and informally visit the classroom at any time; this "open door" policy enhanced communication with parents, and was particularly beneficial in acquainting new families to the classroom's routines

There are many other ways to involve parents in schools, including inviting their participation on school councils, forming parent-led committees or Parent-Teacher Organizations, and using parents as math or reading tutors. Many schools have a volunteer or part-time Parent Coordinator, who greets families as they enter the school, directs them to classrooms, informs families about school policies, and keeps data on parental involvement. Parent Coordinators are very visible signs of a school's commitment to family involvement.

There are many benefits to including parents and families in school activities. These benefits include:

- Increasing students' language achievement
- Enhancing students' achievement
- Increasing students' attitudes toward school
- Improving students' morale
- Increasing students' positive behaviors and emotional development
- Reducing students' drop-out rate
- Reducing destructive behavior in school
- Reducing the likelihood that students will become involved with drugs, violence, or teen sex
- Increasing parents' self-confidence
- Increasing parents' attitudes about teachers and their own aspirations for their children (Cordry, 2004; Pena, 2004; Quesada, Diaz, & Sanchez, 2003)

**Cultural Barriers to Involvement**    Despite the many benefits of parental involvement, many family members simply choose not to become involved with their children's school experiences. Many factors can contribute to these perceived barriers, including parents' intimidation of school "jargon," issues of transportation and childcare, parents' own negative experiences with schooling, lack of effective communication, and overall misperceptions of the roles of parents and families in schools.

For those parents and family members that are minorities, disadvantaged, and/or who do not speak English, these challenges are particularly difficult to overcome. In her study of Mexican-American families, Pena (2004) found that the following factors influenced the level of parental involvement:

1. *Language.* This was particularly influential in determining activities in which parents chose to participate
2. *Parent cliques.* The existence of "cliques" of parents that dominated school activities limited the participation of others, particularly those that were new to the community
3. *Parents' education.* Many parents felt that they could not help their children in school because of their own limited knowledge; some also found it difficult to complete school paperwork, such as applications for free or reduced lunch, because of limitations in reading skills or in English
4. *Attitudes of school staff.* Unfortunately, parents perceived that some teachers felt that parent involvement was an extra burden and therefore discouraged these activities
5. *Cultural influences.* The cultural values of the family also influenced the degree to which some parents participated in the school. For example, in some more traditional households, it was expected that mothers stay home and were therefore not available to attend school functions
6. *Family issues.* Day-to-day realities, such as transportation, childcare, and work schedules, also impeded the involvement of many families in school activities

**Overcoming Barriers**    Teachers and schools can incorporate many different strategies to encourage the participation of parents and family members in their children's learning experiences. While particularly important in overcoming cultural barriers, these are effective regardless of the families with whom you will soon be working.

- Offer flexible schedules, to accommodate for parents' work and other family obligations
- Provide transportation to the school for conferences, meetings, or other school events
- Conduct home visits, where individual invitations can be made to involve families in school experiences
- Seek parents' input on ideas for family workshops or training
- Send written communication home to families in both English and the parents' native language

- Provide a translator at school meetings and conferences
- Use a variety of modes of communication and personal contacts to invite participation
- Use technology as a tool for communication (while being sensitive to those families who may not have access to this technology)
- Provide parents with clear directions on how they can become involved with their children's school and classroom experiences
- Get to know the cultures of families in the community
- Involve parents in school-based planning and decision-making
- Create social functions, such as dinners or picnics, where teachers and families can become better acquainted and build personal relationships
- Acknowledge parents' contributions (Halsey, 2005; Halsey, 2004; Quesada et al., 2003)

**Think About It**

In addition to these strategies, how else can teachers work with parents to increase their involvement in schools?

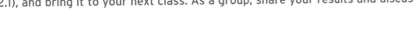

Consider the school where you are volunteering. Are parents welcomed? Involved in the classroom? Participating in other activities? Why do you think that parents feel welcomed—or don't feel like they belong in the school?

**Group Talk**

Attend a parent meeting—such as a PTO meeting or workshop. Or, if your school doesn't hold meetings or events that include parents, talk to a parent of a child that attends your school. Fill out the discussion sheet (Figure 2.1), and bring it to your next class. As a group, share your results and discuss the following questions:

- Do any barriers exist that prevent parents from being involved at your school?
- Why do these barriers exist?
- How is the school encouraging parental involvement?
- What suggestions would you have to improve parental involvement at this school?

**Figure 2.1 ↓ Parental Involvement**

**Parental Involvement Discussion Guide**

- Event or meeting attended:

- Describe what you observed:

- Topics of discussion:

- Level of parent involvement: (Did one group of parents dominate the activity? Did teachers or the principal dominate the activity?)

- Level of involvement of teachers/administrators: (Were teachers present at the event? What role did they play?)

- Questions/Concerns that parents raised:

Effective schools begin with effective, well-prepared teachers!

# What Makes Schools Effective?

It is probably no surprise that effective teachers are usually found in effective schools, which have the direct support and participation of parents and family members. No matter how good your intentions and abilities are individually, it is very difficult to teach students effectively when you have little support from administration, inappropriate or inadequate resources, and an unsafe school environment. All the pieces need to be in place in order for teachers to have the most positive impact on students' learning.

In the 1960s a paper was commissioned by the U.S. Office of Education to assess the effectiveness of American education. Written by James Coleman, the report concluded that public schools didn't make a significant difference in a student's academic achievement. Instead, Coleman's report credited the student's family background as the main reason for student success in school. His findings proposed that children, who were from poor families or homes, lacked the values to support education. Therefore, these children could not learn, regardless of what schools did. (Coleman, 1966)

These highly controversial findings generated a great deal of subsequent research, particularly from the Center for Urban Studies at Harvard University. Edmonds, Brookover, Lezotte, and others began to look at a wide range of variables within school buildings that appeared to consistently contribute to higher rates of student achievement—particularly in urban environments. (e.g., Brookover & Lezotte, 1977; Edmonds, 1979) Their research revealed significant differences in student achievement from one school to the next. While some schools were highly successful, others in virtually the same neighborhood were not. Characteristics describing both types of schools were observed and documented. The basic conclusion of this comparative research was:

- Public schools can and do make a difference, even those composed of students from poverty backgrounds

- Children from poverty backgrounds can learn at high levels as a result of public schools
- There are specific characteristics common to all the schools where **all** children are learning, regardless of family background

**Characteristics of Effective Schools**   The studies by Edmonds (1979), and Brookover and Lezotte (1977) then began to describe the characteristics of schools that demonstrate high rates of student academic performance—regardless of the students' race, ethnicity or socioeconomic status. The following list delineates these characteristics:

- *Clear School Mission*—there is a clearly articulated school mission that is shared by all staff and faculty. There is an explicit understanding of and commitment to instructional goals, priorities, assessment procedures, and accountability.
- *High Expectations for Success*—there is a climate of expectation in which the staff and faculty believe and demonstrate that all students can master of the content.
- *Instructional Leadership*—the principal acts as an instructional leader and effectively and persistently communicates that mission to the staff, parents, and students.
- *Frequent Monitoring of Student Progress*—student academic progress is measured with a variety of assessment procedures. The results of the assessments are used to guide and improve instruction.
- *Opportunity to Learn and Student Time on Task*—teachers allocate a significant amount of classroom time to instruction in the content and skills. Teachers use classroom time efficiently.
- *Safe and Orderly Environment*—there is an orderly, purposeful, businesslike atmosphere which is free from the threat of physical harm. The school climate is caring and is conducive to teaching and learning.
- *Home School Relations*—parents understand and support the school's basic mission and are given the opportunity to play an important role in helping the school to achieve that mission.
- *Highly Trained Effective Teachers*—the teacher is the most powerful variable that the child encounters on a regular basis. The teacher is well-prepared and develops effective teaching practices. (Allington & Cunningham, 1996; Kauchak, Eggen, & Carter, 2002)

What is unique about these characteristics is that they are the only set of research-based variables that are consistently associated with better student learning.

**Looking Inside Effective Schools**   Let's step inside an effective school. What might you see? How do the characteristics of this school parallel with the components of effective teaching outlined above?

In slicing through the question of effective schools, we've identified four categories:

- Teachers
- Students
- Instruction
- Organization

1. *Teachers.* As noted previously, effective teachers are those most often found in effective schools. Specifically, in effective schools:

- Teachers are involved in decision-making and take responsibility for instruction
- Teachers are made a part of the school's change or reform process
- Teachers are active members of site-based management teams
- Time is provided for teachers to meet regularly in order to plan and collaborate

- Special education teachers connect with classroom teachers to increase student inclusion and align curriculum
- An investment is made in teachers' professional development

2. *Students.* Effective schools also consider students as having a critical role in their success. In effective schools:

- A commitment is made to the belief that all students can be successful
- High expectations are articulated for all students
- Teachers are expected to be in regular contact and communication with students' families
- Students' families are involved in the school's activities, and in making decisions that affect students' learning
- Families in need are provided with a variety of services

3. *Instruction.* The quality of instruction is also critical to the success of a school and its students. In effective schools:

- The primary mission is to promote student learning
- The majority of time in the school day is allocated to instruction
- Assessments are tied to everyday and authentic experiences
- Administrators don't over-rely or overemphasize standardized tests, which are instead considered as only one part of the total assessment package
- The curriculum is flexible, to allow for a variety of teaching and learning styles

4. *Organization.* How a school is organized, and the physical facilities themselves, are also important. In effective schools:

- The physical environment is safe for all students
- Playground equipment is safe, and inspected often

Teachers play a prominent role in the success of their school and it's students.

- A consistent and fair management system is adopted
- The normal day is extended to include programs before and after school
- Class scheduling accommodates for large, uninterrupted chunks of instructional time
- Summer programs are provided for a variety of learning needs
- Class size is kept small enough to optimize student learning

While all of these components are critical, many educators believe that it is the teacher who makes the most difference in the lives of students. Richard Allington and Patricia Cunningham, noted educational researchers, suggest that, "effective classroom teachers are the only absolutely essential element of an effective school" (1996, pg. 81).

## What about Schools at Risk?

Effective schools, and effective teachers, exist in every type of community across all types of geographic regions. However, some educators argue that schools at risk—for example, those that serve children of poverty or those that are in rural communities—don't have the same access to resources as other successful schools that might reside in more affluent communities. Educators (and the media!) often talk about the *"achievement gap,"* and how some communities' schools are not as effective as compared with others in assuring students' academic success. Some suggest that these gaps are influenced by such societal factors as poverty, SES, ethnicity, and native language. What does it take to be effective under the most challenging conditions?

We believe that there is equal potential with all students, and that effective schools and teachers recognize that it is the individual—not outside circumstances—that determine success. Schools at risk, in particular, require that teachers and administrators set *high expectations* for their students, focus on the *curriculum,* and understand students as *unique individuals*. However, these are components of success for any school!

Educators also note the following elements of effective schools for students and communities that are at risk. As you read this list, consider how these are different—or identical to— components for success in *any* school:

- Schools adopt a "no excuses" mindset
- A primary focus is placed on maximizing instructional time
- Teachers get to know students academically, socially, and culturally
- Support programs are provided for students and their families
- Instruction is guided by regular assessment
- Instructional grouping remains flexible and varied
- Instruction builds on students' knowledge and experiences
- Students are treated as being competent individuals
- The culture and language of students is valued, and used as part of instruction
- Teachers and administrators have faith in students' potential and abilities

Teachers, parents, and administrators who truly care about their students create effective schools—in any community—! Figure 2.2 overviews the connectedness of all the roles within a school community; these roles will be explored further in this section.

## Keys to Effective Schools: School Personnel

In this chapter, we have explored the components that contribute to making schools more effective. While it is obvious that effective schools require quality teachers and students ready to learn, there is an additional key that is critical to success: school personnel. In this section,

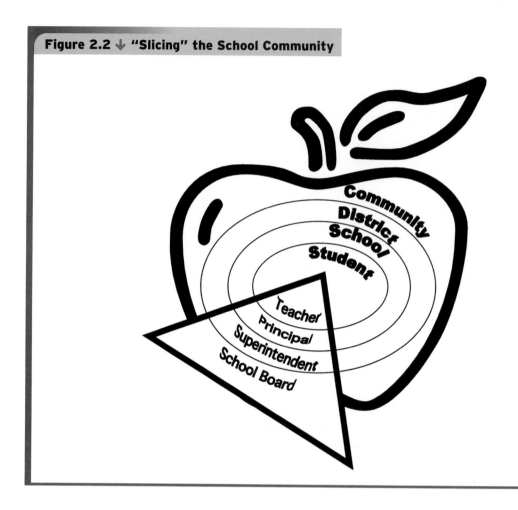

**Figure 2.2 ↓ "Slicing" the School Community**

**Group Talk**

What do you think are the characteristics of effective schools? Are those characteristics different for elementary, junior high, and high schools?

This section has listed four categories for components of effective schools: *teachers*, *students*, *instruction*, and *organization*.

- First, review the list of components for each of these categories (pages 53-55). What additional components can you add?
- Next, brainstorm other categories, in addition to teachers, students, instruction, and organization.
- Which of these characteristics have you found to be most prevalent in schools that you have visited?

**Think About It**

Think about a "typical" school day. How many different people influence what students do both inside and outside the classroom, in addition to their teachers? You might be surprised!

we'll describe the many types of people in schools that contribute to success. All roles are critical and interconnected.

## Paraprofessionals

Paraprofessionals, which are also referred to as paraeducators or instructional aides, are most often part-time school employees that provide a variety of instructional and clerical support to teachers and students. In today's classroom, paraprofessionals are major participants in the delivery of education and special services, from early childhood through high schools, to students with a range of abilities and for those students who are learning English as a second language (Ashbaker & Morgan, 2001). Specifically, paraprofessionals are found in inclusive classrooms to support students with disabilities as part of their special education program.

Paraprofessionals look very different today than they did fifty years ago. In the 1970s, paraprofessionals most often had clerical and noninstructional roles, such as copying materials and monitoring lunch breaks. In the 1980s, their role expanded to include tutoring individual students, in order to allow classroom teachers to have more time for whole group ***direct instruction.*** Currently, the role of the paraprofessional focuses primarily on instructional support, including monitoring behavior, individual and small group instruction, and assistance in skill acquisition (Wadsworth & Knight, 1996). Often, their roles overlap those of the classroom teacher. Their role is particularly critical in full ***inclusion*** environments, where children with special needs are placed in regular classroom settings. Paraprofessionals provide an essential link between the special education teacher and the classroom teacher.

Paraprofessionals perceive their role to be multifaceted, and to include a range of activities (Downing, Ryndak, & Clark, 2000):

- *Providing behavioral support*—such as keeping students with disabilities from disrupting their classmates and keeping students on task
- *Monitoring students*—ensuring that students understand their tasks and providing assistance as needed
- *Teaching*—including the direct instruction of specific skills in a range of academic and nonacademic subjects
- *Adapting and modifying curricular, materials, and activities*—which allows students with special needs to be involved in class activities
- *Supporting personal care*—by helping students at lunch or when using the restroom
- *Facilitating interactions with peers*—by prompting students to work together and suggesting ways for classmates to be effective helpers
- *Completing clerical work*—such as copying materials for the classroom teacher, filing, grading, checking homework, or putting up bulletin boards

Paraprofessionals that are assigned to students who are older or who have multiple disabilities may also be responsible for the following non-academic tasks (Carroll, 2001):

- *Daily living skills*—which include changing diapers, teaching self-feeding skills, dispersing medications, and other health needs
- *Community skills*—including accompanying students to community college classes, teaching students how to use public transportation, and assisting with shopping skills
- *Domestic skills*—such as cooking, laundry, and cleaning

Paraprofessionals can have a very positive impact on the students with whom they work. Woolfson and Truswell (2005) found that some of the many strengths of paraprofessionals, as perceived by parents and teachers, included supporting the following:

- Learning on all levels
- Children with challenging behavior problems
- Positive relationships with students
- Emotional needs of students
- Social and developmental needs of students
- Home-school links
- Parental initiatives

It is expected that the demand for paraprofessionals will continue to rise, especially to keep up with the demands for quality inclusion practices and to support the needs of an increasing number of students who are learning English as a second language. Because of their increased importance in the school, many paraprofessionals have a high degree of responsibility and independence in decisions regarding instructional adaptations and modifications, behavioral support, and information that is shared with parents. However, because paraprofessionals often do not have specific training, and often note that their training consists of "trial by fire" or learning on the job, concerns regarding the preparation of paraprofessionals are emerging across the country.

What is the training required of paraprofessionals? Most paraprofessionals today must meet one of the following requirements:

- Associate's degree or equivalent number of credit hours
- Passing score on a state exam

The requirements will differ depending on the school's Title I status, the funding sources for the paraprofessionals, and whether or not the paraprofessional's duties are instructional or nonacademic. These regulations have changed substantially under the "No Child Left Behind" Legislation of 2001. Do you know if you could be a paraprofessional in your state?

**A Look Inside the Paraprofessional Role**   Becoming a paraprofessional, or instructional aide, might be an excellent option for many of you who are considering a career in education. Through this important job, you will get an insider's look at the role of teaching, learn a variety of instructional strategies hands-on, and make a positive impact on students' learning! Lyndsey Dickenson balances her job as a paraprofessional with her full-time course load in a teacher preparation program. She shares her experiences below.

Do you have the preparation and qualifications necessary in your state to be an aide? We would recommend that you look into this exciting possibility!

## Team or Department Chair

The teacher is only one part of the team of educators in an effective school (though arguably the most important part!). Many individuals contribute to a school's climate, the development of curriculum, and instructional decisions that impact what is actually taught in the classroom. One of these roles is the *team* or *department chair.*

In elementary schools, a veteran teacher is often selected as a mentor for novice teachers or as a "chair" that organizes grade level team meetings. This position varies considerably among schools. Sometimes, these teachers receive extra pay, or a stipend, for their extra services. Most often, however, they do not. Usually, these lead teachers are selected by the school administers, though sometimes they might be voted on by their peers.

**Classroom Glimpse**

My typical day as an aide begins at 8:30. This year I go to five classrooms throughout the day. I pull out students who are in resource to work with them if the teacher asks me to; otherwise I help out in the classroom so the students can stay in class.

The greatest benefit I feel from the job is the students cannot wait for me to come into their classroom. I love when the students feel they can talk to me because they trust me, and they ask me to always come to their class.

The greatest challenge of being an aide is to work with teachers who do not appreciate the extra assistance, and make you copy papers!

I would recommend for every student to be an aide. I feel everything I know and have learned is from the experiences I have had from working at a school. ■

In middle schools, junior highs, and high schools, each content area (e.g., math, science, English) often has a department chair. Like in the elementary schools, department chairs are usually selected from amongst the school's most experienced teachers. Unlike the chairs or lead teachers in elementary schools, the roles of these lead teachers are much more defined, and more uniform across school systems. Usually, chairs have a reduced teaching load and work more days than regular classroom teachers. Consequently, department chairs usually receive a higher salary.

One of the primary roles of the department chair is to act as the liaison between his/her teachers and the school administrators. In effect, the chair is the advocate for the classroom teachers. Other typical tasks include: (Armstrong, Henson, & Savage, 2001)

- Ordering supplies
- Evaluating faculty
- Coordinating staff development
- Disseminating information on district policies
- Mentoring new teachers
- Allocating the department's materials budget
- Arranging for the distribution of textbooks

Being a chair allows an experienced teacher to assume new responsibilities and grow professionally, while remaining in the classroom where he/she will have the most impact on students' learning.

**A Look Inside the Role of Team or Department Chair**   What does a "typical" day of a chair really look like? As you read the two different vignettes that follow, think about what tasks are different—and the same—with two very different educators.

### First look: Middle school science

Debi Molina-Walters is an eighteen-year classroom veteran, who has most recently been a science department chair in a middle school. What are some of the roles and tasks that Debi describes?

The job of a middle school department chair has changed for me over the past ten years of my experience. In my first few years as chair, the traditional department chair duties centered on ordering textbooks, equipment, and department supplies. It was also my responsibility to organize department meetings where I passed out and collected paperwork as well as disseminated news and directives. I performed other bureaucratic duties as assigned by the principal or district administration. I maintained and inventoried department equipment and materials.

As education has changed its view on leadership over the past eight to ten years, this typical department chair description has changed. My most recent and rewarding experience was focused on site-based leadership duties. I was still responsible for ordering textbooks, equipment, and department supplies as well as providing leadership during monthly department meetings. The biggest change was that I became a site-based coach for the implementation of the state's science standards and related teaching strategies. I facilitated department reviews of standards-based lessons, literacy strategies, and the continuous improvement process. I made regular monthly classroom visits and completed department observations of teaching styles and classroom learning environments. I also was responsible for surveying student attitudes about science education and learning. I attended monthly leadership committee meetings and trainings to learn how to do all of the above. As members of the school's leadership committee, the chairs became leaders of school-based professional development sessions and presented model lessons for our department teachers.

**Classroom Glimpse**

My mornings typically started between 6:30 and 6:45. As the department chair, I always opened up the science wing. Each morning I did a quick equipment check. I was responsible for the computer cart and making sure the equipment was stored properly and working. Once a week I flushed all the drains in the science wing to prevent backwash. I arranged for the service of all science equipment and the removal of science waste products. My door was always open and I constantly fielded questions and concerns from my department staff. My "prep time" was spent visiting classrooms, meeting with teachers, talking with students about their science experience, checking equipment, or arranging meetings and/or teaching materials. I was usually the last teacher out of the building, where I did a safety check to make sure all doors were locked and blinds closed. I also organized the cleaning duties of the department's stockroom. I worked at meeting the instructional needs of the other teachers in the department. As the department chair, I was the problem solver. ■

## Second look: English chair

Now let's look into the classroom of another veteran department chair, Gale Olpp Ekiss, who has been a junior high social studies teacher and chair for over twenty years:

When I was selected to become a department chairperson for a social studies department of nine people, I thought, "Yes, someone had noticed my above average teaching abilities!" Little did I know that my being selected to be a department chairperson had a minimal amount to do with my abilities to teach seventh graders. Instead, my duties with my department revolved around my leadership skills that were just in the formative stage early in my career. Luckily, someone noticed this potential. From that moment on, I began to acquire and polish my leadership skills. A typical day for me might include:

7:45—Unlock the door to find a note on your desk: "Child sick. I'll be at home. Here's my sub plans. Good Luck, Teacher A."
Put my lunch in the refrigerator.
Intercom announcement: Department Chairperson meeting in principal's conference room in ten minutes.
Check mailbox in office for new mail.
Look at photos of the principal's secretary's grandchild—smile big.

8:00—At Department Chairperson Meeting: write notes about new policies and procedures as well as details for events coming up.

8:45—Return to room and prepare to start the day.
Unlock classroom door and students enter.
Sub for Teacher A runs in with cryptic lesson plans that need translation.
Sub also needs directions on where to find materials for lessons and directions for the faculty bathroom.

8:55—Class bell rings but still helping the Sub.
Kids are looking around for me or just talking among themselves until the morning announcements and pledge begin.

9:05—Instruction begins.
Interrupted by principal who wants my order forms for materials to be purchased.

10:05—Students leave, and prep time begins.
Take work to copy room to be printed.
Go to bathroom.
Check on Teacher B who wants input on his teaching.
Make phone call to parent.
Get book from school library for a lesson I'm creating.
Grade a couple of papers (hoped to get at least thirty graded).
Teacher C asks you to cover her class so she can go to the bathroom.

*11:05*—Class returns.

*12:05*—Lunch.

Try to eat while sharing the information from morning meeting.

Listen to whiners, support the principal, think of positive spins for the new information, socialize, and encourage professional growth.

Sing *Happy Birthday* to Teacher C and share birthday cake.

*12:30*—Class returns.

*3:30*—Class dismissed.

Teachers D and E want to order materials late—the principal has already taken the order.

Teacher F asks you to cover his morning duty tomorrow since he has a dentist appointment.

Teacher G comes by just to talk—has to be rescheduled to tomorrow afternoon after tutoring.

*4:00*—Attend district meeting on selecting the new social studies book.

Share my concerns on readability and what my students need.

Take more notes to communicate to department members.

*5:30*—Lug six sets of textbooks to my car that are being considered for district adoption, and hope that someone will help me get this 100 pounds of books into the school building.

*6:30*—Return to school for Parent Advisory group meeting.

Represent the teachers and their concerns.

Serve punch and cookies and clean up the utensils.

*8:00*—Go Home.

Grade those other twenty-eight papers that weren't graded this morning.

Gale describes the following roles of department chairs:

1. *Communicator.* As a department chairperson, I was liaison between the school and district administration and the teachers. I needed to communicate the policies and practices to my department and then take their reactions back up the chain of command. Of course, this is not a popular place to be because change is always stressful. So, as I would present the information to the teachers, I would wear a "teacher hat." As I dealt with the administrators, I would wear the "decision-making hat." By wearing two hats, I could be part of both teams.

2. *Instructional Leader.* The principal is the "top dog" for instructional leadership at a school. At least that is his/her label, but in an elementary/secondary setting, it is common to have the principal be someone outside of your grade level or academic area. Therefore, you become the specialist. It is your job to attend district and school level meetings and help create the scope and sequence for the curriculum. You are the textbook selector (hopefully with advice from the rest of the department), and the motivator to attend professional growth opportunities. This also makes you the resident scholar for all questions on campus regarding your grade level or subject area.

3. *Department Morale Builder.* I'm convinced the reason that teachers stay in teaching is that they enjoy their school setting and coworkers. If they have someone who will mentor, listen, engage in social activities, commiserate, and celebrate with them, they will remain in teaching. The burnout comes from alienation from the workplace society. So it is the department chairperson who is to be the cheerleader for the group. Chairs encourage activities, celebrate birthdays, pass around the vacation photos, and provide a support system for the group.

4. *Hand Holder (Advocate).* Many hours are spent in those interpersonal situations. In each department there are the strong (need little hand holding), the loners (won't take the hand holding), and the needy (seek the hand holding). This means the chairperson needs to identify what approach works well with each teacher so that the department functions with smoothness.

**Think About It**

What roles did you recognize in these two vignettes that were similar? Were there any roles or tasks that were different?

5. *Emergency Back-Up (Resource).* The department chairperson is the first person to be called when the substitute teacher doesn't arrive. The chair needs to be prepared to read cryptic lesson plans and translate them for the sub—all while you are also trying to point all where the required materials and equipment are located. Then when there is a fire drill or lock-down, you must make sure your area is secure. You will also be asked to cover classrooms for the teacher who has laryngitis, and you may be asked to attend a parent-teacher conference where fireworks might go off. ■

Department chairs provide essential leadership and mentoring within an effective school team.

**Effective Teachers, Effective Chairs**   Are the roles and tasks of teachers and chairs really that different? Let's use Gale's description of chairs, to compare what we've learned about effective teachers and the roles of chairs (see Figure 2.3):

## School Principals

Within a school building, the principal plays a critical role in assuring the smooth and safe operations of that facility. In order to become a principal, an educator typically must have a graduate degree and three years of classroom teaching. Before being certified, the individual also typically needs to complete an internship, much like your own future student teaching, to learn about the day-to-day tasks of administration under the guidance of another principal.

**Figure 2.3**   ↓ **Characteristics of Effective Teachers and Chairs**

| | Effective Teachers | Effective Chairs |
|---|---|---|
| **Communicator** | • serve as liaison between school and parents<br>• demonstrate high verbal and written communication skills<br>• incorporate student feedback into instruction<br>• stimulate high-order thinking through effective questioning | • serve as liaison between school and district administration<br>• communicate district policies with teachers<br>• communicate teachers' concerns with administration |
| **Instructional Leader** | • have extensive knowledge of pedagogy and subject area content<br>• engage students in their own learning<br>• focus instruction on objectives that are tied to standards | • evaluate teachers in the department<br>• provide professional development<br>• facilitate selection of texts and materials<br>• guide process of curriculum development |
| **Morale-Builder** | • set clear expectations for students<br>• establish a positive and democratic classroom | • mentor new teachers<br>• actively listen to teachers' concerns and share in celebrations |
| **Advocate** | • match instruction to students' needs and abilities<br>• connect school and home/ cultural experiences<br>• challenge students to succeed to their own potential | • support teachers who are struggling; provide guidance and suggestions<br>• find each teacher's strengths and facilitate professional growth<br>• advocate for department at school- and district-wide meetings |
| **Resource** | • utilize a variety of resource materials, content experts, and technologies<br>• incorporate a variety of teaching strategies and methods<br>• include authentic and experiential learning activities | • assist substitutes and provide back-up<br>• find resources and materials for teaching team<br>• assure safety during drills<br>• cover classrooms as needed<br>• provide expertise in text adoption |

Principals often choose this profession because they enjoy working with other adults and have an interest in curriculum development. Effective teachers, including departmental chairs, often have the experience and skills to become effective principals. However, there are other very specific abilities that a principal needs to acquire to be successful. Allington and Cunningham (1996) describe the principal's role as being similar to an architect's, because they offer ideas, plans, sketches, visions, and partial blueprints for reform, delegate most of the actual work to others in their team, and listen to their team for ideas and solutions. Some consider principals as the key to a school's educational climate.

Some of the specific tasks that principals have include:

- Seeking resources for the school
- Observing and monitoring the effects of curriculum changes or reforms
- Preparing budgets
- Developing class schedules
- Completing paperwork for state and federal reports
- Evaluating teachers and staff
- Overseeing academic programs
- Ensuring compliance with state and local regulations
- Coordinating pupil services
- Spearheading the school's discipline program

In effect, the principal is the official representative of the school to the community. Principals need to be skillful negotiators, because they must communicate effectively with many parts of that community—including parents, business leaders, the superintendent, and of course the school's teachers and students. Principals usually have a longer contract than teachers, but they also put in many extra hours attending school functions and district meetings.

**A Look Inside the Principal's Office**   Below, three school principals share their stories about their experiences as administrators. As you read these stories, think about the principals' roles, and how they might differ across different school communities.

**Classroom Glimpse**

## A First Look: Charlene

Charlene Smith is a retired elementary school principal from urban schools in both California and New England. She describes her role in the following way:

In general, the elementary principal is the person responsible for the total operations of all of the activities at a school site. This includes the instructional program, community support and relations, and the maintenance of the equipment, grounds, and supplies.

On a daily basis, the principal accepts the responsibility of the instructional program by:

- Visiting classrooms
- Introducing new materials and teaching methods
- Facilitating the use of district and community resources
- Interpreting academic accountability (e.g., testing) to parents and the community
- Serving as a model instructor to teachers by instructing in the classroom
- Providing a system of periodic evaluation of all personnel, including classified and certified professionals

Activities that may occur on a typical day (though there is no such thing as "typical" at a school site):

- Holding staff meetings (before the start of the school day); agenda items could include district announcements, introduction of new materials and software, grade level and/or content area chats, and staff development activities
- Being visible at bus duty (before and after school), during recess, and at lunch

- Opening announcements from the office
- Teaching in at least three classrooms a week (to model good instructional practices)
- Making classroom observations and holding follow-up conferences with teachers (immediately afterwards if possible, using chairs or other support staff to cover classes)
- Meeting with parents or PTA groups

Being an elementary principal encompasses the best of all worlds. It gives one the opportunity to be in the world of children (in a learning environment) and lets one slide comfortably into the adult sector without changing the setting. The most important aspect of the job for the principal is to be the instructional leader. This must be radiated to the staff, the students, and the community at all times. Since the school's primary function is instruction, this is where the bulk of the principal's energy should be focused.

Principals should eliminate as many non-instructional activities as possible from the duty list of teachers. Good instruction every hour of the school day is the ultimate goal for every school. The principal's effort in curriculum, in-service training, fair discipline, maintaining equipment, providing supplies, and guiding and evaluating personnel should be aimed towards creating a school that provides an exemplary education for its students. ■

## A Second Look: Gina

Gina Vukovich is currently an elementary school principal in a community that primarily serves Hispanic families. A majority of her students enter school speaking Spanish, and many initially have limited English proficiency. Gina describes an "ideal" school day as the following:

*7:45*—Arrive on campus prior to students.

*7:50*—Assist in the cafeteria during the morning breakfast rush.

*8:15*—Place new students into classrooms and prepare for morning announcements.

*8:30*—Make morning announcements.

*8:35*—Answer phone calls and emails from faculty, parents, district administrators.

*9:00*—Conduct informal observations in classrooms or a scheduled formal observation of a new teacher.

*10:30*—Return phone calls and emails.

*10:50*—Assist in the cafeteria through all lunch periods.

*12:45*—Tackle one or two quick tasks.

*1:00*—Conduct informal observations in classrooms or a scheduled formal observation of another new teacher.

*2:45*—Assist in parking lot with after school pick-up and traffic.

*3:15*—Attend scheduled meetings.

This schedule is an administrator's dream. In reality, the only guaranteed events an administrator can count on within any given school day are students arriving, eating lunch, and leaving the same time each day. Each of these events requires the supervision and the direction from the administrator. The time in between leads one on an adventure of twists and turns. Sometimes the best-laid plans can be followed, whereas other times one must find the flexibility to go with the flow. In either case, the day never ends as scheduled and the "To Do" list increases with each passing day. Discipline, parent conferences, district meetings, faculty meetings, fire and lockdown drills are some the events that alter the course of the day. The reality is that principals stay late to complete all the tasks that could not be accomplished during the regular school day. ■

### A Third Look: Jacqueline

The two previous vignettes have described very typical routines and duties of a school princi-pal. However, depending on the community and specific mission of the school, the day can look very different. Dr. Jacqueline Bell-Jones has been an administrator at an alternate coed junior high/high school for pregnant and parenting students. While her school days also included holding faculty meetings, prioritizing budgets, and working with parents, her "typi-cal" duties could also include:

- Managing student numbers when the school is filled to capacity
- Maintaining adequate class size and finding funding for additional teachers
- Finding alternative daycare for students' children
- Working with the Dropout Specialist to ensure that students stay in school
- Ensuring that students have access to WIC and other social service agencies
- Coordinating with parole officers and Child Protection Services
- Coordinating school surveillance with area law enforcement ■

**Summing Up the Principal's Role**   What do these vignettes tell you about the roles of school principals? Dr. Jacqueline Bell-Jones describes the functions of administrative manage-ment to be:

- Planning
- Organization
- Development
- Supervision
- Coordination/Collaboration
- Reporting
- Budgeting

As seen in the vignettes, the manner and degree to which these functions are actualized and applied is dependent on the situation and the school setting. Jacqueline also suggests that *decision-making* is at the core of a leader's ability to perform these functions effectively. In fact, decision-making differentiates between poor, good, and great leaders. A leader MUST be effective in this essential leadership task. Making decisions and problem solving affects every aspect of an administrator's ability to lead. On any given day, the decisions a principal must make can number into the thousands.

## District Superintendent

If the teacher's "slice" of the educational community is the classroom and its students, and the principal's "slice" is the operations at the school, the role of the superintendent deals more broadly with issues and concerns of the community as well as the day-to-day administration of the district itself. The superintendent works directly with the school board, and shares responsibility in areas related to the curriculum, personnel issues, and district policies. All other district employees are accountable to the superintendent—either directly or indirectly.

Usually, district superintendents have been both classroom teachers as well as building principals (though the recent trend in some urban communities is to hire individuals with business backgrounds to run the district). It is typical for superintendents to have an advanced degree, such as a doctorate, and to have completed specific training for this role.

Unlike teachers, superintendents typically do not have *tenure*. Instead, the school board determines the length of their employment. Superintendents often have three-year contracts.

Administration must make many critical decisions throughout the school day, which directly affect  what teachers and students do in the classroom.

Reread the three vignettes about school principals, highlighting the decisions that these professionals are making. Then use this information to fill in the "Administrator Decision Chart" (Figure 2.4), below.

- Which decisions have the most impact on what teachers do on a day-to-day basis?
- Which decisions are most critical for operating an effective school?
- When are students most impacted by the decisions of administrators?

### Figure 2.4  ↓ Administrator Decision Chart

**Directions:** The following chart lists the primary functions of a school principal. Reread the three administrator vignettes, considering these seven functions. On the chart below, jot down the decisions that principals must make within each of these functions. What additional decisions can you include?

| Function | Administrative Decisions |
| --- | --- |
| Planning | |
| Organization | |
| Development | |
| Supervision | |
| Coordination/Collaboration | |
| Reporting | |
| Budgeting | |

However, because of the complexities, politics, and stress of their positions, superintendents typically do not stay in their positions for more than three to five years.

The specific responsibilities of the district superintendent include:

- Implementing all school board policies, once they are adopted
- Officially recommending candidates for school positions to the board
- Monitoring all of the district's academic programs and providing status reports to the board
- Overseeing the maintenance of buildings and equipment
- Overseeing the preparation of the annual budget, which is submitted to the board for final approval

School superintendents in some districts are responsible for only one or two schools and, in these cases, are often also the building principal. In large urban districts, superintendents are responsible for several hundred schools, and consequently have a very visible role in the community and/or state. However, whether they serve two schools or two hundred, the basic roles and responsibilities of the superintendents are the same.

**Think About It**

How are the leadership responsibilities of superintendents similar to, or different from, those of a school principal or a department chair?

**Examining the Superintendent's Responsibilities**   Dr. Donald Enz, an experienced school administrator, notes that the school superintendent has a broad and diverse role in the educational system. The school superintendent has the primary role of working directly with the school board to develop and implement the policies of the school district. In addition, it is important that the superintendent understand how to improve student achievement by implementing, defining, and monitoring the necessary changes to improve the school district within the educational organization and greater community.

The superintendent is expected to provide the leadership necessary to shape the vision of the school district using the various stakeholders in the district. The climate of the organization is an important consideration that also must be addressed by the superintendent. Assuring equity, compliance, and effective policies is another important role, as are effectively communicating strategies to improve learning, responding to feedback, and encouraging participation in the system. The effective management of an educational organization will require the superintendent to:

- Demonstrate knowledge of quality school improvement efforts affecting student achievement
- Implement and manage school finances
- Direct the management of the school plant
- Implement the human resource policies of the district

   As described in depth below, Dr. Enz identifies the roles of a superintendent to include:
- Visionary
- Educator
- Community Leader
- Manager
- Financier

**The Superintendent as a Visionary and Decision Maker**   It is very important that the superintendent define and develop a strategic mission statement for the organization. The primary and overall role of the superintendent is to work with members of the educational community and all stakeholders to develop effective goals and action plans that will promote the fulfillment of the strategic mission. It is important to create a climate of innovation and change in support of student achievement. Linking student achievement to the ongoing nature of the educational organization and community is the superintendent's primary role.

**Superintendent as Educator**   The superintendent will be required to understand the principles and characteristics of curriculum planning, design, and implementation. He or she will need to know how to match curriculum, instruction, and assessment to the state standards. A clear understanding of the different learning styles, cultural backgrounds, abilities and disabilities within the superintendent's own district is crucial. Identifying research-based effective strategies, and using data and best practice research, are both essential in implementing the school's mission of student achievement. The superintendent must assure that the educational organization educates all of the stakeholders (e.g., parents, community members, school staff). Identifying strategies for effective professional development programs is vital to this mission. Promoting activities that assure the staff is learning quality, best practice teaching methods, as well as strategies for personal, professional development growth, is a crucial role the superintendent must undertake as an educational leader in the district.

**Superintendent as Community Leader**   The superintendent should be an effective communicator. It is important that the mission, goals, and priorities of the educational program are effectively communicated to students, staff, parents, and the greater community. The superintendent has the responsibility to work collaboratively with school board members and policymakers to assure the organizational goals and priorities are implemented within the greater community. It is important that the superintendent understand the legal rights and responsibilities of the educational community. He or she should ensure equal educational opportunities, promote an appreciation of diversity, and encourage respect—both in cultural and learning styles—to promote equity in the educational program.

**Superintendent as Manager**   In addition to the many educational goals, it is important that the superintendent apply the quality principles of school management in the organization procedures. Understanding how to identify problems and formulate a plan are essential. Using data to support decision-making and understanding how to frame and solve problems are key roles of the superintendent.

**Financier**   Understanding the legal requirements of school finance is crucial to the superintendent's role. Demonstrating knowledge of public school financing and the appropriate use of a variety of funds is also essential. Involving members of the community and stakeholders in the development of budgets and resources is necessary for proper financial management.

Dr. James Bailey [a pseudonym], a former superintendent in a rural school system, identifies the following characteristics of a superintendent's role:

- Leadership
- Organization
- Vision
- Focus on Organizational Goals

## A Wednesday in April

*7:15*—Struggle to catch up to a speeding school bus, only to observe that it is one of ours. Use cell phone to report incident to Supervisor
*Background*—Bus was coming from an Indian reservation fifteen miles from our district. We have been besieged with complaints from parents regarding the driver's sporadic pick-up and drop-off schedule.

*7:30*—Arrive at office, debrief with administrative assistant, check emails, phone messages; return urgent calls and messages, and then work with assistant to review the daily schedule and deadlines

*8:00*—Visit high school to meet with teacher association president regarding a meet and confer session planned for 3:30 in the afternoon
*Background*—The teacher association president met the previous evening with her leadership to share a "straw" design of a salary and benefit proposal that was drafted by the "meet and confer" team.

*8:20*—Travel to the maintenance yard and bus barn to meet with the classified employee President to discuss the result of their "loop-out" meeting

*8:35*—Go to elementary school to meet with a class of first grade students in the library where I read from a Tommie DePaola book

**Classroom Glimpse**

**Classroom Glimpse**

*9:15*—Hustle back to the district office to meet the superintendent's leadership team to discuss the following topics:

1. Assistant Superintendent for Human Relations and Support Services
   - Status of resignations/retirements
   - Results of bus accident investigation
   - Update on unprofessional conduct complaint against teacher
2. Special Education Director
   - Concern about growing costs and inability to provide services in the area of Physical Therapy and Speech and Language Therapy
   - Recruiting efforts to do same
   - Possible Office of Civil Rights complaint from parent who disagrees with the services provided in her child's Individualized Educational Plan
3. Finance and Construction Director
   - Bids on large technology upgrade projects
   - Budget figures in light of yesterday's legislative session
   - School Land donation terms with Real Estate Developer

*10:00*—Bi-weekly Administrative Meeting
   *Topics:*
   1. School updates
   2. Budget override needs
   3. Staffing requirements for following year
   4. Final recruiting trip arrangements
   5. Summer school planning
   6. Meet and confer status
   7. Final prep regarding state standardized testing
   8. Discussion regarding need to revisit and reprioritize capital outlay furniture and equipment requests
   9. Initial planning for administrative planning retreat in June
      - Principals need to review past efforts to increase student achievement, especially in mathematics, and begin to work with staffs and analyze new test data so that goals can be re-established
   10. High school graduation dilemma (low graduation rate)
   11. Middle school progress on transition to low-key eight grade promotion
   12. Report from administrative year-end party committee

*11:50*—Check with administrative assistant, check emails, phone messages, return urgent ones

*12:30*—Meet for informal lunch with city manager to discuss joint library use plan

*1:15*—Back in office to prep for administrator evaluation meeting

*1:30*—Meet with administrator to conduct annual performance evaluation
   *Background*—The evaluation instrument is composed of administrative competencies, approved by the governing board, systemic goals set annually, and specific areas of personal professional growth, set mutually between the administrator and superintendent. This evaluation is more sensitive because during the year there were examples of behavior that resulted in a letter of direction; therefore, the evaluation will include an improvement plan, which must be followed under threat of termination.

*2:15*—Meet with chair of technology committee to discuss budget issues and seek a reprioritized request list, less twenty percent of the requested budget

*2:40*—Call from director of the state school administrators association seeking assistance at the capitol the following week in a small group lobbying effort

*2:50*—Return phone calls, emails, write memos

*3:00*—Return phone call to editor of newspaper regarding clarification on one or two items listed in budget override

*3:15*—Return call to parent angry that her son was suspended from school for fighting; he is a baseball player and may lose his scholarship

*3:30*—Attend meet and confer meeting
*Topics:*
1. Follow-up on loop-out regarding salary and benefit "straw design"
2. Discuss new information regarding local and state budget
3. Work with certified and classified representatives their optional positions
4. Discuss reclassification of school secretaries and bus drivers
*Background*—The meet and confer process is unique in that it consists of twenty representatives from throughout the faculty, staff, administration and school board. The group operates from an "interest-based" approach rather than a "positional" one. This means that, as a group, they identify common interests and then work on solutions together. This collaboration results in decisions that are mutually supported. Facilitation is shared by a paid facilitator and one from the state education association, both trained in the same technique.

*5:30*—Sandwich dinner with the school board president in preparation for the evening study session

*6:30*—Governing board study session
*Topic*—proposed budget override election in the fall
*Background*—District is in the sixth year of a seven-year override. Revenues have already begun to decrease at a rate faster than student growth will compensate. Annual health insurance and retirement benefit rate increases are causing extreme difficulty in maintaining staff and programs, let alone raising salaries.

*8:15*—Head for home

The schedule described above is representative of the scope and pace of activities for two and three nights a week during most of months from mid-January through May. Thankfully, the pace decreases in June and July, though of course it gradually increases throughout the summer and fall. The role characteristics mentioned earlier are essential to provide effective and meaningful leadership. Those who strive to work at this level must realize that there is no closure to your responsibilities. The biggest challenge, however, is to adapt an attitude and schedule that affords a balance between personal and professional life; and that affords a quality of life for you and your family. ■

- Emphasis on Student Welfare and Achievement
- Decision-making
- Foresight and Proactivity
- Continuous Improvement
- Accountability
- Collaboration
- Patience

These characteristics are applied daily in addressing a wide variety of issues and in dealing with uniquely different groups of people. In the "Wednesday in April" vignette, Dr. Bailey walks you through a "typical" day in the life of a school Superintendent.

**Comparing School Leaders**   The role of the superintendent is to provide the necessary leadership to bring together diverse groups in the school system for common purposes. The superintendent must promote strategies that see to the welfare of all students. He or she must

**Figure 2.5** ↓ **Comparing the Roles of School Leaders**

| Department Chair | School Principal | District Superintendent |
|---|---|---|
| Communicator | Collaborator | Community Leader |
| Instructional Leader | Supervisor | Educator |
| Morale-Builder | | |
| Advocate | | |
| Resource | Developer | Visionary |
| | Planner | |
| | Organizer | Manager |
| | Reporter | |
| | Budgeter | Financier |

understand how to set priorities and apply resources to those priorities to assure effective implementation. Above all, the superintendent must understand and use effective communication strategies to improve the learning environment for all students in the school district.

But how is this different from the role of other educational leaders in a school district? The chart in Figure 2.5 overviews the ways in which these important positions intersect. What other roles do these leaders share?

In what other ways do the roles of these educational leaders intersect? What can be added to this chart? As you learn more about the roles and responsibilities of Chairs, Principals, and Superintendents, revisit this chart to make additional comparisons between the responsibilities of these critical educators.

## The School Board

Sometimes referred to as boards of trustees or school councils, the school board serves a critical function in the overall "apple" that is public education. These significant and unique governmental entities have a great deal of autonomy and power. School boards vary in size, though they typically range between five and nine members. The community elects most school boards, though a major or city council appoints some. Most school board members are not compensated monetarily, and many use this role as a stepping-stone to other political positions.

School boards provide the link between the local school district and the state's department of education. Their primary responsibility is to establish basic policies for the district and to oversee the implementation of state requirements.

The National School Boards Association has defined the governance responsibilities of boards to include:

- Establishing a long-term vision for the school system
- Maintaining the basic organizational structure of the district (e.g., employing the superintendent, adopting the budget, approving policies)
- Insuring accountability to the community

- Making the final decisions in collective bargaining
- Advocating for children and public education (Campbell & Green, 1994)

The specific roles of school boards can be broken down into nine different areas:

1. *Finance.* One of the most important roles is to raise money through taxes and distribute funds to schools. Board members must also make decisions about school services, and how much teachers and other professionals in the schools are to be compensated (i.e., salaries).

2. *Policy.* Another primary function of the school board is to set policies on a range of topics that are to be implemented across the district.

3. *Personnel.* Teachers' contracts are offered by the school board, which has the legal authority to hire and fire district personnel. School board members are also responsible for matters associated with personnel relations.

4. *Communication.* The responsibility of the school board is to maintain communication with the schools, specifically through the superintendent, parents, and the constituents who elected them. School board members also often find themselves needing to clearly communicate policy with the media.

5. *Community.* The community members typically hire school board members; therefore, they have a responsibility to listen to their constituents and to bring their ideas and concerns to the board for discussion and possible action.

6. *Administration.* The need for clear communication is perhaps most critical between the school board and the superintendent. This administrative relationship is pivotal to the success of the board.

7. *Instruction.* School boards flesh out and implement the state's guidelines regarding curriculum. They also work with the superintendent to adopt specific educational programs for the district, and react to curricular recommendations brought to the board by the superintendent.

8. *Schools.* School boards are responsible for the infrastructure of their district, including insuring that buildings and buses are safe and well maintained.

9. *Students.* While implemented at the building level, school boards set policy in a number of student-related areas, including attendance policies, dress codes, and conduct and discipline standards.

(Anderson, 1992; Armstrong, Henson, & Savage, 2001)

**Effective School Boards**   Because they are most often elected by their communities, school board members often find themselves in a balancing act between the desires of the constituents who elected them and the needs and recommendations of the district administration. While they are expected to defer to the superintendent on best educational polices, for example, they may find this difficult if the superintendent's philosophy differs from their community members' perspectives. There is no doubt that individual school board members bring to the table the specific agendas and educational priorities of the community from which they are elected.

There is no better way to understand the complexities and political nuances of the school board's role than to visit an actual meeting. Figure 2.6 provides a checklist that can be used when determining how effective individual school boards are in conducting their district's business.

# Looking Forward

In this section, we have explored insights into how the role of teaching fits within the classroom specifically, and within the broader educational community. Teaching is indeed a multifaceted career, and is one that grows more multidimensional as the needs of society and communities continue to change. We have no doubt that you will find these many dimensions of teaching to be fascinating—and perhaps at times overwhelming—and that you will continue to be rewarded by the many ways that you will positively change the lives of your students.

**Figure 2.6** ↓ **School Board Observation Sheet**

**Directions:** Listed below are some of the most common components of an effective school board. Attend one of your community's school board meetings. As you observe the interactions between the school board members, note if the members' actions match the elements below.

**1. Finance**
___Members have read a prepared budget and bring it to the meeting
___Members ask for clarification of issues related to the budget
___Budget decisions are fair to all schools within the district

**2. Policy**
___Members don't make decisions based on constituent pressures
___Members are knowledgeable about the law
___Policies are implemented consistently
___Members filter fact from opinion
___Members come to the meeting prepared

**3. Personnel**
___Objective criteria are used in hiring
___Professionals are compensated appropriate to their qualifications and responsibilities

**4. Communication**
___Members display appropriate decorum during meetings
___Members display respect for each other, and for those attending the meeting
___Members stay on task and stick to the agenda
___Members are team players, not prima donnas
___Members encourage divergent opinions
___Members display a positive attitude
___Members display a high level of professionalism

**5. Community**
___Policies are sensitive to broad public need, and not to special interest groups
___The public is invited to respond to policies
___Community members are treated respectfully
___Members understand their roles and responsibilities

**6. Administration**
___The superintendent is encouraged to recommend policy action
___Complaints from special-interest groups are channeled to administrators
___Administrators' expertise is recognized on curricular issues
___Members show respect for the superintendent
___Members understand the superintendent's role

**7. Instruction**
___Members support innovation and excellence
___Teaches are given room to experiment
___Teachers are involved in decision-making
___Superintendents are viewed as curriculum leaders
___Adequate funding is provided for instruction
___Curriculum is given a priority at meetings

**8. Schools**
___Members are concerned for school safety
___Members insist that schools are free of prejudice and discrimination
___Members have adopted long-range plans for facilities and maintenance
___Members are concerned with facility appearance
___Members understand the schools' mission

**9. Students**
___Students' needs are placed ahead of politics
___Students are the members' priority
___All students are expected to succeed
___Members are concerned about student needs across the entire district
___Programs reflect many different student needs

(Anderson, 1992; Campbell & Greene, 1994; Council, 1994; Marlowe, 1997)

# Talking to Teachers—The Motivation to Teach

Why do individuals choose to become a teacher? Perhaps because the challenges of teaching are outnumbered only by the rewards that come from helping students realize their dreams. The following teacher shares his reasons for becoming an educator. Review his story and see if you understand and relate to his feelings and experiences.

Dan Alderson teaches English at Lake Stevens High School.

Why did I become a teacher? I really hate that question. Interviewers frequently ask it, and it seems as though they expect some deeply philosophical reason in reply, some great and grand idea or some life-changing event that acted as an impetus or a starting gun, if you will, that released me from the chute and sped me down the track toward my first classroom. I suppose the reason I hate that question is because I have never had the type of answer I assume people are seeking. I've never had an answer; instead, I have a story.

I was twenty-six years old, married (with two children), successfully climbing the management ladder at the local grocery store, making good money, driving newer vehicles, and acquiring the "necessary toys." My future was bright. There was only one problem: I wasn't fulfilled. Oh sure, I enjoyed being with my family, tucking my kids in at night, and working with customers at the store, but there was something missing. That something was a sense of accomplishment, a feeling that I was making a real difference in the world—the kind of difference Mr. Whalen made in my life.

Mr. Whalen arrived during my freshman year in high school. His quick smile and quicker laugh made him an instant favorite among his students. Though he taught the world's most boring subject (history), his energy and enthusiasm made the past come alive. He also made me come alive. He saw students not as they were, but as the potential they had to become. He saw what we could be in the future, if we could believe in ourselves as he believed in us. His belief changed us. Mr. Whalen made a difference.

Because he made a difference, I am currently engaged in the most challenging, exhilarating, exhausting, refreshing, difficult, rewarding, frustrating, amazing, demanding, and stunningly miraculous profession in the world. I am a teacher because Mr. Whalen believed. Now I make a difference.

**What is Mr. Alderson's motivation to teach?**

**What are some of your reasons for becoming a teacher?**

## Research Citations

Allington, R. L., & Cunningham, P. M. (1996). *Schools That Work: Where All Children Read and Write.* New York: HarperCollins.

Anderson, C. G. (1992). Behaviors of most effective and least effective school board members. *ERS Spectrum, 10*(3), 15–18.

Armstrong, D. G., Henson, K. T., & Savage, T. V. (2001). *Teaching Today: An Introduction to Education,* 6th ed. Upper Saddle River, NJ: Merrill Prentice Hall

Ashbaker, B. Y., & Morgan, J. (2001). Paraeducators: A powerful human resource. *Streamlined Seminar, 19*(2), 1–4.

Brookover, W. & Lezotte, L. (1977). Changes in school characteristics coincident with changes in student achievement: Schools can make a difference. New York: Praeger.

Campbell, D. W., & Greene, D. (1994). Defining the leadership role of school boards in the 21st century. *Phi Delta Kappan, 75,* 391–395.

Carroll, D. (2001). Considering paraeducator training, roles, and responsibilities. *Teaching Exceptional Children, 34*(2), 60–64.

Coleman (1966). Equality of Educational Opportunity. Washington, DC: U.S. Department of Health, Education, and Welfare.

Cordry, S. (2004). Parents as first teacher. *Education, 125*(1), 56–62.

Council, B. (1994). Steer a steady course: Nine navigational lessons for school board members. *The American School Board Journal, 181*(1), 25–27.

Downing, J. E., Ryndak, D. L., & Clark, D. (2000). Paraeducators in inclusive classrooms: Their own perceptions. *Remedial and Special Education, 21*(3), 171–181.

Edmonds, R. R. (1979). Some schools work and more can. Social Policy, 10, 28–32.

Greene, K. R. (1992). Models of school board policy-making. *Educational Administration Quarterly, 28*(2), 220–236.

Halsey, P. A. (2005). Parent involvement in junior high schools: A failure to communicate. *American Secondary Education, 34*(1), 57–69.

Halsey, P. A. (2004). Nurturing parent involvement: Two middle level teachers share their secrets. *Clearing House, 77*(4), 135–137.

Kauchak, D., Eggen, P., & Carter, C. (2002). *Introduction to Teaching: Becoming a Professional.* Upper Saddle River, NJ: Merrill Prentice Hall.

Marlowe, J. (1997). Good board, bad board. *The American School Board Journal, 184*(6), 22–24.

Pena, D. C. (2004). Parent involvement: Influencing factors and implications. *Journal of Education Research, 94*(1), 42–54.

Quesada, R. L, Diaz, D. M., & Sanchez, M. (2003). Involving Latino parents. *Leadership, 33*(1), 32–34, 38.

Rancic, E. (1992). Happily ever after? *The American School Board Journal, 179*(9), 31, 33.

Rogers, J. J. (1992). Good-bye, honeymoon. *The American School Board Journal, 179*(9), 30, 32.

Rude, R. (1999). Lessons from the top. *The American School Board Journal, 186*(1), 41–42.

Stronge, J. H. (2002). *Qualities of Effective Teachers.* Alexandria, VA: ASCD.

Wadsworth, D. E., & Knight, D. (1996). Paraprofessionals: The bridge to successful full inclusion. *Intervention in School and Clinic, 31*(3), 166–172.

Woolfson, R. C., & Truswell, E. (2005). Do classroom assistants work? *Educational Research, 47*(1), 63–75.

Wyman, W. (2001). Teaching quality. *Progress of Education Reform, 2*(4), 1–6.

Zemelman, S., Daniels, H., & Hyde, A. (1998). *Best Practice: New Standards for Teaching and Learning in America's Schools,* 2nd ed. Portsmouth, NH: Heinemann.

# Teacher as Scientist and Scholar

Section A provided many examples of the numerous roles and responsibilities teachers enact on a daily basis, but perhaps the most important role is that of helping students to become successful learners. Today's teachers, more than ever before, must be scholars of learning and scientists of teaching. Today's teachers have a professional mandate to continually search for new and better ways to help their students learn. Hence, understanding the learning process is a critical part of becoming a teacher.

In Section B we will briefly discuss how teachers are active scientists and scholars. We will discuss dominant learning theories that have influenced the way you were taught and how these theories affect what classroom teachers practice today. In addition, we will review an emerging perspective—the biological foundations of learning. Then, we will describe how a teacher's philosophy helps him/her to utilize these learning theories in actual classroom practice. Finally, we will present what research has discovered about effective schools and effective teaching practices.

## Chapter Three: Understanding Learning Theories

- Behaviorist Learning Theories
- Cognitive Learning Theories
- Constructivist Learning Theories
- Biological Foundations for Learning
- Applying Learning Theories to Classroom Practice

## Chapter Four: Understanding Educational Philosophy and Your Professional Beliefs

- Classical Philosophies
- Teaching Styles in Practice
- Exploring Careers in Education

# Understanding Learning Theories

# 3

Learning is an ongoing and neverending process. It begins prior to birth and continues through an entire lifespan. Learning takes place at home, in school settings, during social and recreational activities, and at work. In this chapter, we will explore the *theories* that describe our development and how these impact instructional decisions in the classrooms.

**Definitions**

**Perception** the result of perceiving, which is the process of using the senses to acquire information about the surrounding environment or situation.

**Phenomena** a fact or occurrence that can be observed. Something that is out of the ordinary and excites interest and curiosity.

**Programmed instruction** a teaching method involving sequences of controlled steps in which a student has to thoroughly learn the material covered in one step before proceeding to the next.

**Psychology** a study of the human mind and mental states—or study of animal and human behavior.

**Reciprocal** given or done in return for something else.

**Reinforcement** either a positive (reward) or negative (punishment) action that strengthens the likelihood of repeating or avoiding the stimulus.

**Schema** our mental image of an object or action, which is in large part determined by our personal prior experiences. For example, your schema for the concept of "dog" might be a specific breed of dog—such as a beagle—because that is the breed of dog that you had as a child. Others will have different conceptions, based on their own personal experiences.

**Scholar** a person who has vast knowledge and expertise in a specific area of study.

**Scientists** is a person who has developed a systematic knowledge of a particular phenomenon. This knowledge is gained through having a theoretical background enhanced through observation and experimentation.

**Stimulus** an agent or factor that provokes interest.

**Theory** a set of ideas that form an explanation that helps explain complex phenomena.

## As you read, think about how you learned . . .

★ To read

★ To do math

★ To write stories

★ To conduct a science experiment

★ To combine all these skills and knowledge to develop original ideas

## Focus Questions

★ How have theories of learning evolved over the years?

★ What theorist do you most agree with? Why?

★ What theories of learning influenced your schooling?

★ What theories of learning do you think will have the most impact on your own teaching?

Theories are propositions that help explain complex *phenomena.* The question that has long mystified scholars is whether a single theory can describe, in all situations, how humans learn. Such a comprehensive theory must account for all the facts of how children learn language, math, social interactions, solve problems, etc. Theories are also dynamic and fluid—they must continue to evolve as our understanding of human development, science, and the impact of social and cultural influences expand (Cromer, 1997; Schunk, 2003).

The study of learning is primarily the product of philosophical writings regarding the nature of knowledge, which can be traced as far back as Plato. Early philosophers and scientists attempted to answer the question: "How do we think, reason, learn or know?" but it was not until the nineteenth century that attempts were made to study these topics experimentally (Driscoll, 1994). Though there are many learning theories in current literature that attempt to explain these phenomena, most of these theories can be organized into three broad categories:

- Behaviorism
- Cognitivism
- Constructivism

In Chapter 3 we will discuss these theories and provide a brief biography of the major theorists that have influenced educational theory and practices over the last 150 years.

# Behaviorist Learning Theories

Beginning in the late nineteenth century, theorists began to formalize the study of learning. Theorists such as Ivan Pavlov (see Box 3.1) studied the process of learning and how humans can be taught to remember. Pavlov found an association between a *stimulus* and a response that is called classical conditioning. Classic conditioning occurs when a natural reflex responds to a stimulus. The most popular example is Pavlov's observation that dogs salivate when they eat or even see food. Essentially, animals and people are biologically "wired" so that a certain stimulus will produce a specific response (Cromer, 1997).

Pavlov's work was extended by John Watson (see Box 3.2) and and B. F. Skinner (see Box 3.3). **The behaviorists believe environment shapes behavior. They are concerned with the changes in a student's behavior that occur as a result of learning. Behaviorist theory emerges in the form of operant conditioning, using *reinforcement*—or rewards for the desired behavior.** Behavioral or operant conditioning occurs when a response to a stimulus is reinforced. Basically, operant conditioning is a simple feedback system: If a reward or reinforcement follows the response to a stimulus, then the response becomes more probable in the future (Sherwood & Sherwood, 1970). This practice is reflected in the classroom by the use of gold stars, time at the computer, choice time on Friday afternoons, and so on.

For most of the twentieth century, behavioral theory provided the foundation of most of the learning theory that was applied to child-rearing and in classrooms. Parents and teachers still find that, in many instances, individuals do learn when provided with the appropriate blend of stimuli, rewards, and negative reinforcement (Kohn, 1993). Behavioral principles are often most effective with young children and simpler tasks. For instance, how many of us were rewarded with dessert when we ate all of our vegetables at dinner? However, there have been many criticisms of behaviorism, including the following:

*1.* Behaviorism does not account for all kinds of learning, since it disregards the independent activities of the mind. There are many activities children engage in that are not reinforced with rewards or praise.

*2.* Behaviorism alone can't fully explain how children learn language. While children may imitate adult use of language, imitation and reinforcement does not account for the development of new

**Box 3.1** ⇩ **More About Ivan Pavlov**

**Ivan Pavlov** (1849–1936) was born in a small village in central Russia. His family hoped he would become a priest and he attended a theological seminary. After reading Charles Darwin, he became more interested in science and began attending the University of St. Petersburg where he studied chemistry and physiology. Pavlov received his doctorate in 1879 and continued his studies and doing his own research in topics that interested him: digestion and blood circulation. His work became well known and he was appointed professor of physiology at the Imperial Medical Academy.

Pavlov studied the digestion system. He was especially interested in the interaction between salivation and the action of the stomach. Without salivation, the stomach wasn't able to initiate digestion. Pavlov wanted to see if external stimuli could affect this process, so he rang a metronome at the same time he gave the experimental dogs their food. After a while, the dogs—which before only salivated when they saw and ate their food—would begin to salivate when the metronome sounded, even if no food was present. In 1903 Pavlov published his results calling this a "conditioned reflex." This is different from an innate reflex, such as yanking a hand back from a flame, in that it had to be learned. Pavlov called this learning process "conditioning" (in which the dog's nervous system comes to associate the sound of the metronome with the food, for example). He also found the conditioned reflex will be repressed if the stimulus proves "wrong" too often. If the metronome sounds repeatedly and no food appears, eventually the dog stops salivating at the sound (Todes, 2000).

**Box 3.2** ⇩ **More About John Watson**

**John Watson** (1878–1958), often called the founder of the science of Behaviorism, was born in South Carolina and grew up on a farm. John entered Furman University at age sixteen. He received a master's degree after five years and went on to the University of Chicago to pursue a doctorate in psychology, which he received in 1903. Five years later, Johns Hopkins University appointed him professor of experimental and comparative psychology.

In 1913 he published an article outlining his ideas and essentially establishing a new school of psychology, in which Watson described the goal of psychology as the prediction and control of animal/human response and behavior. (Brewer, 1991)

Inspired by the work of Ivan Pavlov, Watson studied the biology, physiology, and behavior of animals. At that time he also began studying the behavior of children, concluding that humans were simply more complicated than animals, but operated on the same principles. All animals, he believed, were extremely complex machines that responded to situations according to their "wiring," or nerve pathways, conditioned by experience. He also dismissed heredity as a significant factor in shaping human behavior (Todd & Morris, 1994). Watson strongly sided with nurture in the nature-nurture discussion, and is perhaps most well-known for the following quote:

> Give me a dozen healthy infants, well-formed, and my own specified world to bring them up in and I'll guarantee to take any one at random and train him to become any type of specialist I might select—doctor, lawyer, artist, merchant-chief and, yes, even beggar-man and thief, regardless of his talents, penchants, tendencies, abilities, vocations, and race of his ancestors. (Watson, 1930)

**Box 3.3 ↓ More About B.F. Skinner**

**Burrhus Frederic Skinner** (1904–1990), often called the father of applied behaviorism, dedicated his life's work to studying the relationship between reinforcement and observable behavior. He is considered by many to be one of the most important figures in twentieth-century psychology. The principles of reinforcement he outlined were built upon by clinical psychologists and applied to the treatment of mental disorders. The application of behaviorism to clinical psychology still appears today in treatments for anxiety disorders and reflects many approaches to classroom management (Bjork, 1997).

Skinner's work in education began in the early 1950s during a visit to his daughter's fourth grade math class. This experience provided insight into current teaching practices to shape the remainder of his career. His observations revealed that the instructional process was violating the basic principals of learning. He saw that the teacher's instruction was not supporting the current level of learning for all individuals in the classroom. In behaviorist terms, instruction (shaping) should adapt to each child's current performance level. However, in the math class, he clearly observed that some of the students had no idea how to solve the problems, while others knew the material and learned nothing new. In shaping, each best response is immediately reinforced. Skinner had researched delay of reinforcement and knew how it hampered performance. But, in the math class, children did not find out if one problem was correct before doing the next; they had to answer a whole page before getting any feedback, and then probably not receiving any until the next day. But how could one teacher with twenty or thirty students possibly shape mathematical behavior for each one simultaneously? Clearly teachers needed help. That afternoon, Skinner constructed his first teaching machine (O'Donohue & Ferguson, 2001).

Skinner's first teaching machine simply presented problems, in random order, for students to do with feedback after each one. This machine did not teach new behavior; all it did was give more practice on skills already learned. Within three years, however, Skinner developed **programmed instruction.** Through careful sequencing, students responded to material broken into small steps. The steps were similar to what a skilled tutor would ask of a student with whom they were working one on one. The first response of each sequence was prompted, but as performance improved, less and less help was given. By the end, a student was doing something he or she could not have done at the beginning (Skinner, 1987).

Some of the better programs from the 1960s are still used, and with the coming of the computer and internet, the sophisticated perfect machine Skinner lacked is now available (Hergenhahn & Olson, 2004).

---

language patterns (grammar). For instance, when a child uses the phrase *"We goed to the zoo,"* he is not imitating what an adult has spoken, rather the child is over-applying the grammar feature, language pattern, for past-tense "ed." (Chomsky, 1969).

## Behaviorism in the Classroom

A typical behaviorist approach in the classroom often occurs as the teacher models the correct response to new information. As the children practice the correct response she provides positive reinforcement for the correct response. If an incorrect response is made, the teacher quickly re-teaches and models the correct response before the lesson can proceed. Usually the information is very logically presented in a highly sequenced series of steps. (See the following Classroom Glimpse.)

**Classroom Glimpse**

Mrs. Barr is presenting a lesson on the sound of the letter Bb. She asks her kindergarten students to listen to the sound and say it with her. She points to the letter symbol and says bah-bah-bah. The children listen and then repeat what she says. She praises the children and gives them a positive reinforcement by putting a marble in a small glass jar. The children are pleased to hear the clinking sound—they know if they earn ten marbles in the jar by the end of the day they will earn a sticker!

Next, Mrs. Barr tells the children to listen as she says three words. Baby, Button, Bottle. She asks them to repeat the words with her. As she says the words she emphasizes the b sound. She asks the children what sound starts each of the words. The children excitedly reply Bah! Once again a smiling Mrs. Barr rewards their efforts with another bright colored marble clinking in the jar.

Now Mrs. Barr tells the children to listen carefully. She says three words: Cat, Bunny, Dog. She asks the children which one begins with the b sound. The children reply BUNNY! She smiles and repeats their correct answer. For the third time the marble clinks in the jar.

Finally, Mrs. Barr gives the children a worksheet that has ten rows of pictures. Each row has three pictures. The children are told that they need to circle all the pictures that start with the letter sound of Bb. The children quickly return to their desks, grab a crayon and wait until Mrs. Barr does the first practice row with them as a whole group. ■

This very brief vignette illustrates the modeling, reinforcement and step-by-step instructional sequence. While effective, can you imagine how tedious the day might become if all lessons were taught in this one instructional approach?

Eventually, educators began to feel that, while although stimulus-response does explain many human behaviors and has a legitimate place in instruction (for instance, behaviorist theories still provide the foundation for programmed learning and all computer-assisted instruction used in classroom today), behaviorism alone was not sufficient to explain all the phenomena observed in more complex learning situations. These realizations brought more prominence to the cognitive theories of learning (Hergenhahn & Olson, 2004).

# Cognitive Learning Theories

Cognitive theories (sometimes called information processing) first appeared in the 1920s, but were usurped by behavioral theories for a number of years, only to re-emerge as a dominant force again in the mid-1950s. **This theory views learning as an active mental process of acquiring, remembering, and using knowledge. Learning is evidenced by a change in knowledge that makes a potential change in behavior possible, but not necessary** (Schunk, 2003).

Cognitive theorists, like R.M. Gagne, are concerned with the operations that happen inside the brain as we learn (see Box 3.4). Other cognitive theorists, like Jean Piaget and Albert Bandura, take the perspective that students actively process information. These individuals believe learning takes place through the efforts of the individual as they organize, store, and then find relationships between information, linking new to old knowledge. Piaget also viewed learning as a changing process and children as individuals that developed over time (see Box 3.5). Albert Bandura, also believed that the environment and the individual influenced each other and learning occurs within that interaction (see Box 3.6).

## Box 3.4   ↓ More About Robert Gagne

**Robert Gagne (1916–2002)** is often credited for helping turn the art of instruction into science. The beginning of Gagne's unique contributions were developed during World War II when he was asked to find a way to instruct non-teachers to make airplane mechanics out of farmers in thirty days, instead of two years of trial and error. Through this experience, Gagne identified the five kinds of performance that require unique types of instruction.

A leader in the field of instructional design since the 1940s, Gagne identified five major categories of learning. The significance of these classifications is that each type requires different instruction. The five major categories of learning are: verbal information, intellectual skills, cognitive strategies, motor skills, and attitudes. Different internal and external conditions are necessary for each type of learning. This work led to the publication of *The Conditions of Learning* (Gagne & Medsber, 1965), which outlined the relation of learning objectives to appropriate instructional designs.

Gagne further suggests that learning tasks for intellectual skills can be organized in a hierarchy according to complexity: stimulus recognition, response generation, procedure following, use of terminology, discriminations, concept formation, rule application, and problem solving. The primary significance of the hierarchy is to identify prerequisites that should be completed to facilitate learning at each level. Prerequisites are identified by doing a task analysis of a learning/training task. Gagne believes that learning hierarchies provide a basis for the sequencing of instruction (Gagne, Wager, Golas, & Keller, 2004).

As a professor of psychology at Princeton University, his interest in research shifted toward the learning of school subjects. The Information Processing Model, described later, helps teachers to deliberately arrange the learning conditions to promote the achievement of an intended goal (Driscoll, 1994). Cognitivists see instruction as a way of supporting the various internal processes by activating mental sets that:

- affect attention and selective perception
- enhance encoding
- provide an organization of the new data

Cognitivists, like Gagne, view the teacher's role as coordinating the learning environment so that learning remains focused on the goal of instruction.

## Cognitivism in the Classroom

Cognitive learning theories emphasize how information is processed. Cognitive theorists believe a teacher can encourage learning by providing information to students and helping them organize the information in such a way they are able to recall it later (Hergenhahn & Olson, 2004). Figure 3.1 offers the sequence of learning from a cognitive theorist perspective.

This learning sequence is called the Information Processing Model. It provides a blueprint of how the mind senses, processes, stores, and recalls information. Cognitivists believe this information can help teachers design instruction with particular concern to content, sequence, and structure.

## Box 3.5 ↓ More About Jean Piaget

**Special Feature by Nancy Perry, Ph.D.**
**Jean Piaget 1896–1980** was born in Neuchâtel, Switzerland on August 9, 1896. As a child he had a strong interest in nature and biology; in fact, he published his first paper on albino sparrows at age eleven! Graduating with a Doctorate in Zoology from the University of Neuchâtel in 1918, Piaget took a position teaching psychology and philosophy at Sorbonne University in Paris. While at Sorbonne, Piaget worked on the development of intelligence tests with Alfred Binet. During this time, Piaget became intrigued by children's erroneous responses to various test items. When Piaget began to ask the children about how they arrived at their answers to the questions, he came to realize there was  a pattern in the logic children used to solve the problems. Younger children were using one set of strategies and logical thought processes to arrive at their answers, and older children another. Based on this discovery, Piaget came to believe the answers to our questions about cognitive development might be discovered by studying how children's ability to logically reason grows over time (Piaget, 2000; Piaget, 2001 reissue of earlier work).

To study how knowledge develops, Piaget and his students interviewed, observed, and conducted simple experiments with thousands of elementary school children. Piaget also conducted in-depth observations on each of his three children. Through these clinical investigations, Piaget discovered that we progress through four stages of cognitive development: **sensorimotor, preoperational, operational, and formal operations.**

During the *sensorimotor stage* of cognitive development, infants use their senses to gather knowledge. They learn by manipulating objects and creating **schemas,** or categories of thought, about how the objects feel, taste, smell, move, and act.

At the *preoperational stage*, roughly between the ages of two and seven, children combine their sensory abilities with their newly acquired symbolic abilities (e.g., language and imagination) to gather information. The combination of these abilities helps young children connect their past experiences with new experiences more quickly, which deepens their understanding of the world. However, children of this age still experience difficulties with cause and effect because they cannot fully focus on all of the possible variables that cause an object to act in the way it does. Children of this age also experience difficulty understanding that others may think differently about an object or event, or have a different opinion about how these objects and events actually work. Piaget calls this **egocentrism**—the inability to view objects and situations from another person's perspective.

During the *concrete operational stage*, between the ages of seven and nine, children gain more flexibility in their thinking. They are able to coordinate information more precisely and consider several possible outcomes to problems based on the information they have collected. However, children in this stage of development still need concrete manipulatives to understand unfamiliar concepts and principles such as mathematical ideas not easily visualized.

Finally, during the *formal operational stage*, from about age eleven or twelve to adulthood, children master the ability to use abstract reasoning to solve problems. They can imagine all of the variables that might influence the outcome of their actions and systematically analyze each part of a problem without the use of concrete examples.

Although many people contend that Piaget's stages of development are static, they are not. Piaget believed the development of knowledge is a process of continual construction and reorganization. Knowledge constructed at each stage of development is reorganized in the following stage, leading toward progressively refined reasoning abilities and ideas about any given subject. This construction and reorganization is made possible by the dynamic and continuous processes of *adaptation, reflective abstraction, and equilibration*. These three processes are evident in all stages of cognitive development, including infancy, but our use of them becomes more flexible over time.

*Adaptation* consists of the dual processes of *assimilation* and *accommodation*. According to Piaget, assimilation and accommodation are how our minds make sense of objects and situations in our environment and how they work. For example, when we are faced with an unfamiliar stimulus, such as a platypus, we attempt to *assimilate*, or take in, and categorize all of the characteristics of the platypus, to our existing knowledge base. Now, if we have experience with platypus-like creatures, we fit the platypus into our understanding of these creatures—perhaps we connect it to our existing understanding of ducks or seals. In this case, not much changes in our thinking. But, if we are totally perplexed by this platypus, and are not satisfied that its characteristics relate to our current understanding of ducks or seals, we have to *accommodate* the structures of our thinking to add the platypus into our existing knowledge base. In this case, our thinking changes— we create a new schema; either by adapting our thinking about ducks and/or seals, or by creating an entirely new category of thought for large creatures with a bill like a duck and a body like a seal.

*Reflective abstraction* is the process of drawing out, interpreting, and coordinating information from the things we observe. It is our search for relationships, such as similarities and differences, between what we currently know and what we are learning about. This process enters into the knowledge construction process during assimilation. As we **abstract** or gather information about objects, we assimilate the observable properties of the object, as we did with our platypus. We then investigate the actions of the object or the object's responses to our actions. Finally, we seek information about unobservable properties of the platypus such as purpose or intent. Once we have done all of this, we **reflect** upon the information we have acquired and begin searching our existing schema to determine how it applies to what we already know. In essence, we put the new information into a relationship with our old body of knowledge to determine if we need to accommodate our thinking. If we determine our old thought patterns are sufficient enough to aid in our understanding of the new stimuli, nothing changes. If not, we create a new schema, or category of thought, to account for the platypus.

It is our desire to achieve *equilibrium*, a sense of comfort our current line of thinking sufficiently explains that way the world works, which fuels the construction of knowledge. Each time we assimilate something that does not fit within our view of the world we experience *disequilibrium*, or cognitive conflict. It is this sense of uneasiness or internal contradiction that pushes us to reflect upon and adapt our own thinking. This, in turn, begins the continuous process of adaptation, reflective abstraction, and equilibration that leads to our ever-growing knowledge of the world and how it works (Piaget, 2000, Piaget, 2001).

## Box 3.6 ↓ More about Albert Bandura

Albert Bandura (1925– ) received his Ph.D. in 1952 from the University of Iowa where he was initially influenced by behaviorist theory. In 1953, he started teaching at Stanford University. However, Bandura felt behaviorism, with its limited emphasis on observable variables, avoided understanding mental processes. Bandura found this a bit too simplistic for the phenomena he was observing—aggression in adolescents—and so decided to add a little something to the formula. He suggested that, while environment did cause behavior, behavior causes environment as well. He labeled this concept **reciprocal determinism:** The world and a person's behavior cause each other.

Later, he went a step further. He began to look at personality as an interaction among three dynamic variables—the environment, behavior, and the person's psychological processes. These psychological processes consist of the ability to entertain images in the mind and language. At the point where he introduces imagery, in particular, he ceases to be a strict behaviorist, and begins to join the ranks of the cognitivists. Adding imagery and language to the mix allows Bandura to theorize much more effectively about learning through observation and self-regulation (Evan, 1989; Bandura, 1997).

**Attention**—You learn through observation of a model (something to learn); you need to pay attention. Extreme emotions like fear or anger can impede your ability to pay attention, as can physical states like sleepiness or hunger.

**Retention**—Once you have observed the model, you must be able to remember what you have paid attention to. You store what you have seen in the form of mental images or verbal descriptions. When information is stored, you can later "bring up" the image or description, so you can reproduce it with your own behavior.

**Reproduction**—The ability to translate the images or descriptions of the model into actual behavior; for example, completing long division, doing back flips, or writing an essay. Your ability to imitate improves with practice—and your ability improves even when you just imagine yourself performing! Many athletes, for example, visualize their performance prior to competing.

**Motivation**—Even considering all of the factors above, you're still not going to learn or do anything unless you are motivated to. You must have some reason, or motivation, for doing it. Bandura mentions a number of motives:

- **past reinforcement**—traditional behaviorism.
- **promised reinforcements**—(incentives) we can imagine.
- **vicarious reinforcement**—seeing and recalling the model being reinforced.

Notice that reinforcement is traditionally considered to be the cause of learning. Bandura differs by saying that reinforcement doesn't cause learning, but gives us a reason to demonstrate what we have learned. (Bandura, 1986)

**Figure 3.1   ↓ Cognitive Theory Processing**

| Sequence | Description of Learning Function | Example of Learning Experience |
|---|---|---|
| Sensory reception | One or more of the body's senses (e.g., sight, smell, touch, sound, and taste) perceive the information. | While shopping at the mall, Mary sees, hears, and smells hundreds of pieces of information. |
| Sensory memory | Acts as a buffer for information received by the senses. Filters the vast array of information to only those of interest at a given time. | Amid all the sights and sounds, Mary hears a few notes coming through the clutter. |
| Paying attention | Immediately, after sensing information, the act of selective perception. | Mary begins to recognize the notes. |
| Short-term memory | Serves as a temporary note pad for new information. Short-term memory is usually forgotten quickly. However, some information (based on the individual's level of interest) is processed. | Mary recognizes the song as one of her favorites, but it is a different version than the one she has sung to dozens of times before. |
| Semantic encoding | Information meaningful to the individual is encoded for emotional content, personal relevance and is reviewed in terms of prior experiences. | Mary remembers the last time she heard this song played was when she met her new boyfriend. |
| Long-term memory | Intended for long-term storage of interpreted information. Information from the long-term memory can be retrieved and brought to consciousness. | Mary continues to remember other times she has heard this song. She decides she likes the "old" version better. |
| Response generator | If warranted, the response generator causes muscles to take action and the response may or may not be emitted back to the environment. | Mary decides to buy the old version of the song to give to her new boyfriend. |

What does this sequence look like instructionally? Consider the egg lesson outlined below.

| Sequence | Example of Learning Experience |
|---|---|
| Sensory reception | Students come into the class. They see the teacher has put an egg, in a plastic cup, paper, and a magnifying glass at each student's desk. Each groups of four desks also has a jug of water. |
| Sensory memory | Teacher has written question on the board. *What do you know about eggs?* She asks her class this question. The students begin to answer and as they do the teacher writes their responses on the board. *Eggs are smooth, can be eaten, can grow into little chicks. Have yolks, whites.* |
| Paying attention | The teacher now draws the student's attention to the materials on the student's desk. The teacher asks the students to take the magnifying glass to examine the use the magnifying glass to examine the shell of the egg. |

**These first three steps help to focus student attention, stimulate their interest and prior knowledge about the topic the teacher intents to introduce.**

| | |
|---|---|
| Short-term memory | The teacher asks the students to draw what they see and share that information with a partner. The students quickly discover that the egg is not smooth as they initially predicted, rather it has tiny little holes. The teacher asks, *"Why do you think the egg has holes?* The students suggest that the eggs have holes to let light in the shell, or to let air in the shell. |
| Semantic encoding | The teacher tells the students to fill their cups half full with water and to place their eggs into the cup. Then asks them to observe what happens. As they watch the teacher continues to guide their observations with questions. Does the egg float or sink to the bottom of the glass? What does the egg look like in the water? Do you see little bubbles? Which part of the egg is giving off bubbles? What are the bubbles telling us? |
| Long-term memory | The students are beginning to change their perceptions and knowledge about eggs and their structures. The many questions the teacher is posing is helping the students to reshape and refine their prior knowledge of eggs. The discussion between the students and the writing down and sharing their information with the group is also helping this new knowledge go from short-term memory to long-term memory. |
| Response Generator | The talking and writing and exploring serves as a part of the physical actions as they continue to motivate new learning and encourage the students' retention of this information. |

**Think About It**

Contrast this lesson with the behaviorist lesson plan (the sound of the letter Bb). What differences do you notice in the:

Teacher role:

Student's role:

In the 1980s several lesson plan formats were developed to help teachers create lessons that would help children move from simple memorization of facts—the egg shell has holes that allows for air exchange—to a deeper understanding of that fact which then allows for better retention of information. Chapter 5 in Section C offers more information about these lesson formats.

Cultural factors that may affect a child's learning development include language, morality, belief systems, religion, and socialization.

# Constructivist Learning Theories

Constructivism also began in the 1920s. Its leading theorist, Lev Vygotsky, believed culture to be the prime factor of individual development. (See Box 3.7). Humans create culture, and every child is raised in the context of that particular culture. Therefore, culture affects a child's learning development. Cultural factors include:

- language
- morality
- belief systems
- religion
- socialization

**Culture teaches children what to think and how to think. Cognitive development results from an interactive process, whereby a child learns through problem-solving experiences shared with someone else, usually a parent or teacher, but sometimes a sibling or peer** (Hergenhahn & Olson, 2004). Initially, the person interacting with the child assumes most of the responsibility for guiding the problem solving, but gradually this responsibility transfers to the child.

Constructivism is founded on the premise that, by reflecting on our experiences, we construct our own understanding of the world we live in. Each of us generates our own "rules" and "mental models" which we use to make sense of our experiences (Schunk, 2003). Learning,

### Box 3.7 ↓ More about Lev Vygotsy

**Lev Vygotsky (1896-1934)** graduated with degrees in law, history, and philosophy earned concurrently at two different Moscow universities in 1917, at the ripe old age of twenty-one. Though Vygotsky never had formal training in psychology, his pioneering work in developmental psychology has had a profound influence on education since the 1930s. Though Vygotsky produced most of this work in the 1920s, the Russian Revolution and Stalinist suppression prevented most of Vygotsky's theories from being available in the West until the 1980s.

Vygotsky argued that a child's development cannot be understood by a study of just the individual. Instead, to understand development and learning, we must also examine the child's social and cultural world (home, school, community). The major theme of Vygotsky's theoretical framework is that social interaction plays a fundamental role in the development of cognition. Vygotsky described learning as being embedded within the social events and occurrences as a child interacts with the people, objects, and events in his/her environment.

A second aspect of Vygotsky's theory is the idea that the potential for cognitive development is limited to a certain time span that he calls the *"zone of proximal development"* (ZPD). This is the distance between the child's actual developmental level (as determined by independent problem solving) and the level of potential development as determined through problem solving under adult guidance or in collaboration with more capable peers. The zone of proximal development represents the amount of learning possible by a student given the proper instructional conditions (Newman, 1993).

The theory of social constructivism translates into current classroom practice in the use of **curriculum** that is based on solving real-world concerns and problems in small groups that emphasize interaction between learners and learning tasks. **Instruction** should occur with appropriate adult help, as students are often able to perform tasks they are incapable of completing on their own. This support is called scaffolding—where the adult continually adjusts the level of his or her help in response to the child's level of performance—and is an effective form of teaching. Scaffolding not only produces immediate results, but also instills the skills necessary for independent problem solving in the future. **Assessment** methods must take into account the zone of proximal development. What children can do on their own is their level of *actual development*, and what they can do with help is their level of *potential development*. Two children might have the same level of actual development, but given the appropriate help from an adult, one might be able to solve many more problems than the other. Assessment methods must target both the level of actual development and the level of potential development (Wertsch, 1988).

therefore, is simply the process of adjusting our mental models to accommodate new experiences. There are several guiding principles of constructivism:

- Learning is a search for meaning. Therefore, learning must start with the issues around which students are actively trying to construct meaning.

- Meaning requires understanding **wholes** as well as parts. And parts must be understood in the context of wholes. Therefore, the learning process focuses on main concepts, not isolated facts.

- In order to teach well, we must understand the mental models students use to perceive the world and the assumptions they make to support those models.

## Case Study 3.1

**Annie's Construction**   When Annie was ten months old she began to call her Daddy "Dada" and her Mommy "Mama." Annie also imitated what her family called her Grandma, "Gi-Gi." Though her family called her Grandpa "Papa," Annie refused to call him by that name, instead she called him "Da-Gi." Annie's personal construction of "DaGi" for Grandpa is an example of a personal mental model based on rules Annie determined.

■ What "rules" might Annie have developed?

- The purpose of learning is for an individual to construct his or her own meaning, not just memorize the "right" answers and regurgitate someone else's label or meaning (see Case 3.1: Annie's Construction).
- Since education is inherently interdisciplinary, the only valuable way to measure learning is to make the assessment part of the learning process, ensuring it provides students with information on the quality of their learning.

## Constructivism in the Classroom

Constructivist theory is seen in the classroom in the form of cooperative learning and learning investigations initiated by the students' own interests. With appropriate adult help, students can often perform tasks they are incapable of completing on their own. With this in mind, scaffolding—where the teacher continually adjusts the level of his or her help in response to the student's level of performance—is an effective form of teaching. Scaffolding not only produces immediate results, but also instills the skills necessary for independent problem solving in the future. Constructivism in middle and high school classrooms also takes on another dimension—the expertise of the young adults and the context of solving real problems and doing real work. The following vignette illustrates this process.

In the fall of 2005, hurricane Katrina slammed the gulf coast of Louisiana, Mississippi, and Alabama. The electronic media featured the horrors of the natural disaster for hours on end. Many of the students in a lower socioeconomic middle school in urban Phoenix had relatives who lost everything in this event. One story that especially touched the hearts and minds of the students in this poor Arizona middle school was the complete loss of a New Orleans middle school library. The students began to share their concerns with their teachers. After a few days of discussion in their social studies class, the students decided to take action. They determined that they wanted to raise funds to purchase books for the New Orleans middle school. Working with their own school library-media specialist, and their English, social studies, and math teachers, they began to research the costs of the literature books and contacted the New Orleans school district to determine the titles in the destroyed library's inventory. With the help of the school principal and the English teacher, the students contacted local community leaders (including some of their own parents) to determine the best way to raise the money. For nearly four weeks, part of their work at school consisted of interacting in cooperative groups, with each group charged with researching part of the solutions to this larger problem. They wrote letters to book clubs, local businesses, local philanthropists, and local media. They figured the costs for the books (they soon realized they couldn't replace all the books but they could replaced the fiction section in the library) so they took a class vote and decided the students would prefer to have books like Harry Potter, than reference texts. The students coordinated three fundraising drives:

- A donated dinner by a local restaurant where parents and community members bought tickets
- A silent auction at the donated dinner (goods were donated by local businesses)
- A community dance where a local radio personality donated his time to be the DJ

**Think About It**

Though no test will record these students' learning, what do you think they learned through this effort?

By the end of November, one hundred determined twelve-year-olds had raised nearly 7,000 dollars to help replenish the library in New Orleans.

Who drove the curriculum and efforts of this event?

What math did the students need to do to determine how much money to raise?

What English skills did the students need to use contact local community leaders?

Teachers today have the opportunity to choose from a diverse set of learning theories when designing their lessons. However, it must be noted that no single theory currently offers an adequate explanation for the remarkably complex phenomena of human intelligence. As a result, perhaps the best approach is for future teachers to consider an eclectic approach that draws on the idea of a learning theory continuum (see Figure 3.2).

**Group Talk**

What learning theories do you see reflected most often in the K through 12 classrooms where you are observing?

What theory does your professor most often use in this class?

Which theory do you feel most comfortable with in terms of your own future instruction?

Understanding learning theories not only helps us understand others' instructional practices, but this knowledge also helps us make good decisions in our instruction so that our students' learning experiences can be optimized.

**Figure 3.2** ↓ **Comparing and Contrasting Learning Theories**

| Major Theory | Key Principles | Types of Learning |
|---|---|---|
| **Behaviorism** | • Behavior is repeated until it becomes automatic.<br>• The behavior of the learner indicates learning has occurred.<br>• The influence of the external environment contributes to the shaping of the individual's behavior.<br>• The environment presents a stimulus that prompts a behavior.<br>• Whether the behavior occurs again is dependent on the consequence that follows it. | • New physical skills<br>• Recall of basic facts<br>• Performing well defined procedures or skills |
| **Cognitivism** | • Learning is influenced by existing knowledge.<br>• Learning is based on the thought process behind the behavior.<br>• Leaning is governed by internal processes rather than by external circumstance (behaviorism).<br>• Defines the process of selecting information (attention), translating information (encoding), and recalling information when appropriate (retrieval). | • Problem solving<br>• Reasoning<br>• Information processing<br>• Classifications |
| **Constructivism** | • Learning occurs when the learner applies current knowledge to solving new problems.<br>• Learning occurs through interaction with others.<br>• Individuals construct knowledge by working to solve realistic problems, usually in collaboration with others.<br>• Learning is seen as a change in meaning constructed from new experience.<br>• Suggests that individual interpretation of experience vs. objective representation (information processing perspective). | • Need for creativity<br>• Complex problem solving<br>• Need to apply knowledge to changing situations |

# Biological Foundations for Learning

The behaviorists, cognitivists, and constructivists who developed the three preceding theories of learning had to infer the process of learning from careful, long-term observations of external behavior. Since the 1980s, technological innovations have enabled neuroscientists to study the living brain. Brain imaging techniques such as functional magnetic resonance imaging (fMRI) are non-invasive procedures that allow researchers to graphically record and simultaneously display three-dimensional, color-enhanced images of a living brain as it processes information (Sochurek, 1987). These data provide researchers with a new way to understand the organization and functional operations of the brain as it relates to human learning (see Box 3.8).

This emerging learning theory is based on the biological structures and functions of the brain, and reinforces various aspects of the propositions put forth by behaviorists, cognitivists, and constructivists. However, this theory also focuses heavily on the role of emotion, personal interest, and motivation in the learning process. Humans do not simply learn things devoid of feeling (Wolfe, 2001). What we learn is influenced by prior personal experience and interests, biases, and prejudices. All of these elicit emotion, which can inhibit or encourage subsequent learning. Emotions and thoughts literally shape each other and cannot be separated (see Figure 3.3).

The premise of the biological view of learning suggests that, as long as the brain is not prohibited from fulfilling its normal processes (due to medical or physical conditions), learning will occur. Every person is born with a brain which functions as an immensely powerful

## Box 3.8 ↓ More about fMRI

Magnetic resonance imaging (MRI) is an technique used primarily in medical settings to produce high quality images of the organs and systems inside of the human body. MRI provides an unparalleled view inside the human body (Schwartz, 2002).

*Functional* Magnetic Resonance Imaging (fMRI) is a relatively new imaging technology most often utilized to study the brain. Investigations in the fields of vision, language, motor function, memory, emotion, and pain have been greatly assisted by fMRI technology.

fMRI can be used to map changes in the blood-oxygen flow, which allows for functional mapping of the human brain. Consequently, an fMRI can provide high resolution, noninvasive reports of neural activity. For instance, fMRI allows us to see how speech is processed and when and how we receive visual information. This new ability to directly observe brain function opens an array of new opportunities to advance our understanding of brain organization, as well as a potential new technique for assessing neurological health and cognitive development (Smilkstein, 2003).

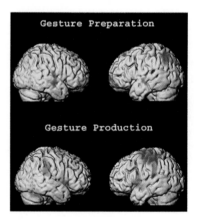

fMRI has been the single most useful innovation for brain research to date.

© Visuals Unlimited/CORBIS

Though this science is relatively new, it is producing important new information about how children learn to read and do arithmetic. Scientists now have a fair idea of where in the brain these skills reside and which skills are acquired quickly and slowly. For example, it seems that turning groups of letters into words is, initially, a relatively slow process, while making sense and meaning of these words is extremely rapid (Wolfe, 2001). Likewise, mental arithmetic once learned seems to work in the same way in children as adults. These scanning techniques may one day also help tell teachers objectively what methods are best to help children learn. It may also help to support specific types of learning strategies for children who have learning difficulties (Posner, 2003).

processor (Sylwester, 2000; Caine & Caine, 1991). The core principles of a biological view of learning state:

1. The brain is a parallel processor, meaning it can perform several activities simultaneously, like seeing, tasting, and smelling.
2. Learning engages the whole physiology.
3. The search for meaning—making sense of what is happening—is inborn.
4. The search for meaning comes through organization and categorization of information (called patterning; cause and effect).
5. Emotions are critical to the ability to detect patterns.
6. The brain processes wholes and parts simultaneously.
7. Learning involves both focused attention and peripheral **perception.**
8. Learning involves both conscious and unconscious processes.
9. Learning is enhanced by challenge/curiosity and inhibited by threat.
10. Each brain is unique.

The three instructional techniques associated with biological learning theory are:

- *Orchestrated immersion*   Teachers create learning environments that fully immerse students in an educational experience—engaging as many senses as possible.
- *Relaxed alertness*   Teachers eliminate fear in learners while maintaining a highly active and challenging environment.
- *Active processing*   Teachers allow learners to strengthen and internalize information by actively processing it with peers and through hands-on learning activities.

The "Classroom Glimpse" offers an illustration of how emotions influence learning.

The following Group Talk activity offers an opportunity for you to process this new information about the emotional learning cycle. Take a few minutes to read this information. After you have read the information, consider the questions. Share your thoughts with a peer.

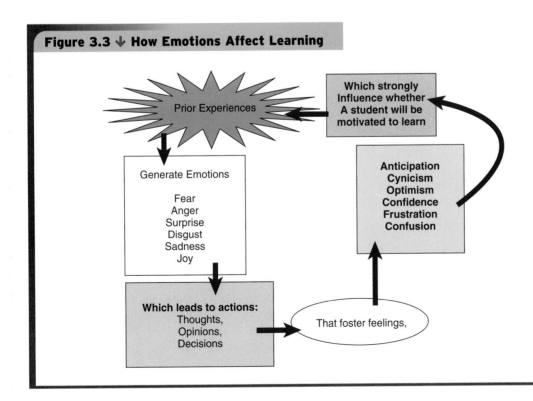

**Figure 3.3 ↓ How Emotions Affect Learning**

Prior Experiences

Which strongly Influence whether A student will be motivated to learn

Generate Emotions

Fear
Anger
Surprise
Disgust
Sadness
Joy

Anticipation
Cynicism
Optimism
Confidence
Frustration
Confusion

**Which leads to actions:**
Thoughts,
Opinions,
Decisions

That foster feelings,

**Classroom Glimpse**

Tara loves to sing **(prior experiences).** Every time she sings her teachers, family and friends praise her beautiful voice (**generates emotions** such as happiness, joy, pride). Subsequently, these positive feelings encourage Tara to make the decision to practice and work even harder on her singing **(actions).** She takes vocal lessons and tries out for the school choir. Her decision to practice and take lessons continues to deepen her love of music and her improve her vocal skills. This new knowledge further inspires confidence **(feelings).** Tara's motivation to learn more about music and singing creates a continuous self-propelling cycle of **motivation and learning.**

**Group Talk**

## Examining the Connections Between Emotions and Learning

As you read the following vignette about Ms. Nora's fourth grade class, consider your own experiences in school and what you have just learned about the biological foundation of learning. Then, consider what might have influenced the academic outcomes for James, Jose, and Derrick.

Ms. Nora calls her fourth grade students in from lunch recess. It is hot outside and the children are sweating. Ms. Nora can feel the temperature rising as they enter the room. James, Jose, and Derrick are not only physically hot, their tempers are flaring from a contested game of playground soccer. As they come into the classroom the boys are shouting, calling each other names, and shoving each other.

Ms. Nora brusquely reminds them to put their playground disputes behind them and immediately starts to distribute "Mad Math Minutes" worksheets. The goal of this exercise is to do as many single-digit multiplication problems—correctly—in one minute. This drill is to help the students practice for the state-mandated accountability test at the end of month.

At the end of the one-minute activity Ms. Nora asks the children to exchange papers to do the grading. Most of the children score fairly well—ranging from twenty-five to thirty correct responses out of fifty. However, James, Jose, and Derrick have only answered ten to fifteen problems and all three of them have made several computational mistakes. Ms. Nora is frustrated with the boys and chastises them loudly in front of their peers.

At the end of the day, as Ms. Nora records their daily grades, she notices that these three normally well-behaved boys continued to have difficulty on the spelling test and their comprehension counts worksheet.

*1.* What factor(s) do you think contributed to the boys' academic difficulty in class today?

*2.* What might you (as teacher) have done when the boys entered the classroom?

*3.* Though the vignette describes an elementary school experience with young boys, are adults' ability to learn affected by their emotions in similar ways? Provide a personal example.

# Applying Learning Theories to Classroom Practice

In the previous sections, we have explored a variety of learning theories: behaviorism, cognitivism, constructivism, and biological foundations. While it is important to understand these theories in terms of human development, how do these theories help explain and/or enhance classroom instruction?

The following vignette examines one high school dance teacher's class. As you read about her lesson, consider what learning theory(s) underlies each particular part of the lesson. Use Group Talk 3.2 to identify the theories.

**9:00—Warm up.** Ms. Denay always begins her fifty-minute high school dance class with a ten-minute ballet warm-up. While the students practice the warm-up skills she has taught them, she moves among them, refining the placement of arms, legs, and torso. As she observes their movements she verbally praises their efforts.

**9:10—Group Directions.** The next part of the lesson involves the students practicing a rather complex jazz dance. The three-minute dance has multiple sections where three different groups of dancers enter and leave the stage at various times; but there are also times when all groups of dancers are all on the stage performing all movements, hopefully, in perfect synchronization. To rehearse the various components of the dance, Ms. Denay asks groups A, B, C to practice each of their parts separately.

**9:15—Group Practice.** The three groups move to three corners in the gym. During the first part of the practice, Ms. Denay instructs the students to perform using only counts. In other words, all of the students count, in sets of four, as they rehearse the choreography. Counting enables the students to slowly practice the series of movements and encourages their efforts to move in unison. Next, Ms. Denay plays the music and once again the students—this time more rapidly—practice dancing their parts.

**9:25—Whole Class Practice.** After the class has practiced the dance twice as separate groups, Ms. Denay brings the class together to perform the entire dance. She has set up the video camera to record their effort in order for the students to critique and improve their piece.

**9:30—Whole Group Observation.** Before they watch the video, Ms. Denay asks the students to consider what they should look for. As a group they decide they need to watch the performance twice. First, they will watch for their own group effort, then they will watch the video as a whole performance. They decide to focus their observation on moving in unison (this has been somewhat problematic in the past and they have been working on this aspect of their performance in their practice) and entering the stage on time.

**9:35—Discussion/Feedback/Problem Solving.** The dancers reassemble quickly to discuss what they saw in their group performance and then to discuss what they saw in the routine as a whole. Groups A and C were pleased—they felt they had done an excellent job at moving in unison and were right on time with their on-stage entry. Group B had hesitated with one of its entries on the stage, and they felt the hesitation created the secondary problem of causing them to be out-of-step with each other. Ms. Denay asked the class to offer Group B suggestions on how to solve this problem. Group A offered that they had a lead dancer who the others followed to be sure they entered exactly on time. Group B accepts the suggestion and appoints Sherre to be lead.

**9:40—Whole Group Performance.** The class performs the entire dance once again. Ms. Denay videotapes the dance.

**9:45—Observation.** The class observes the second performance. Clearly, Group B's decision to have a lead dancer helped them significantly. Mrs. Denay dismisses the class to start dressing for their next course. ■

**Classroom Glimpse**

## Group Talk

### Identifying Learning Theories in Practice

Using Figure 3.2 (page 95) Comparing Learning Theories, consider what Ms. Denay did at each part of her lesson to ensure her students learned. What learning theory was reflected in her actions?

9:00 — Warm-up

9:10 — Group Directions

9:15 — Group Practice

9:25 — Whole Class Performance

9:30 — Whole Class Observation

9:35 — Group Discussion–Feedback–Problem solving

9:40 — Whole Class Performance

9:45 — Whole Class Observation and Feedback

As you consider this lesson as a whole, did one instructional theory dominate or did Ms. Denay use a range of approaches? How do you believe this influenced the effectiveness of the lesson?

If you were Ms. Denay, describe how you might build on this lesson tomorrow?

What learning theory would be reflected in this strategy?

## Looking Forward

In this chapter we reviewed the three major learning theories and their proponents. In addition we briefly discussed the emerging neurological perspective of how learning occurs. Interesting, it reflects the views of all three learning theories, depending on the type of learning the student is trying to accomplish.

In the following chapter, we will review the major philosophies of education. A philosophy, reflects a system of thought. In this case the philosophies reveal distinct perspectives of the purpose and approaches to education. Similarly, we will discuss teaching styles, which are more contemporary. You will find yourself relating to these beliefs and subsequent approaches to education. Finally, we will look at the different levels of teaching, from early childhood to secondary education and the newest field of study, special education.

## Research Citations

Bandura, A. (1986). *Social Foundations of Thought and Action.* Englewood Cliffs, NJ: Prentice Hall.

Bandura, A. (1997). *Self-Efficacy: The Exercise of Control.* New York, NY: Freeman.

Bjork, D. W. (1997). *B.F. Skinner: A Life.* Washington, DC: American Psychological Association.

Brewer, C. L. (1991). Perspectives on John B. Watson. In G. A. Kimble, M. Wertheimer, & C. L. White (Eds.), *Portraits of pioneers in psychology.* Washington, DC: American Psychological Association.

Buckley, K.W. (1989). *Mechanical Man: John B. Watson and the Beginnings of Behaviorism.* New York, NY: Guilford Press.

Caine, R. & Caine, G. (1991) *Making Connections: Teaching and the Human Brain.* Alexandria, VA: Association Supervision and Curriculum Development.

Chomsky, C. (1969). *The acquisition of syntax in children from 5 to 10.* Cambridge, MA: M.I.T. Press.

Cromer, A.H. (1997). *Connected Knowledge : Science, Philosophy, and Education.* New York, NY: Oxford University Press.

DeNicolas, A. T. (1989). *Habits of Mind: An Introduction to the Philosophy of Education.* St.Paul, MN: Paragon House Publishers.

Driscoll, M. P. (1994). *Psychology of learning for instruction.* Needham Heights, MA: Allyn & Bacon.

Evan, R. I. (1989). *Albert Bandura.* Westport, CN: Praeger Publishers.

Gagne, R. M. & Medsker, K. L. (1995). *The conditions of learning: Training applications.* Belmont, CA: Wadsworth Publishing.

Gagne, R.M., Wager, W. W., Golas, K. & Keller, J. M. (2004). *Principles of instructional design,* 5th Ed. Belmont: CA. Wadsworth Publishing.

Hergenhahn, B.R. & Olson, M.H. (2004). *Introduction to the theories of learning,* 7th Ed. Upper Saddle River, NJ: Prentice Hall.

Kohn, A. (1993). *Punished by rewards: The trouble with gold stars, incentive plans, A's, praise, and other bribes.* Boston, MA: Houghton Mifflin.

Newman, F. (1993). Lev Vygotsky; revolutionary scientist *Critical Psychology.* Bath, UK: Routledge.

O'Donohue, W. T. & Ferguson, K.E. (2001). *The Psychology of B F Skinner.* London, UK: Sage Publications.

Piaget, J. (2000). *The Psychology of the Child.* New York, NY: Basic Books.

Piaget, J. (2001). *Psychology of Intelligence.* Bath, UK: Routledge.

Posner, M.I. (2004). *Cognitive neuroscience of attention.* New York, NY: Guilford Press.

Schunk, D. H. (2003). *Learning Theories : An Educational Perspective,* 4th Ed. Upper Saddle River, NJ: Prentice Hall.

Sherwood, E. & Sherwood, M. (1970). *Ivan Pavlov.* Heron Books, London, Eng.

Skinner, B.F. (1987). *Upon further reflection.* Upper Saddle River, NJ: Prentice-Hall, Inc.

Sylwester, R. (2000). *A biological brain in a cultural classroom: Applying biological research to classroom management.* Thousand Oaks, CA: Corwin Press.

Todd, J.T., & Morris, E. K.(1994). *Modern perspectives on John B. Watson and classical behaviorism.* Westport, CT: Greenwood Press.

Todes, D. P. (2000). *Ivan Pavlov: Exploring the animal machine.* New York, NY: Oxford University Press.

Watson, J.B.(1930). *Behaviorism.* Chicago, IL: University of Chicago Press.

Wertsch, J.V. (1988). *Vygotsky and the Social Formation of Mind.* Boston, MA: Harvard University Press.

Wolfe, P. (2001). *Brain matters: Translating research into classroom practice.* Alexandria, VA: ASCD.

## Reading on the Human Brain and Neuroscience

- Bransford, J., Brown, A. & Cocking, R. (2000). *How people learn: Brain, mind, experience and school.* Washington, D.C: National Academy Press.

- Butterworth, B. (1999). *What counts: How every brain is hardwired for math.* New York, NY: Free Press.

- Byrnes, J. (2001). *Minds, brains, and learning: Understanding the psychological and educational relevance of neuroscientific research.* New York, NY: The Guilford Press.

- Calvin, W. (2002). *A brain for all seasons: Human evolution and abrupt climate change.* Chicago, IL: University of Chicago Press.

- Damasio, A. (1999). *The feeling of what happens: Body and emotion in the making of consciousness.* New York, NY: Harcourt.

- Diamond, M. & Hopson, J. (1998). *Magic trees of the mind: How to nurture your child's intelligence, creativity, and healthy emotions.* New York, NY: Dutton Press.

- Fauconnier, G. & Turner, M. (2002). *The way we think: Conceptual blending and the mind's hidden complexities.* New York, NY: Basic Books.

- Freeman, W. (2000). *How brains make up their minds.* New York, NY: Columbia University Press.

- Goldblum, N. (2001). *The brain-shaped mind: What the brain can tell us about the mind.* Cambridge, UK: Cambridge University Press.

- Greenspan, S. & Shanker, S. (2004). *The first idea: How symbols, language, and intelligence evolved from our primate ancestors to modern humans.* Cambridge, MA: Da Capo Press.
- Johnson, S. (2004). *Mind wide open: Your brain and the neuroscience of everyday life.* New York, NY: Scribner.
- LeDoux, J. (2002). *Synaptic self: How our brains become who we are.* New York, NY: Viking Press.
- Klein, S. (2000). *Biological psychology.* Upper Saddle River, NJ: Prentice Hall.
- Kotulak, R. (1996). *Inside the brain: Revolutionary discoveries of how the mind works.* Kansas City, MO: Andrews McMeeley Publishing.
- Pinker, S. (2002). *The blank slate: The modern denial of human nature.* New York, NY: Penguin Books.
- Ratey, J. (2001). *A user's guide to the brain.* New York, NY: Pantheon Books.
- Smilkstein, R. (2003). *We're born to learn: Using the brain's natural learning process to create today's curriculum.* Thousand Oaks, CA: Corwin Press.
- Schwartz, J. (2002). *The mind and the brain: Neuroplasticity and the power of mental force.* New York, NY: Harper Collins Publishers.

# Understanding Educational Philosophy and Your Professional Beliefs

*In modern times there are opposing views about the practice of education. There is no general agreement about what the young should learn either in relation to virtue or in relation to the best life; nor is it clear whether their education ought to be directed more towards the intellect than towards the character of the soul. . . . And it is not certain whether training should be directed at things useful in life, or at those conducive to virtue, or at non-essentials. . . . And there is no agreement as to what in fact does tend towards virtue. Men do not all prize most highly the same virtue, so naturally they differ also about the proper training for it.*

Aristotle wrote that passage more than 2,300 years ago, and since that time educators are still debating the issues he raised. There are many different views regarding the purpose of education and the best manner in which to teach them. These views are called philosophy.

**Definitions**

**Case Study**   an instructional technique that provides students an opportunity to apply what they learn in the classroom to real-life experiences.

**Cooperative Learning**   an instructional technique that uses small teams, each with students of different levels of ability, and uses a variety of learning activities to improve their understanding of a subject. Each member of a team is responsible not only for learning what is taught, but also for helping teammates learn, thus creating an atmosphere of achievement.

**Empathetic**   the ability to identify with and understand another person's feelings or situation.

**Discussion**   an instructional technique that engages students in carefully planned classroom verbal interactions.

**Drill**   an instructional technique used when students need to learn information at an automatic response level; for instance, "drilling" math facts. Drill is also used when students need to practice a skill to perfect a performance, such as a dance routine or a musical piece.

**Inclusive**   an instructional environment that includes students with special needs into the regular classroom setting for part or all of their instruction.

**Lecture**   an instructional technique where the instructor provides information in a direct manner, with little verbal exchange between the participants (i.e., little student interaction).

**Philosophy**   a branch of knowledge or academic study devoted to the systematic examination of basic concepts such as truth, existence, reality, causality, and freedom. A set of basic principles underlying a particular sphere of knowledge. A set of beliefs underlying someone's practice or actions.

**Profession**   an occupation that requires extensive education or specialized training.

**Professional**   a person who demonstrates a high degree of skill or competence in an occupation.

**Pre-professional**   one who is studying a profession, but still lacks the full range of knowledge or competence to practice.

**Problem-Based Learning (PBL)**   an instructional technique that challenges students to "learn to learn," working cooperatively in groups to seek solutions to real-world problems.

## As you read, think about . . .

★ What type of high school did you go to?

★ Did this high school reflect a specific philosophy?

★ What philosophy described in Chapter 4 best reflects the philosophy of your high school?

## Focus Questions

★ What is important for children to know?

★ What knowledge and beliefs do you want them to have?

★ What is the best way to teach this knowledge and these beliefs?

In Chapter 2, the History of American Education section, we began to establish a sense of the different purposes of education. For example, the Puritans believed that the purpose of learning was to enable children to learn to read the Bible. They felt this was important because it prevented Satan from tempting the child's soul. While a hundred years later, Benjamin Franklin helped to establish Academies—he believed education should lead to practical training. These two purposes for education reflect belief systems, which in turn echo different philosophies of education. These philosophies ultimately determine what content is taught, how the content is taught, and even the nature of teacher-student interactions.

# Classical Philosophies

The *philosophy* of education is the study of the purpose, nature, and content of education. Other questions that philosophy answers include the nature of the knowing mind and the human subject, problems of authority, and the relationship between education and society (Murphy, 2005; Nodding, 1995). Philosophers have proposed a number of purposes for education:

1. The success of any society depends on educating its young to become responsible, thoughtful, and productive citizens. In addition to understanding children and the role of children in society, educators must consider the far-reaching outcomes of the curriculum, including ethical principles and moral values.

2. Progress in all aspects of society—cultural, economics, religious, agriculture—depend upon having capacities that schooling can educate. Education thus is a means to fostering the individual's, society's, and even humanity's future development and prosperity.

3. An individual's development and the ability to reach a personal goal often depends upon an appropriate and sufficient education in childhood and preparation in adulthood. Education can provide a firm foundation for future achievement and personal fulfillment.

While there are many philosophers and philosophies, there appear to be four dominant schools of philosophical thought, which haves strong support in American education today. We will briefly discuss these philosophies to help you build a framework from which you can better understand the type of schooling you received as an elementary and secondary student, and then help you develop your own educational philosophy and practices.

- *Essentialism* assumes there is a core body of knowledge that must be mastered in order for a person to be considered "educated." It focuses on the "essentials" and is subject oriented. Essentialism could be summed up in this phrase: "Information is the key to a good education" (see Box 4.1).

- *Perennialism* is more "idea" oriented, and considers education to consist of becoming acquainted with the great writing and thinking throughout history. To perennialists, "understanding is the key to a good education" (see Box 4.2).

- *Progressivism* seeks to make education practical and applicable to the needs of students and society. It assumes that making knowledge and skills meaningful are the keys to a good education (see Box 4.3).

- *Existentialism* stresses "authenticity"—the commitment to finding true being. To the existentialist, discovering one's own meaning in life is the key to a good education (see Box 4.4).

Figure 4.1 summarizes these major philosophies. On the following pages, we provide more information about the goals of each philosophy and profile the major founder philosopher for each system of thought. We also will offer our thoughts on how these philosophies "look" inside today's classrooms.

Box 4.1  ↓ More about Essentialism

**Essentialism** refers to the "traditional" approach to education. It is so named because it strives to transmit the "essentials", such as traditional moral values and intellectual knowledge students need to become model citizens. While the term essentialism as an educational philosophy was originally popularized in the 1930s by the American educator **William Bagley** (1874–1946), the philosophy itself had been the dominant approach to education in America from the beginnings of American history (Wesley-Null, 2003; Bagley, 1909).

American essentialism is grounded in a conservative philosophy that accepts the social, political, and economic structure of American society. It contends that schools should not try to radically reshape society. Rather, essentialists argue that American schools should instill such traditional American virtues such as respect for authority, perseverance, fidelity to duty, consideration for others, and practicality (Nodding, 1995; Pring, 2005).

Box 4.2  ↓ More about Perennialism

**Perennial** means "everlasting," like a flower that blooms year after year. Perennialists support the view that some core ideas have lasted over the millenniums and are as important today as when they were first conceived. A major proponent of the perennialist philosophy, **Robert Hutchins** (1899–1977), believed these eternal concepts should be the focus of education.

The *Great Books of the Western World* (published by Encyclopedia Britannica) is a series originally published in 1952. The series contains sixty volumes and forms the basis of the perennialist curriculum (Mayer & Hicks, 1992). The series began when the University of Chicago's president, Robert Hutchins, collaborated with Mortimer Adler (chairmen of the board of Encyclopedia Britannica).

Perennialists believe students, who are engaged in learning profound and enduring ideas, will come to appreciate learning for its own sake. Like an Essentialist, Hutchins believed schools should focus on these ideas rather than practical or applied knowledge. However, unlike an Essentialist, he believed schools should not teach values. He believed that this effort would weaken the intent and outcome of learning (Ashmore, 1989).

Box 4.3  ↓ More about Progressivism

**John Dewey** (1859–1952) is the person most responsible for the success of the Progressivist educational philosophy. A social reformer and professor of philosophy and psychology at the University of Chicago, Dewey founded the famous Laboratory school as a place to pilot his educational ideas. This work has had a major impact in American schools since the 1920s (Martin, 2003; Hook, 1995).

The progressive movement encouraged schools to broaden their curriculum to reflect the needs and interests of the students. Dewey believed children learned best through active interactions and play with others. He believed children learned best when they were engaged in activities that had meaning to them. Dewey believed children acquire knowledge when they applied their previous experience to solving new, meaningful problems and he developed a five-step method for solving problems (Nodding, 1995).

**Box 4.4   ↓ More about Existentialism**

**Educational existentialism** sprang from a strong rejection of the traditional essentialist approach to education. Existentialism rejects the existence of any source of objective, authoritative truth. Instead, individuals are responsible for determining for themselves what is "true" or "false," "right" or "wrong," "beautiful," or "ugly." For the existentialist, there exists no universal form of human nature; each of us has the free will to develop as we see fit.

**Søren Aabye Kierkegaard** (1813–1855) was a nineteenth century Danish philosopher and theologian generally recognized as the first existentialist philosopher. Kierkegaard was deeply influenced by the work of the writer Rousseau.

In the existentialist classroom, subject matter takes second place to helping the students understand and appreciate themselves as unique individuals who accept complete responsibility for their thoughts, feelings, and actions. The teacher's role is to help students define their own essence by exposing them to various paths they may take in life and creating an environment in which they may freely choose their own preferred way. Since feeling is not divorced from reason in decision-making, the existentialist demands the education of the whole person, not just the mind. (Garff & Kimmse, 2004)

**Jean Jacques Rousseau** (1712–1778) was a Franco-Swiss philosopher of Enlightenment period whose political ideas influenced the French Revolution. His revolutionary legacy is perhaps best demonstrated by his most famous line in *The Social Contract:* "Man is born free, and everywhere he is in chains." His career began in 1749, when Rousseau won first prize in a contest, held by the Academy of Dijon, on the question: "Has the progress of the sciences and arts contributed to the corruption or to the improvement of human conduct?" Rousseau took the negative stand, contending that humanity was good by nature and had been fully corrupted by civilization. His essay made him both famous and controversial. Few people have equaled Rousseau's influence in politics, literature, and education. Many attribute his writing to influencing the Existentialist philosophy of education (Damrosch, 2005).

Rousseau illustrates his views on education in Émile, a story describing the growth of a young boy of that name, presided over by Rousseau himself. He brings him up in the countryside, where he believed humans are most naturally suited, rather than in a city, where we only learn bad physical and intellectual habits. The aim of education, Rousseau says, is to learn how to live, and this is accomplished by following a guardian who can point the way to good living. He minimizes the importance of book-learning, and recommends that a child's emotions should be educated before his reason. He placed a special emphasis on learning by experience. Rousseau views education as the "drawing out" of what already exists in the child—the fostering of what is native—allowing the freed development of the human potential (Starobinki, 1988).

| Figure 4.1 | ↓ Comparison of Educational Philosophies | | | |
| --- | --- | --- | --- | --- |
| **Philosophies** | **Perennialism** | **Essentialism** | **Progressivism** | **Existentialism** |
| **Basic Belief** | The acquisition of knowledge of the great ideas of western culture | Core body of basic knowledge and skills | As society is ever changing; new ideas are important | There exists no universal form of human nature; all humans have free will |
| **Curricular Emphasis** | Curriculum should remain constant over time | Emphasis on intellectual and moral standards | Student interest and motivation are important | Individual student interest drives the learning |
| **Teaching Method** | Teachers should directly instruct and guide students' understanding | Teachers transmit instruction in a logical and systematic manner | Hands-on inquiry, field trips; integration on thinking, feeling, and doing | Learning is self-paced, self-directed; teacher is co-learner |
| **Character Development** | Cultivation of the intellect is the highest priority of education | Students should be taught respect for discipline, hard work, and authority | Schools should help students develop personal and social values | Schools help students appreciate themselves as unique individuals who take responsibility for their actions |

## Philosophies in the Classroom

How do these common philosophies relate to classrooms, or classroom practice? The philosophy that is held by a teacher, administrator, or even a community will directly mold what teachers implement and how they deliver their lessons. Let's take a closer look at how this philosophical impact relates to classrooms today.

**Essentialist Theories**  Essentialists urge that essential academic skills and knowledge be taught to all students. Traditional disciplines such as math, natural science, history, foreign language, and literature form the foundation of the essentialist curriculum. Essentialists frown upon vocational content (e.g., learning skills needed to be an auto mechanic or hygienist).

Students are required to master a body of information and basic techniques, gradually moving from less to more complex skills and detailed knowledge. Only by mastering the required material for their grade level are students promoted to the next grade.

Essentialist programs are academically rigorous, for both slow and fast learners. It calls for more core requirements, a longer school day, a longer academic year, and more challenging textbooks. Moreover, essentialists maintain that classrooms should be oriented around the teacher, who ideally serves as an intellectual and moral role model for the students. The teachers or administrators decide what is most important for the students to learn and place little

Teachers who believe in the Progressivist Theory use hands-on experiences to stimulate interests and opportunities to learn.

emphasis on student interests, particularly when they divert time and attention from the academic curriculum. Essentialist teachers focus heavily on achievement test scores as a means of evaluating progress (Murphy, 2005).

In an essentialist classroom students are taught to be "culturally literate," that is, to possess a working knowledge about the people, events, ideas, and institutions that have shaped American society. Reflecting the essentialist emphasis on technological literacy, *A Nation at Risk* recommends all high school students complete at least one semester of computer science. Essentialists hope that when students leave school, they will possess not only basic skills and an extensive body of knowledge, but also disciplined, practical minds, capable of applying schoolhouse lessons in the real world (Wesley-Null, 2003; Bagley, 1909).

**Perennialism Theories**   While both perennial and essentialist philosophies believe in rigorous intellectual curriculum and accept little flexibility, the perennialist differs in the belief that factual knowledge is more important than conceptual understanding. For example, science is not about the current facts, but rather the act of investigation (Murphy, 2005).

In classroom practice, the teacher who follows a perennial philosophy conducts seminars where students and teachers engage in mutual inquiry sessions—called Socratic dialogues—to develop an understanding of history's most critical and timeless concepts.

**Existentialist Theories**   Although many existentialist educators provide some curricular structure, existentialism, more than other educational philosophy, affords students great latitude in their choice of subject matter. In an existentialist curriculum, students are given a wide variety of options from which to choose (Garff & Kirmmse, 2004).

Vocational education is regarded more as a means of teaching students about themselves and their potential than of earning a livelihood. In teaching art, existentialism encourages individual creativity and imagination more than copying and imitating established models.

Existentialist teaching methods focus on the individual. Learning is self-paced, and self-directed. It also includes a great deal of individual contact with the teacher, who relates to each student uniquely and freely. Although elements of existentialism occasionally appear in public schools, this philosophy has found wider acceptance in private schools and alternative public schools founded in the late 1960s and early 1970s (Pring, 2005).

**Progressivist Theories**   Progressivists believe education should be a perpetually enriching process of ongoing growth, not merely a preparation for adult lives. They stand in direct contrast to essentialists and perennialists in the belief that the study of core-traditional subject matter is appropriate for all students. Progressivists believe that the home, workplace, and schoolhouse can ideally blend together to generate a continuous and fulfilling learning experience in life.

Today's progressivists center the curriculum on the experiences, interests, and abilities of the student. Teachers plan lessons that encourage curiosity and guide students' greater levels of learning. Teachers use games and hands-on experiences to stimulate interests and opportunities to learn. Children work together to solve problems, generate ideas, and create new knowledge for themselves.

## Group Talk

### The Influence of Educational Philosophy on Your Current Thinking

In a small group, discuss your educational background using these questions to guide your discussion.

*1.* What classic philosophy best represents the education you received?

*2.* How has this philosophy influenced your thinking about education?

*3.* You may have attended more than one school system as you grew up. Were these systems different in philosophical stance? If so, did that have an impact on your education?

# Teaching Styles in Practice

When you are asked about your philosophy of education, most people asking this question are referring to your personal notions about how you plan to teach and why. In most cases we do not explicitly consider learning theory or classical philosophies as we form our own teaching philosophy; instead, teaching philosophies begin at a much more personal level and are usually formed by the experiences we have had in classrooms as we were going to school. In most cases, we are responding to the teaching styles of our past teachers. Use the following two "processing activities" to consider your own former influential teachers.

# Processing Activity

## The Best Teacher

**Directions**   **Take a few moments to consider your schooling experience. Please respond to the following questions.**

Who was your favorite teacher?

What grade or subject did they teach?

Why was this particular teacher your favorite?

What type of adjectives did you and your classmates use to describe this teacher?

What specific practices did this teacher use to motivate students?

What did this teacher do to help you learn?

# Processing Activity

## The Worst Teacher

**Directions:**   **Take a few moments to consider your school experience. Please respond to the following questions.**

Who was your worst teacher?

What grade or subject did they teach?

Why was this particular teacher your least favorite?

What type of adjectives did you and your classmates use to describe this teacher?

What specific practices did this teacher use to motivate students?

What did this teacher do to keep you from feeling successful in their class?

Hopefully, most of us have had several teachers we considered as we completed this exercise. However, our experiences as students, and our discussions with pre-service teachers over the last forty years, suggest that nearly all of us have had a negative experience with a teacher. These individuals may also cause us residual feelings of frustration, anger, and self-doubt. Take a few moments to consider the *worst* teacher you have had during your schooling experience.

Our prior experiences in school continue to have both positive and negative influences on our lives long past childhood and adolescence. Likewise, these experiences may also impact your views of teaching and the teaching style you adopt for your own classroom (Steffy, Wolfe, Pasche & Enz, 1997).

As a *preservice professional,* your philosophy of education is still being formed; yet, these early beliefs have a profound influence on your everyday classroom practices. Take a moment to complete the Instructional Beliefs Survey (Figure 4.2), then add your points. The Special Feature by Jill Stam (Box 4.6), which follows this survey, will provide you with insight regarding your choices and philosophies.

---

### Box 4.6 ↓ Exploring Teaching Styles in Practice

**Special Feature by Jill Stamm**

After you have added your points on the Belief Survey, you will most likely notice that one column has received more points than the others. The column that you awarded the most points reflects your current view about teaching and learning. The following pages label and more fully describe the four philosophies of education that are prevalent in the field of education today.

It is important to remember that one teaching style is not better than another. Each style has terrific advantages and some disadvantages. Often times, you may have two columns that have similar scores. This usually suggests that, as a student, you have had a range of teachers who had divergent teaching practices that deeply influenced your views of teaching and learning.

Our teaching styles usually do not change dramatically **until** we have had a great deal of time developing our own teaching styles through experience in the classroom.

## Figure 4.2 ↓ Instructional Beliefs Survey

**Directions:** Each box below contains descriptive phrases. Score each group giving yourself a 4 for the most like you, 3 for the next, 2 for the next, and 1 for the least like you. Be sure to put a score in **each** box. Score across each category. Next, add scores in each column A, B, C, D to obtain column totals. [Adapted from the Instructional Orientation Profile, (Stamm, J., Enz, B., Wactler, C. and Freeman, D. 1996). Stamm, J., & Wactler, C. (1997). *Philosophy of Education Workbook:* New York: McGraw-Hill.]

### I believe Classroom Environments should be/should have:

| | | | |
|---|---|---|---|
| • Task-oriented<br>• Organized & Structured<br>• Commercially prepared material | • Student-oriented<br>• Flexible-Spontaneous activity<br>• Student-generated material | • Content-oriented<br>• Goal-directed/ Semi-structured<br>• Teacher-prepared material | • Technology-oriented<br>• Production-dominated activity<br>• Materials created on computer |

### I believe Lesson Plans should be/should have:

| | | | |
|---|---|---|---|
| • Specific objectives are clearly defined<br>• Essential elements of instruction<br>• District guidelines and scope and sequence | • Long-term, loosely structured outcomes<br>• Thematic units and Integrated curriculum<br>• Student choice of what to learn | • Extentions beyond district guidelines<br>• Emphasis on depth of knowledge<br>• Extensive resources (outside speakers, field trips) | • Open-ended and information driven<br>• Multi-level inquiry planning<br>• Emphasize technological skills and information interpreting techniques |

### I believe Discipline should include:

| | | | |
|---|---|---|---|
| • Positive reinforcement for desired behaviors<br>• Teacher/School-developed rules<br>• Consistent consequences for undesired behaviors | • Classroom community meetings to discuss behavior<br>• Rules established by teacher and students<br>• Serious problems dealt with on individual contract basis | • Teacher modeling of desired behavior<br>• Student responsibility for his or her own conduct<br>• A focus on ethics and moral development | • An emphasis on community responsibility<br>• Teacher and students dialogue to clarify expectations<br>• Procedures to govern student interaction with technology |

### I believe Classroom Activities should include:

| | | | |
|---|---|---|---|
| • Independent/Seat work<br>• Lecture–Direct instruction<br>• Daily or weekly homework assignments/projects | • Student choices<br>• Cooperative learning<br>• Student-chosen activities and projects | • In-depth research on topics<br>• Lecture/discussion questions<br>• Extensive reading | • Students working on-line<br>• Peer teaching<br>• Student created presentations and projects |

### I believe Grading and Student Evaluation should include:

| | | | |
|---|---|---|---|
| • Mastery testing<br>• Progress measured objectively and frequently<br>• Tests that assess stated objectives | • Ongoing portfolio assessment<br>• Grades for effort as well as achievement<br>• Self and peer evaluating process as well as product | • Essay and objective tests<br>• Grades on ability to apply knowledge<br>• High standards | • Grading student work on decision making, resources used<br>• Evaluation of students' technical competence<br>• Feedback given via E-mail |

### I believe Knowledge and Instruction should include:

| | | | |
|---|---|---|---|
| • Logical step-by-step instruction<br>• Drill and practice focused on specific outcome<br>• Focus on mastering the basic/ essential skills | • "First-hand" experiences<br>• Manipulation and experimentation<br>• Students construct their own meaning/ develop personal understanding | • Intense study and immersion in content<br>• Teacher transmission/model<br>• Depth of knowledge as a goal | • Teaching students how to search for information<br>• Exploration/student interest<br>• An emphasis on meaning of information |

### I believe the Teacher's Role is:

| | | | |
|---|---|---|---|
| • Manager<br>• Organizer<br>• Planner | • Facilitator<br>• Explorer<br>• Co-learner | • Expert<br>• Mentor<br>• Guide | • Interpreter<br>• Consultant<br>• Connector |

| Column A total | Column B total | Column C total | Column D total |
|---|---|---|---|
| | | | |

# Column A: Executive

If you awarded Column A the most points you favor have the **Executive** teaching style. The executive approach is very skills-oriented, and is so labeled because it reflects many of the same values and outcomes that are found in business and industry. This approach utilizes elements of the behaviorist and cognitivist learning theories and more clearly reflect the **Essentialist** philosophy of education.

The executive teacher is a manager. The teacher, as manager, directs students' learning and focuses on end products that can be measured accurately. District guidelines and grade-level scope and sequence determine what will be taught. Such teachers are efficient in lesson planning, devising materials to meet student needs, and in testing of the objective.

The student is seen as the consumer of information. The content to be learned is highly specified and is taught to students in the exact form they will need to know it for a test. The content is usually "delivered" to the awaiting student by a *lecture* method.

High achievement in recalling a great deal of information is the goal. Student learning is considered the goal, and achievement scores the end product.

The classroom environment is highly structured, and it is extremely efficient and is organized around accomplishing tasks.

## Positive Factors

- Because both the content to be taught and the outcomes to be achieved are so clearly stated and well defined, new teachers are usually able to find early successes and therefore greater comfort by using this approach.

- Teachers using the executive approach often place a very high value on the use of research-based strategies.

- Administrators, state legislators, and many parents have high praise for teachers who use this approach. It gives comfort to be able to "see clearly" what is expected of each student.

- Teachers who enjoy and excel in being well organized thrive in this environment.

## Negative Factors

- Teachers who teach with this approach often suffer from greater "burn-out." Because they incorporate each new research-based strategy into their repertoire, when new research comes along, the executive teacher keeps creating additional demands on his/her teaching, but does NOT give up any past techniques! Eventually, they cannot keep up with their own demands for high performance; they become overwhelmed and often quit teaching.

- Students who need special attention, have cultural or language differences, or have exceptional skills, are often not able to have their needs met in this structured, prescribed environment.

# Column B: Humanist

If you awarded Column B the most points you favor a **Humanist** teaching style. This approach may be familiar because it shares common elements with current trends in education including student choice of what to study, *cooperative learning,* self-evaluation, and grading for effort. This teaching philosophy is most aligned with the constructivist learning theory and the **Progressivist** philosophy of education.

The humanist teacher is a facilitator of learning. The teacher, as facilitator, is an *empathetic* person who guides the student in the process of self-discovery. The teacher's role is to prepare students to learn how to make good choices both academically and personally. The student is seen as an authentic person with a unique personal history and culture, and individual competencies are valued.

Choice is central to this approach, both in what to learn and how to learn it. In order to help students acquire knowledge, the teacher makes sure the information, resources, and relevant equipment are accessible to students.

The classroom environment is rich with books, tapes, objects, animals, and equipment. Learning through multiple forms of media and materials is considered essential. There is usually a sense of loosely organized clutter.

### Positive Factors

- Because meeting a student's individual needs is the focus of this approach, many students thrive in this setting. Each student has a tailored set of expectations for achievement and progress is tracked by the attainment of individual goals.
- Because the environment is rich with a variety of resources, student interest in new topics and ideas is aroused.
- Teachers experienced in this approach often feel that they are connecting deeply with children to teach them personally what they need at a given time. This is often a joyful experience for the teacher.
- Many parents like this approach because they recognize their own child's individual needs are being valued.

### Negative Factors

- Teaching from this orientation can be very difficult for the beginning teacher. It often takes several years of teaching experience within a more traditional executive approach before the teacher has the confidence to address the needs of the individual student.
- Administrators, legislators, and some parents are frustrated by this approach because it is more difficult to know exactly what is expected of children at each grade/age level. It is more difficult to track and to develop a standard of comparative progress.
- Teachers who teach from this philosophical orientation sometimes feel they have to "hide" their humanist practices in order to comply with district testing and tracking demands. The feeling of being "subversive" is uncomfortable and frustrating.

## Column C: Classicist

If you awarded Column C the most points you favor a **Classicist** teaching philosophy. The roots of the classicist approach date back to ancient Greece. The goal of the teaching philosophy is to develop well-rounded citizens through an intense liberal arts curriculum. A classicist teacher often reflects the cognitive learning theories within their instructional practices and reflects the **Perennial** educational philosophy.

The teacher is a model that inspires passion for a particular content area. The teacher, as model, "lives" his or her subject matter and demonstrates high levels of scholarship for the student to emulate. The classicist prepares extensively for lessons and includes many types of supplemental materials, speakers, field trips, and so on, so the subject "comes alive" for students.

The student is seen as a potential scholar, capable of great contributions if inspired to study hard. Because each content area has a structure of its own, the teacher of a specific content models the manner and principles of procedures appropriate to that field.

The classroom environment reflects the essence of the values of the particular content area. The classicist focuses upon content and arranges for students to confront the subject matter in the way the specialist in the field experiences the content.

### Positive Factors

- Teachers who teach from this philosophical orientation are often a favorite "teacher of the year." The teacher's passion for his/her subject is very appealing and inspiring to students. The excitement shared for the subject matter is enjoyable for teacher and student alike.
- Administrators and parents often have high praise for this type of teacher because they get noticed for their excellence and for their ability to inspire students who model their enthusiasm for the subject.

- Students are encouraged to delve deeply into the subject matter and achieve a higher level of understanding.
- Because there is intrinsic reward for this teacher, there is less "burn out"; they often retire only after a long teaching career.

### Negative Factors

- Some students who do not share this teacher's love of the particular subject matter can become "invisible" to the teacher who goes on to focus only on those students who share the teacher's enthusiasm.
- Students who are not talented in the subject area may become easily lost as the level of expected scholarship increases throughout the course. The often rapid pace makes catching-up more difficult.

## Column D: Informationist

If you awarded Column D the most points, you favor an **Informationist** teaching style. This technological approach is just emerging in classrooms across the country. The information age, which dominates the business world, is manifesting itself in the classroom and is changing not only the role of the teacher, but also of the nature of the pursuit of knowledge itself. This teaching philosophy uses an interesting combination of behaviorism, cognitive information processing, and a constructivist perspective. Since this approach offers the greatest personal freedom and instructional options (the Internet is virtually the world at your fingertips), it most closely reflects the **Existentialist** philosophy of education.

The informationist teacher is an assistant. Since no one person can possibly "know everything" about a topic, the teacher's role is becoming less of an authority and more of a co-learner/explorer.

The student is seen as a "user" of information. Each student is encouraged to search for information relevant or interesting to him or her. Student progress is monitored via e-mail and computer logs.

The environment supports these new forms of communication, rich with online computers and hardware and software to make multiple application of knowledge possible. The focus of the informationist classroom is on worldwide communication. This approach stresses the role of information in everyone's life.

### Positive Factors

- As society becomes more technologically dependent, the skills emphasized in this orientation will be more and more valued.
- As our world's knowledge base increases exponentially, it is recognized that no one can stay an expert in an area of knowledge easily. This approach validates the role of every person as a co-learner and explorer of knowledge.
- Teaching and learning is no longer limited to space and time constraints. Therefore, the number of potential learning opportunities for all computer users vastly increases.

### Negative Factors

- Some students feel detached, and therefore alone in their learning process. Some may feel a lack of human caring and connection with other students and their instructor.
- If there are technical failures, the learning process is impaired.
- There are risks in relying on information that is "out there" which is inaccurate, misleading, or potentially dangerous to the learner.
- There is a tendency to overload an instructor with too many students, because there is the perception of efficiency and economy of scale that may not be accurate.

## Defining Your Own Unique Philosophical Statement

Now that you have read about the four types of teaching philosophies, let's take a few moments to think about how you would begin to write your own philosophy. Rarely is a real-life teacher neatly categorized into completely one or the other philosophy. Generally the strongest teachers are a blend of beliefs and practices. It is the quality of that unique blend that makes teaching an art.

---

**I believe Classroom Environments should be:**



**I believe Lesson Plans should be:**



**I believe Classroom Management should use:**



**I believe Learning Activities should include:**



**I believe Grading and Student Evaluation should include:**



**I believe students learn through:**



**I believe the Teacher's Role is best described as:**

---

## Group Talk

### Identifying Learning Theories in Practice.

Directions: Consider the three major learning theories you read about in Chapter 3: behaviorism, cognitivist, and constructivism. Identify which learning theory(s) is reflected in the following instructional practices, and explain why you chose that theory.

Which instructional approaches do you find the most helpful in your learning? Why?

| Approach | Explanation |
|---|---|
| *Drill* | This technique is used when students need to learn information at an automatic response level (for instance, math facts). Another time is when students need to practice a skill to perfect a performance, such as a dance routine, or a musical piece.<br><br>**Theory:**<br><br>**Why:** |
| *Lecture* | The classroom lecture is a special form of communication in which the instructor provides information in a direct manner. Although lecture can certainly be an efficient means of instruction, it often functions as an information delivery system rather than a learning experience.<br><br>**Theory:**<br><br>**Why:** |
| *Discussion* | Engaging students in a carefully planned classroom discussion stimulates a more active role in the learning process. Learning is rooted in experiencing information, not in the information itself. Discussion encourages the student to respond to the information being presented.<br><br>**Theory:**<br><br>**Why:** |
| *Case Study* | This approach provides students an opportunity to apply what they learn in the classroom to real-life experiences. This instructional strategy can highlight fundamental dilemmas or critical issues and provides a format for analyzing controversial scenarios.<br><br>**Theory:**<br><br>**Why:** |
| *Cooperative Learning* | This teaching strategy uses small teams, each with students of different levels of ability, and uses a variety of learning activities to improve their understanding of a subject. Each member of a team is responsible not only for learning what is taught but also for helping teammates learn, thus creating an atmosphere of achievement.<br><br>**Theory:**<br><br>**Why:** |
| *Problem-Based Learning (PBL)* | This instructional method challenges students to "learn to learn," working cooperatively in groups to seek solutions to real world problems. These problems are used to engage students' curiosity and initiate learning the subject matter. PBL prepares students to think critically and analytically, and to find and use appropriate learning resources.<br><br>**Theory:**<br><br>**Why:** |

Projected higher enrollment growth for pre-school age children will create many new jobs for preschool teachers.

# Exploring Careers in Education

Theories of learning and philosophies of education, combined with your preferences in instructional styles, provide a foundation of knowledge for exploring the range of careers in education. All levels of teaching careers, from preschool, kindergarten, elementary, special education, middle and secondary school teaching, requires a variety of skills and aptitudes, including:

- a talent for working with children
- organizational, administrative, and recordkeeping abilities
- research and communication skills
- the power to influence, motivate, and train others
- patience and creativity (Steffy, Wolfe, Pasche, & Enz, 1999)

In this decade, preschool, kindergarten, elementary, special education, middle, and secondary school teachers will hold about four million jobs in the United States. Through 2015, overall student enrollments in elementary, middle, and secondary schools—a key factor in the demand for teachers—are expected to rise dramatically (Taylor, 1997). Another factor in these job openings will result from the need to replace the large number of baby boomers who are expected to retire from teaching in this period. In addition to enrollment growth and retirement, some states are also instituting programs to improve early childhood education, such as offering full-day kindergarten and universal preschool. These last two programs, along with projected higher enrollment growth for preschool-age children, will create many new jobs for preschool teachers, which are expected to grow much faster than the average for all occupations nationally (Brewer, 2004).

The supply of teachers is expected to increase in response to reports of improved job prospects, better pay, more teacher involvement in school policy, and greater public interest in education. In recent years, the total number of bachelor's and master's degrees granted in education has increased steadily. Because of a shortage of teachers in certain locations, and in anticipation of the loss of a number of teachers to retirement, many states have implemented policies that will encourage more students to become teachers (Taylor, 1997).

What level of teaching do you wish to pursue? We have provided information about the specific talents and skills each major of teaching requires.

## What Is Early Childhood Education?

This educational level prepares educators to work with the academic, social, emotional, and physical needs of a child from infancy to age eight. The major focus of the early childhood curriculum encompass a thorough knowledge of child development, including:

- *Physical development*—Concerns the physical growth and control of the body
- *Perception and sensory development*—How a child functions using the senses and the ability to process the information gained
- *Communication and language development*—Using visual and sound stimuli, especially in the acquisition of language and in the exchange of thoughts and feelings
- *Cognitive development*—How the child thinks and processes information
- *Emotional development*—Involves how children manage their feelings
- *Social development*—Concerns the child's identity, his/her relationship with others, and understanding his/her place within a social environment
- *Neurological development*—Recent studies on infant brain development show most of a person's neurons are formed from ages zero through five. If a young child doesn't receive sufficient nurturing, nutrition, parental/caregiver interaction, and stimulus during the crucial ages of zero through five, the child may be left with a developmental deficit that hampers his or her academic success.

A wide array of educational philosophies circulate through the field; however, today most early childhood teacher preparation programs strongly favor a **Constructivist** learning theory. The curriculum is child-centered and there is a focus on the importance of play. Play provides children with the opportunity to actively explore, manipulate, and interact with their environment. It encourages children to investigate, create, discover, and be motivated to take risks and add to their understanding of the world. It challenges children to achieve new levels of understanding of events, people, and the environment by interacting with concrete materials (Seefeldt & Barbour, 1997). Hands-on experiences create authentic experiences in which children begin to feel a sense of mastery over their world. This philosophy follows with Piaget's ideals that children should actively participate in their world and various environments, to ensure they are not "passive" learners but "little scientists" who are actively engaged (Brewer, 2004; Wardle, 2002).

The major national associations for early childhood *professionals* are:

- National Association for the Education of Young Children (NAEYC) *http://www.naeyc.org/*
- National Association of Early Childhood Specialists in State Departments of Education (NAECS/SDE) *http://naecs.crc.uiuc.edu/*
- Association of Childhood Educators International (ACEI) *http://www.acei.org/*

## What Is Elementary Education?

Elementary school teachers reflect the broadest range of age certification (typically K through 8). These teachers play a vital role in the development of children. What children learn and experience during their early years can shape their views of themselves and the

Elementary school teachers play a vital role in the development of children.

world, and can affect their later success or failure in school, work, and their personal lives. Elementary school teachers introduce children to mathematics, language, science, and social studies. They use games, music, artwork, films, books, computers, and other tools to teach basic skills.

Most elementary school teachers instruct one class of children in several subjects. In some schools, two or more teachers work as a team and are jointly responsible for a group of students in at least one subject. In other schools, a teacher may teach one special subject—usually music, art, reading, science, arithmetic, or physical education—to a number of classes. A small but growing number of teachers instruct multilevel classrooms, with students at several different learning levels. For example, a multilevel class may be comprised of children who are both six and seven, representing first and second grade levels (Cruikshank & Sheffield, 1991).

Elementary teachers use many instructional methods to help children learn. In addition to direct instruction (lecture), teachers use group work, often called cooperative learning, to encourage collaboration in solving problems. As you read in Chapter 1, elementary teachers plan, evaluate, and assign lessons; prepare, administer, and grade tests; listen to oral presentations; and maintain classroom discipline. Elementary teachers, like all teachers, work with students from varied ethnic, racial, and religious backgrounds. With growing minority populations in most parts of the country, it is important for teachers to work effectively with a diverse student population. Likewise, elementary teachers work with students who face a range of learning and physical challenges and emotional problems. Elementary teachers form partnerships with special education teachers to provide appropriate education and support to all students (Walmsley, 1994).

Requirements for regular licenses to teach K through 8 vary by state. However, all states require general education teachers to have a bachelor's degree and to have completed an

Middle school teachers need a strong knowledge of content matter, knowledge of how to teach that content, and experience with young adolescents.

approved teacher training program with a prescribed number of subject and education credits, as well as supervised practice teaching (i.e., student teaching). Some states also require technology training and the attainment of a minimum grade point average. A number of states require that teachers obtain a master's degree in education within a specified period after they begin teaching (Taylor, 1997).

Professional organizations for elementary teachers include:

- Association for Supervision and Curriculum Development (ASCD) *http://www.ascd.org/*
- International Reading Association (IRA) *reading.org*
- National Council for the Teaching of Mathematics (NCTM) *http://www.nctm.org/*
- National Science Teachers Association (NSTA) *http://www.nsta.org/index.html*

## What Is Middle School Education?

As you think back to your schooling during the time you were eleven to thirteen, were you attending an elementary school? If you did, you most likely had one teacher who provided most of the basic curriculum. While you may have had art, music, or physical education teachers, you still spent most of the day with one teacher and one class of students. Or did you attend a middle (sometimes called junior high) school? If you attended a middle school, you most likely had several teachers; one teacher taught math, another science, and still another taught English.

The middle school movement in the United States began in the 1950s. The intent behind the creation of middle schools was to better meet the academic, social, and developmental needs of young adolescents in a school setting separate from K through 8 schools, K through 5 elementary schools, and high schools. Adolescents between the ages of ten and fourteen are experiencing a period of dramatic physical and cognitive growth, developing a new and untested ability to think in abstract and complex ways (Hernandez, 2000). Middle school is designed to provide continued work in learning skills while bringing more depth to the cur-

Secondary teachers have the opportunity to greatly influence their students' career choices.

riculum than is the case in elementary schools. It emphasizes guidance and exploration, independence and responsibility.

To prepare someone to teach middle school students requires a strong knowledge of content matter (typically defined as a bachelor's degree or twenty-four hours of content), knowledge of how to teach that content (called pedagogy), and a great deal of experience working with young adolescents (Powell, 2004). An expertly prepared middle school teacher must exhibit:

- *Academic excellence.* Middle-grades teachers must have a deep understanding of the subjects they want to teach (typically a bachelor's degree or twenty-four hours of coursework).

- *Content pedagogy.* Middle-grades teachers need a equally strong knowledge of how to teach the content. This skill helps young adolescents learn the concepts and skills of a demanding curriculum.

- *Developmental responsiveness.* Middle-grades teachers must have a solid understanding of early adolescence, as well as the skills and dispositions to work with young adolescents' unique developmental challenges. These teachers should know how to motivate and engage young adolescents in their own learning.

- *Equity and cultural diversity.* Middle-grades teachers must have a wide repertoire of skills, mixed with a sustained sense of hope, support, and expectations for achievement, to enhance learning and development for the most racially and ethnically diverse school population in our nation's history.

The major national association for middle school professionals is the National Middle School Association, *http://www.nmsa.org.*

## What Is Secondary Education?

Secondary schools typically represent grades 9 through 12. Secondary teachers must be content specialists, typically with a bachelor's degree in the content area or a minimum of twenty-four hours of content coursework. In addition, excellent secondary teachers must have the ability to communicate, inspire trust and confidence, and motivate students, as well as understand their young adult students' educational and emotional needs. Secondary teachers have the opportunity to greatly influence their students' career choices (Armstrong & Savage, 2001). Billie vividly remembers two charismatic high school teachers—one a dance teacher and the other a child development teacher. These two women strongly influenced her decision to become both a dance and primary teacher! Did you have a high school teacher with whom you felt you related well?

**Basic Curricular Structure**   At the high school level, students take a broad variety of classes. Typically, American high schools require that courses in the areas of English, science, social science, and mathematics be taken by the students every year. Specifically, most high school students must take:

- Three science courses: biology, chemistry, physics, geology, and forensics
- Three math courses: algebra, geometry, trigonometry, pre-calculus, calculus, and statistics
- English classes, which are usually required all four years of high school
- Two courses in social science content, often including American history, civics, and world history; other courses in law (constitutional, criminal, or international), economics, and *psychology* may be offered
- A year of physical education (usually referred to as gym or PE by students)

High schools offer a wide variety of elective courses, although the availability of such courses depends upon each particular school's financial situation. Most states require students to earn a few credits of classes considered electives, including:

- Visual arts (drawing, sculpture, painting, photography)
- Performing arts (choir, drama, band, orchestra, dance, film)
- Vocational education (woodworking, metalworking, automobile repair)
- Computer science/business education (word processing, programming, graphic design, Web design)
- Physical education (American football, baseball, basketball, track and field, swimming, gymnastics, water polo, soccer)
- Journalism/publishing (school newspaper, yearbook)
- Foreign languages (French, German, and Spanish are common; Chinese, Latin, Greek, Japanese, and Russian are less common, though Latin is gaining increased popularity)
- Family and consumer science/health ("home economics," nutrition, child development)

## What Is Special Education?

Special education teachers work with children and youths who have a variety of physical, emotional, or learning challenges. Special education teachers must be patient, able to motivate students, understand their students' special needs, and accept differences in others. Teachers must be creative and apply different types of teaching methods to reach students who are having difficulty learning. Communication and cooperation are essential skills, because special education teachers spend a great deal of time interacting with others, including students, parents, and school faculty and administrators (Deutsch-Smith, 2003).

The majority of special education teachers work with children with mild to moderate disabilities, using and modifying the curriculum to meet the child's individual needs. Most special education teachers instruct students at the elementary, middle, and secondary school level, although some teachers work with infants and toddlers. Some special education majors work with children with severe physical handicaps, autism, or mental retardation (Heward, 2002). The various types of disabilities that qualify individuals for special education programs include:

- specific learning disabilities
- speech or language impairments
- mental retardation
- emotional disturbance
- hearing impairments or visual impairments
- autism
- combined deafness and blindness
- traumatic brain injury

Students are classified under one of the categories, and special education teachers are prepared to work with specific groups. Early identification of a child with special needs is an important part of a special education teacher's job. Special education teachers use various techniques to promote learning. Depending on the disability, teaching methods can include individualized instruction, problem-solving assignments, and small-group work.

Special education teachers help to develop an Individualized Education Program (IEP) for each special education student. The IEP sets personalized goals for each student and is tailored to the student's individual needs and ability. When appropriate, the program includes a transition plan outlining specific steps to prepare students with disabilities for middle school or high school or, in the case of older students, a job or postsecondary study. Teachers review the IEP with the student's parents, school administrators, and the student's general education teacher. Teachers work closely with parents to inform them of their child's progress and suggest techniques to promote learning at home (Heward, 2002).

Special education teachers design and teach appropriate curricula, assign work geared toward each student's needs and abilities, and grade papers and homework assignments. They are involved in the students' behavioral, social, and academic development, helping the students develop emotionally, feel comfortable in social situations, and be aware of socially acceptable behavior. Preparing special education students for daily life after graduation also is an important aspect of the job. Teachers provide students with career counseling or help them learn routine skills, such as balancing a checkbook or manipulating the public transportation system.

As schools become more *inclusive,* special education teachers and general education teachers are increasingly working together in general education classrooms. Special education teachers help general educators adapt curriculum materials and teaching techniques to meet the needs of students with disabilities. They coordinate the work of teachers, teacher assistants, and related personnel, such as therapists and social workers, to meet the individualized needs of the student within inclusive special education programs. A large part of a special education teacher's job involves interacting with others. Special education teachers communicate frequently with parents, social workers, school psychologists, occupational and physical therapists, school administrators, and other teachers (Deutsch-Smith, 2003).

Special education teachers work in a variety of settings. Some have their own classrooms and teach only special education students; others work as special education resource teachers and offer individualized help to students in general education classrooms; still others teach together with general education teachers in classes composed of both general and special education students. Some teachers work with special education students for several hours a day in a resource room, separate from their general education classroom.

Special educators who work with infants usually travel to the child's home to work with the child and his or her parents. Many of these infants have medical problems that slow or preclude normal development. Special education teachers show parents techniques and activities designed to stimulate the infant and encourage the growth and development of the child's skills. Toddlers usually receive their services at a preschool where special education teachers help them develop social, self-help, motor, language, and cognitive skills, often through the use of play.

Special education teachers enjoy the challenge of working with students with disabilities and the opportunity to establish meaningful relationships with them. Although helping these students can be highly rewarding, the work also can be emotionally and physically draining. The major national associations for special education professionals include:

The Council for Exceptional Children, 1110 N. Glebe Road, Suite 300, Arlington, VA 22201-5704. Internet: *http://www.cec.sped.org*

National Center for Special Education Personnel & Related Service Providers, National Association of State Directors of Special Education, 1800 Diagonal Road, Suite 320, Alexandria, VA 22314. Internet: *http://www.personnelcenter.org*

**Think About It**

What career path is best for you? Which position best matches your philosophy or theories of education? Use the activities in Figure 4.3 and 4.4 to explore your best career goals.

**Figure 4.3  ↓ Thinking about Becoming a Teacher**

*Directions:* As you read the descriptions of the different types of teachers, you could see that while all teachers need to have a bachelor's degree, the training and preparation for each level is very specific. When you apply to a teacher preparation program, you will be asked to determine an explicit level or preparation focus. Take a few minutes to consider, from your perspective, the pros and cons of each level.

| Level | Pros | Cons |
|---|---|---|
| Early Childhood | | |
| Elementary | | |
| Middle | | |
| Secondary | | |
| Special Education | | |

At this point, what appears to be your top choice? Why?

**Figure 4.4   ⬇ Interview a Teacher**

*Directions:* Interview a teacher (one who represents the level that you are most interested in becoming). The interview will probably take about twenty to thirty minutes to conduct.

Teacher's name

Teacher's level

| How long has the teacher been teaching? | How long at this level? |
|---|---|

Why did this teacher choose this **profession?**

Where did they receive their teacher preparation?

Do they have an advanced degree or endorsement?

What do they like best about their teaching position?

What do they like least?

What have been some of the greatest challenges they have faced in this position?

What are some of the rewards of their profession?

# Looking Forward

What motivates us to become teachers? Is it our theories, our philosophies, our past experiences—or a unique combination of both? Read the following special vignette to learn what motivated one Nationally Board Certified teacher to become a professional educator.

While everyone has participated in schooling, very few individuals become teachers. Through education, training, and experience, teachers develop a specialized knowledge base that enables them to analyze the content to be learned, comprehend their students' needs and interests, and determine the best methods and strategies to teach the students who will be learning it. All this mental processing is usually done in seconds, as the needs of students change within minutes in an average learning situation. How do teachers become so proficient? **Section 3—Teacher As Craftsman** provides some beginning answers to this question.

# Talking to Teachers–The Motivation to Teach

Why do individuals choose to become a teacher? Perhaps because the challenges of teaching are outnumbered by the rewards that come from helping students realize their dreams. The following teacher shares her reasons for becoming an educator. Review her story and see if you understand and relate to her feelings and experiences.

Sarah Wolfe has been a classroom teacher for ten years and is currently an Organizational Staff Development Coordinator in Prince William County Schools.

I have had several memorable teachers in my life, but my parents modeled teaching best. They were teachers in their real lives but vastly different in their approaches. From my mother, I learned the love of reading. Each day she made time to read to herself, or us, and taught us how to live through the pages of a book. From my father, I learned dedication to the craft. Preparation is what makes it look easy; expectation is what makes learning hard. Many nights there were piles of books, articles, and papers on our dining room table and Dad would heave through it, take in information, then write out page after page in long hand on dusty yellow legal pads. Writing was one of his gifts, speaking and engaging audiences were his others. I build on these memories each day I walk to the front of the classroom.

I am a teacher and a student of children. I thrive on the enlightened looks and confident strides children make when they learn something new. Teaching is problem solving and problem making. I always felt like a conductor—an engineer of learning. I know what the coordinates (standards) of the curriculum are, but the journey always takes different paths and forks depending on how the children decide to get there. I supply the tools, the compass, and the travel brochures. They learn how to use them to set their own courses.

One of my most memorable days at school came when I had an instructional brainstorm around ten PM on a Thursday; the night before I was to teach a science lesson about the scientific process and extinction of living things. I decided my second graders would connect more to the objective if they became members of several dinosaur digs. Each student was given a "real" job on the dig site. I had researchers, engineers, draftsmen, paleontologists, photographers, editors, and reporters. Each played an essential role in the discovery of the dinosaur. It took most of the day and each child, regardless of his/her disability, talent or instructional need, was completely enthralled with the process. I knew I had truly accomplished my objectives when I was walking the class out to the buses and my most challenging child hugged my waist and said, "I really want to come back tomorrow and do it again!"

*What philosophy of education is most consistent in Sarah's actions?*

*What teaching style is the most reflective of her practices?*

*What continues to inspire her career efforts?*

*Who initially inspired you to consider teaching as a profession?*

## Research Citations

Armstrong, D. G. & Savage, T. V. (2001). *Teaching in the Secondary School: An Introduction,* 5th Ed. Upper Saddle River, NJ: Prentice Hall.

Ashmore, H. S. (1989). *Unseasonable Truths: The Life of Robert Maynard Hutchins.* Boston, MA: Little Brown & Co.

Bagley, W. C. (1909). *Classroom Management: Its Principles and Technique.* London, UK: Macmillan.

Brewer, J. A. (2004). *Introduction to Early Childhood Education : Preschool Through Primary Grades,* 5th Ed. New York, NY: Allyn & Bacon.

Cruikshank, D. E. & Sheffield, L. J. (1991). *Teaching and Learning Elementary and Middle School Mathematics.* London, UK: Macmillan.

Damrosch, L. (2005). *Jean-Jacques Rousseau: Restless Genius.* Boston, MA: Houghton Mifflin.

Deutsch-Smith, D. (2003). *Introduction to Special Education: Teaching in an Age of Opportunity,* 5th Ed. New York, NY: Allyn & Bacon.

Garff, J. & Kirmmse, B.H. (2004). *Soren Kierkegaard: A Biography.* Boston, MA: Princeton University Press.

Hernandez. M. A. (2000). *Middle school years: Achieving the Best Education for Your Child:* Grades 5–8. Clayton, UK: Warner Books

Heward, W. L. (2002). *Exceptional Children: An Introduction to Special Education,* 7th ed. Upper Saddle River, NJ: Prentice Hall.

Hook, S. (1995). *John Dewey: An Intellectual Portrait.* Amherst, NY: Prometheus Books.

Martin, J. (2003). *The Education of John Dewey.* New York, NY: Columbia University Press.

Mayer, M. S. & Hicks, J. H. (1992). *Robert Maynard Hutchins: A Memoir.* Berkeley, CA: University of California Press.

Murphy, M. (2005). *The History and Philosophy of Education : Voices of Educational Pioneers.* Upper Saddle River, NJ: Prentice Hall.

Noddings, N. (1995). *Philosophy of Education.* Boulder, CO: Westview Press.

Powell, S. D. (2004). *Introduction to Middle School.* Upper Saddle River, NJ: Prentice Hall.

Pring, R. (2005). *Philosophy of Education.* London, UK: Continuum International Publishing Group.

Seefeldt, C., & Barbour, N. H. (1997). *Early childhood education: An introduction,* 4th Ed. Upper Saddle River, NJ: Prentice Hall.

Starobinki, J. (1988). *Jean-Jacques Rousseau: Transparency and Obstruction.* Chicago, IL: University of Chicago Press.

Steffy, B., Wolfe, M., Pasche, S., & Enz, B. (1999). *Life Cycle of the Career Teacher.* Thousand Oaks, CA: Corwin Press.

Taylor, F. (1997). *Careers in teaching,* 7th Ed. London, UK: Kogan Page Ltd.

Walmsley, S. A. (1994). *Children Exploring Their World: Theme Teaching in Elementary School.* Portsmouth, NH: Heinemann.

Wardle, F. (2002). *Introduction to Early Childhood Education: A Multidimensional Approach to Child-Centered Care and Learning.* New York, NY: Allyn & Bacon.

Wesley-Null, J. (2003). *A Disciplined Progressive Educator: The Life and Career of William Chandler Bagley.* History of Schools and Schooling, V. 43: Peter Lang Publishing.

## Reading on the Human Brain and Neuroscience

• Bransford, J., Brown, A. & Cocking, R. (2000). *How People Learn: Brain, Mind, Experience and School.* Washington, DC: National Academy Press.

• Butterworth, B. (1999). *What counts: How Every Brain is Hardwired for Math.* New York, NY: Free Press.

• Byrnes, J. (2001). *Minds, Brains, and Learning: Understanding the Psychological and Educational Relevance of Neuroscientific Research.* New York, NY: The Guilford Press.

• Calvin, W. (2002). *A Brain for all Seasons: Human Evolution and Abrupt Climate Change.* Chicago, IL: University of Chicago Press.

- Damasio, A. (1999). *The Feeling of What Happens: Body and Emotion in the Making of Consciousness.* New York, NY: Harcourt.
- Diamond, M. & Hopson, J. (1998). *Magic Trees of the Mind: How to Nurture Your Child's Intelligence, Creativity, and Healthy Emotions.* New York, NY: Dutton Press.
- Fauconnier, G. & Turner, M. (2002). *The Way We Think: Conceptual Blending and the Mind's Hidden Complexities.* New York: Basic Books.
- Freeman, W. (2000). *How Brains Make up Their Minds.* New York, NY: Columbia University Press.
- Goldblum, N. (2001). *The Brain-Shaped Mind: What the Brain Can Tell us About the Mind.* Cambridge, UK: Cambridge University Press.
- Greenspan, S. & Shanker, S. (2004). *The First Idea: How Symbols, Language, and Intelligence Evolved From our Primate Ancestors to Modern Humans.* Cambridge, MA: Da Capo Press.
- Johnson, S. (2004). *Mind Wide Open: Your Brain and the Neuroscience of Everyday Life.* New York, NY: Scribner.
- LeDoux, J. (2002). *Synaptic Self: How Our Brains Become Who We Are.* New York, NY: Viking Press.
- Klein, S. (2000). Biological Psychology. Upper Saddle River, NJ: Prentice Hall.
- Kotulak, R. (1996). *Inside the Brain: Revolutionary Discoveries of How the Mind Works.* Kansas City, MO: Andrews McMeeley Publishing.
- Pinker, S. (2002). *The Blank Slate: The Modern Denial of Human Nature.* New York, NY: Penguin Books.
- Ratey, J. (2001). A User's Guide to the Brain. New York, NY: Pantheon Books.

# Teacher as Craftsman

Research consistently shows that teachers have the greatest potential to influence children's education. But what knowledges, skills, and dispositions make a teacher effective? In this section we will examine the profession from the lens of a craftsman.

We will synthesize current research on the personal characteristics of effective teachers and the types of practices effective teachers use. In particular, we will focus our efforts on the knowledges, skills, and dispositions beginning teachers need to have in order to be successful in the classroom. Specifically, this section will discuss:

**Chapter Five: What Makes a Teacher Effective?**

- What Characteristics Do Effective Teachers Possess?
- What Skills Do Effective Teachers Have?

**Chapter Six: Examining Effective Teaching**

- Beginning the Day with Proactive Management
- Planning a Good Beginning
- Using Miniature Closures

**Definition**

**Craftsman**   a person with specific skills, expertise, ability, and techniques.

# What Makes a Teacher Effective? 5

Research in this area reveals that effective teachers possess many positive characteristics, such as professional integrity, task *perseverance,* and a deep commitment to their students (Brophy & Good, 1986). Teaching also has an ethical dimension that requires a teacher to consistently consider the needs of the students (and the students' families), colleagues, administration, and the community at large (Borich, 2004). These personal attributes are considered essential to success in the teaching profession.

Personal attributes are the foundation to building a long-term career in education.

**Definitions**

**Attributes**   a quality, property, or characteristic assigned to someone or something.

**Characteristics**   a distinguishing feature or quality that makes somebody or something recognizable.

**Colleagues**   others you work with, especially in a professional or skilled job.

**Diagnostic Assessment**   an assessment used to find out what a student's strengths and/or weaknesses are in a certain area. For example, schools might use a diagnostic reading assessment to determine students' reading levels or needs in skill development.

**Disposition**   an inclination or tendency to act in a particular and predictable way; often referred to in teaching as professional attitudes or values.

**Hierarchy**   an organization of people or information arranged in a particular order, typically from least to most important.

**Performance Assessment**   a type of assessment that involves students in "doing" tasks that are authentic and have real-world applicability; students are typically solving a problem or creating a project that has meaning. A portfolio is an example of a performance assessment.

**Perseverance**   steady or continued actions or belief, usually over a long period and especially despite difficulties or setbacks. Staying with a task or assignment.

**Simulation**   a type of learning strategy that involves students in a real-life situation, in which they typically solve a problem. In a civics course, for example, students might have a simulation that involves a court case.

**Tact**   an intuitive sense of what is right and appropriate, and the skill to consider other's feelings in varied situations.

**Taxonomy**   the science of classifying or organizing people, animals, plants, and ideas.

## As you read, think about . . .

★ Your favorite teachers. Why were they your favorite?

★ What made them effective?

★ How did this teacher help you feel successful?

★ How did your teachers support your learning?

## Focus Questions

★ What are the national expectations for new teachers?

★ What professional characteristics are most directly linked to student achievement?

★ How does a positive learning community influence students' learning?

# Characteristics of Effective Teachers

Effective teachers, from preschool through the university level, are somehow able to connect with all the students in the class. They are also able to motivate their students and create an interest in learning, whether the ABCs or calculus (Cruickshank, Jenkins, & Metcalf, 2003). Research in teacher effectiveness has consistently demonstrated that when students are interested in a subject they usually perform better. In addition, effective teachers enjoy and are enthusiastic about the teaching and learning process, as enthusiasm appears to promote student interest, motivation, and inspiration (Bettencourt, Gillett, Gail, & Hull, 1983; Borich, 2004). Effective teachers are deeply committed to helping students learn, and work tirelessly to develop effective lessons and learning experiences.

Take a few moments to assess your favorite teacher's professional *characteristics.* Use Figure 5.1, **The Professional Characteristics Checklist.** Place a check by the attributes you felt your favorite teacher(s) possessed. (Enz, Honaker, & Kortman, 2002)

---

**Figure 5.1   ⬇ The Professional Characteristics Checklist**

*Directions:* Picture one of your favorite teachers in you mind. Make a check next to the following attributes that accurately describe that teacher.

_____ **Commitment**—Teacher had a genuine concern for students and was dedicated to helping them become successful learners.

_____ **Creativity**—Teacher sought opportunities to provide unique learning experiences and developed imaginative lessons.

_____ **Enthusiasm**—Teacher showed delight in teaching students and content. High levels of energy and effort were observable.

_____ **Flexibility**—Teacher responded to unforeseen circumstances in an appropriate manner and modified actions or plans when necessary.

_____ **Integrity**—Teacher maintained high ethical and professional standards and responded to student needs appropriately.

_____ **Organization**—Teacher was efficient and successfully managed multiple tasks simultaneously and established/maintained effective classroom routines/procedures.

_____ **Perseverance**—Teacher gave best effort, strove to complete tasks and improve teaching skills and management strategies.

_____ **Positive Disposition**—Teacher possessed pleasant interpersonal skills and was patient, resilient, optimistic, and approachable.

_____ **Professional Appearance**—Teacher dressed in a manner that inspired confidence and public trust.

_____ **Reliability/Dependability**—Teacher took responsibility for students' academic, emotional, and physical well-being.

_____ **Self-Confidence**—Teacher gave students a sense of assurance and inspired confidence.

_____ **Self-Initiative/Independence**—Teacher was a creative problem-solver.

_____ **Tact/Judgment**—Teacher was diplomatic and courteous when handling difficult situations.

---

As you assessed your favorite teacher's personal and professional characteristics, did you think about your own? Do you possess these *attributes?* The following list includes many of the attributes mentioned, and a few more. The additional characteristics include oral and written expression and collegiality. These qualities are also essential to be an effective teacher. Take a few moments to reflect upon these professional characteristics by using Figure 5.2, **The Professional Characteristics Self-Assessment Checklist.**

**Think About It**

Look through your responses on the checklist.

- Where do you excel?
- Where are there potential areas of difficulty?
- If you have marked "sometimes" how could you strengthen this quality?

## Figure 5.2 ⬇ The Professional Characteristics Self-Assessment Checklist

This checklist is designed to help potential teachers appraise their personal and professional attitudes and actions. Scale Guide: **S**=Sometimes, **U**=Usually, **A**=Always. Provide a concrete example of how you demonstrate this attribute.

| S | U | A | Professional Characteristics |
|---|---|---|---|
| | | | **Oral Expression**—I am articulate and communicate concisely. I model fluent and grammatically correct language. *Example:* |
| | | | **Written Expression**—I communicate clearly and concisely and use grammatically correct language and appropriate mechanics. *Example:* |
| | | | **Tact/judgment**—I am diplomatic and courteous when handling difficult situations that may arise with family, friends, and colleagues. *Example:* |
| | | | **Self-Initiative/Independence**—I am an active and creative problem solver. I take responsibility to solve problems that arise. *Example:* |
| | | | **Self-Confidence**—I am a thoughtful, independent problem-solver and make decisions based on multiple sources of information. *Example:* |
| | | | **Collegiality**—I take advantage of working with, and learning from others. I enjoy sharing my ideas. *Example:* |
| | | | **Commitment**—I am able to commit to projects and sustain my interests over time. *Example:* |
| | | | **Creativity**—I actively seek opportunities to learn new information. I am imaginative and like to try new things. *Example:* |
| | | | **Flexibility**—I respond to unforeseen circumstances in an appropriate manner and modify my actions or plans when necessary. *Example:* |
| | | | **Integrity**—I maintain high ethical and personal standards. *Example:* |
| | | | **Organization**—I am efficient and successfully manage multiple tasks simultaneously. *Example:* |
| | | | **Perseverance**—I give my best efforts consistently and strive to complete tasks in my daily life. *Example:* |
| | | | **Positive Disposition**—I possess pleasant interpersonal skills and am patient, resilient, optimistic, and approachable. *Example:* |
| | | | **Reliability/Dependability**—I take responsibility for my actions, thoughts, and behaviors. *Example:* |

Adapted from Enz, B.J., S. Hurwitz, & Carlile, B.J. (2005). *Coaching the Student Teacher: A Developmental Approach.* Dubuque, IA: Kendall/Hunt Publishers.

## What Is a New Teacher Expected to Do?

In the mid-1990s a committee of teachers, teacher educators, and state agency officials created the Interstate New Teacher Assessment and Support Continuum (INTASC). The standards developed by INTASC outlined the knowledge, *dispositions,* and performances deemed essential for all new teachers regardless of subject or grade level (Darling-Hammond, 2000). These standards represent a shared view among states and within the profession of what constitutes competent beginning teaching. These standards are often used in teacher education programs to guide the planning of courses or how pre-service teachers are assessed (see Box 5.1. **More About INTASC Standards**). The INTASC Standards include:

1.  *Content Pedagogy*—The teacher understands the central concepts, tools of inquiry, and structures of the discipline he or she teaches and can create learning experiences that make these aspects of subject matter meaningful for students.

2.  *Student Development*—The teacher understands how children learn and develop and can provide learning opportunities that support a child's intellectual, social, and personal development.

3.  *Diverse Learners*—The teacher understands how students differ in their approaches to learning and creates instructional opportunities adapted to diverse learners.

4.  *Multiple Instructional Strategies*—The teacher understands and uses a variety of instructional strategies to encourage student development of critical thinking, problem solving, and performance skills.

5.  *Motivation and Management*—The teacher uses an understanding of individual and group motivation and behavior to create a learning environment that encourages positive social interaction, active engagement in learning, and self motivation.

6.  *Communication and Technology*—The teacher uses knowledge of effective verbal, nonverbal, and media communication techniques to foster active inquiry, collaboration, and supportive interaction in the classroom and with professional peers.

7.  *Planning*—The teacher plans instruction based upon knowledge of subject matter, students, the community, and curriculum goals.

8.  *Assessment*—The teacher understands and uses formal and informal assessment strategies to evaluate and ensure the continuous intellectual, social, and physical development of the learner.

9.  *Reflective Practice: Professional Growth*—The teacher is a reflective practitioner who continually evaluates the effects of his or her choices and actions on others (students, parents, and other professionals in the learning community) and who actively seeks out opportunities to grow professionally.

10. *School and Community Involvement*—The teacher fosters relationships with school *colleagues,* parents, and agencies in the larger community to support students' learning and well-being.

# Skills of Effective Teachers

In Section 1 we introduced you to the concept of effective teachers and effective schools. You quickly learned that effective schools take a great deal of thought, knowledge, skill, and effort on the part of many dedicated educators. But the most important components in an effective school are the teachers. In Section Three we will examine the deliberate actions teachers engage in that help them be more effective in helping students achieve and develop positive attitudes toward school and learning. Like the research about effective schools, research on effective teachers has been conducted by comparing high-achieving classrooms to low-achieving classrooms. Extensive classroom observations of virtually hundreds of teachers over the past two decades, have examined the differences between these two groups (Borich, 2004; Brophy & Good, 1986). Qualitative analysis found that highly effective teachers share many common features and tend to behave and teach in similar ways, regardless of school, subject, or the ability level of their students. Effective teachers

## Box 5.1   ↓ More about INTASC

The **Interstate New Teacher Assessment and Support Consortium** (INTASC) is a consortium of state education agencies and national educational organizations dedicated to the reform of the preparation, licensing, and ongoing professional development of teachers. Created in 1987, INTASC's primary constituency is state education agencies responsible for teacher licensing, program approval, and professional development. Its work is guided by one basic premise: An effective teacher must be able to integrate content knowledge with the specific strengths and needs of students to assure that *all* students learn and perform at high levels.

The mission of INTASC is to provide its member states a forum to learn about and collaborate in the development of

- compatible educational policy on teaching among the states
- new accountability requirements for teacher preparation programs
- new techniques to assess the performance of teachers for licensing and evaluation
- new programs to enhance the professional development of teachers

INTASC believes that all education policy should be driven by what we want our P–12 students to know and be able to do. Thus, all aspects of a state's education system should be aligned with and organized to achieve the state's policy as embodied in its P–12 student standards. This includes its teacher licensing system. Teacher licensing standards are the state's policy for what all teachers must know and be able to do in order to effectively help all students achieve the P–12 student standards. The teacher licensing standards become the driving force behind how a state's teacher licensing system (program approval, licensing assessments, professional development) is organized and implemented. Thus, a state's process for approving teacher preparation programs should be designed to verify that a program is aligned with the teacher licensing standards and provides opportunities for candidates to meet the standards. The state licensing assessments should verify that an individual teacher candidate has the knowledge and skills outlined in the licensing standards.

INTASC has been working to develop model policy that states can use as a resource as they work to align their own teacher licensing systems. To date, INTASC has accomplished the following:

- Developed model "core" standards for what all beginning teachers should know, be like, and be able to do in order to practice responsibly, regardless of the subject matter or grade level being taught.
- Translated the core standards into model licensing standards in mathematics, English language arts, science, special education, foreign languages, and arts; and are developing standards for elementary education and social studies/civics.
- Initiated development of a new licensing examination, the Test for Teaching Knowledge, which will measure a beginning teacher's knowledge and skill in the core standards.
- Developed and validated a model **performance assessment** in the form of a candidate portfolio in math, English/language arts, and science that is linked to INTASC's standards.
- Developed principles for quality teacher preparation programs to guide teacher preparation programs on how to incorporate INTASC's performance-based standards.

Adapted from tahttp://www.ccsso.org/projects/Interstate_New_Teacher_Assessment_and_Support_Consortium/

**Overall Tone**

· Classroom community
· Classroom management
· Task orientation
· Student success
· Student outcomes

**Thoughtful Clear Lessons**

· Students
· Content
· Materials
· Lesson presentation
· Student assessment

**Instructional Strategies**

· Drill—practice
· Lecture
· Discussion
· Case study
· Cooperative learning
· Problem-based learning

engage students in discussions more than lectures. But while lecturing, effective teachers combine a variety of visual aids in their teaching. Effective teachers require students to be active learners by engaging students in a wide range of activities (Marzano, Pickering, Polack, 2001; Daniels & Bizar, 1998). They have students work in small groups and have students answer each other's questions. Though there have been whole texts devoted to this topic, we will briefly synthesize this information into three intertwined layers:

*1.* The overall tone of the classroom

*2.* The thoughtfulness and clarity of the lessons

*3.* Variety of instructional strategies

This chapter will now explore the craft of teaching by magnifying critical competencies in the standards that have the most direct daily impact on students: instructional planning, instructional strategies, management, and assessment.

# Overall Tone—Building Classroom Community

As you reviewed your favorite and worst teacher in Chapter 4, you may have remembered a sense of classroom environment these teachers created. In most cases, we remember our favorite teacher as having a predictable and orderly classroom, where the teacher treated students with respect and kindness. These teachers had the ability to create a class community— a learning environment where all students supported one another. Interestingly, research suggests most students (regardless of age) do better academically in classrooms where they feel safe and respected (Nodding, 1984). Conversely, less effective teachers usually appear to have classes that are unpredictable and chaotic, or extremely rigid and strict (Irvine, 2001). Less effective teachers often appear disorganized and are frequently inconsistent in teaching methods and classroom management (e.g., one day the teacher is overly strict, the next day he/she is lax with discipline).

**Figure 5.3  ↓ Building Classroom Community**

| Feature | Descriptions |
|---|---|
| Climate | • Establishes a class in which students can respectfully express feelings/opinions<br>• Uses students' interests to build and extend curriculum<br>• Is interested in the students as individuals<br>• Encourages a "safe" place for students to learn |
| Classroom Management | • Uses classroom rules established with students<br>• Uses instructional routines<br>• Recognizes students' positive efforts |
| Student Success | • Believes all students are capable of learning<br>• Understands students learn differently<br>• Uses a variety of different approaches to accommodate students<br>• Understands the role of family/community in the schooling process<br>• Invites students to offer feedback and support to each other's work and efforts |

A strong classroom community is extremely conducive to learning. Classrooms that have a positive classroom community contain an aura of tolerance where no one student or group of students is ridiculed or excluded based on any educational, social, or emotional concerns. In classrooms where teachers have established a positive classroom community, students learn how to participate in class meetings, work flexibly *and* collaboratively in small groups, and resolve conflicts peacefully. A successful classroom community promotes social competence and academic success and a sense of safety and belonging. Effective teachers take deliberate actions that establish and continually build a positive classroom community (Cabello & Terrell, 1994). Figure 5.3 **Building Classroom Community** offers a few of the beliefs effective teachers hold and the deliberate actions these teachers take in order to develop a positive classroom climate.

**Theory Into Practice**  Creating a sense of community in the classroom enables teachers to address students' social, emotional, and cognitive development. Abraham Maslow's "*Hierarchy* of Needs" (1957) (Figure 5.4) illustrates that having one's basic needs met is the foundation for building "higher levels" of knowing and understanding (see Box 5.2 for more information about Maslow). Only after the first three basic needs are met can human beings begin to focus energy and effort and learn efficiently.

When basic needs have not been met, children may have great difficulty learning and relating positively to others. Creating a caring community in the classroom is one of the most effective strategies for addressing children's basic needs for physical and emotional comfort so that they can be open to learning, feel hopeful about the future, and reach their full potential.

**Figure 5.4** ↓ **Maslow's Hierarchy**

Being Needs

Self-actualization
(Achieving individual potential)

Esteem Needs
(Self-esteem and esteem of others)

Belonging Needs
(Love, affection, being a part of groups)

Safety Needs
(Shelter, removal from danger)

Physiological Needs
(Health, food, sleep)

Deficit Needs

| Need and Definition | Classroom Impact |
| --- | --- |
| **Physiological needs**—These are biological needs. They consist of needs for oxygen, food, water, and a relatively constant body temperature. They are the strongest needs because, if a person were deprived of all needs, the physiological ones would come first in the person's search for satisfaction. | Students who are hungry or thirsty think about their physical needs for food or water instead of learning. Students' physical needs must be met before they are able to learn; that is why many schools provide breakfast, snacks, and lunch for students who otherwise might not receive a meal. |
| **Safety needs**—When all physiological needs are satisfied and are no longer controlling thoughts and behaviors, the needs for security can become active. Safety needs deal with the feeling of security, comfort, and being out of danger. | For many students today, danger has replaced the sense of safety they need in order to learn. Some students live in communities where violent acts happen daily and they have had experiences that threaten their feelings of safety. Students who feel unsafe cannot devote energy to learning. Instead, they focus their energy on protecting themselves from potential harm. When teachers create a safe classroom community, students are better able to relate positively to others and engage in learning. |
| **Belonging needs**—When the needs for safety and for physiological well-being are satisfied, the next class of needs for love, affection, and belongingness can emerge. This involves both giving and receiving love, affection, and the sense of belonging. | Students who do not experience a sense of belonging often exhibit aggressive behavior, because they are angry or hurt. These children need adults who can create a classroom environment where everyone feels accepted and valued. |
| **Esteem needs**—When the first three classes of needs are satisfied, the needs for esteem can become dominant. These involve needs for both self-esteem and for the esteem a person gets from others. Humans have a need for a stable, firmly based, high level of self-respect, and respect from others. When these needs are satisfied, the person feels self-confident and valuable as a person in the world. When these needs are frustrated, the person feels inferior, weak, helpless, and worthless. | Students acquire self-esteem when they do things every day that make them feel competent. Esteem basically is about self-esteem, which is feeling good about ourselves. We can get such esteem in two ways. Internally, we can judge ourselves and find ourselves worthy by our own defined standards. Most people, however, start with the outside, seeking social approval and esteem from other people, judging themselves by what others think of them. Teachers who create a positive classroom community increase the likelihood that all children will build internal and external self-esteem. |
| **Self-actualization needs**—When all of the foregoing needs are satisfied, then and only then are the needs for self-actualization activated. Maslow describes self-actualization as a person's need to be and do that which the person was "born to do." "A musician must make music, an artist must paint, and a poet must write." | Positive classroom communities help children to feel physically and psychologically safe. In these environments they feel as though they belong. These feelings then allow children to learn and feel capable and confident, which then encourages high levels of competence. |

---

**Box 5.2  ⬇ More about Abraham Maslow**

**Abraham Maslow** (1908–1970) was an American psychologist. He received his BA in 1930, his MA in 1931, and his PhD in 1934, all in psychology and all from the University of Wisconsin.

He is mostly noted today for his proposal of a hierarchy of human needs, which he often represented as a pyramid. The base of the pyramid consists of the *physiological* needs, which are necessary for survival (1954). Once these basic needs are taken care of (resolved), an individual can concentrate on the second layer, the need for *safety and security*. The third layer is the need for *love and belonging*, followed by the need for *esteem*. Finally, *self-actualization* forms the apex of the pyramid.

In this scheme, the first four layers are what Maslow called *deficiency needs* or D-needs. If they are not filled, you feel anxiety and attempt to fill them. If they are filled, you feel nothing; you feel only that something is lacking. Each layer also takes precedence over the layer above it; you do not feel the lack of safety and security until your physiological needs are taken care of, for example. In Maslow's terminology, a need does not become salient until the needs below it are met.

Needs beyond the D-needs are "growth needs" or *"being values,"* which Maslow called B-needs. When fulfilled, B-needs do not go away. Rather, B-needs motivate us further. He outlines about fourteen of these values or B-needs, including beauty, meaning, truth, wholeness, justice, order, simplicity, richness, and so on.

Maslow also proposed that people who have reached self-actualization will sometimes experience a state he referred to as "transcendence," in which they become aware of not only their own fullest potential, but the fullest potential of human beings at large (Maslow, 1971).

## Thoughtful, Clear Lessons—Planning for Student Success

Effective teachers are also incredibly good planners. They think ahead and deliberately plan for student success. Writing lesson plans is like planning a journey. If you expect to get where you want to go, you need to map your route carefully to make the most efficient use of time and resources (Hunter, 1994; Enz, Hurwtiz, & Carlile, 2005). Likewise, teachers need to plan carefully to help students learn what is being taught, and how to make full use of opportunities to connect curriculum content and involve students in the learning process. Basically, a lesson plan is a simple document that answers three questions:

1. What do you want students to be able to know or do?
2. How will you teach the lesson?
3. How will you assess what students have learned?

During the process of answering these three basic questions, effective teachers also make highly creative decisions. In fact, effective teachers consider all of the following variables as they plan instruction (Borich, 2004; National Board Certified Teachers, 1987):

1. *Knowledge of Students*—Effective teachers know their students and what their students need to be successful. Effective teachers consider and design instruction that will meet the needs/interests of their students. Specifically, effective teachers know their students':

   • ability levels
   • backgrounds

- interest levels
- ability to work together in groups
- prior knowledge and learning experiences
- special needs or accommodations
- learning preferences

2. *Knowledge of Content*—Effective teachers know the content they teach. They use local school district curriculum guides but also utilize national and state curriculum standards in designing instruction. Likewise, they determine ways to connect student interests to the new content to be taught.

3. *Knowledge of Materials*—Effective teachers use a wide variety of materials to teach their students the content to be learned. They know that nearly all students do better if they can be exposed to content in a variety of ways. For example: technology, software, audiovisuals, community resources, equipment, manipulatives, library resources, local guest speakers, and volunteers, can assist in teaching and will help students learn new content.

4. *Knowledge of Lesson Presentation*—Effective teachers use variety in lesson planning and structure based on attributes of the content to be taught and the needs of their learners. There are different types of lesson structures. Some examples of lesson formats are provided at the end of this chapter.

5. *Knowledge of Instructional Strategies*—Effective teachers have a wide range of teaching strategies, and know that determining which method is "right" for a particular lesson depends on many things. Among them are age and developmental level of their students; what the students already know; what they need to know to succeed with the lesson; the subject-matter content; the objective of the lesson; the available people, time, space and material resources; and the physical setting.

6. *Knowledge of Student Assessment*—Effective teachers use student assessment to guide their understanding of student learning and their own classroom teaching. Effective teachers know that how a student performs is a good reflection of the instruction they received, therefore effective teachers develop many strategies to informally assess students' progress throughout the lesson.

Now let's return to our three questions that describe the components of an effective lesson plan.

**Planning Question 1: What do you want the students to know and be able to do?**   To answer this question, an effective teacher must first determine the learner outcome(s) (sometimes called lesson objective)—this is the term educators use to describe what the students need to know and be able to do by the end of the lesson.

Learner outcomes usually contain an **observable** verb such as *recall, solve, measure,* or *construct,* which allows the teacher to be able to determine the students' comprehension and level of involvement at given points in the lesson (Hunter, 1994). For example:

**The student will be able to:**

- *Define* the term photosynthesis
- *Label* the parts of an insect
- *Calculate* the diameter of a circle

Learner outcomes are clearly stated and help make student progress easier to determine. In addition learner outcomes should be clear that students can "know" about a topic or subject at different levels. The major idea of the *taxonomy* is that educational objectives can be arranged in a hierarchy from less to more complex. (See Box 5.3 and Figure 5.5., **More About Benjamin Bloom,** and **Bloom Cognitive Taxonomy.**) Bloom's Taxonomy (1957) provides a range of educational objectives, verbs that reflect students' knowledge level, questions that would typically illicit the level of response, and possible outcomes that would reflect that particular level of learning.

## Box 5.3   ↓ Learn More about Benjamin Bloom

**Benjamin Bloom** (1913–1999) was an American educational psychologist at the University of Chicago in the 1960s. Dr. Bloom's two most significant contributions to the field included his classification of educational objectives (mid-1950s) and the theory of mastery learning.

Bloom's Taxonomy (classification system) was a way to categorize performance objectives that commonly occur in educational settings. Dr. Bloom and his colleagues identified three broad categorizes of performance: affective, psychomotor, and cognitive learning.

**Affective learning** is demonstrated by behaviors indicating attitudes of awareness, interest, attention, concern, and responsibility; ability to listen and respond in interactions with others; and the ability to demonstrate those attitudinal characteristics or values that are appropriate to the test situation and the field of study. This domain relates to emotions, attitudes, appreciations, and values such as enjoying, conserving, respecting, and supporting. Verbs applicable to the affective domain include accepts, attempts, challenges, defends, disputes, joins, judges, praises, questions, shares, supports, and volunteers.

**Psychomotor learning** is demonstrated by physical skills such as coordination, dexterity, manipulation, grace, strength, speed; actions that demonstrate the fine motor skills such as use of precision instruments or tools; or actions that evidence gross motor skills such as the use of the body in dance or athletic performance. Verbs applicable to the psychomotor domain include bend, grasp, handle, operate, reach, relax, shorten, stretch, write, differentiate (by touch), express (facially), perform (skillfully).

**Cognitive learning** is the ability "to learn new information." Cognitive objectives revolve around knowledge, comprehension, and application of any given topic. (See Figure 5.5. Bloom's Cognitive Taxonomy).

Another important contribution made by Bloom was his theory on **mastery learning.** Mastery learning is an instructional method that presumes all children can learn if they are provided with the appropriate learning conditions. Specifically, mastery learning is a method whereby students are not advanced to a subsequent learning objective until they demonstrate proficiency with the current one.

Mastery learning curricula generally consist of content that all students begin together. Students who do not satisfactorily complete a topic are given additional instruction until they succeed. Students who master the topic early engage in enrichment activities until the entire class can progress together. In a mastery learning environment, the teacher directs a variety of group-based instructional techniques, with frequent and specific feedback by using *diagnostic assessment,* as well as regularly correcting mistakes students make along their learning path. Mastery learning requires well-defined learning objectives organized into smaller, sequentially organized units. Mastery learning includes:

- Activities emphasizing problem solving and other "higher-order" thinking skills.
- Students actively engaging in the learning process with frequent interaction and feedback with the instructor and other students.

Successful interactions with the curriculum and positive relationships with the instructor should result in increased student self-concept and lead to happier, more productive individuals (Bloom, 1956; 1980)

**Figure 5.5   ↓ Bloom Cognitive Taxonomy**

**Research into Practice: Bloom Cognitive Taxonomy**

| LEVEL | DEFINITION | VERBS |
|---|---|---|
| *Knowledge* | Student recalls or recognizes information, ideas, and principles in the approximate form in which they were learned. | Write<br>List<br>Label<br>Name<br>State<br>Define |
| *Comprehension* | Student translates, comprehends, or interprets information based on prior learning. | Explain<br>Summarize<br>Paraphrase<br>Describe<br>Illustrate |
| *Application* | Student selects, transfers, and uses data and principles to complete a problem or task with minimal direction. | Use<br>Compute<br>Solve Demonstrate<br>Apply<br>Construct |
| *Analysis* | Student distinguishes, classifies, and relates the assumptions, hypotheses, evidence, or structure of a statement or question. | Analyze<br>Categorize<br>Compare<br>Contrast<br>Separate |
| *Synthesis* | Student originates, integrates, and combines ideas into a product, plan, or proposal new to him or her. | Create<br>Design<br>Hypothesize<br>Invent<br>Develop |
| *Evaluation* | Student appraises, assesses, or critiques on a basis of specific standards and criteria. | Judge<br>Recommend<br>Critique<br>Justify |

Eby, J. (1984). *Taxonomy of Educational Objectives: Handbook I: Cognitive Domain*, New York: NY: Longman Publishing Group.

In addition, when teachers develop instructional outcomes, it is important for these learning goals to be:

- **Logically Sequenced**—When students are asked to complete tasks in an order that is logical and builds naturally from one step to another, the teacher will spend more time teaching and less time keeping students on task.

- **Appropriate to Student Achievement Level(s)**—Students are more likely to stay with a task, and subsequently learn more of the material taught, *if* the material presented is already part of the students' prior experience. In addition, students must be presented materials with which they will experience a high rate of success. Students in fourth grade and higher should experience a success/accuracy rate of at least eighty percent. Students in kindergarten through third grade should experience a success rate of at least ninety percent.

- **Directly Linked to Unit Goals and to State/District/School Standards**—Students will learn best when the information builds upon and reinforces knowledge presented in previous days/weeks. This does not mean learning always develops in a "lock-step," linear progression. Integrated instruction brings ideas together and forms connections in the learner's mind. Teacher's who integrate curricula and relate the information to be learned to their students' lives, increase the likelihood that the new information will be meaningful and relevant.

Many studies show that learning is enhanced when students become actively involved in the process.

**Group Talk**

Take a few minutes to determine if the following statements are well-written, observable objectives:

**Students will be able to:**

| Yes | No | Objective |
|-----|-----|-----------|
|  |  | Appreciate the story |
|  |  | Analyze a story |
|  |  | Summarize the story |
|  |  | Invent a story |
|  |  | Critique a story |
|  |  | Illustrate a story |

Share your responses with your group.

1. Can you come to consensus on all of the sample objectives, above?

2. Which objectives were harder to determine? Why?

**Planning Question 2: How will you teach the lesson?**   Knowing what needs to be taught/learned is only the first step in lesson planning. Just as critical is determining *how* to effectively deliver instruction (Cruickshank, Jenkins, & Metcalf, 2003). The opportunity for creativity starts when a teacher considers the procedures for the lesson.

One goal all teachers should strive for is **active learning.** Active learning is instruction that allows students to talk, listen, read, write, and reflect as they approach course content through problem-solving exercises, informal small groups, *simulations,* case studies, role-playing, and other activities—all of which require students to apply what they are learning. Many studies show that learning is enhanced when students become actively involved in the process. Instructional strategies that engage students in the learning process stimulate critical thinking and a greater awareness of other perspectives (Brophy & Good, 1986). Although there are times when lecture is the most appropriate method for disseminating information, research in learning and retention suggests that the use of a variety of instructional strategies can positively enhance student learning (Cotton, 1995; Marzano, Pickering, & Pollock, 2001). Obviously, teaching strategies should be carefully matched to the teaching objectives of a particular lesson. In Chapter 4, we provided a description of a variety of effective **instructional strategies,** including:

- Drill
- Lecture
- Discussion
- Case Study
- Cooperative Learning
- Problem-Based Learning (PBL)

**Planning Question 3: How will you assess what the students have learned?**   While there are many types of "tests" available to teachers, we will discuss *ongoing assessment,* which relies heavily on teacher observation of students' performance or the collection of student products, often called artifacts. When students are assessed as part of the teaching-learning process, then assessment information tells teachers what each student knows and can do, and what he or she is ready to learn next (Daniels & Bizar, 1998). Teachers also use their assessment of students' learning to reflect on their own teaching practices so they can adjust and modify curricula, instructional activities, and classroom routines that are ineffective (Danielson, 1996). Other questions teachers need to consider when determining how and when they will assess students' progress, include:

- **When should the teacher assess student progress?** Students' understanding should be assessed at significant points throughout the entire lesson. This includes constant monitoring of students' performance or occasionally pausing the lesson to ask all students to demonstrate their understanding of the information being taught.
- **How can the teacher determine if all students can perform correctly?** Beyond observation, the teacher may ask students to write the answer, tell a neighbor, respond in unison, indicate the answer on individual slates, signal the answer, demonstrate the skill, and so on.
- **Why should teachers assess students frequently?** Before the teacher proceeds from one goal to the next, all students need to demonstrate an understanding of the content presented. If all students do not understand the lesson, the teacher will need to adjust

teaching strategies, try again, and then re-assess the students' progress to determine understanding before moving on to the next objective.

- **How do teachers collect information about students' progress?** In addition to instructional strategies, effective teachers use a variety of tools to gather information about their students. Teachers then use the information when planning future lessons, and/or for making accommodations for students who are struggling. These tools can include: observations, interviews, student self-assessment, student artifacts, and portfolios.

**Think About It**

Which information-gathering tools have you seen teachers use? Which tools do *your* college instructors use?

While teachers do not use all of these tools in every lesson, each tool does provide unique and important information about what the students are learning and how effective the instruction has been (Newman, 1996; Schmoker, 1999). Therefore, it is important to incorporate each of these tools systematically as a lesson unit is planned. Figure 5.6. **Information-Gathering Tools Checklist,** provides an overview of each of these information-gathering tools.

**Lesson Plans in Review**  We now know that effective teachers use effective plans, which include *clear objectives,* a variety of *instructional strategies,* and *appropriate assessments.* What do these components look like in action?

Let's observe Mr. Flynn as he develops his lesson plan. Mr. Flynn has planned a lesson for his sophomore English class. The students are learning about factual writing, and part of their culminating project will be to publish a class newspaper. Today they will learn about the parts of a lead paragraph, in preparation for writing a lead paragraph for a topic they have selected. The lesson outcomes/objectives are:

- Explain that the lead paragraph of a news story usually answers who, what, when, where, why, and how.
- Determine, from selected newspaper articles, the information that answers who, what, when, where, why, and how.

Mr. Flynn is establishing foundational background, so the level of objective he is writing reflects the knowledge and comprehension levels of Bloom's Cognitive Taxonomy. The objectives he has written also define the outcome he expects his students to demonstrate at the end of the lesson.

Mr. Flynn has decided the best way to share this foundational information with his students is through a brief lecture and modeling the expected outcome. The students work together to discuss their answers and reinforce the information their teacher has presented.

**Think About It**

Take a few moments and use Figure 5.7. **Lesson Planning Checklist,** and review Mr. Flynn's lesson plan. What are the strengths of his lesson plan? How might it be improved?

Mr. Flynn also knows that when he asks the students to work together to determine the components of a lead paragraph, it will enable him to circulate about the room to gather information to confirm the students' comprehension of the lesson. These observations enable him to check student understanding and provides a feedback loop to himself— a way to reflect upon his own teaching.

There are many types of lesson plan formats that teachers use. How a teacher selects a format often depends on his/her philosophy of education, theories of learning, or personal past experiences. We will share two formats with you:

- Direct Instruction
- Five E's (Inquiry)

As you are reading, think about your own philosophies and theories, and which plans—or combinations—might best suit your own style of teaching.

## Figure 5.6   ↓ Information-Gathering Tools Checklist

*Directions:* Interview a teacher about the information-gathering tools he or she typically uses to collect information about children's development and their progress. Place a check by the tools/techniques used; write any comments, suggestions, or additions he/she describes; then summarize what you learned about assessment from this interview.

**I. Teacher Observations**—The most sensitive student assessment is teacher observation. In all cases, the teacher labels, dates, and organizes the observation records to document development over time.

- ❑ Checklists—sometimes called structured observation. The teacher uses predetermined observation guides to document students' development and progress on specific skills or concepts.
- ❑ Anecdotal records—sometimes called unstructured observation. The teacher records student interactions with peers, print, literature, writing process, in-class discussion, center activities, etc.
- ❑ Vignettes—sometimes called teacher reflections. The teacher recalls student interactions and records them after the event has occurred.

**II. Interviews/Questions Techniques**—Interviews may be conducted with the student, parents, and special area teachers. Interviews may occur informally during the school day or may be formalized when the teacher needs to narrow the focus of the questions to reflect a previously identified concern. Teachers may consider four types of interview questions:

- ❑ Descriptive—What did you do during _____?
- ❑ Structured—Can you tell me when _____?
- ❑ Contrast—How are these stories alike/different?
- ❑ Process—How did you decide to _____?

**III. Student Self-Assessment Techniques**—Students should be actively involved in assessing their own work, reflecting upon their progress, and establishing new learning goals.

- ❑ Teacher-made questionnaires/surveys.
- ❑ Teacher-student conferences.

**IV. Products, work samples, and artifacts**—Teacher collects multiple examples of student-created products to assess each child's development. For example, in the area of literacy, these items could include:

Reading
- ❑ List of books "read"
- ❑ List of questions about books
- ❑ List of favorite stories

Writing
- ❑ Journal entries
- ❑ Learning Logs
- ❑ Formal Written Assignments

**V. Portfolio Management System**—Teacher devises a management system to collect and analyze samples of students' work, teacher's anecdotal notes, and formal and informal assessment measures. A portfolio allows the teacher to document a student's progress over time and share that information with the student, the student's parents, and other teachers and administrators.

> **Figure 5.7   ↓ Lesson Planning Checklist**
>
> **1. What do you want the students to be able to know or do?**
> - Desired learner outcome(s) are described in clear observable terms.
> - The outcomes are logically sequenced.
> - The outcomes are measurable.
>
> **2. How will you teach the lesson?**
> - The activities selected will accomplish the objective(s)/outcomes.
> - Procedures engage students in active learning.
> - Transitions are planned from one activity to another.
>
> **3. How will you assess what the students have learned?**
> - Assessment focused directly on instructional outcomes.
> - Assessment technique provided options for immediate feedback (teacher/student).
> - Written lesson plans include informal assessments of student learning.

# Direct Instruction Lesson Plan

The *direct instruction* (or *direct presentation*) lesson plan is usually a reflection of the behaviorist and cognitive processing perspectives of learning (Hunter, 1995; Enz, Hurwitz, & Carlile, 2005). This type of lesson is best used when introducing new information and when covering a great deal of information. Figure 5.8. **Direct Lesson Outline** provides a structure for this direct lesson plan format, and Figure 5.9. **Direct Lesson in Action** provides you with a sample format for using this approach.

# Five E's Lesson Format

The Five E's (Engagement, Exploration, Explanation, Extension, and Evaluation) (Figure 5.10) is designed for the inquiry nature of guiding and science lessons (Gagne, Briggs & Wager, 1992). It more closely aligns with a combination of the cognitive information processing and constructivist perspectives of learning. Figure 5.11 provides a sample lesson using this inquiry approach to teaching and learning.

# Looking Forward

In this chapter, we have explored a variety of concepts related to effective teachers—including their characteristics and how they plan their lessons. We also explored how effective lessons incorporate three interrelated elements: objectives, instructional strategies, and assessments. These elements may be implemented differently, depending upon which lesson plan format that the teacher implements.

Is any one lesson plan design better than the other? No, each design has its pros and cons depending on the audience. The important thing is to know what you want your students to learn and then map it out so you know the direction that is best for your students. It might be the long and winding road that takes you where they need to go, but the destination is the same.

**Figure 5.8   ↓ Direct Lesson Outline**

**Objectives:**
- What do you want the students to learn?
- What do you want the students to demonstrate?

State Standard:                                    District Curriculum Goal:

**Introduction:**
- How will you gain the students' attention?
- How will you connect students' prior knowledge to new learning?
- How will you motivate students?

**Instructional Content:**
- What strategies will you use to teach the content?
- How will you sequence the delivery and learning of the content?
- How will students be actively engaged?

**Assessment:**
- How will you determine the students' level of understanding?
- How will you document the students' learning?
- How will you differentiate to accommodate all learners?

**Closure:**
- How will you help students retain information learned?
- How will you help students apply knowledge learned?

**Resources/Materials:**
- What resources/materials/equipment will you use to teach the content?
- What preparations are necessary?

## Figure 5.9 ↓ Direct Instruction in Action

**Learner Outcomes: Lesson objective and sub-objectives**

**Unit of Study:** Newspaper    **Daily Lesson Plan:** Lead Paragraph

**Lesson Outcomes: Students will be able to:**

- Explain that the lead paragraph of a news story usually answers who, what, when, where, why, and how.
- Determine from selected newspaper articles the information that answers who, what, when, where, why, and how.

### Introduction—Focus, anticipatory set, motivation

In yesterday's class we learned that the headlines of newspapers are designed to help you read the paper. You all were very good at reading headlines and predicting what the article would be about. Now we're going to learn another way to get the news quickly and easily. The first paragraph of an article is called the lead paragraph; it is designed to help you read the paper and quickly learn all about the outcome of the state basketball tournaments or the latest on state or national events.

### Instructional Input (Content)—Teaching procedures and student activities

- Write who, what, when, where, why, and how in a vertical column on the board **(modeling).** Ask students to write these words in their notes **(active participation).** Tell them they will need to use these words in the activity they are about to begin. Tell students that with the help of their partner they will be asked to find information in a newspaper article and write it in a column to the right of their "who, what, when, where, why, how" column. Demonstrate on the board where information is to be written.
- Walk around room. Ensure students list the information in their notes **(check for understanding).** Students are more likely to stay on task if teacher is in close proximity.
- Ask students to listen carefully as the teacher reads a lead paragraph from a selected article. Ask the class to listen for who the article is about, what happened, when it happened, where it happened, why it happened, and how it happened. As students hear the answer to each question, they should write the answer in the designated column of their notes **(guided practice).**
- When the class is finished writing their answers, ask them to share the answers to the following questions: who, what, when, where, why, and how. If all/most students appear to say the correct answers, move on to the next activity.

### Assessment: Checking for understanding and lesson assessment

- Have students work in pairs. Hand out selected news stories, one per student.
- Explain that students are to take turns reading the first paragraph out loud to their partners. Then, with the partner's help, each student is to identify the who, what, when, where, why, and how information from the article.
- Ask students, "In which paragraph did you find this information"?
- Tell students to write the information in the appropriate column in their notes.
- Partners are to check for accuracy of the information recorded.

### Closure: Lesson summation of learner's new knowledge

- Observe students' responses. Ensure the tasks are being completed correctly **(Check for understanding).** When each pair has finished, challenge students to pull information together by asking them to remember, without looking at their notes, all six questions usually answered in the lead paragraph of an article.
- Ask students to remember in which paragraph they found the information.
- After a brief wait ask students to share with their partner those six questions and the name of the paragraph where the answers were found.

### Resources: Equipment, materials, teaching aids

Sample article with appropriate lead paragraph—for guided practice.
Sample articles with appropriate lead paragraphs—one per student.

## Figure 5.10 ↓ Five E's Science Lesson Plan

**Engagement:** The activities in this section capture the students' attention, stimulate their thinking, and help them access prior knowledge.

- Demonstration
  - teacher and/or student
- Reading from a
  - current media release
  - science journal or book
  - piece of literature (biography, essay, poem, etc)
- Free write
- Analyze a graphic organizer

**Exploration:** In this section students are given time to think, plan, investigate, and organize collected information.

- Reading authentic resources to collect information
  - to answer open-ended questions
  - to make a decision
- Solve a problem
- Construct a model
- Experiment design and/or perform

**Explanation:** Students are now involved in an analysis of their exploration. Their understanding is clarified and modified because of reflective activities.

- Student analysis and explanation
- Supporting ideas with evidence
- Reading and discussion

**Extension:** This section gives students the opportunity to expand and solidify their understanding of the concept and/or apply it to a real-world situation.

- Problem solving
- Experimental inquiry
- Thinking Skills Activities
- Classifying, abstracting, error analysis
- Decision-making

**Evaluation:** By the end of the lesson there should be a means of determining how well students have learned and can apply the new concepts and the related vocabulary. Such evaluation does not have to be at the end of the lesson. It can be embedded in other phases.

- Teacher- and/or student-generated scoring tools or rubrics

**Figure 5.11   ↓ Five E Lesson Plan**

**Lesson Title:** Camouflage: Eating All the Little Fishes

**Lesson Outcome:** The first graders will learn how camouflage helps animals survive.

**Engagement:** Teacher reads the story "How to Hide a Butterfly and Other Insects" by Ruth Heller. This simple text has color pictures that demonstrate how insects use camouflage to hide from their enemies and prey. The first graders have fun looking for the hidden insects.

**Exploration:** The teacher breaks the children into six groups of four students each.
- Each group has a different colored, patterned cloth that is placed on the table, and each table had a tiny cup containing many different colored paper "fishes."
- The "fishes" are sprinkled on the cloth.
- The teacher turns out the lights.
- The children are asked to find as many of the fishes as they can and remove them from the cloth.
- The children have 20 seconds to find all the fish they can.
- The teacher turns the light back on and the children freeze.
- The fish left are sorted and counted by color.

**Explanation:** The teacher asks the children if they notice anything about the fish that are left on the cloth. The children in each group should realize that the fish left are the same color as the cloth.

**Extension:** The teacher asks the children to think about, then write, their explanation of how the fishes in their experiment are like the butterflies and insects in the story, "How to Hide a Butterfly and Other Insects." The teacher gives each group chart paper and markers to record their thoughts.

**Evaluation:** The teacher gives each child drawing paper and crayons. The teacher asks the children to draw a habitat (a concept previously learned), and to draw pictures of camouflaged animals that might live in this habitat. As the children complete this task, the teacher circulates and asks children about their unique creations.

## Research Citations

Bettencourt, E., Gillett, M., Gall, M., & Hull, R. (1983). Effects of teacher enthusiasm training on student on-task behavior and achievement. *American Educational Research Journal, 20,* 435–450.

Bloom, B. S. (1956). Taxonomy of educational objectives: Classification of educational goals. *Handbook 1: Cognitive domain* (pp. 201–207). New York, NY: Longman.

Bloom, B. S. (1980). *All our children learning.* New York, NY: McGraw-Hill.

Borich, G. (2004). *Effective teaching methods.* Upper Saddle River, NJ: Merrill/Princeton Hall.

Brophy J. & Good, T. (1986). Teacher behavior and student achievement. In M. C. Wittrock (Ed.), *Handbook of research on teaching* (3rd ed., pp. 328–375). Upper Saddle River, NJ: Merrill/Prentice Hall.

Cabello, B., & Terrell, R. (1994). Making students feel like family: How teachers create warm and caring classroom climates. *Journal of Classroom Interaction, 29,* 17–24.

Cotton, K. (1995). *Research you can use to improve results.* Alexandria, VA: Association for Supervision and Curriculum Development.

Cruickshank, D. R., Jenkins, D. B., & Metcalf, K. K. (2003). *The act of teaching.* New York, NY: McGraw-Hill.

Daniels, H. & Bizar, M. (1998). *Methods that matter.* Portland, ME: Stenhouse.

Danielson, C. (1996). *Enhancing professional practice: A framework for teaching.* Alexandria, VA: Association for Supervision and Curriculum Development.

Darling-Hammond, L. (2000). Reforming teacher preparation and licensing: Debating the evidence. *Teachers College Record, 102,* (1): 28–56.

Enz, B. J., Honaker, C, & Kortman, S. (2002). Trade secrets: Tips, tools and timesavers for middle/secondary teacher 2nd Ed. Dubuque, IA: Kendall/Hunt.

Enz, B. J., Hurwitz, S. & Carlile, B. J. (2005). *Coaching the student teacher: A developmental approach,* 3rd Ed. Dubuque, IA: Kendall/Hunt.

Eby, J. (1984). *Taxonomy of educational objectives: Handbook I: Cognitive domain.* New York: Longman.

Gagne, R., Briggs, L. & Wager, W. (1992). *Principles of instructional design* 4th Ed. Fort Worth, TX: HBJ College.

Hunter, M. (1994). *Mastery teaching.* Thousand Oaks, CA: Corwin.

Irvine, J. J. (2001). *Caring, competent teachers in complex classrooms.* Washington, DC: American Association of Colleges of Teacher Education.

Marzano, R. J., Pickering, D. J., & Pollock, J. E. (2001). *Classroom Instruction that works: Research-based strategies for increasing student achievement.* Alexandria, VA: Association for Supervision and Curriculum Development.

Maslow, A. (1954). *Motivation and personality* (2nd ed). New York, NY: Harper.

Maslow, A. (1957). *The search for understanding.* New York, NY: West.

Maslow, A. (1971). *The farther reaches of human nature.* New York, NY: Viking.

National Board Certified Teachers (1987). Last accessed date, from *http://www.nbpts.org/about/coreprops.cfm*

Newmann, F. M. (1996). *Authentic achievement: restructuring schools for intellectual quality.* San Francisco, CA: Jossey-Bass.

Noddings, N. (1984). *Caring: A feminine approach to ethics and moral education.* Berkeley, CA: University of California.

Schmoker, M. (1999). *Results: The key to continuous school improvement.* (2nd ed.). Alexandria, VA: Association for Supervision and Curriculum Development.

# Examining Effective Teaching 6

Many things influence a teacher's actions in the classroom. As we have explored in previous chapters, these influences include educational theories and philosophies, a teacher's dispositions and abilities, lesson formats, and even educational leaders from centuries ago. We hope that it is becoming very apparent that effective teaching requires a careful balance and understanding of both science and artistry in order to meet the unique needs of every student in the classroom.

This chapter focuses on three important elements in an effective lesson plan:

- Proactive management
- Lesson beginnings
- Miniature closures

**Definitions**

**Anticipatory set**   the way the teacher starts the lesson, which helps to capture students' attention. The initial actions and statements made by the teacher help the students to become interested in the subject and also relate to the prior experiences students have with the objectives of the lesson.

**Classroom Routines/Procedures**   these are explicit tasks or activities that the teacher expects the students to perform to maintain classroom organization and efficiency. For example, teachers might establish routines for lining up, taking attendance, and handing out materials in class.

**Closure**   the end of a lesson. Closures often include reviewing and clarifying the key points of a lesson, tying them together into a coherent whole, and emphasizing how students will apply new knowledge to real-world concepts.

**Genre**   different categories of something, such as types of literature. Book genres include fiction, non-fiction, mysteries, fantasy, and science fiction.

**Modalities**   different ways, or modes, of learning. Learning modalities can include visual, auditory, or body/kinesthetic. Because each student learns through a different modality, teachers should incorporate activities that maximize multiple modalities so that all learning needs can be met.

**Participation**   the act of taking part in the learning activity. Active involvement in the lesson increases the likelihood that the student will comprehend and retain the new information being taught. Active participation can occur in one of two ways:
- *Covert participation*–nonobservable actions, such as thinking about something.
- *Overt participation*–observable actions, such as talking in groups, raising hands, or completing a study guide.

**Proactive Management**   taking the initiative to organize a classroom through the use of specific classroom procedures and routines.

**Transitions**   the time between one classroom activity and another. In teaching, it is important to minimize transitions so that students have more time focusing on instructional tasks.

## As you read, think about . . .
★ How did your high school teachers begin class?
★ What did your elementary teachers do to get your attention?
★ Did you enjoy learning new information? Why? Why not?

## Focus Questions
★ How do classroom procedures and routines help a teacher to teach?
★ How does the use of anticipatory sets help students to learn new information?
★ How can teachers consistently engage students in learning?
★ How do closures help teachers to monitor student learning?

# Beginning the Day with Proactive Management

What a teacher does to prepare his or her classroom prior to the beginning of school and the beginning of a lesson makes a big difference in how successful the lesson will be and, consequently, how much the child will learn. This is called *proactive management.*

To ensure an effective learning environment that enables all students to learn, students need to have a well-established set of *classroom procedures* or *routines.* Students must know what to expect from the teacher on a daily basis regarding classroom activities and *transitions* (Wong & Wong, 2004; Kronowitz, 1999; Enz, Kortman, & Honaker, 2002). A clear set of procedures benefits all students as they will know what to expect every day.

Let's observe two new teachers, Ms. Jordon and Ms. Terry, start the day with their third-grade students. Though it is only mid-September, these two teachers are definitely using instructional time in very different ways. See if you can determine what makes the teachers' interactions with students more or less effective.

### First Example: Ms. Jordan

**8:30** Ms. Jordon's children begin to line up outside the door in a quiet and organized line. Before the children enter the room, she uses a special signal to gain their attention. Once everyone is looking at her, she reminds the students to:

- Make their lunch decisions now, and
- Turn in their permission slips and check off their names.

As soon as the students enter the classroom they use the *"I'm Here Chart"* (Figure 6.1) to signal both their presence and their lunch choices, by placing a distinctively colored and labeled popsicle stick in their name pockets located on the attendance chart. The sticks represent different things:

- The white "milk" sticks signal that the child has brought lunch and intends to purchase milk only;
- The red "hot meal" sticks signal that the child will be purchasing the hot lunch; and
- The green "salad bar" sticks signal that the child will be purchasing the salad bar.

If a lunch stick is not placed in a name pocket, it signals that the child is absent. The last child in line is the week's classroom recorder. Using a form Ms. Jordon has developed, the recorder will count up the attendance, note who is absent, and tally how many hot meals, salad bars, and milks Ms. Jordon's room will be ordering from the cafeteria. Ms. Jordon is also checking for permission slips for an upcoming field trip. After the students have signaled their attendance, they place their permission slip (if they have brought one) into the wire basket and check off their name on the clipboard placed beside the basket. Next, the students move to their seat or to the Library Center to return books to the classroom library using the Library Loan System. Several students check in their books. (Each book has a card with the title on it. Children remove the card and place it in their name pocket when they check out the book. When they check in the book, they return the book's card to the book.) Then students return the books to the appropriate *genre* basket (the books have stickers on them and the students place them in the basket with the corresponding sticker).

As soon as the students are in their seats they start to work on the *Morning Mind Challenge* (MMC). Ms. Jordon had written the MMC, a sponge activity (see **Instructional Inspiration 6.1**), on the board the night before. Today it is a math question, some days it is a riddle, some times a "Do you remember. . . ." question.

**8:40** Nearly every day at this time, the students in Ms. Jordon's class are in their seats and already working. While all the checking-in was going on automatically, Ms. Jordon used the time to move among the students, welcome them, ask questions, follow up on home correspondence, and electronically send the attendance and lunch information to the school office.

**8:45** Ms. Jordon begins to ask the children about the Morning Mind Challenge, and by 8:45 she begins to teach her math lesson (scheduled until 9:30). ∎

**Figure 6.1** ↓ **I'm Here Attendance and Lunch Chart**

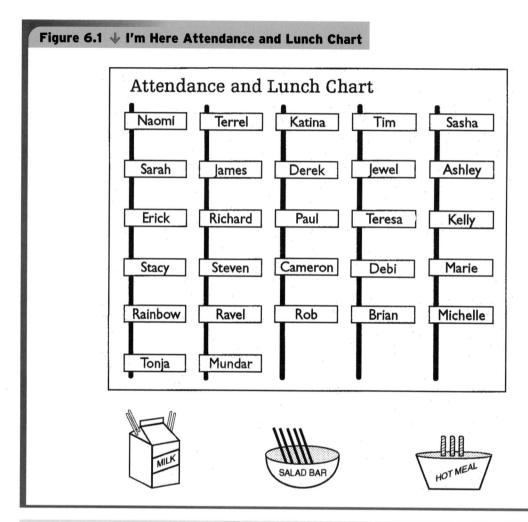

## Attendance and Lunch Chart

| Naomi | Terrel | Katina | Tim | Sasha |
| Sarah | James | Derek | Jewel | Ashley |
| Erick | Richard | Paul | Teresa | Kelly |
| Stacy | Steven | Cameron | Debi | Marie |
| Rainbow | Ravel | Rob | Brian | Michelle |
| Tonja | Mundar | | | |

MILK   SALAD BAR   HOT MEAL

## Contrasting Practice: Ms. Terry

**8:30** As soon as the bell rings the students charge into the room, as Ms. Terry is finishing writing the Morning Mind Challenge (MMC) on the board. She casually greets her students as they come into the room. As the students enter, they talk to each other and move leisurely. Ms. Terry asks the children to settle down.

**8:40** Ms. Terry asks the students to start working on the MMC. As the students begin to work, Ms. Terry stands before the class computer to begin taking roll on the electronic form. She calls on the children one-by-one (many of the children are still talking while she takes attendance). After she completes attendance, Ms. Terry asks the students to raise their hands if they want to buy hot lunch. She counts the hands and enters the number on the electronic form. Next she asks the children to raise their hands if they want salad bar but, before she is able to count their hands, she has to stop and deal with a discipline problem. As Ms. Terry turns back, two students raise their hands to tell her they have changed their mind and want salad bar instead. Ms. Terry makes the change on the computer and goes on asking students to raise their hands if they want milk.

**8:50** Ms. Terry now asks the students who brought back classroom library books to put them on their desks. Ms. Terry collects the books in a basket. Later today, she will organize the books (alphabetically) and reshelf them. (This will take approximately 15 minutes a day.)

**8:55** Next, she asks if any of the students have permission slips to return. She asks the students to pass them forward. She will check the forms in during lunch or after school. (This will take approximately 5 minutes.)

**9:00** Finally, Ms. Terry is ready to start the math lesson (scheduled until 9:30). ■

## Taking a Closer Look

As we analyze the difference between these two classrooms, it must be noted that both teachers care deeply about their students' learning. However, one teacher is making much better use of classroom time – a critical factor in effective teaching and ultimately higher student achievement. How would you analyze these differences, to "take a closer look" into these very different classrooms? To begin the analysis, consider the following comparison grid. (See Figure 6.2, **Proactive Management: Teacher-Student Actions**.)

**Figure 6.2    ↓ Proactive Management: Teacher-Student Actions**

| Ms. Jordon | | Proactive Management: Teacher/Student Actions | Ms. Terry | |
|---|---|---|---|---|
| Yes | No | | Yes | No |
| | | Teacher greets students at the door.<br>• INTASC 5: Motivation & Management<br>• Personal Characteristic: Positive Disposition | | |
| | | Students complete routine tasks, such as attendance and collecting/returning assignments/books.<br>• INTASC 2: Student Development<br>• Personal Characteristic: Creativity | | |
| | | Teacher has completed all instructional preparation before the students enter the door.<br>• INTASC 7: Planning<br>• Personal Characteristic: Organization | | |
| | | Clear, logical sequenced directions are given *only* when teacher has students' attention.<br>• INTASC 6: Communication<br>• Personal Characteristic: Oral Expression | | |
| | | Teacher physically circulates and visually scans room to make sure students understand the task.<br>• INTASC 3: Diverse Learners<br>• Personal Characteristic: Flexibility | | |
| | | Transition (the time from one activity to another) is smooth, taking less than two minutes.<br>• INTASC 5: Motivation & Management<br>• Personal Characteristic: Organization | | |

**Let's Do the Math**   Take a few minutes to calculate the difference in math instruction the children will receive in Ms. Terry and Ms. Jordan's classes.

How much more time will Ms. Jordon's class receive in:

- One week? One month? Nine months?

How much time will Ms. Terry spend working to reshelf library books?
- In one week? In one month? In nine month?

It took Ms. Jordan five hours prior to school starting to set up the Library Loan System. The system is self-managing. How much more time will Ms. Terry spend each year?

A comparison of these two teachers clearly reveals that Ms. Jordon has developed a number of techniques that help her manage her students and instructional time very efficiently. Ms. Jordon **knows** that instructional time is precious. The more instructional time she has, the more her students will learn. Therefore, she knows she needs to manage simple management tasks with student routines and use as little time as possible. Let's identify the simple management routines she used in only the first ten minutes of her class day.

- Attendance - Lunch Chart
- Check-In Form
- Library Book Check-In Chart
- Library Re-Shelving System
- Student Helpers

All classrooms have tasks and procedures that must be performed on a daily basis. Well-developed management routines serve as proactive tools that save both student and teacher time and ensure a smooth functioning classroom. During the first week of school, Ms. Jordon **skillfully** and explicitly taught her students these simple management routines. While it may initially appear as though it takes a great deal of time to develop the check-in charts, ultimately these devices will save hours of time and a great deal of frustration. Ms. Jordon's **disposition** to have a well-managed class determined it was time well spent.

Ms. Terry's lack of management routines cost the students time and makes extra work for her throughout the day. For instance, she will have to take time later in her day to re-shelf the library center books and check in the permission slips.

Experienced teachers and classroom-effectiveness researchers suggest that the establishment of these routines should begin on the first day and continue through at least the first two weeks of school. Classroom management experts stress that using this time to teach routines will actually give you more total teaching time during the year, plus you will benefit from having a well-managed, organized classroom (Enz, Honaker, Kortman, 2002; Wong & Wong, 2004; Kronowitz, 1999).

There are virtually dozens of routine tasks that could make classroom life easier and more organized – for both students and teachers. Figures 6.3. and 6.4. list a number of routines and procedures used in effective classrooms.

## Figure 6.3   ↓ Examining Proactive Routines for the Elementary Classroom

**Directions:** Observe an elementary classroom, focusing on any routines the teacher uses. Using the checklist below, place an X by the routines you observe occurring.

What grade are you observing?                                What time of day is it?

Choose one routine to describe. How does that routine work?

**Beginning Class**

___ Enter/Exiting the Classroom
___ Attention Signal
___ Attendance Procedures
___ Lunch Count
___ Tardy Students

**Classroom Management Procedures**

___ Rules of Respect
___ Out-of-Room Policies
___ Restroom Procedures
___ Drinking Fountain
___ Pencil Sharpening
___ Fire/Earthquake/Bomb Threat Drills
___ Noise Control
___ Movement in Classroom

**Instructional Activities**

___ Assignment Calendar
___ Distributing Supplies
___ Seeking Teacher's Help
___ Storing/Filing Work
___ Computer Access
___ Finishing Work Early
___ Study Buddy System

**Other Routines**

**Grading and Checking Assignments**

___ Self-Checked Work
___ Editing Checklist
___ Grading Criteria/Rubrics
___ Recording Grades

**Work Expectations and Requirements**

___ Heading Papers
___ Name/Number/Class Information
___ Quality of Work
___ Incomplete/Incorrect Work
___ Turning in Completed Work
___ Homework Check-In

**Dismissing Class**

___ Putting Away Supplies and Equipment
___ Cleaning Up
___ Going to Special Support Services,
         Speech, and Resource
___ Lining up and moving in line

Adapted from Enz, B.J., Kortman, S., & Honaker, C. (2002). *Trade Secret: for Primary/Elementary Teachers.* (2nd ed.). Dubuque, IA: Kendall/Hunt.

**Figure 6.4** ↓ **Examining Proactive Routines for the Secondary Classroom**

**Directions:** Observe a middle or secondary classroom, focusing on any routines the teacher uses. Using the checklist below, place an X by the routines you observe occurring.

What grade/subject are you observing?

Choose one routine to describe. How does that routine work?

*Beginning Class*
___ Enter/Exiting the Classroom
___ Attention Signal
___ Attendance Procedures
___ Tardy Students

*Classroom Management Procedures*
___ Classroom Rules
___ Out-of-Room Policies
___ Movement in Class
___ Drinking Fountain
___ Noise Control
___ Fire/Earthquake/Bomb Threat Drills

*Instructional Activities*
___ Assignment Calendar
___ Distributing Supplies
___ Seeking Teacher's Help
___ Storing/Filing Work
___ Computer Access
___ Finishing Work Early
___ Study Buddy System

*Other Routines*

*Grading and Checking Assignments*
___ Self-Checked Work
___ Editing Checklist
___ Grading Criteria/Rubrics
___ Recording Grades

*Work Expectations and Requirements*
___ Heading Papers
___ Name/Number/Class Information
___ Quality of Work
___ Incomplete/Incorrect Work
___ Turning in Completed Work
___ Homework Check-In

*Dismissing Class*
___ Putting Away Supplies and Equipment
___ Cleaning Up
___ Returning Resource Materials

Adapted from Enz, B. J., Honaker, C., & Kortman, S. (2002). *Trade Secret: for Middle/Secondary Teachers.* (2nd ed.). Dubuque, IA: Kendall/Hunt.

# Instructional Inspirations 6.1

**Sponge Activities:** Transitions between activities, classes, or periods are a major source of lost time. In the average classroom, one hour a day is lost in transitions. This adds up to five hours a week. Statements and directives such as the following will reduce time lost in transition. Sponge activities can be used to minimize wasted time. For example:

**When the students first enter the room, before the bell has rung:**
*"On your paper, write three things that you remember from yesterday."*
*"Read the first page of the story and think of a question to ask a friend."*

**As the teacher or student helper passes out the materials:**
*"Students, be thinking about _____. Turn to your neighbor and share your answer."*
*"Think of a question about _____."*

Sponge activities such as these are quick and effective ways to review lesson content with your students and maximize transitional time.

---

Complete Figure 6.3 (Elementary) or 6.4 (Secondary) the next time you visit a classroom to learn how teachers use routines to manage their class.

During your next college class session, meet in groups of four to six to compare responses.

**Group Talk**

■ What routines are most common?

■ What difficulties did you see arise when routines were not in place?

■ What routines were most effective and why?

■ If you were teaching the lesson you observed, which routines would you change? Why?

■ What routines did you observe that weren't on the checklist?

# Planning a Good Beginning

How a teacher begins his or her lesson, how he or she captures the students' interest and sustains student attention, is critical to student learning and achievement (Lowman, 1996). We are now turning our attention to the lesson itself by analyzing two new seventh-grade teachers, Mr. Boyd and Ms. Wiley. Both teachers are science teachers, and both classrooms have just started the study of genetics.

**Classroom Glimpse**

### First Example: Ms. Wiley

As the students take their seats in Ms. Wiley's room, she has placed a vividly colored transparency of a DNA sequence on the overhead and tells the students they are going to be learning about genetics. She asks them to begin reading in their biology book, Chapter 2, which begins to describe the work of a monk named Gregor Mendel and how his study of differences in pea plants led to the science of genetics. Within a few minutes, Ms. Wiley begins to have some very restless students. After about twenty minutes, many of the students are daydreaming, passing notes, or text messaging. She has become frustrated and has started to write detention notices. Thirty minutes into class she asks the students to share with her what they learned about Gregor Mendel, but her question is met with blank looks. The students start flipping pages and offer a few half-hearted answers. Finally, she turns to the eye grid transparency and handout (see Mr. Boyd's classroom vignette) but the students are not responding to her. Several students are already complaining that genetics is boring!!!! ∎

**Classroom Glimpse**

### Contrasting Practice: Mr. Boyd

As soon as the students walk into Mr. Boyd's room he looks directly at their eye color and begins to take a tally. The students are curious as to what their teacher is doing. On the overhead he has placed a transparency, which asks the students to think about their parents' eye color. In a few moments he replaces the question transparency with the one he has just completed, based on the tally of his students' eye color.

| Blue (bb) | Brown (BB or Bb) |
|-----------|------------------|
| 8         | 18               |

Mr. Boyd asks the students a series of no-risk questions:

- Who has parents with brown eyes?
- Who has blue-eyed parents?
- Who has eyes that are a different color than their parents?

He tells the students, "Today we are going to learn why some of us have blue eyes and some of us have brown eyes." He says each parent contributes one gene for eye color. He tells the students that brown is a dominant color (more people have brown eyes) and is represented with a big B. He further explains that blue is a recessive color (fewer people have blue eyes) and is represented with a b. If you have blue eyes you will have two recessive genes (bb) for eye color. If you have brown eyes it could be represented like this BB or Bb.

| Blue eyes are recessive bb | Brown eyes are dominate BB or Bb |
|----------------------------|----------------------------------|
| b from mom                 | B from mom                       |
| b from dad                 | B from dad                       |

He works out this chart on the overhead, and the students have an exact handout like this at their desks. They work out the genetic equation together. Mr. Boyd watches to make sure all the students are working with him.

*Genetic Equation 1*

| Mom (Blue = bb)<br>Dad (Brown = BB) | b | b |
|---|---|---|
| B | Bb | Bb |
| B | Bb | Bb |
| How many children would have blue eyes? 0<br>How many children would have brown eyes? 4 | | |

Next, Mr. Boyd asks the students to figure out what happens if one parent has Bb like all of the offspring in the first genetic equation. Once again they work out the equation with him.

*Genetic Equation 2*

| Mom (Blue = bb)<br>Dad (Brown = Bb) | b | b |
|---|---|---|
| B | Bb | Bb |
| b | bb | bb |
| How many children would have brown eyes? 2<br>How many children would have blue eyes? 2 | | |

Finally, Mr. Boyd asks the students to consider how two brown-eyed parents could have a blue-eyed child. He lets the students begin to work together to solve this genetic mystery. As they work together, he circulates the room to make sure all the students have been engaged in responding to the lecture and taking their notes. He is not surprised to discover that all his students have been working along with him. He had been able to observe their active **participation** while he was lecturing and discussing. As he moves among the students, many of them point to the equation they think is most like their family. He smiles and nods at their comments, and offers verbal reinforcement to their hypothesis. After a few minutes he returns to the overhead and asks for the students to share their findings.

*Genetic Equation 3*

| Mom (Brown = Bb)<br>Dad (Brown = Bb) | B | b |
|---|---|---|
| B | BB | Bb |
| b | Bb | bb |
| How many children would have blue eyes? 1<br>How many children would have brown eyes? 3 | | |

He then asks the students to consider how many children from these three mathematic grids would have blue eyes and how many would have brown. The students add up the numbers and realize that only three out of twelve children would be blue eyes; nine would have brown. Mr. Boyd congratulates the students for their efforts and then asks them to consider how humans first figured out genetics. He asks them to predict how long ago this discovery was first made. He asks them to write that prediction on their papers and then assigns them to read Chapter 2 in class. ■

## Taking a Closer Look

What instructional strategies is Mr. Boyd using that are helping his students stay involved and enthusiastic with the topic? Active engagement is a critical factor in effective teaching and ultimately higher student achievement (Marzano, Pickering & Pollack, 2001). To begin the analysis, consider the following comparison grid. See Figure 6.5. **Teaching Strategies.**

Comparisons of these two teachers clearly reveal that Mr. Boyd is using a number of effective instructional strategies that help his students connect to the new information he is teaching and stay actively engaged with him throughout the entire lesson:

- Beginning lessons effectively
- Presenting information clearly
- Encouraging student responses
- Maximizing participation

**Figure 6.5   ↓ Teaching Strategies**

| Ms. Wiley | | Teaching Strategies | Mr. Boyd | |
|---|---|---|---|---|
| Yes | No | | Yes | No |
| | | Teacher stimulates interest in lesson by actively involving students or by asking thought-provoking questions. *INTASC 6: Communication* *Personal Characteristic: Creativity* | | |
| | | Teacher connects new learning with something familiar. *INTASC 2: Student Development* *Personal Characteristic: Commitment* | | |
| | | Teacher provides appropriate concrete visual models *INTASC 4: Multiple Instructional Strategies* *Personal Characteristic: Written Expression* | | |
| | | Teacher provides opportunities for overt participation, such as simultaneous note taking and small group activities. *INTASC 4: Multiple Instructional Strategies* *Personal Characteristic: Flexibility* | | |
| | | Teacher presents information in a logical sequence, going from the simplest to more difficult concepts. *INTASC 1: Content Pedagogy* *Personal Characteristic: Organization* | | |
| | | Teacher models appropriate responses using overhead or board. *INTASC 6: Communication & Technology* *Personal Characteristic: Written Communication* | | |
| | | Teacher writes critical information on board, chart, or overhead. *INTASC 6: Communication & Technology* *Personal Characteristic: Written Communication* | | |
| | | Teacher checks student understanding and responses throughout lesson. *INTASC 8: Assessment* *Personal Characteristic: Commitment* | | |

**Beginning Lessons Effectively**   What the teacher does in the first few minutes of the lesson is essential for motivating students' interest and sets the stage for further learning. Mr. Boyd piqued the students' interest by checking their eye color as they walked into the door. The question on the overhead, *"What is the color of your parents' eyes?"* was something the students knew and directly related to what they would be learning in class. These activities *activate students'* prior knowledge. To activate prior knowledge, the teacher often uses a technique called an *anticipatory set.* An anticipatory set:

- Helps students become ready to learn
- Gets the learner's attention
- Often involves overt (observable) participation
- Connects prior knowledge to new information
- Helps the student learn faster
- Reduces discipline problems

## Examples of anticipatory sets:

> *Before we read the story, The Lottery, I want to finish grades. I've decided to fail three students and have placed three fail slips among these thirty pass slips in this hat. Now, we'll pass the hat and everyone takes a slip.*

> *Raise your hand if you will be looking for a summer job when school gets out. Most employers will require you to fill out an application. Today, we'll learn how to fill out an application to improve your chances of getting a summer job.*

Clearly, starting the lesson successfully requires more than "turn to page . . ." Ms. Wiley basically lost most of her students' interest, and thus lost their ability to learn about genetics, by not activating their prior knowledge (Bettencourt, Gillet, Gail, & Hull, 1983). Asking them to read unfamiliar information did not build an adequate fund of knowledge or interest. So most students in her class became bored and stopped participating in the lesson. Next, Ms. Wiley had discipline concerns and, when the active part of the lesson was offered (eye-grids), she had little enthusiasm for the topic.

**Presenting Information Clearly**   When students are learning something for the first time, teachers need to thoughtfully consider how information is presented. To do this the teacher needs to consider how to present information in a logical sequence (Hunter, 1994). And while new knowledge is not always gained in step-by-step progression, knowledge does build upon prior information. When lessons build from known to new, from simple to complex, the teacher increases the likelihood that students will learn and retain the information (Enz, Hurwitz, & Carlile, 2005). Mr. Boyd's use of the eye grids built from the simplest combination to the more complex and supported the students' learning by keeping them engaged—he used an eye-grid handout that matched his overhead exactly. As he worked through the genetic combination, he was able to observe the students as they followed along with him. The answers to the questions he asked also confirmed their growing understanding of genetic combinations.

Mr. Boyd's use of visual models (eye grids) also provided every student an opportunity to use multiple *modalities*—students were *hearing, seeing,* and *writing* through the entire lesson.

Research has consistently revealed that when students are encouraged to ask questions and give responses throughout the lesson, they are more likely to be motivated to stay on task and learn throughout the entire lesson.

While Ms. Wiley's use of a vividly colored DNA double helix transparency was interesting, she did not refer to it nor did it relate directly to the learning objectives, which were:

1. Students will understand that for each physical trait, such as eye color, each parent contributes one gene to the offspring.
2. Often a trait has a dominant and recessive characteristic. The dominant characteristic governs the actual expression of the trait, for instance, the color of the eye.

**Encouraging Students' Responses and/or Questions**  When Mr. Boyd asked no-fail questions (How many of your parents have brown eyes?) he made it easier for all students to participate. Research has consistently revealed that when students are encouraged to ask questions and give responses during a lesson, they are more likely to be motivated to stay on task and learn throughout the entire lesson. In addition, Mr. Boyd responds to the students' questions and answers positively using both verbal comments and nonverbal gestures.

**Maximizing Opportunities for All to Participate**  Studies reveal that students who actively participate in a lesson tend to be more accountable, responsible, and successful than students who are merely bystanders (Marzano, Pickering & Pollack, 2001). The following information also explains why Mr. Boyd wanted the students to work together to figure out the last genetic equation. Students remember:

- **10%** of what they read
- **20%** of what they hear
- **30%** of what they see
- **50%** of what they see and hear
- **70%** of what they say
- **90%** of what they say while doing

Figure 6.6 provides a guide for observing teachers' instructional strategies in the classroom. While you may not see *all* of these strategies used in *every* lesson, each strategy is important and will enhance students' learning.

**Figure 6.6   ↓ Examining Instructional Strategies**

*Directions:* Using the checklist below, place an X by the actions you observe.

What grade/subject are you observing?

Describe the classroom environment:

**Begins Lesson Effectively**
- ❑ Teacher activates/establishes students' prior knowledge of current lesson.
- ❑ Teacher helps students understand the purpose or importance of the lesson.
- ❑ Teacher stimulates interest in the lesson by actively involving students.

**Presents Information Clearly**
- ❑ Teacher presents information in a logical sequence.
- ❑ Teacher provides concrete and/or visual models when appropriate.
- ❑ Teacher uses vocabulary appropriate to students' level of understanding.

**Gives Clear Directions and Explanations**
- ❑ Teacher presents directions in a logical sequence.
- ❑ Teacher writes critical information on the board, chart, or overhead.
- ❑ Teacher checks students' understanding of directions before independent practice.

**Encourages Student Responses and Questions in Teaching**
- ❑ Teacher encourages students' responses and/or questions.
- ❑ Teacher responds in a positive and supportive manner to questions.
- ❑ Teacher uses responses to monitor student understanding of information presented.

**Maximizes Opportunities for All to Participate**
- ❑ Teacher asks questions of whole group first, rather than individuals.
- ❑ Teacher offers frequent opportunities for student-to-student interactions/inquiry.
- ❑ Teacher provides opportunities for overt participation, such as working on handout, manipulations, small group activities, discussions.

Adapted from Enz, B. J., S. Hurwitz, & Carlile, B. J. (2005). *Coaching the Student Teacher: A Developmental Approach.* Dubuque, IA.: Kendall/Hunt.

## Classroom Strategies

Use the Examining Instructional Strategies guide during your next classroom visit. Watch closely to see how many of the strategies are used. During your next college course session, meet in pairs to share your responses.

- ■ Were any of the strategies missing?
- ■ Did it make a difference in the lesson's success?
- ■ Which strategy was used most effectively? Describe this strategy.
- ■ How would you improve the lesson by changing just one of the strategies?
- ■ Which strategy do you think you would be most comfortable using the next time you make a presentation?
- ■ How do these strategies relate directly with the INTASC standards for effective teaching?

**Maximizing Student Learning**    Effective teachers have always known that what they do makes a difference in how their students learn. The goal, then, should be to apply effective instructional strategies to every lesson, every day. As the last chapter illustrated, students learn more when they are actively engaged in learning (Hunter, 1994). Student learning is increased when teaching is presented in a manner that assists students in mentally organizing the information they are learning. How teachers organize and present their lesson directly impacts how children learn (Enz, Hurwitz, & Carlile, 2005; Lowman, 1996).

# Miniature Closures

Just as the beginning of a lesson is important in gaining students' attention, the *closure* of a lesson is also critical. Effective closures provide students with a review of the material they learned and provide the teacher with a quick check to see if students understood the material presented (Daniels & Bizar, 1998). In the following vignettes, read carefully to see how each teacher is using closures to wrap up a science lesson for kindergarten students.

**Classroom Glimpse**

### First Example: Ms. Marks

Ms. Marks' kindergarten lesson objective is "Children will be able to label the parts of a seed." This is part of a larger instructional unit called "Living Things Grow." She has started the lesson by using a KWL chart (See Figure 6.7 **KWL Chart**). Ms. Marks gives each table of children a small cup that contains several different types of seeds. She asks the children to tell her if they know what kind of seeds are in the cup. They name the different seeds—lima bean, pinto bean, corn, kidney bean. She tells them that today they will be learning about the different parts of seeds. She asks the students to share what they already know about seeds (**anticipatory set**—to activate the children's prior knowledge). As the students share what they know, Ms. Marks writes the information on the chart.

Ms. Marks congratulates the children on their good questions. She tells them today they are going to learn about the different parts of a seed. She asks each table to find the lima bean seeds. There are enough for each child to have one lima bean. She passes out a small plastic magnifying glass and paper to each child. She asks the students to examine their seeds and report what they see. As the students work, Ms. Marks walks around the room and listens to their comments. This information helps her to hear their views and helps her to know what misconceptions they may have about seeds. She has also found that walking around the room is a good way to make sure all students stay on task.

### Figure 6.7    ↓ KWL Chart

| What we **K**now | What we **W**ant to learn | What we **L**earned |
|---|---|---|
| Seeds are baby plants. | How does a seed become a plant? | |
| Different plants have different seeds. | How long does it take a seed grow into a plant? | |
| Seeds need water to grow. | Why do plants need water and dirt to grow? | |

After a few minutes, she asks the students to share what they have learned about the first examination of the seeds and she writes this down on the chart. Next, Ms. Marks gives the little scientists lima beans that have been soaking in water for a couple of hours. The children marvel at how large the beans have become. Within a few moments, the children realize that the outside of the seed has slid off. Almost immediately, the lima bean opens into two halves.

At this point, Ms. Marks uses a "get attention signal" (she claps her hands three times, and the students respond by clapping back and then become quiet and listen). She asks the children to share what they have just discovered. The students tell her that the lima bean had a covering. She tells them that this is called the seed coat. This direct input of new information is called **instructional input.** The children also share that the lima bean seed has two halves. She writes this information into the chart. This immediate confirmation of verbal and written feedback helps students know they are correct. Next, Ms. Marks hands them a paper to draw what they see as they examine their lima bean seed. The students draw the two halves and they also draw the "baby plant" inside the seed. Once again, she signals for their attention. She asks them to describe what they see and she writes this on their KWL chart.

Now Ms. Marks tells the students that the tiny plant needs help to grow. It needs food. She asks the children *"Where do you think the baby plant gets food?"* There are several guesses including incorrect answers. She listens and replies that it is a good guess. But she doesn't confirm that the responses are correct. Within a few moments one child offers the correct answer, that the two sides of the seed are the food for the baby plant. She writes this information on the chart. Now she asks the students to review with her what they learned during their experiment today. The students re-read the *What We Learned* part of the KWL chart. (See Figure 6.8. **Completed KWL Chart**).

To summarize or close the lesson, Ms. Marks gives the children a drawing of the seed and asks the children to label it. (See Figure 6.9. **Diagram of a Lima Bean Seed.**) After the students complete the labeling, Ms. Marks puts a completed diagram on the overhead and asks the students to check their answers.

In addition to serving as a closure activity, the diagram is also a good assessment tool to document the children's learning and participation. Later in the day, Ms. Marks reviews the papers and makes observational comments on two. One student had used a number of excellent descriptions in his group. Another child was having difficulty following directions and needed to be redirected. She makes these anecdotal notes to help remind her of students' behavior patterns and possibly share with parents later in the year during parent-teacher conferences. ■

---

### Figure 6.8  ↓ Completed KWL Chart

| What we know | What we want to learn | What we learned |
|---|---|---|
| Seeds are baby plants. | How does a seed become a plant? | Seeds are hard. We think this helps to protect them. |
| Different plants have different seeds. | How long does it take a seed grow into a plant? | The seeds have a shell-like covering called a _seed coat_. |
| Seeds need water to grow. | Why do plants need water and dirt to grow? | The lima bean seed has two halves. |
| | | There is a _little plant_ inside the seed. It has two tiny leaves and a root. |
| | | The little plant needs food to grow; it gets it _food_ from the rest of the seed. |

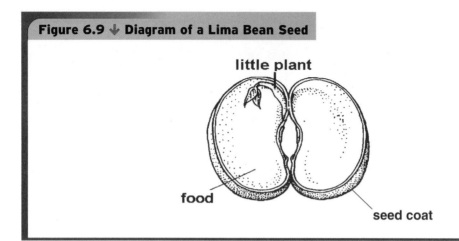

**Figure 6.9 ↓ Diagram of a Lima Bean Seed**

little plant

food

seed coat

### Contrasting Practice: Ms. Cayman

Next door, Ms. Cayman is also introducing her five-year-olds to the parts of seed. Like Ms. Marks she has provided each table of six children with a sack of seeds. She asks the students to see if they recognize the different types of seeds in the sack. The students begin to list the beans: lima bean, pinto bean, corn, kidney bean.

Ms. Cayman asks the students to tell her how the seeds were alike and different. She begins to write down what the children share with her.

Next she passes out the lima beans seeds that have soaked in water. Then she provides them with magnifying glasses and paper. She asks the students to work in pairs and dissect their seed. The children quickly discover that after the seed coat falls away the seed actually has two parts. They also find the tiny little plant inside. She asks the children to draw what they see. The children discuss a great deal at the table—they enjoy using the magnifying glass.

To summarize the lesson Ms. Cayman provides the students the same seed diagram that Ms. Marks provided her students. However, Ms. Cayman, is quite surprised that her students had difficulty completing the form correctly. Most of the students could only label the little plant. ■

### Taking a Closer Look

What instructional strategies is Ms. Marks using that are helping her students extend their knowledge of the parts of a seed? Critical to her success are:

- Active student engagement
- Explicit input
- Summarizing at strategic points in the lesson

Students need a chance to see and say what they are learning. To begin the analysis, consider Figure 6.10. **Building the Lesson.**

## Putting It All Together

In this section, we have introduced three additional strategies to use when planning an effective lesson:

- Promoting student retention and understanding
- Using effective closures
- Assessing student progress

## Figure 6.10 ↓ Building the Lesson

**1. Begins Lesson Effectively**
- ❏ Activates/establishes students' prior knowledge of current lesson.
- ❏ Helps students to understand the purpose or importance of the lesson.
- ❏ Stimulates interest in lesson by actively involving students.

Marks:

Cayman:

**2. Presents Information Clearly**
- ❏ Presents information in a logical sequence.
- ❏ Provides concrete and/or visual models when appropriate.
- ❏ Uses vocabulary appropriate to students' level of understanding.

Marks:

Cayman:

**3. Gives Clear Directions and Explanations**
- ❏ Presents directions in a logical sequence.
- ❏ Writes critical information on board, chart or overhead.
- ❏ Checks students' understanding before they practice on their own.

Marks:

Cayman:

**4. Encourages Student Responses and Questions**
- ❏ Encourages students' responses and/or questions.
- ❏ Responds in a positive and supportive manner to questions.
- ❏ Uses responses to monitor student understanding.

Marks:

Cayman:

**5. Maximizes Opportunities for All to Participate**
- ❏ Asks questions of whole group first, rather than individuals.
- ❏ Offers frequent opportunities for student interactions/inquiry.
- ❏ Provides opportunities for overt participation, such as working on handout, manipulations, small group activities, discussions.

Marks:

Cayman:

**6. Provides Students Feedback Through the Lesson**
- ❏ Provides feedback to students as soon as possible.
- ❏ Provides feedback to students in a positive manner.
- ❏ Helps students evaluate their own performance.

Marks:

Cayman:

**7. Instruction Promotes Student Retention**
- ❏ Defines or models the expectations of the lesson or learning.
- ❏ Offer chances for students to demonstrate their understanding.
- ❏ Monitors student responses and adjusts instruction accordingly.

Marks:

Cayman:

**8. Uses Closure-Summarization Techniques**
- ❏ Offers closure at the end of distinct segments in the lesson.
- ❏ Provides opportunity for the students to summarize.
- ❏ Actively involves students in their own closure/summarization.

Marks:

Cayman:

**9. Assesses Student Progress**
- ❏ Teacher observes students working.
- ❏ Assessment focuses directly on lesson goals and objectives.
- ❏ Teacher maintains an accurate record of student performance.

Marks:

Cayman:

Questions can serve as a way to increase a student's attention and assess student understanding.

As we observed Ms. Marks' lesson, it becomes apparent that she was using these strategies in a overlapping manner. Her use of effective closure strategies helped her to assess the students' progress, and simultaneously allowed her to reinforce their learning.

**Promoting Student Retention and Understanding**   Obviously, the goal of instruction is to have students retain the information presented. As we examined Ms. Cayman and Ms. Marks' lesson we noticed that both teachers had the same objective/outcome "students will be able to label the parts of a seed."

Both teachers were using the techniques to activate the children's prior knowledge. But almost immediately, Ms. Marks began to guide the students to spotlight on the objective of the lesson. She guided her students by using questions to focus the children's observations. She reinforced their learning of new information by writing down what the children were learning on the KWL chart; this action *promoted students' retention* of information.

Effective closures summarize students' understanding of the material (Cotton, 1995; Newman, 1996; Hunter, 1994). Ms. Marks knew there were three parts of the seed, so she knew she would have to briefly stop the students' observations to *assess their progress* of the information and reinforce their learning at least three times during the lesson. These brief checks for understanding or miniature closures helped her to observe the students' ability to label the parts of the seed. Ms. Mark's use of the seed diagram as an *assessment tool to document students' progress* was appropriate as it directly matched her objective. The seed diagram was also a way to gain immediate responses from all the students.

Figure 6.11 **Examining the Lesson** combines all of the instructional strategies we've described so far in this chapter. In order to better understand how teachers use all of these strategies together, use this guide as a reference to review the lessons you just read, during an actual classroom visit, or as you view a classroom video case study.

## Figure 6.11 ↓ Examining the Lesson

*Directions:* Using the checklist below, place an X by the actions you observe. Then describe specifically the actions the teacher took to accomplish this goal.

**Begins Lesson Effectively**
- ❏ Teacher activates/establishes students' prior knowledge of current lesson.
- ❏ Teacher helps students to understand the purpose or importance of the lesson.
- ❏ Teacher stimulates interest in lesson by actively involving students or by asking questions.

Describe the strategies.

**Presents Information Clearly**
- ❏ Teacher presents information in a logical sequence.
- ❏ Teacher provides concrete and/or visual models when appropriate.
- ❏ Teacher uses vocabulary appropriate to students' level of understanding.

Describe the strategies.

**Gives Clear Directions and Explanations**
- ❏ Teacher presents directions in a logical sequence.
- ❏ Teacher writes critical information on board, chart, or overhead.
- ❏ Teacher checks students' understanding of directions before they practice independently.

Describe the strategies.

**Encourages Student Responses and Questions in Teaching**
- ❏ Teacher encourages students' responses and/or questions.
- ❏ Teacher responds in a positive and supportive manner to questions.
- ❏ Teacher uses responses to monitor student understanding of information presented.

Describe the strategies.

**Provides Students With Feedback Through the Lesson**
- ❏ Teacher provides feedback to students as soon as possible.
- ❏ Teacher provides feedback to students in a positive manner.
- ❏ Teacher helps students evaluate their own performance.

Describe the strategies.

**Maximizes Opportunities for All to Participate**
- ❏ Teacher asks questions of whole group first, rather than individuals.
- ❏ Teacher offers frequent opportunities for student-to-student interactions/inquiry.
- ❏ Teacher provides opportunities for overt participation, such as working on handout, manipulations, small group activities, discussions.

Describe the strategies.

**Promotes Student Retention and Understanding**
- ❏ Teacher defines or models the expectations of the lesson or learning.
- ❏ Teacher provides opportunities for students to demonstrate their understanding of lesson.
- ❏ Teacher monitors student responses, interprets, and adjusts instruction accordingly.

Describe the strategies.

**Uses Effective Closure or Summarization Techniques**
- ❏ Teacher gives students an opportunity for closure at the end of distinct segments in the lesson.
- ❏ Teacher provides opportunity for the students to summarize at the end of each lesson.
- ❏ Teacher actively involves students in their own closure/summarization.

Describe the strategies.

**Assesses Student Progress**
- ❏ Teacher observes students working.
- ❏ Assessment focuses directly on lesson goals and objectives.
- ❏ Teacher maintains an accurate record of student performance.

Describe the strategies.

Adapted from Enz, B. J., S. Hurwitz, & Carlile, B. J. (2005). *Coaching the Student Teacher: A Developmental Approach.* Dubuque, IA.: Kendall/Hunt.

**Box 6.1** ⇓ **More About Madeline C. Hunter—A Teacher's Teacher**

Madeline Cheek Hunter (1916-1994) was an influential American educator who developed a model for teaching and learning that was widely adopted by schools during the last quarter of the twentieth century.

From her position at University of California at Los Angeles (UCLA) campus school, she synthesized many research findings and research-based practices from various sources and produced her TIP (theory into practice) model. Hunter's plan had seven steps and a closure activity. Most importantly, it also gave educators a common vocabulary of classroom planning that teachers still use today:

Madeline Hunter developed a **teacher "decision-making" model** for planning instruction. Her model is called ITIP (Instructional Theory into Practice) and is widely used in school districts around the country. There are three categories which are considered basic to ITIP lesson design.

**Content:** Within the context of grade level, content standards, student ability/needs, and rationale for teaching, the teacher decides what content to teach.

**Learner Behaviors:** Teachers must decide what students will do (a) to learn and (b) to demonstrate that they have learned.

**Teacher Behaviors:** Teachers must decide which "research-based" teaching principles and strategies will most effectively promote learning for their students. This was translated into a seven steps lesson plan.

1. Before the lesson is prepared, the teacher should have a clear idea of what the teaching **objectives** are. What, specifically, should the student be able to do, understand, and care about as a result of the teaching. The teacher needs to know what **standards** of performance are to be expected and when pupils will be held accountable for what is expected. **The pupils** should be informed about the standards of performance.

2. **Anticipatory set**—sometimes called a "hook" to grab the student's attention: actions and statements by the teacher to relate the experiences of the students to the objectives of the lesson. Anticipatory sets put students into a receptive frame of mind, focus student attention on the lesson, create an organizing framework for the ideas, and extend the understanding and the application of abstract ideas through the use of example or analogy.

3. **Teaching/presentation**—includes Input, Modeling, and Checking for Understanding.

   a. **Input**—The teacher provides the information needed for students to gain the knowledge or skill through lecture, film, tape, video, pictures, etc.

   b. **Modeling**—Once the material has been presented, the teacher uses it to show students examples of what is expected as an end product of their work. The critical aspects are explained through labeling, categorizing, comparing, etc. Students are taken to the application level (problem-solving, comparison, summarizing, etc.).

   c. **Checking for Understanding**—Determination of whether students have "got it" before proceeding. It is essential that students practice *doing it right* so the teacher must know that students understand before proceeding to practice. If there is any doubt that the class has not understood, the concept/skill should be retaught before practice begins.

4. **Guided practice**—An opportunity for each student to demonstrate grasp of new learning by working through an activity or exercise under the teacher's direct supervision. The teacher moves around the room to determine the level of mastery and to provide individual remediation as needed.

5. **Closure**—Those actions or statements by a teacher that are designed to bring a lesson presentation to an appropriate conclusion. Used to help students bring things

together in their own minds, to make sense out of what has just been taught. "Any questions? No. OK, let's move on" is not closure. Closure is used:

- to cue students to the fact that they have arrived at an important point in the lesson or the end of a lesson
- to help organize student learning, to help form a coherent picture, to consolidate, eliminate confusion and frustration
- to reinforce the major points to be learned
- to help establish the network of thought relationships that provide a number of possibilities for cues for retrieval

Closure is the act of reviewing and clarifying the key points of a lesson, tying them together into a coherent whole, and ensuring their utility in application by securing them in the student's conceptual network.

6. **Independent practice**—Once pupils have mastered the content or skill, it is time to provide for reinforcement practice. It is provided on a repeating schedule so that the learning is not forgotten. It may be homework or group or individual work in class. **The failure to do this is responsible for most student failure to be able to apply something learned.**

7. **Summary**—You told them what you were going to tell them with the anticipatory set, you tell them with **presentation,** you demonstrate what you want them to do with **modeling,** you see if they understand what you've told them with **checking for understanding,** and you tell them what you've told them by tying it all together with **closure.** (Hunter, 1994)

# Looking Forward

Who knew that it took so much time and effort to effectively start your day on the right foot? Ok, well not all that time is spent in one day, or at least it doesn't have to be. Be prepared. Prepare tools to make your life easier. If you can predict and prepare ways to streamline tasks that are done daily, take the time to do it before your students arrive. It may not seem like much time, but you will soon see that there is no such thing as free time when it comes to a typical day in the life of a teacher. So, do what you can to save those precious minutes . . . they add up! We all know it is important to evaluate our students; we need to put into our minds that this is something we do daily in many different ways. We have to continually assess their progress, essentially assessing our teaching, on a daily basis. We want our students to be successful, and there is not one way to insure the success of all students. We have to be willing to adapt our teaching to meet the needs of our students and assess them on *what we teach them,* not what we expect them to know.

## Building Effective Lessons

In groups of four to six, select one of the case studies accompanying this text to review together. As you read the case, record your observations individually on Figure 6.10, **Building the Lesson,** then compare your thoughts with those of your colleagues.

- As a group, pick one area the teacher excelled in. Why did you choose that strategy?
- Are there any discrepancies in your group's responses? If so, defend your position to the group.
- As a group, make recommendations for this teacher to improve his/her lesson.
- How do these lesson components align with the professional characteristics of teachers described earlier in this chapter?

Group Talk

## Research Citations

Bettencourt, E., Gillett, M., Gall, M., & Hull, R. (1983). Effects of teacher enthusiasm training on student on-task behavior and achievement. *American Educational Research Journal, 20,* 435–450.

Cotton, K. (1995). *Research you can use to improve results.* Alexandria, VA: Association for Supervision and Curriculum Development.

Daniels, H. & Bizar, M. (1998). *Methods that matter.* Portland, ME: Stenhouse.

Enz, B. J., Honaker, C, & Kortman, S. (2002). Trade secrets: Tips, tools and timesavers for middle/secondary teacher (2nd ed.). Dubuque, IA: Kendall/Hunt.

Enz, B. J., Hurwitz, S. & Carlile, B. J. (2005). *Coaching the student teacher: A developmental approach.* (3rd ed.). Dubuque, IA: Kendall/Hunt.

Enz, B. J., Kortman, S. & Honaker, C. (2001). Trade secrets: Tips, tools and timesavers for primary and elementary teacher (2nd ed.). Dubuque, IA: Kendall/Hunt.

Hunter, M. (1994). *Mastery teaching.* Thousand Oaks, CA: Corwin.

Kronowitz, E. (1999). *Your first year of teaching and beyond.* New York, NY: Addison-Wesley.

Lowman, J. (1996). Characteristics of exemplary teachers. *New Directions for Teaching and Learning, 65,* 33–40.

Marzano, R. J., Pickering, D. J., & Pollock, J. E. (2001). *Classroom Instruction that works: Research-based strategies for increasing student achievement.* Alexandria, VA: Association for Supervision and Curriculum Development.

Newmann, F. M. (1996). *Authentic achievement: restructuring schools for intellectual quality.* San Francisco, CA. Jossey-Bass.

Wong, H. K. & Wong, R. (2004). *The first days of school: How to be an effective teacher.* Mountain View, CA: Harry K. Wong.

## Additional Sources

Rice, J. K. (2003). *Teacher quality: Understanding the effectiveness of teacher attributes.* Washington, D.C.: Economic Policy Institute.

Wayne, A. M., & Young, P. (2003). Teacher characteristics and student achievement gains: A review. *Review of Educational Research, 73* (1), 89–122.

Wolfe, P. (1998). Revisiting effective teaching. *Educational Leadership, 56* (3), 61–64.

# Teacher as Politician

What does politics have to do with teaching? Everything! Because our public educational system is governed and funded by state and national governmental regulations, much of what you will do as a teacher will be a direct result of a politician's educational decisions. The amount of funding that your school has access to, the standards that frame your curriculum, and even the content of your instruction is very much guided through political policy.

Therefore, in your career as a teacher it is important for you to assume the role of "politician," so that you can not only understand the political nature of education in your community, but so that you can also become a policy leader in order to guide and change regulations. As stated in the quote below, teachers share the same political responsibilities as any citizen.

> *The role of a teacher, as an individual in politics, differs little from that of any other citizen. There are basic responsibilities in which all citizens share alike . . . A teacher has, with all mature citizens, the responsibility for law observance, for unfailing exercise of the privilege and duty of voting, and for taking active part in politics at the community level to the extent to which time will allow.*
> (R. R. Knutson)

In this section, we will be exploring the following issues as they relate to teaching and politics:

**Chapter 7: Politics in the School**

- Politics in Your Community
- Accountability and Academic Standards
- Standardized Testing
- School Funding
- School Branding

**Chapter 8: Politics in Your Community**

- Racial Equity
- Gender Equity
- Religion in Schools
- School Choice
- Home Schooling

In this section, we'll focus on current issues that relate to "schooling" in a broader sense, and how politics affects the advocacy decisions that you will be making on behalf of your school and your students. To be an effective advocate for your students, you need to fully understand the context in which you will be teaching on a political level.

# Politics in the School

**7**

In this chapter, we'll turn to those political issues that have the closet impact on the school itself; in Chapter 8, we'll broaden the political scope to include community issues. As you read through and discuss these two chapters, reflect on how these national issues may or may not be influencing policies in the communities where you live. Also reflect on your stance toward these issues, and how you might respond to them when you are in the classroom.

**Definitions**

**Adequate Yearly Progress (AYP)**   how a school's success or performance is measured under current "No Child Left Behind" legislation. This formula includes students' performance on state exams and attendance.

**Branding**   the practice of using product or brand names to provide funding for schools or other organizations. For example, schools use "branding" when they contract with specific soda companies to have exclusive rights to sell their products in the school.

**Constituents**   people who reside in a specific area, to whom you are often accountable. As a school teacher, your constituents will include parents, businesspeople, council members, and other residents in the community surrounding your district.

**Extracurricular Activities**   programs or activities that are in addition to a school's regular academic curriculum. Sports and clubs are examples of extracurricular school activities.

**Merit Pay**   extra pay that is received because of exceptional performance. In education, merit pay is typically determined by the academic performance of the teacher's students, and may also include a teacher's participation as a school leader or in mentoring.

**Politics**   n 1. relating to governance structure, 2. a point of view reflecting beliefs and values.

**Sight Words**   words that are used with the most frequency in our language. Early literacy instruction often focuses on sight word vocabulary. English sight words include *the, a, and, he, she, you, it, on, in,* and so on.

## As you read, think about . . .

★ When you think about "school politics," what current issues come to mind?

★ Think about the teachers you most admire. Which would be considered as political leaders? What issues do they support?

★ Think about your own political beliefs. How might these impact your decisions and actions in the classroom?

## Focus Questions

★ What are the types of standards that impact what teachers do in their curriculum and instruction? In their professional lives?

★ What is the role of standards in defining classroom curriculum?

★ How are standards used for accountability?

★ What is the difference between performance and content standards? What role does each play in planning curriculum?

★ What has been the impact of "No Child Left Behind" legislation on the lives of students and their teachers?

★ What impact does high-stakes testing have on students? On teachers and schools?

★ How are schools funding, and why is this a political issue?

# Politics in Your Community

What are the hottest educational issues in your community? And what are the issues that are being debated most vehemently in your state's legislature? As a teacher, it is very important that you keep up to date with those issues that are impacting the field of teaching. The decisions that are made in your school boards, within the state legislature, and even in the nation's capital will have a profound effect on what you will do in the classroom.

Sometimes, policy-driven changes are very supportive of effective practices in education, and clearly advocate for the needs of students. However, the reality is that many issues are politically motivated by individuals who may—or may not—have any background in education. Some even push certain agendas simply to gain votes for upcoming reelections or to gain favor with *constituents* by endorsing what might be controversial views of educational policies.

Does this sound cynical? It isn't intended to! However, political pressures and agendas are realities in the changing field of education. Therefore, you not only need to know what those agendas are, but you also need to have the most updated information on the issues so that you can debate them articulately with others. A teacher who is also a politician will be a formidable force for leadership in any school system.

*The political venue is not new to education. Refer back to the quote by Knutson that opened this section. When do you think this quote was written? A few years ago? More recently? It may come as a surprise, but this quote is actually from* **October of 1952,** *over half a century ago! Like many educational issues, teaching and politics has a long history in our country. As you read the next two chapters, look for the historical quotes. Are you surprised at how similar the concerns were at such a different time in our history? We suggest that you do some historical sleuthing yourself, and add to this fascinating look into our profession's political past.*

**Initial reflection: Current hot topics**   But where do we start in looking at current political issues? What is most impacting your communities and state? We have identified six distinct areas, which we'll discuss in more depth later in the next two chapters.

First, however, it would be useful for you to reflect on those issues that will be most closely impacting your future practices in the classroom. Take a few minutes to complete the "Group Talk" exercise. It would be most helpful to first fill out the **Hot Topics** (Figure 7.1) chart, based on articles in your newspaper or on your local news. What is politically hot where **you** live?

## Politics in Your Community

What are the hottest political topics in your community or state? Specifically, which issues impact schools and the education profession?

Before you meet in your discussion group, complete the **Political Issues** chart (Figure 7.1). Use local newspapers, newscasts, the Internet, or other media sources to determine which topics are getting the most "press" in your area. Then, discuss the following with your group:

- Which issues were most commonly identified amongst your group members?
- How do these specific issues impact teachers' performance in the classroom?
- What political agendas might be driving these decisions?
- As a teacher, what might you do to advocate for—or against—these issues? Where you do stand?

Now, look back at the beginning of this section where we list the School and Community issues that will be covered in the Chapters (page 181). How many of these issues are included on your group's list? Which of your community's issues are therefore also reflected in the broader context of our national politics?

| Figure 7.1 ↓ Political Issues in Your Community | | | |
|---|---|---|---|
| **Political Hot Topics** | | | |
| **Issue** | **Political Ties** | **Your Stand** | **Group's Stand** |
|  |  |  |  |
|  |  |  |  |
|  |  |  |  |
|  |  |  |  |

# Accountability and Academic Standards

Read any educational news story or article today, and two of the most common buzzwords that you will encounter will likely be *accountability* and *standards*. What is all the fuss about? What do these terms really mean, particularly in the context of day-to-day teaching?

Simply stated, *accountability* refers to holding public educators accountable—or responsible—for teaching the essential material of the curriculum. Accountability describes the process of connecting incentives and supports to results (Gandal & Vranek, 2001). *Performance-based accountability,* or tying the teacher's responsibility to how they actually *perform* in the classroom—is designed with the purpose of ensuring that all students will master crucial knowledge and skills (Hess, 2003).

The term *standards* refers to a set group of objectives that teachers must teach to in order to be accountable. There are many sets of educational standards, including the following:

- **Academic standards**—these outline what students should learn across content and across grade level. These can include:

  - *State standards*—these set the guidelines for your classroom curriculum.

  - *National standards*—these are set by professional groups and are often used as the basis for the state standards. Organizations such as the International Reading Association, National Council for Teachers of Mathematics, National Science Teachers Association, and National Council for Teachers of English are just a few of the organizations that develop content standards (see also Chapter 12 for more information on standards).

- **Professional standards**—these outline what teachers should know and be able to do in order to be successful in the classroom. These also include:

  - *State professional standards*—which are often used as the basis for your state's licensure exam and/or licensure renewal.

  - *National standards*—which, like the content standards, are often used to guide in the development of state standards. Standards from the Interstate New Teacher Assessment and Support Consortium (INTASC), which were discussed in Chapter 5, and the National Board for Professional Teaching Standards (NBPTS), which will be discussed further in Chapter 12, are perhaps the most common national standards for teachers.

Professional standards were discussed in the previous chapter, as they related to certification and licensure. *Academic standards* are the focus for this chapter.

Gandal and Vranek (2001) provide the following elements to describe appropriate academic standards.

### Academic standards:

- Define what students should learn each year
- Are simultaneously reasonable and rigorous
- Are achievable by all students
- Represent the skills and knowledge that are essential to student learning
- Need to be teachable
- Must be clear, with enough detail and precision so that students, teachers, and parents know what students need to learn

These concepts are politicized when the public desire for accountability drives the need for standards. Teachers' ability to prove their accountability is reflected in how well they implement their state's required standards. This "proof" is often provided through standardized testing—which we will explore next in this chapter. The goal of the standards and accountability movement is to help all students achieve at high levels of knowledge and skill.

**Standards in the classroom**   As a classroom teacher, it is critical that you become very familiar with your state's academic or content standards. Your district's curriculum will be based on these standards. It is also very likely that your performance evaluation will be based on how well these standards are implemented and learned by your students.

States do require that teachers follow the standards in their instruction. Some states are very explicit in their directions regarding standards. Compare the following statements, found on state Department of Education web sites (Figure 7.2), and jot down your responses to the following questions.

1. When comparing the states' definitions of standards, which components are similar?
2. How do these states differ in their descriptions of standards?

**Figure 7.2   ↓ Sampling State Standards**

**Student Performance Standards (Kentucky)**

In June, 2001, the Kentucky Board of Education accepted new performance standards that resulted from a comprehensive process involving more than 1,600 Kentucky teachers, various advisory groups, and which provided for public input.

These new standards set the stage for the work that lies ahead of Kentucky's educators: To improve the academic achievement of all our students.

The new standards are important because they define what we mean when we say a student has performed at the "novice," "apprentice," "proficient" or "distinguished" level. They clarify for teachers, students and parents how we evaluate student work, and they explain for students what we expect of them.

*http://www.education.ky.gov*

**Academic Standards (Ohio)**

Clearly defined statements and/or illustrations of what all students, teachers, schools, and school districts are expected to know and be able to do. Educators generally discuss three types of standards—**Content Standards, Performance Standards, and Operating Standards.**

***Content Standards***—describe the *knowledge and skills* that students should attain - often called the "what" of "what students should know and be able to do." They indicate the ways of thinking, working, communicating, reasoning, and investigating the important and enduring ideas, concepts, issues, dilemmas, and knowledge essential to the discipline.

***Performance Standards***—are concrete statements of *how well* students must learn *what* is set out in the content standards - often called the "be able to do" of "what students should know and be able to do." Performance standards specify "how good is good enough." They are the indicators of quality that specify how adept or competent a student demonstration must be.

***Operating Standards***—describe the conditions for learning. These can include specific expectations and additional guidelines for school districts, communities, and families to use in creating the best learning conditions for meeting student needs and achieving state and local educational goals and objectives.

*http://www.ode.state.oh.us/academic_content_standards*

**State Learning Standards (New York)**

At the approach of the twenty-first century, the Board of Regents approved a new set of learning standards for all students in New York State. They represent the core of what all people should know, understand and be able to do as a result of their schooling. As such, these learning standards are to form the basis for a re-vision of education in New York.

With this re-vision, students may expect an intellectually powerful education no matter where they live; in which teaching, assessment, and the provision of supports for learning are to be closely linked; and in which schools and parents share the same high expectations of youngsters.

Learning standards have two primary dimensions. Content standards describe what students should know, understand and be able to do. Performance standards define levels of student achievement pertaining to content. However, the teaching and learning which takes place in between is the heart of the matter. This addresses opportunity to learn standards and is, perhaps, the most crucial element of the entire process.

*http://www.emsc.nysed.gov/ciai/describe.html*

*3.* How does your state define standards (check your state's Department of Education web site)?

*4.* Based on your analysis of state descriptions, how would you define academic standards?

> *The realization of objectives is an intimate process of social change that involves reorientation of teacher perspectives based upon new knowledge that is carefully worked into the culture of the school (and community!) . . .*
>
>       *. . . the person who realizes educational objectives at the classroom level—meaning the teacher—must be intimately involved in the entire process of change.* (Shaftel, 1957, pgs. 297, 298)

Generally speaking, state academic standards have the following elements in common:

**Standards. . . .**

- Define what students know and are able to do
- Are tied to student performance
- Describe the conditions for student learning
- Set high expectations for *all* students
- Are intended to improve students' academic achievement
- Tie together the processes of teaching and learning
- Form the backbone for a district's curriculum
- Are closely aligned with a state's accountability system—especially through standardized testing

## Standards in Action

What do these standards look like in an actual classroom? First, consider the vignette below, which describes a second-grade reading lesson:

### Reading Lesson

Mr. Landers and his students are gathered at the reading corner, which houses his classroom library. This library includes books on many reading levels and topics, to accommodate for the many reading levels and interests of his students. He is also very careful to include a variety of genre in his classroom library—including nonfiction and poetry.

The book that Mr. Landers is reading today is about the solar system, which is also the topic for his afternoon science lesson. Before reading the book, the class had generated a variety of questions about the solar system that they hoped the book would answer. These questions are listed on a chart, also located in the reading corner. Mr. Landers reviews these questions with the class. As he previews the book, Mr. Landers asks if this section would be considered fiction or nonfiction. He also points out the author's use of bold print when introducing new terms, which are repeated in the book's glossary. These words will be added to the class Solar System vocabulary list.

At the conclusion of the book, Mr. Landers and the class return to their initial question chart. Mr. Landers transcribes their responses, as the students provide answers based on the book's contents. Mr. Landers also uses this time to review concepts that the class has previously studied. For example, he draws their attention to the plural of sky [skies], which has an irregular spelling pattern. On a new chart paper, the class generates a list of other words that follow this pattern [e.g., flies, spies]. ■

**Classroom Glimpse**

How many reading standards are included in this brief lesson? Using state standards from Arizona for Grade 2 reading, we found the following:

- Recognize plurals and irregular plurals
- Ask relevant questions in order to comprehend text
- Identify differences between fiction and nonfiction
- Locate facts in response to questions about expository text
- Locate specific information by using organizational features in expository text
- Recognize high frequency words and irregular *sight words*

**Think About It**

How similar are your state standards to those identified above? What is missing from our list that might be included in your state?

Although it's useful to match standards to an existing lesson, as we had you do when reading this vignette, it is important to remember that teachers need to **start** with the standards. Standards provide the guidance from which a lesson evolves.

## Politics and State Standards—The NCLB Issue

As we have explored, academic standards provide the framework for a teacher's instruction. But why is that considered a political issue? The answer lies in the evolution of the standards movement. Although good teaching has always evolved from a teacher's understanding of what his/her students are to know and do—or knowledge of standards—the difference today is that these standards are being initiated and enforced from **outside** of the classroom. Because of an increased focus by the public on accountability, the public has demanded the creation of uniform standards against which teachers and their students can be measured.

The movement toward standards-based reform began in the 1990s, which gave rise to state-level accountability systems. The standards and accountability movement today is perhaps most notably defined through *"No Child Left Behind" (NCLB),* which was legislated in January of 2002 (see Figure 7.3 for a NCLB primer). NCLB was generated by politicians and enacted at a national level, and marks an important departure from the federal government's role in education by moving decision-making from a local to a national level (Abrams & Madaus, 2003). In essence, NCLB made performance-based education accountability a federal mandate. At its heart, NCLB requires that schools and teachers enact a mission that "all children can learn."

Mandates associated with NCLB include accountability and testing requirements that substantially increase student testing and hold all schools and their teachers accountable for student performance. NCLB requires states to meet **adequate yearly progress (AYP)** to insure that schools are accountable for student achievement on state tests (a more in-depth look at standardized testing is included in this chapter). Schools that fail to meet these AYP goals face corrective actions, which can include removing school faculty, implementing new curriculum, extending the school day and/or year, giving parents choices to send their children to other schools, or completely dismantling the failing school (Abrams & Madaus, 2003). These are very serious consequences for schools, and their teachers!

This legislation has had very concrete impacts on what teachers teach, how students are assessed, and how "success" is defined. These decisions were made at the political level, with very little consultation with educators—particularly classroom teachers.

NCLB, and the standards movement overall, does have positive influences on the learning process, including (Gandal & Vranek, 2001; Hess, 2003):

- Ensuring that all students will master crucial knowledge and skills
- Holding public educators accountable for teaching essential material
- Giving schools and districts the incentive to seek out and cultivate excellence
- Holding schools and their personnel accountable for the success of their students, and providing the mechanism for closing those schools that are not successful

**Figure 7.3** ↓ **NCLB Primer**

**NCLB—No Child Left Behind.** The NCLB Act, which reauthorized the Elementary and Secondary Education Act, became law in 2001 and was enacted in January of 2002. *No Child Left Behind (ESEA,* Title II) provides federal funding to states and districts for activities that will strengthen teacher quality in all schools, especially those with a high proportion of children in poverty. It requires that all children in America learn at grade level by 2014. It requires states to label schools as "meeting standards" or "failing" based on standardized test scores. NCLB reform is based on the following four "pillars":

- *Stronger accountability for results*
  - Closing the achievement gap and making sure all students, including those who are disadvantaged, achieve academic proficiency.
  - Requiring annual state and school district report cards to inform parents and communities about state and school progress through reports on *adequate yearly progress.*
  - Requiring that schools that do not make progress provide supplemental services, such as free tutoring or after-school assistance; take corrective actions; and, if still not making adequate yearly progress after five years, make dramatic changes to the way the school is run.
  - Requiring that schools hire only those teachers who are *highly qualified* in their content.
- *More freedom for states and communities*
  - Providing states and school districts with increased flexibility in how they use federal education funds.
  - Allowing districts to use funds for their particular needs, such as hiring new teachers, increasing teacher pay, and improving teacher training and professional development.
- *Encouraging proven education methods*
  - Emphasizing educational programs and practices that have been proven effective through rigorous *scientifically-based research.*
  - Targeting federal funding to support these programs and teaching methods that work to improve student learning and achievement.
- *More choices for parents*
  - Providing parents of children in low-performing schools with increased options in where to send their child.
  - Allowing parents to transfer their children to a better-performing public school, including a public charter school, within their district if their neighborhood school does not meet state standards for at least two consecutive years.
  - Providing students from low-income families in schools that fail to meet state standards for at least three years with supplemental educational services, including tutoring, after-school services, and summer school.

**AYP—Adequate Yearly Progress.** AYP is a key component to the NCLB law. Schools are required to demonstrate that 95% of their students have met AYP goals, which are largely based on student attendance and standardized test scores. Districts are also accountable for AYP goals.

**Highly Qualified Teachers.** NCLB requires local school districts to ensure that all teachers hired to teach core academic subjects in Title I programs are highly qualified. Requirements for "highly qualified teachers" include:

- full certification,
- a bachelor's degree,
- and demonstrated competence in subject knowledge and teaching. (Core subjects include English, reading or language arts, mathematics, science, foreign languages, civics and government, economics, arts, history and geography.)

**Scientifically-Based Research.** NCLB supports those curricular programs that are found to be effective through research that is empirically based. Specifically, it supports research that uses quantitative methodology and has randomized control and treatment groups in its design. Randomized controlled trials are studies that randomly assign individuals to an intervention group or to a control group, in order to measure the effects of the intervention.

**Think About It**

How does your community feel about NCLB, and its related accountability mandates? This is one political issue that certainly has caught the attention of the public and media. It is useful to search through your local newspapers to ascertain how it is impacting schools in your community. Politically speaking, where does your community stand in regards to NCLB?

- Expecting a richer and more challenging curriculum
- Creating more productive dialogue between educators and parents
- Focusing everyone's attention on student achievement

However, there are many critics of standards, and particularly of how this movement is implemented through current politics. Some contend that it is the single largest nationalization of education policy in our country's history (Elmore, 2003). Other criticisms of NCLB and its associated mandates include (Elmore, 2003; Harvey, 2003):

- Creating an artificial learning environment that bears little resemblance to the real work of schools
- Setting goals that are unrealistic
- Not providing adequate funding to implement associated mandates (such as requirements for state testing) by either federal or state allocations
- Losing local control by moving educational decisions as far as possible from the classroom
- Using single test scores to determine what students know and are able to do
- Basing educational decisions on ungrounded theories of improvement and reform
- Perverting incentives for quality and performance and using federal funding as leverage for prescribed change

**Group Talk**

## Content Standards

Effective lessons *begin* with clear content standards. Standards provide the framework from which teachers plan their instructional activities. Consider the list of content standards for a Grade 6 social studies lesson, taken from the *Texas Essential Knowledge and Skills.*

If you were required to teach these standards, how might you construct a lesson that would motivate and interest your students? After you jot down your lesson ideas, discuss your plans with your group.

- Was this process easy, or difficult? Why or why not?
- In what ways were your lessons similar? Different?
- What are the best elements of your group's lesson ideas?
- What assessments might you use to determine if your student learned the standards that were presented to them? (accountability!)

### Content Standards (Grade 6 Social Studies):

- The student understands that historical events influence contemporary events
- The student uses maps, globes, graphs, charts, models, and databases to answer geographic questions
- The student understands the impact of interactions between people and the physical environment on the development of places and regions
- The student applies critical-thinking skills to organize and use information acquired from a variety of sources including electronic technology

### Lesson Ideas

- Introducing the Lesson:

- Engaging the Students:

- Closing the Lesson:

- Assessing the Standards:

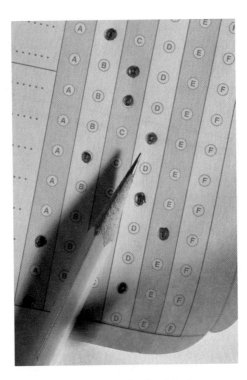

Well constructed standardized test can provide useful information to guide instruction and support student success.

# Standardized Testing

Integral to the accountability and standards movement is a renewed and quite vigorous interest in *standardized testing*. Standardized testing refers to those assessment tools that are standard, or uniform, for a body of students. Standardized tests provide a consistent way of measuring progress so that educators and parents know if students are meeting required standards.

Standardized tests are most often grouped into the following categories:

- *Norm-referenced tests*—measure how an individual scores as compared to other students
- *Criterion-referenced tests*—measure how well an individual compares to a standard or set of established criteria

Because they are most often given to large numbers of students, standardized tests typically use a multiple-choice format in order to facilitate the process of scoring and analysis. This format can be problematic, however, because it typically doesn't allow students to demonstrate higher-level skills, such as creative problem solving. The test would be able to determine if students knew the correct *definition* of an electric charge, for example, but not if a student could actually *construct* a working circuit.

Standardized tests not only are used to measure an individual student's achievement or ability, but also are often used to determine how accountable a school's curriculum is to its predetermined standards. Therefore, the tests are ideally tied directly to those standards. Because of regulations in the NCLB law, states are establishing statewide tests that are directly aligned with their content standards. Specifically, NCLB requires that public schools in every state assess students in reading and math on an annual basis in Grades 3 to 8, and again before they graduate from high school. The content of science will be added to the testing process in 2007.

Not all standardized tests are the same in terms of quality. When poorly constructed, they can become a distraction and source of frustration for students and their teachers. When well designed, however, they can provide useful information to guide instruction and support student success. Gandal and Vranek (2001) suggest that effective and appropriate tests should:

1. Be tied **directly to standards**
2. **Include high-level concepts** in order to tap breadth and depth of content and skills
3. **Become more challenging** in each successive grade

## High-Stakes Testing

Some standardized tests, such as the state tests described above, are often referred to as *high-stakes tests*. This refers to the potential consequences associated with failure on the tests. For example, your state's teaching certification exam is a high-stakes test. If you fail this test, you won't be eligible for certification!

Similarly, state testing has its share of consequences. For example, some districts will not promote a student to the next grade level if they fail to pass the state exam. Many are also using the state test to determine if students receive their high school diploma. In other words, students would be denied a diploma even in those cases when they receive passing scores in all their high school coursework.

For districts and their teachers, the stakes are high as well. Schools must report their test scores to the state, and scores are publicly reported. If you check your state's Department of Education web site, you will more than likely see the test reports from schools across your state.

These standardized tests are used to "label" schools as successful or failing. In Arizona, for example, the state uses the following labels to classify its public schools:

- Excelling
- Highly Performing
- Performing
- Underperforming
- Failing

Most states, however, simply label schools as "Meeting Adequate Yearly Progress" or "Not Meeting Adequate Yearly Progress." In other states, schools are given a letter grade, with those falling below a D designated as Needing Improvement. These labels are published in local newspapers, on district websites, and on the state's Department of Education web site. The labels are therefore easily accessible to anyone—including realtors who use this information to influence home sales!

What do the consequences of these labels look like in action? Figure 7.4. **AYP and Consequences for Schools** provides an overview of the consequences that can occur if schools continue to be unsuccessful in producing students who perform well on the state exams—or who don't make *adequate yearly progress*. These are based on reports from the state of Arizona. How different—or similar—are these consequences for districts in your own communities?

> *There are a number of sources to which curriculum planners can turn for evidence useful in making decisions about the broad outlines of the instructional program. One of the sources is the body of data that can be accumulated about the students. To be genuinely useful for making important decisions such data would need to include more than achievement test scores, important as these results may be. Interests, attitudes, values, vocational plans, home backgrounds, out-of-school activities, are among the items upon which helpful information can be collected. (Rehage, 1956, pg. 416)*

## Teaching to the Test

It can be argued that, with the implementation of NCLB, test taking has become more pervasive in our classrooms (e.g., Amrein & Berliner, 2003), and that these tests in fact distract teachers away from their "real" job of teaching. Because of the consequences of low test scores—including negative labels for schools, potential loss of teacher's *merit pay*, and even

## Figure 7.4   ↓ AYP and Consequences for Schools

Consequences for Schools Not Making Adequate Yearly Progress (AYP)

| | Arizona's Consequences | Consequences in Your State |
|---|---|---|
| *Year 1* | No Consequences | |
| *Year 2* | School Improvement<br>• Develop improvement plan<br>• Notify families of school's status<br>• Offer option to transfer<br>• District provides technical assistance | |
| *Year 3* | School Improvement<br>• Revise improvement plan<br>• Notify families of school's status<br>• Offer option to transfer<br>• District provides technical assistance<br>• Offer eligible students supplemental services | |
| *Year 4* | Corrective Action<br>• Revise improvement plan<br>• Notify families of school's status<br>• Offer option to transfer<br>• District provides technical assistance<br>• Offer supplemental services<br>• Choose at least one corrective action to implement | |
| *Year 5* | Restructuring<br>• Revise improvement plan<br>• Notify families of school's status<br>• Offer option to transfer<br>• District provides technical assistance<br>• Offer supplemental services<br>• Choose corrective action<br>• Develop restructuring plan | |
| *Year 6* | Restructuring<br>• Implement restructuring plan | |

the possibility of losing a job—teachers often feel pressured by their community and administrators to insure that their students excel. This leads to what we often refer to as "teaching to the test," or concentrating the curriculum solely on the isolated facts or information that will be covered on a high-stakes test.

It is of course important to insure that your students do well on tests, particularly if there are consequences to them or your school if they fail. But how do you balance between preparing students for the test and engaging in unethical practices to insure high scores?

Consider the vignette, below, which is taken from an experience that one of Bette's college students faced.

What would you do if you were in Suzette's position? As much as we all would like to "bend the rules" a bit to insure that our students are successful—particularly those who might be at risk and at an unfair disadvantage—Suzette would more than likely be breaking the law if she followed through with her teacher's requests. However, how fair is the testing situation if children who are learning English can only have the test question read once—if at all?

What can you do to avoid a similar situation? We would recommend the following:

### Proper Testing Procedures

- Make sure you are very familiar with the testing requirements for your state.
- Ask your host teacher if it would be permissible for you to read the instructor's manual before the test is administered. This will provide guidance for the level of assistance that can be offered during the testing administration.
- Make sure you are clear about the level of assistance that can be offered to English Language Learners and to students who are receiving special education services.

**Classroom Glimpse**

### High-Stakes Testing

Suzette was a college sophomore, and was completing her first field experience in a high school math class. The high school was located in an urban center, and the families of most of the students were struggling economically. The student population also reflected a high percentage of non-English speakers who had recently immigrated to the community.

Suzette's primary responsibility during her internship was to assist students who struggled with assignments and to observe the teacher's practices to learn effective management techniques. She found that she really enjoyed working with these at-risk students, and had developed a very positive rapport with them.

During one of Suzette's class visits, the students were taking the state's high-stakes graduation test. Her host teacher asked Suzette to erase any stray marks on the test booklets, fill in bubbles on incomplete exams, and to assist non-English-speaking students by rereading the exam directions. The teacher explained to Suzette that this would help insure that students in this school were not penalized unnecessarily because of their unfamiliarity with formal testing procedures. The teacher made it very clear, however, not to directly tell any students the answers to any test questions.

Suzette needed to have a good grade in her interning so that she could continue into the teacher preparation program, and she also wanted to make sure that the students were as successful as possible with this critical exam so that they could be eligible to graduate from high school. However, she suspected that what she was being asked to do was not in compliance with the state's testing procedures. Should she advocate for the students by assisting them on the exam, or support the state's rulings regarding the proper administration of the exam? ■

- If you suspect you are being asked to do something improper, ask your teacher first for clarification. Perhaps you misunderstood your teacher's request.
- If the teacher persists in his/her questionable demand, request that your university place you in another classroom immediately. Report the teacher's actions to your university supervisor.

**High-stakes testing as public policy**    Even prior to the adoption of NCLB mandates, the use of high-stakes testing has been on the rise in this country. Just in your own pursuit of a teaching degree, you will have taken—or need to take—an assortment of tests that could include:

- American College Testing (ACT) or Scholastic Aptitude Test (SAT) to get into college
- Test of English as a Foreign Language (TOEFL) if you are a non-native English speaker
- College placement exams, particularly for math and reading
- Pre-Professional Skills Test (PPST) or a Professional Assessment of Beginning Teachers (such as PRAXIS) to get into teacher education
- Exit exam from your teacher education program
- State Licensure exam in order to be certified

How do high-stakes tests impact the students who take them? Supporters of high-stakes tests contend that these assessment benefit the educational system and policy by (Gandal & McGiffert, 2003; Gandal & Vranek, 2001; Heubert, 2002/2003):

- Changing the nature of teaching and learning
- Focusing attention on the achievement of students
- Fostering the development of richer, more challenging curriculum
- Adding significant value to school improvement efforts
- Articulating the same high expectations for every student
- Providing information on where students and schools need to improve
- Providing the incentives for making necessary improvements
- Identifying and addressing students' learning needs
- Providing a lever to improve both teaching and learning

Conversely, critics of high-stakes testing argue that this practice has the following negative impacts on students and schooling (Abrams & Madaus, 2003; Amrein & Berliner, 2003; Heubert, 2002/2003; Neill, 2003):

- Increasing the risk of low-achieving students to leave school without a high school diploma, therefore diminishing opportunities for future economic success
- Disadvantaging some groups of students over others, particularly in relation to ethnicity, disability, income, and language
- Distracting educators away from central learning objectives
- Increasing the likelihood that teachers will "teach to the test"
- Defining curriculum solely by what is covered on the test
- Pressuring teachers to raise test scores, no matter the means
- Providing an incomplete and inaccurate picture of what an individual student knows and can do
- Increasing teachers' control over the learning experience to the expense of students' own directed learning

---

**Figure 7.5   ↓ Strategies for Success**

**Positive Solutions to the High-Stakes Challenge:**

✓ Establish and insist on high expectations for all of your students; make sure that you provide students with explicit definitions of those expectations

✓ Become very familiar with your state's academic standards, and insure that your instruction directly aligns with what is expected for your grade and content

✓ Be politically savvy—keep in tune with what is being said and written about high-stakes testing in your community, and how to separate opinion from actual policy

✓ Get to know your students—make adjustments and accommodations so that students will be successful

✓ Learn how to interpret test data and use that information in planning your instruction

✓ Avoid the temptation to narrow your curriculum to "fit" the test; instead, employ high-level thinking and performance activities with your students (which will in turn *improve* their test scores)

✓ Use multiple forms of assessments in your classroom, and share results regularly with students and their caregivers; make the case that wise decisions are made from *many sources* and not a single test

✓ Provide students with opportunities to become familiar with the construction of the test, but avoid taking valuable instructional time to work through drill and skill booklets

✓ Collaborate with your school administrator and other teachers to develop effective strategies for curricular improvement—based on standards and best instructional practices

✓ Work on state committees to insure that what is on state tests is aligned with standards that are appropriate for your students' grade level and content

---

**Think About It**

What other solutions can you and your classmates suggest to insure success in a high-stakes environment? How do teachers in your community feel about high-stakes testing? Use the interview in Figure 7.6 to discover how high-stakes assessment is affecting teaching and learning in P-12 schools near you.

- Reducing time scheduled for art, music, and physical education
- Decreasing student motivation
- Increasing the proportion of students who drop out of high school
- Propelling teachers to leave the profession

Wherever you might stand on high-stakes testing, be assured that this is one hot political issue that will impact you—and your students—into the foreseeable future!

**Finding solutions**   Because high-stakes testing will be an inevitable part of your expectations and accountability as a classroom teacher, it is important for you to develop strategies so that you—and your students—can be successful. Figure 7.5. **Strategies for Success** provides some solutions to this politically charged mandate.

> *From his continuing contacts with each pupil, the teacher can achieve a knowledge and an understanding that will far surpass that obtainable from any test battery no matter how it is administered. With this understanding, the teacher is in the most effective position to bring to realization the intellectual potential of each child. . . . . A score or a report upon a test is something sterile. Grave consequences can stem from accepting mental measurement as the last word . . .*
> *Make the tester prove the score.* (Brown, 1957, pgs. 162, 165)

# School Funding

Where does school funding come from? When one of our colleagues raised this question to students in an Introduction to Education course, the response was, "through bake sales!" If that were indeed the case, education would certainly be in dire straits today!

**Figure 7.6** ↓ **Teacher Interview: High-Stakes Testing**

*Directions:* How do teachers in your community feel about issues related to high-stakes tests? Interview a teacher in your neighborhood to find the answers to the following questions.

Teacher's name

Teacher's level

How long has the teacher been teaching?          How long at this level?

1. What types of high-stakes tests are used in this teacher's district?


2. What are the purposes of these tests?


3. What is his/her view on high-stakes tests?


4. What does this teacher see as the benefits of high-stakes testing?


5. The disadvantages or challenges of high-stakes testing?


6. How are student scores used by the school or district?


7. In addition to high-stakes testing, how does this teacher collect more comprehensive information about student performance?


8. How does this teacher explain student achievement to families or caregivers?


9. What advice would this teacher give to novices in regards to high-stakes testing and accountability?

Keeping up with the computer and telecommunications revolution can drain a school district's funding.

School funding, as we will explore, actually comes from a variety of sources. Bake sales, car washes, and rummage sales do help, in that they support a variety of *extracurricular activities* and programs. Be assured, however, that the bulk of funding for *public* education comes from the taxpayer. States allocate funding to a school on a per pupil basis, which is supplemented by federal agencies targeted at very specific programs or populations. When looking at the total funding picture, however, the vast majority of a school's budget relies directly on local property taxes.

But how is funding a political issue? By focusing on accountability, standards-based education is pushing districts and schools to more clearly define their goals and priorities for student learning. Appropriate budget choices, in turn, are clearly aligned with stated district/school goals. Funding is also tied to accountability and student performance. Teachers who have high-performing students, as measured on state exams, may receive more money through merit pay. Schools that are labeled as low performing may receive funding for specific programs—or may lose their funding entirely if they are forced to close.

School funding is also political in terms of how budgets are distributed across districts and states. In some states, schools receive part of their funding through the tax base of their constituents. Therefore, schools in high-income areas receive a higher level of funding than their low-income neighbors. These inequities often lead to widening gaps in the educational experiences of low- and high-income students, and heated political battles in the legislature. Shouldn't students receive the same level of funding, regardless of where they live? Or should communities decide what level of financial support they are willing to provide their own children?

## The Downside of School Funding

One of the primary areas of concern as it relates to education budgeting is the increasing practice of *unfunded mandates.* When laws are adopted that impact educational policy, the funding to implement the required changes often does not accompany these changes. Cetron and

Classroom Glimpse

## School Funding

To improve math scores in the third grade, a critical year for state testing, the Brookside School District decided to adopt a new textbook which the school administrators believed was better aligned with state and federal curriculum standards. These texts were, indeed, a better curricular match with the state math standards.

However, the district's limited funding only allowed for the purchase of the texts themselves, and did not allow the district to purchase the $1,000 worth of manipulatives, per class, which were critical to the success of this math program.

As a third-grade teacher, what would you do? ■

Cetron (2003/2004) point to the underfunding of initiatives as they relate to NCLB as a demonstration of the government's inability to adequately supply sufficient resources to support its reforms.

Many educators believe that the increased requirements for state testing, for example, are not appropriately funded by the federal policymakers that enacted this legislation. School boards can also be guilty of unfunded mandates, by requiring that certain curriculum be implemented without providing schools with increased revenue to insure that the new requirements are put into place. Ramirez (2002/2003) argues that unfunded mandates divert money to specialized programs that could have been better used in the classroom or in increasing teacher pay. Consider, for example, the vignette above.

The dilemma faced by Brookside is unfortunately all too common. Often, schools are given a mandate (such as increased test scores) and suggestions on how to address the mandate (such as adopting certain required curriculum), but are not provided the financial means for making these changes happen in the classroom.

Ramirez (2002) also suggests that the computer and telecommunications revolution has consumed vast amounts of schools' funding. In their attempt to "keep up," districts have poured large amounts of money into technology infrastructure, equipment, software, and training with little or no support from state or federal governments. Ironically, while these changes have led to improved access to technology for students and their teachers, there is inconclusive evidence that technology in itself leads to either improved learning and teaching or to improved test scores.

Some argue that national deficits are also a threat to our education system, as they lead to further reductions in federal assistance to states and cities. These reductions can have serious consequences for public schools, and may force local taxpayers to absorb more of the education budget (Cetron & Cetron, 2003/2004). Reductions in funding make it increasingly challenging for schools to maintain even their most important programs.

As frustrating as this dilemma is today for schools and their teachers, the issue of school funding is a long-standing problem that has been faced by many generations of educators. Box 7.1 explores a very current topic and challenge—inequities in public school funding.

*The problem of achieving a more adequate level of state support for schools is the No. 1 problem in American education. Without adequate funds it is impossible to provide educational services of acceptable quality. Everything associated with good education is directly related to the level of financial support . . . The resulting inequalities of educational opportunities, inequal tax burdens, and the general low level of education are to be observed in every state.*
(Pryor, 1950, p. 335)

## Box 7.1  ↓ Funding Inequities

### Special Feature by Conrado Gomez

Different states throughout the country have made attempts at equalizing funding among districts within their particular jurisdictions. Success in these attempts varies from state to state. As can be seen in the synopsis of one state's funding practices, the system is far from equitable. And as a result, a great portion of the state's student population gets the brunt of a system that favors one segment of the population.

Arizona public schools operate under the "equalized" finance system that limits the individual school district's expenditures through a "weighted student count" formula. The "weights" include such variables as district size, location, grade levels, and special education. The limit on the Maintenance and Operation (M & O) expenditures budget is derived from the "weighted student count." M & O, through its limitation, is the main source of funding for Arizona public schools.

The "equalization" process purports to guarantee that all Arizona school districts access their expenditure limit. However, there are some factors that allow funding to be disproportional from district to district. Take for instance the legal proviso available to school districts to appeal to their voters to approve a budget override to be funded from local property tax levies. Traditionally, poor school districts have been unable to get support from voters to pass budget overrides. Wealthier districts, however, generally embrace budget overrides. Parents in these wealthier districts see the advantages of the additional funds coming to their children's schools. Developers and real estate agents, on the other hand, benefit by the appeal that strong schools have on newcomers searching for a place to live.

Another factor that plays a role in the inequality of funding between districts is the juxtaposition of Average Daily Membership—ADM—and Average Daily Attendance—ADA—in the final funding school allocations. The Arizona Revised Statutes define ADM as the total enrollment of each school day through the first 100 days. ADA is calculated by dividing the total membership days of all students by the total number of days in the reporting period. ADM, on the other hand, is the actual average daily attendance through the first 100 days in session for the current school year. ADA is calculated by subtracting the total absence days from the total membership days and dividing that by the total number of days in the reporting period. The end result of factoring in the ADA into the formula is that school districts plagued by poor student attendance are directly impacted in the M & O funding they get. Generally speaking, poorer families have less access to medical care than wealthier families can afford. This access to medical care impacts the amount of time a child is absent as a result of an illness.

Several years ago, the Arizona state legislature approved tax credits for public schools to be used for enrichment activities that usually depend on fees from students. Taxpayers are allowed a tax credit of up to $250 which is subtracted directly from the amount of taxes they owe the state. Even though taxpayers get this money back when they file for income tax returns, they must be able to afford being without this money for a few months. Wealthier taxpayers can afford it; poorer taxpayers cannot. As a result, wealthier districts can offer many more enrichment activities such as field trips, after-school sports, after-school activities, and summer school than poorer school districts cannot afford.

Budget overrides, better student attendance, and tax credits give wealthier districts an advantage over poorer school districts to offer more and better quality programs for their students. As a result, poorer districts lack the funds to implement the types of programs that their students so desperately need. Since many parents in the poorer school districts lack the political clout that wealthier district possess, institutional change is not likely to take place any time soon. Meanwhile, poorer school districts lag further behind in academics—to no fault of their own.

## Funding and Teacher Quality

Unfortunately, inequities or inadequacies in school funding also can lead to inequities in teacher quality. While we would hope that all students, regardless of the community in which they live, have access to the same quality of instruction—the realities are staggering:

### Teacher Quality Inequities

- Our most disadvantaged students often have the most ineffective and inexperienced teachers.
- Poor and minority children are considerably more likely to have uncertified "emergency" teachers, or those teaching out of their area of content expertise.
- In high-poverty schools, approximately thirty percent of core academic subjects are taught by teachers who lack the certification to teach in those subjects.
- Students who attend high-poverty schools are also more likely to have novice teachers, or those with three or fewer years of experience.
- Minority students and those from low-income backgrounds are more likely to have teachers who themselves were unsuccessful on high-stakes exams, such as college admissions tests and teacher licensure exams (Haycock, 2002/2003).

Why does this matter? It matters because the most important factor in a student's learning experience is the teacher who is in the classroom. If low-income or minority students are denied the highest quality teachers, then they are also denied the same quality of experience as their more affluent peers.

Although part of the problem is with funding—low-income schools have less of a tax base, and therefore a smaller funding source for schools—the problem also lies within our profession. Too often, teachers "reward" themselves by moving into schools and neighborhoods that are more prestigious. Unfortunately, our professional culture too often links teacher status with the elite backgrounds of their students.

> In a teacher-shortage study, the U.S. Office of Education points out that teacher shortages may cause fully as much damage to the American schools through lowered standards of teacher competency as through the actual closing of classrooms. . . . Of the many remedies suggested for taking care of the growing teacher deficit, providing higher salaries is believed to hold greatest promise . . .
>
> In the coming school year, tens of thousands of America's children will suffer from the closing of classrooms and the employment of incompetent teachers. Their educational opportunity is being reduced more drastically than any mere statistics on teacher shortages or lower qualifications standards might reflect. [Dawson, 1943, pg. 7, 8]

## What Can Be Done?

As future teachers, it is your generation that can make the difference in the quality of instruction for those students who most need your expertise. You will make some degree of impact no matter what school you choose—but you will make a *tremendous* and *far-reaching* impact if you choose to teach in those schools that most need qualified teachers! We've included some political advocacy hints to make this difference in Figure 7.7.

It is quite possible that your teacher education program offers options to intern in high-need schools or urban areas, or offers special programs to volunteer with students at risk. (See Figure 7.8. **Summer Project** for a description of a summer program that was designed by teacher education students.) Take advantage of these opportunities so that you can become one of those teachers that makes a significant difference!

**Figure 7.7  ↓ Advocacy Hints for Public Educators**

**Making a Difference for High-Needs Schools**

Politically, you can advocate for changes that will bring teachers and funding into those schools that need them the most. We've listed some of those policy strategies below; what additional policies could be implemented to bring quality teachers—and appropriate funding—into the highest-need schools?

- ✓ Find out what your state is doing to implement strategies and programs for students at risk, and write to your representatives to encourage their support of these critical programs
- ✓ Advocate for policies that support salary increases or bonuses for fully qualified teachers that choose to teach in high-poverty schools
- ✓ Support special financial awards for teachers with National Board Certification or advanced degrees who teach and/or mentor in high-poverty schools
- ✓ Insist on intensive professional development that keeps teachers in the classroom; the longer they stay in the classroom, the more effective the teachers will become
- ✓ Write to state policymakers, and insist that states subsidize master's degree programs or housing assistance for teachers who choose rural, urban, and/or high-poverty schools
- ✓ Support class size reduction policies and increased support services for students
- ✓ Demand that school leaders are supportive of quality teaching for all students
- ✓ Restore honor to the profession by keeping the media and the public apprised of the many positive ways in which teachers impact the learning lives of students in your community

**Figure 7.8  ↓ Summer Project**

**"Project eXcellence!"**

"Project eXcellence" enhances the academic opportunities for at-risk K-12 students through innovative curriculum in math, science, and technology. A primary focus is on serving students who represent the state's diverse minority and urban populations, and providing the university's pre-service teachers with a greater respect and understanding of the diversity that exists in today's classrooms. Project eX is directed by Dr. Janel White-Taylor.

Project eX has two components: "**ex Zone,**" a Saturday School program offered during the academic year; and "**eX City,**" a comprehensive summer school experience. Both are provided to K-12 students at no cost. The summer "eX City" experience brings students from a variety of urban districts together for a four-week summer program. The innovative curriculum developed for this program centers on the creation of a K-12 micro-society. The curriculum is created entirely by pre-service teachers. The specific goals of this summer program are:

- To assist K-12 students in mastering state standards and competencies
- To assist K-12 students in learning the skills necessary to compete in a global marketplace through the implementation of a microsociety

- To bridge the digital divide with innovative curricula that are enriched via technology
- To develop and enhance academic skills and self-esteem of K-12 students
- To create an environment where K-12 students are excited about learning

The summer experience centers on a micro-society theme where all students are citizens of "eX City." In the city, students experience real-life events such as purchasing items in the school's store (food items are donated by a local food bank), pay bills on a selected house and car, read city e-mail and news, review and change their own budgets, vote, attend court, and participate in city elections.

Students also choose three other activities to participate in during the day in "eX City." These are grouped into technology, science, math, and fine arts themes. The following classes are offered:

- *Technology*
    - **Newspaper:** Students participate in writing, editing, taking pictures, and using technology to put a newspaper together. Students are also visited by local newspaper journalists and editors.
    - **TV Station:** Students cover stories as they occur in the "Ex City," create weather and sports segments, and edit the final production that is shown on video.
    - **Cyber Café:** Students create their own web site, based on their summer experiences.
- *Science*
    - **Neighborhood:** Students learn about science that surrounds them in their community, including the science of hospitals, parks, and pools.
    - **Innovation Center:** Students use their creativity to invent new products and build robots.
    - **Science Center:** Students discover science in everyday life as they learning about and build a solar system, explode volcanoes, and create an earthquake.
- *Math*
    - **Cool Eats:** Students solve everyday math problems through the use of food, which they create and sell.
    - **The Store:** Students operate the eX Zone store, while learning the basics in how to run a successful business.
    - **The Vault:** Students have the responsibility of managing the eX City's money and to play the stock market.
- *Fine Arts*
    - **Art Gallery:** Students learn about painting, drawing, pottery, and other hands-on arts.
    - **Music Hall:** Students explore music through technology, and compose musical masterpieces which are performed for the eX City.
    - **Theater:** Students participate in Reader's Theater, create their own play, and perform for the citizens of eX City.

## Summer School

How could you and your peers become political advocates for students who are in most need of quality, effective teachers?

Read the description of the "eX Zone" (Figure 7.8), which was developed in part through the curricular planning of teacher education students. With your group, plan how you could develop a summer program to meet the needs of students in your community.

- What school or district in your community would you target for this experience? Why?
- The "eX Zone" used a simulated community model as the framework for its design. What unique twist or focus could you incorporate with your plan?
- What might a sample day look like in your program?
- Which academic standards would you align with your program?
- How could you secure the funding for your proposal?

In the Summer School Proposal form provided, write a brief proposal for your summer school program.

## Summer School Proposal

Project Name: _____

Grade Level: _____

*Content Focus:*

*Related Academic Standards:*

*Materials Needed:*

*Funding Sources:*

*Description of Program:*

# School Branding

What is school *"branding"*? How does it relate to school funding and politics in the classroom? Consider the following vignette.

*Branding* refers to the use of outside sponsors to provide materials or funding to schools—with the expectation for product advertising. Some of it is subtle—such as use of free curriculum materials. Others, such as the naming of football fields, are intended to have high impact and visibility in the community.

Branding comes in many forms, including the sponsorship of programs and activities, exclusive agreements (such as with soda companies), incentive programs, appropriation of space (e.g., naming public facilities in return for cash), educational materials, and electronic marketing (e.g., television programming aimed at schools and students).

School leaders are becoming much more accepting of branding and commercialism as a means to reduce their budgetary shortfalls. As we have already seen in this chapter, finding funding for schools is becoming increasingly challenging. Administrators and school boards therefore have the responsibility to find other revenue sources to support their programs and services. Many brand-name companies are more than willing to fill this void!

But is branding the right way to rectify budgeting challenges? While they can bring in much-needed equipment and facilities—such as footfall stadiums and computer labs—they do come with a cost. Molnar (2003/2004) argues that school branding has the potential to:

- Interfere with school operations, instruction, or even student health
- Promote unhealthy practices such as the consumption of junk food and soft drinks
- Are unrelentless in their overt marketing of students
- Manipulate students for the benefit of a special interest group through the use of instructional materials that market targeted items
- Can be destructive pedagogically, particularly when the message of the branding company is in contradiction to the school's curriculum or standards

Where do teachers and their administrators draw the line? We suggest that you interview teachers and/or administrators to determine how branding is being used in your community.

**Think About It**

What other instances of "branding" did you note in the vignette? What forms of branding occur at your university or college?

---

**Classroom Glimpse**

## School Branding

The community of River Heights is very proud of their high school. Last year, a new football stadium was erected. "Langley Air Field" seats over 10,000 fans, which doubled the capacity of their previous stadium. Expectations run high for another winning season. Also new to the school is the "Electra-Line Computer Lab," which features twenty-five newly donated computer stations. Electra-Line has also donated a complete curriculum guide, featuring the newest in productively and graphics tools, that teachers have implemented into their instruction.

For students, the favorite gathering spot is the sunny atrium, where they have access to brand-name sodas and a snack machine that is complete with seven varieties of potato chips. Running throughout the day is programming provided by Channel T, which focuses on news and informational shows targeted at teens.

Currently, the school hallways are filled with posters displaying the success of grade-level teams in the school-wide reading incentive program. The winning class will receive a free barbeque at the conclusion of the program. The school's physical education teacher is using the health-related curriculum that the barbeque company has provided free of cost. Although it doesn't quite align with the state health standards, the materials provided a much-needed supplement to the school's outdated texts. ■

**Figure 7.9** ↓ **Teacher Interview—Branding**

**Directions:** How is branding used in your community? How prevalent practice is this practice? Use the questions below to guide you in determining the appropriateness of branding in your community's schools.

Teacher's name

Teacher's level

How long has the teacher been teaching?                    How long at this level?

1. What are examples of "branding" at this school?

2. Is the donor providing something that the school needs in order to run its programs effectively, but has no other funding sources to secure it (e.g., renovating a football field)?

3. Does the program align with the school's mission or learning goals, or does the program actually contradict those goals?

4. Are the curriculum materials directly aligned with state standards?

5. Does the endorsement promote healthy choices for your students?

6. Is the primary intent of the product instructional—or simply a tool to market a product to students?

7. Are the materials or products age-appropriate for your students?

8. What is the quality of the materials? Did educators assist in the design?

9. Do you or your students need this product in order to be successful in the learning experience?

# Looking Forward

In this chapter, we have explored how politics can be found in the standards that you will teach in the classroom, the tests you will be required to administer, and the funding to implement reforms. While politicians do have the best interests of their communities in mind when these reforms are implemented, we have also seen that politics can complicate the process of teaching and learning. In the next chapter, we will turn to politics within the context of the school community.

## Research Citations

Abrams, L. M., & Madaus, G. F. (2003). The lessons of high-stakes testing. *Educational Leadership, 61*(3), 31–35.

Amrein, A. L., & Berliner, D. C. (2003). The effects of high-stakes testing on student motivation and learning. *Educational Leadership, 60*(5), 32–38.

Brown, W. H. (1957). Behind the test score. *Educational Leadership, 15*(3), 161–164.

Cetron, M., & Cetron, K. (2003/2004). A forecast for schools. *Educational Leadership, 61*(4), 22–29.

Dawson, H. A. (1943). What we're up against. *Educational Leadership, 1*(1), 6–8.

Elmore, R. F. (2003). A plea for strong practice. *Educational Leadership, 61*(3), 6–10.

Gandal, M., & McGiffert, L. (2003). The power of testing. *Educational Leadership, 60*(5), 32–38.

Gandal, M., & Vranek, J. (2001). Standards: Here today, here tomorrow. *Educational Leadership, 59*(1), 6–13.

Harvey, J. (2003). The matrix reloaded. *Educational Leadership, 61*(3), 18–21.

Haycock, K. (2002/2003). Toward a fair distribution of teacher talent. *Educational Leadership, 60*(4), 11–15.

Hess, F. M. (2003). The case for being mean. *Educational Leadership, 61*(3), 22–26.

Heubert, J. P. (2002/2003). First, do no harm. *Educational Leadership, 60*(4), 26–30.

Knutson, R. R. (1952). As viewed by a classroom teacher. *Educational Leadership, 10*(1), 36–37.

Molnar, A. (2003/2004). Cashing in on the classroom. *Educational Leadership, 61*(4), 79–84.

Neill, M. (2003). The dangers of testing. *Educational Leadership, 60*(5), 39–46.

Pryor, L. J. (1950). The listening post. *Educational Leadership, 7*(5), 335, 339.

Ramirez, A. (2002/2003). The shifting sands of school finance. *Educational Leadership, 60*(4), 54–57.

Rehage, K. J. (1956). Getting evidence for making instructional decisions. *Educational Leadership, 13*(7), 415–419.

Shaftel, F. R. (1957). Evaluation—for today and for the future. *Educational Leadership, 14*(5), 292–298.

# Politics in Your Community

*The war has brought additional responsibilities to the teaching profession. We are fighting on far flung fronts to make possible a free world. We must fight on the home front to prepare our future citizens to live and work in such a world. Otherwise victories won at tremendous cost will be lost through ignorance of the principles of democracy. Our children must be worthy of the freedom for which their fathers and mothers are fighting and working. School services must be expanded, not contracted, to stop too early withdrawals, falling attendance and other inroads on the educational well-being of our young people* (Dawson, 1943, p. 6).

Although the quote above was written in the midst of World War II, its message is not far removed from our current national goals and concerns. Public schools serve a critical role in this—or any—democracy.

Also critical, however, is maintaining a focus on the desires and goals of the community that a school directly serves. Five of these community concerns, which have national implications for schooling and instruction, will provide the focus for this chapter:

- Racial equity
- Gender equity
- Religion
- School choice
- Home schooling

How schools respond to these issues reflects the "pulse" of the community. As a teacher, it will be important for you to understand this pulse so that you can be effective as a political advocate for your students and your profession.

**Definitions**

**Assimilate**   to bring a person into a culture or set of beliefs; to absorb. In our educational history, cultural assimilation has sometimes occurred by force or coercion.

**Basic Skills**   usually referring to the content of reading, math, science, history, and the language arts. The "back to basics" movement in this country is currently gaining momentum, and some charter or private schools focus exclusively on the "basics" in academic content.

**Coeducational**   referring to programs or activities that include both male and female participants. Almost all public schools are coeducational, and both boys and girls attend classes together.

**Charter School**   a school that operates independently, outside of the influences of a public district. Charters can be either private (i.e., they charge tuition and control enrollment) or public.

**Choral Reading**   when participants read a text out loud in unison. Choral reading is common in many early elementary classrooms.

**Doctrine**   a set of beliefs that are shared by a group. Religious organizations have guiding doctrines that are adhered to by its followers.

**Ethos**   beliefs, character, and ideals of a community. A school community, for example, has an established ethos or culture.

**GLBTQ**   acronym for individuals who are gay, lesbian, bisexual, transgendered, or queer/questioning.

**Homonegative**   actions, ideas, or behaviors that reflect negativity toward persons who are homosexual or GLBTQ.

**Intelligent Design**   a theory often related to the concept of creationism, in which it is believed that the universe was created by an intelligent being, or God.

**Reciprocal Teaching**   and instructional strategy in which both students and their teacher participate actively in the teaching/learning process. For example, students may take turns asking each other questions, instead of relying only on the teacher.

**Teachable Moments**   taking advantage of opportunities as they occur in the classroom to optimize student motivation and interest. A teacher might use a current news article, unexpectedly brought to class by a student, as a teachable moment to introduce a social studies topic or concept under study.

**Vouchers**   state-supported funds given to parents to use toward tuition at schools of their choice.

## As you read, think about . . .

★ Your own experiences in school. How were boys and girls treated differently, or the same? Students of different cultural backgrounds or religions? Students with different sexual orientations? Did schools have the same rules and expectations for all students?

★ Imagine that you were a different race or gender. How would your P-12 school experiences been different? The same?

★ How do societal norms impact what is expected in schools and how different groups of students are treated?

★ In thinking of your own experiences, which of your teachers were most effective in developing a classroom climate that was respectful of all students? How did that teacher develop that climate?

## Focus Questions

★ What is Title IX, and how does it impact P-12 schools?

★ What forms of discrimination exist in today's P-12 schools?

★ What are the impacts of discrimination on students and their families?

★ What are the best instructional strategies for confronting racism in the classroom?

★ What religious practices—if any—are allowed in today's public schools?

★ What current factors related to parental choice have the most impact on public schools?

It is critical to be able to understand and communicate appropriately with individuals from a variety of cultures.

# Racial Equity

One of the most daunting and controversial political issues in education today is that of racism in our public schools. Racism is a harsh and ugly word—and one that we as educators tend to shy away from. With all of the laws and rights that have been supported by the courts in terms of desegregating educational opportunities, does racism still exist in schools today? Unfortunately, the answer is a disappointing and resounding "yes."

Why does racism matter? Despite recent advances in education, some students are being left behind in their pursuit of excellence—even within affluent communities (Blumer & Tatum, 1999). Students of color are often overrepresented in special education, and under-represented in accelerated or gifted programs. Racism also matters because it has a damaging effect on students of color as well as those who are of the dominant culture (in our country, the dominate culture is currently White). Some of the consequences for children of color include (Spencer, 1998):

- Lack of affiliation or attachment to school
- Loss of social identity
- Lower self-esteem
- Increase in school drop-out
- Decreased achievement

There are also consequences for children who are White, including a distorted sense of cultural superiority, and a fear or misunderstanding of different cultures. In a time when a global economy is crucial to our nation's growth and financial stability, it is equally critical for all citizens to understand and be able to communicate appropriately with individuals from a variety of cultures. Racism, therefore, impedes our personal, educational, moral, and economic well-being.

**Think About It**

Given our historical past, what does racism look like in schools today?

The educational experiences of children throughout our nation's history reflect socialization to racial stereotyping and mono-culturalism (Spencer, 1998). As we explored in Chapter 1, one of the primary purposes of schooling during the Colonial Period was to socialize new immigrants to the Anglo-European culture. Socialization to the dominant culture was perhaps most vividly illustrated through the use of forced "boarding schools" to *assimilate* Native American children into the White culture and traditions.

## Racism in Our Schools

In today's classroom, racism is often very subtle, and usually unintentional. Consider the vignette below.

How was racism subtly enacted in Tamara's lesson? As a White teacher, Tamara relied on a term that she had grown up with through her schooling and cultural experiences. And while sitting "Indian style" was not used out of disrespect for native peoples, it does illustrate one of the many ways that we might use inappropriate cultural or racial terms. But does something as simple as a misunderstanding really make a difference?

Racism today is subtle and often unintentional; however, it still exists and has a damaging effect on all students. For example, racism is propagated through the school's curriculum, which is primarily centered on western civilization, and sometimes through the attitudes and biases of teachers and school personnel. Hanssen (1998) refers to this unintentional or hidden racism as *institutional racism,* which is most often reflected in:

- School curriculum
- Hiring practices
- The *ethos* of the school

The school curriculum is often unintentionally biased because it reflects the traditions of the nation's dominant White culture. For example, the literature that many teachers often choose for their lessons is rarely written by authors from minority cultures. Much of the curricular bias, however, is a result of our reliance on textbooks, which present history from a Western European perspective. For example, think about your own experiences in American History classes. How was the exploration of Columbus presented? As a brave man who "discovered" a new continent, whose actions are celebrated through school pageants and the crafting of paper ships? Or as a cruel and greedy entrepreneur who enslaved native inhabitants and whose actions led to the genocide of those found on this "newly discovered" continent? It is often said that history is written by those who conquer. Take a moment to think about the

**Classroom Glimpse**

### Subtle Racism

Tamara, a first-year teacher, was getting her third-grade students ready for a new lesson on forest habitats. She was planning to begin her lesson using a book on the effects of deforestation. Tamara was in the reading corner, with her students gathered around her on the rug. She first previewed the story by showing the front illustration and soliciting predictions from her students.

As Tamara began reading the story, she noticed that her students had become restless. Many had their legs stretched out in front of them, and were bumping their neighbors' backs. It soon became evident that the students were not attending to the story. At that point Tamara stopped her lesson, and asked her students to sit "Indian style." Perplexed, her students did not know what to do. Repeating the directions, without reaction from her students, Tamara became increasingly frustrated. She finally modeled what she wanted her students to do (sit cross-legged), and proceeded with the lesson. ■

historical stories that you grew up with, and how those histories would be rewritten from the perspectives of other minority or ethnic groups.

Unfortunately, school racism is also reflected in the hiring practices of faculty and the beliefs and biases held by some teachers and administrators. At an inservice workshop on using alternative assessments in elementary classrooms at a school that was experiencing a rapid increase in the number of its minority student enrollment, one teacher proclaimed in the middle of the presentation, "higher order assessment won't work with *those* children," and left the meeting. While bias and racism isn't always quite this evident (or alarming!), it does still exist in the ways that students are treated in today's classrooms.

How do we avoid falling into our own unintentional biases? Schniedewind (2005) suggests that teachers need to acknowledge their own racial identity, in order to be able to recognize the need for students to affirm their own. We also need to reflect upon and acknowledge that our own experiences, identities, beliefs, and values impact our teaching and curricular decisions. Do we choose a story because it is "comfortable" and written by an author with whom we are familiar, or do we purposely choose those pieces that mirror the cultural and ethnic identities of our students?

Schniedewind (2005) also recommends the following practices that teachers can follow to support students of color:

- Examine our own experiences with and attitudes towards racism and other forms of discrimination
- Validate students' racial identities
- Make classrooms protected places for students to discuss difficult issues such as color, bias, and racism
- Use *teachable moments* and planned activities to address stereotyping
- Investigate ways in which bias exists in schools and society
- Attend professional development opportunities that increase the repertoire of skills and strategies for making classrooms more racially supportive and sensitive

A third form of institutional bias is described as occurring through the ethos of the school itself. An ethos refers to the beliefs, character, and ideals of a community. Students of color often don't feel like they belong in the school, and have norms that might contradict the predominant culture of the student body or of the teachers. For example, consider the following vignette.

## High School Play

Mrs. Stanford has taken her tenth-grade English class to a dress rehearsal of Romeo and Juliet, which is being performed by the state's theater troupe. Prior to the trip, her students have read the play, explored the biography of its playwright, and compared how the themes of the play relate to contemporary life. Her students seemed to be quite excited about the field trip.

As soon as the play began, however, the students began to "talk out" to the play's performers. They encouraged the lovers, commented on their costumes, and talked back to the story's antagonists. Embarrassed by her students' behavior, Mrs. Stanford repeatedly tried to quiet her students. The students appeared perplexed by Mrs. Stanford's concern, and continued participating verbally as the play proceeded. ■

**Classroom Glimpse**

What would you have done if you were in Mrs. Stanford's shoes? Does it help to know that Mrs. Stanford is White, and her students are predominately Black? While it is possible that her students are being disrespectful, it is perhaps more likely that they are simply enacting on the accepted social norms of their culture. It is quite acceptable, for example, for churchgoers to verbally participate in services within many Black communities. These norms would be quite different from the expectations of the congregations in many White churches, however.

In order to avoid unintentional biases—and miscommunication with students—it is important for teachers to dialogue with students about what is acceptable and how the norms of different cultures differ. Teachers also need to remain highly observant and analytical concerning those practices in schools that might reflect institutional racism and conflict with the school's norms or ethos (Hanssen, 1998).

## Confronting Racism

Confronting the realities of racism can't be left only to the individual teacher. To be effective, and to make a difference in the learning lives of students, issues of racial equity need to be imbedded in the school ethos and the curriculum. The need to confront racism is not questioned—what is more difficult, however, is determining the best way to guide students in dealing with cultural differences and biases. While there are many programs and theories on this topic, there are three that have garnered the most attention:

- Multicultural education
- Anti-racist education
- Culturally responsive curriculum

**Multicultural Education**   Multicultural education is most often described as a curriculum plan that fosters a celebration of differences, tolerance, understanding, and acceptance of diversity (Raby, 2004). Multicultural education is seen as an important vehicle for increasing awareness and understanding of cultural differences in schools (Spencer, 1998). Multicultural education describes a wide variety of school practices, policies, and programs that are designed to increase cultural awareness. Programs emphasize the notion that all cultures are equally valid, and might include such activities as an ethnic food fair or identifying certain months for a school-wide celebration of selected cultures.

There are many critics of multicultural education, however. Some contend that it overemphasizes ethnic differences in hopes that tolerance and appreciation will automatically follow; others believe that multicultural education trivializes everyday problems and experiences faced by people of different ethnicities (Spencer, 1998). Other critics call for stronger and more comprehensive approaches that address core issues of racism and bigotry.

**Anti-Racist Education**   Anti-racist education begins from a premise that racism exists, recognizes power imbalances that are racially bound, and includes an examination of the roles of schools in perpetrating inequalities (Raby, 2004). Through its curriculum, anti-racist educators tackle and define concepts of racism; identify and explore concepts of racism as they have evolved historically; and examine the power and inequality in our history, language, and global relations. Professional development in anti-racist education would encourage teachers to confront their own stereotypes, and to help them recognize their own personal, cultural, and institutional manifestations of racism to enable them to become more proactive in responding to racism within their own school setting (Blumer & Tatum, 1999).

The aim of an anti-racist education is to work throughout the curriculum, rather than "adding on" to existing instruction. An anti-racist curriculum would support programs that address racism and social injustice through discussions and analyses of inequalities in power and in the economic status of different ethnic groups. The curriculum emphasizes the empowerment of children of color so that they develop a strong self-identity. Activities that might be used within this curriculum could include learning to problem solve discriminatory behavior through role playing, or promoting activism through letter-writing campaigns or speaking with public officials.

**Culturally Responsive Curriculum**   Current concern in education has focused on developing curriculum and classroom instruction that is more responsive to each child's culture and diverse experiences. It is becoming increasingly more evident that the way in which educators and the community respond to issues of diversity will impact the self-esteem and academic success of students (Phuntsog, 1999), and that instruction that has traditionally been offered in schools fails to meet this goal. It is suggested that the problem lies directly within the educational system, which is currently insufficient for students of culturally and linguistically diverse backgrounds (Nichols, Rupley, & Webb-Johnson, 2000). The mismatch that often exists between home and school expectations, for example, often results in misunderstandings between teachers and their students. It is therefore argued that the educational system must be transformed into one that is more culturally responsive to ensure that all students have an equal chance to succeed.

A culturally responsive or relevant curriculum is one that allows students to learn from a familiar cultural base and through which individuals can connect new knowledge to their own experiences (Menchaca, 2001). This curriculum provides an educationally compatible avenue through which all students can benefit and excel (Nichols et al., 2000). A culturally responsive curriculum provides different examples from those prescribed in textbooks, for example, and counteracts traditional views that predominantly place Western heroes into historical contexts. If cultural discontinuity exists between school texts and students' concepts of content, students' potential to learn key information is jeopardized (Nichols et al., 2000). Instruction that is culturally responsive validates students for who they are by allowing all students to learn and respect other cultural groups' heritage and history.

A culturally responsive curriculum benefits all children by building on the richness of varied lived experiences and cultures to make learning more meaningful. Students are more successful when schools honor and value each child as an individual (Menchaca, 2001). Additionally, the academic achievement of students from culturally diverse backgrounds will improve if schools and teachers make an attempt to ensure that instruction is responsive to the students' home culture (Phuntsog, 1999).

Culturally responsive instruction stresses respect for diversity in order to engage the motivation of all learners while creating a safe and inclusive climate (Phuntsog, 1999). Culturally responsive teachers bridge the gap between school and the students' homes by adapting instruction to meet the learning needs of all students and providing consistency with the values of students' own cultures. Responsive practices are integrated across the disciplines and promote social justice and equity. Also effective are activities that highlight social relationships, such as reciprocal interactions and interactive assessments (Nichols et al., 2000).

When considering culturally responsive instruction, Au and Raphael (2000) emphasize the importance of thoughtful engagement with the full range of society's literacy artifacts. The literacy achievement of students of diversity can be strengthened by giving greater consideration to issues of ethnicity, primary language, and social class (Au, 1998). Students' ownership over literacy is also key to effective instruction, as there exists a reciprocal relationship between ownership and proficiency in literacy (Au & Raphael, 2000).

Practices that are effective within a responsive curriculum include *reciprocal teaching* and retelling, which help increase students' ability to recognize important and less important information. Also effective is encouraging students to develop word banks of vocabulary of interest to them, using predictable and patterned reading materials, promoting *choral reading,* adapting poems to cover familiar topics, and developing literacy centers with multiple genres of culturally appropriate literature (Nichols et al., 2000).

**Think About It**

Where do you stand on this controversial, important, and polarizing issue? What programs are most prevalent in the schools and districts in your own communities?

Spencer (1998) suggests that perhaps the greatest challenge to reducing racism in schools is the highly controversial and political nature of the problem. As we debate issues of racism, strong feelings and emotions are often evoked—along with very polarized opinions about how best to confront racism instructionally, and even whether or not racism exists.

Adding to the challenges is current and growing opposition to multicultural education, or any educational programs that focus on diversity. Many conservatives, in particular, would prefer that multicultural education be eliminated from the curriculum, in order to focus instruction on **basic skills.** Other critics will contend that ethnic cultures and languages should not be taught in schools at all, but rather belong to instruction in the home. Use the Group Talk activity to share observations and ideas, and to build dialogue on how you as novice teachers will best confront the issue of racism in your future classroom.

> . . . *we are citizens of a rapidly shrinking and increasingly interdependent world. The world's peoples must somehow learn to live together—with all the richness of their diversity in culture, economic development, aspirations and religious convictions—or face the destruction of civilization as we have known it.*
> (Bush, 1954)

## Group Talk

### Racism in Schools

After you have filled out the chart, meet as a group to discuss the following:

1. What program are group members most comfortable with? Why?

2. What program are group members least comfortable with? Why?

3. What are the best elements of each program?

4. What program do group members see in the classrooms with most frequency?

### Understanding Racism in Schools

*Directions:* In the chart below, first write your own reflections about the three different programs for addressing school racism. Then, think about the activities you've seen incorporated into schools in your community. What programs are they most like? Why?

|  | My Personal Reflections | Observations from Classrooms |
|---|---|---|
| *Multicultural Education* |  |  |
| *Anti-Racist Education* |  |  |
| *Culturally Responsive Curriculum* |  |  |

One of the most visible changes resulting from Title IX was the availability of sporting opportunities for female students.

# Gender Equity

As we have explored in earlier sections of this book, our country's first schools provided very different educational opportunities for boys and girls. In fact, girls were primarily excluded from formal schooling, and their academic experiences focused on preparing them for maintaining a proper household. Boys, on the other hand, were taught the skills needed to be successful in a future vocation in order to support their families.

Without question, much has changed in the past three centuries! However, it is apparent when reading any current newspaper or listening to broadcast media that some inequalities still exist today concerning the educational opportunities for boys and girls in this country. Just exactly what have we accomplished in achieving gender equity in our schools?

Historically, educators have documented how boys and girls are treated differently in schools. For example, boys' "acting out" behavior is often overlooked by teachers, who consider such behavior as just indicative of "boys being boys." Girls who talk or act out, however, are quickly reprimanded. Boys are often more likely to be called on than girls, are expected to enjoy working on computers and engaging in hands-on activities, are encouraged to read nonfiction texts while girls are guided towards fiction, and may even be called on to answer questions more frequently than girls. Books used in classrooms often contain very positive male role models—that often come to the rescue of their female counterparts.

**Think About It**

Think about your own experiences observing in classrooms. How have you seen boys and girls treated differently—unintentionally—by the teachers with whom you've worked?

## Title IX

One of the most influential pieces of legislation that has impacted gender equity in schools was Title IX of the Educational Amendments of 1972. In general, Title IX prohibits single-sex educational programs. This amendment states:

> *No person in the United States shall, on the basis of sex, be excluded from participation in, be denied the benefits of, or be subjected to discrimination under any program or activity receiving federal financial assistance.* (20 U.S.C. § 1682)

The provisions of Title IX have had an important impact on protecting both students and employees, by opening up courses, activities, and jobs to both genders (Newman, 1998).

For example, boys can take courses once dominated by girls (e.g., homemaking and consumer classes), while girls can enroll in industrial arts and agricultural classes that would have been denied to them in many schools prior to 1972. Title IX has also allowed more women to move into male-dominated administrative positions.

One of the most visible changes resulting from this amendment has related to collegiate sports. This mandate called for a proportional number of opportunities for women in U.S. sports, which resulted in the establishment of women's scholarships and programs that never existed before (Hammer, 2003). This access to sports, in turn, also provided women greater access to college.

However, Title IX has recently come under attack by critics who contend that the rules are sabotaging some men's athletic teams. Recently, the U.S. Department of Education is considering whether to make changes to Title IX that some argue will result in fewer opportunities for women to play college sports. The proposed changes include eliminating future cuts in men's teams, bringing about unlimited walk-on spaces for men's sports, and allowing men's teams to creatively raise their own funds rather than be eliminated. Supporters of these changes argue that the current amendment leads to loss of funding for men's sports and enforces what amounts to a quota system. However, others contend that changes to Title IX are too vague and open-ended, and will leave the door open for new interpretations that might be contradictory to the original intent of Title IX (Hammer, 2003).

## Where Are We Today?

There is some debate whether or not schools have achieved equity in their treatment and expectations of boys and girls. Despite implementation of guidelines for nonsexist language, increased laws concerning sexual harassment, and Title IX, some will argue that we have made little progress towards equitable representation of girls. McClure (1999) states that girls "continue to be socialized to take their stereotypically appropriate gendered place in society" (p. 79). Niemi (2005) suggests that, while there is now parity between boys' and girls' academic achievement, the focus on gaining academic achievement overshadows issues of gender. At best, schools are maintaining the inequity of the American gender status quo.

Other educators are concerned with inequities in the area of technology, and suggest that the existence of technology in schools actually exacerbates the inequities by gender in the P-12 curriculum (Butler, 2004). For example, girls tend to rate themselves lower than boys in their self-perceptions and attitudes about their computer ability, boys tend to be encouraged to use computers more at home, games that appeal to boys dominate the popular market, and girls have fewer role models in terms of female technology teachers or technologists.

However, some educators have recently suggested that it is boys, rather than girls, that are increasingly on the short end of the gender gap in schools, particularly in terms of achievement outcomes (Riordan, 2003). Broad nationwide efforts to bring about gender equity in schools have been effective, particularly in positive results for girls, because of the magnitude of intervention focused on providing female students with opportunities to excel that were not afforded to them in decades past. However, because the gender-equity educational policies over the past thirty years have been successful, specific needs of boys now require careful reassessment. For example, recent reports suggest that, while there are not significant gender differences in math or science scores, the following have been noted (Riordan, 2003):

- Boys have lower reading achievement and writing skills, as compared with their female peers
- Boys have lower grades and lower class ranks, as compared with their female peers
- Boys are involved in more crimes, delinquent and violent behavior, and drug and alcohol use
- The percentage of males enrolling in higher education has decreased
- There exists a growing pool of idle men who are out of school and unemployed

Single-sex classes were established to remedy discrimination or alleged disparate educational effects.

McClure (1999) suggests that boys are limited by their gender stereotypes, and are harassed when they engage in activities or interests that are considered feminine. Consider, for example, how middle school boys would treat a male peer who quit the soccer team to join a local ballet troupe. There does seem to be a double standard for boys and girls, however. For example, how would peers treat a girl that quit the cheerleading squad to join the boys' soccer team? Most probably, this action would be met with respect and admiration. What would happen if a girl wore her brother's clothes to school? Perhaps start a chic new trend? Then consider what would happen if a boy wore his sister's clothes? Gender equity can certainly be considered from many angles!

Some states have begun to develop programs that confront gender inequities head-on. These programs establish gender fairness as a primary goal of education, and enable students to explore and address gender inequities. McClure (1999) describes two such programs:

- **ASETS- Achieving Sex Equity Through Students**—this program includes a peer leadership component that trains students to be agents of change in their schools.

- **Vermont Equity Project**—this program helps middle school students begin to recognize and interpret the effects of cultural messages of conceptions of self and others. Students learn to celebrate diversity and recognize the impact of society's influences to fit into stereotypical gender roles.

Other suggestions for supporting gender equities and opportunities in the classroom and schools include:

- Helping students begin to understand how pervasive sexist language and sex-role stereotyping are in our society and through the popular media

- Involving students in investigating research that examines the role of gender in society

- Involving students in analyzing gender roles attributed to characters in fairy tales or animated films
- Asking students to keep logs of commercials, where they record how males and females are portrayed and represented
- Having students write autobiographies from a different gender perspective (how would their lives be different if they were a male/or female?)
- Rewriting fairy tales from a different gender perspective
- Including literature that balances male and female authors, perspectives, and characters

While some of the strategies above would be more appropriate for different age groups of students, the important point to note is that it is critical for all teachers to first recognize that gender inequities do exist—often in very subtle forms—and that we need to be aware of how these inequities impact our practice, our students' development, and the opportunities that schools provide to all of its students.

**Single-Sex Schools**   One of the strategies that is used to confront issues of gender inequality has been the use of single-sex classrooms or schools. This is an uncommon practice; in 2002, only eleven public single-gender schools existed (Mead, 2003). Most of these schools operate as part of some form of parental choice school program, and some have *coeducational* student populations but assign students to classes according to gender.

In the recent past, single-sex schools were established to remedy discrimination or alleged desperate educational effects that were available to girls in coeducational settings (Mead, 2003). More recently, this strategy is used to provide benefits of single-gender education to both sexes. This is accomplished by providing students with some opportunities for learning in coeducational settings, with some activities, such as math or science instruction, separated by gender.

Why use single-sex classrooms or schools? Some educators contend that achievement scores increase with single-sex class groupings; however, there have not been many studies to either support or refute this claim. Others believe that same-sex schools or classes can provide students with a "safe haven," where they can discuss issues that may be uncomfortable within cross-sex settings (Pollard, 1996). This aspect of same-sex learning is particularly relevant with middle school students, who face a multitude of personal and social issues as they emerge into adolescence.

Do single-sex schools or classrooms have a role in our current educational system? Perhaps the best practice is to remain flexible. Schools may want to consider the benefits of providing same-sex educational opportunities in specific contexts, and with particular groups of students. However, with the provision in NCLB legislation to encourage "innovation" in school design and choice, this controversial system may become more prevalent in the next decades.

## Homonegativity in Public Schools: The Silent Discrimination

While it may be easy for us to discuss and debate issues of discrimination as they relate to gender, and even race, it is typically more difficult for us to have an open dialogue about the daily discrimination that occurs in our schools—and our society—related to gay and lesbian youth. Instead of confronting these challenges, too often educators are silent on the issue, perhaps hoping that "those kinds of students" don't exist in their schools or classrooms. However, a sober reality is that, every thirty-five minutes, a gay or lesbian youth commits suicide in this country (MacGillivray, 2000).

Recently, there was a three-day forum that addressed a variety of critical issues in Arizona's P-12 educational system. In attendance were P-12 educational leaders, university faculty, politicians, and businesspeople representing a wide spectrum of ideals and agendas. Important topics such as bilingual education, high-stakes testing, teacher quality, and parental involvement were discussed and resolutions were mutually created and supported. However, in the final debate of the session, the issue of school bullying and safe climates was brought to the floor. An initial draft had been created that included the right of every student, "regardless of race, gender, religion, or sexual orientation," to be protected in order to ensure that every student had access to a safe and supportive learning climate. Of all the controversial issues confronted by the attendees at the forum, this simple statement drew the most debate and public ire. While everyone supported the notion that every student should be protected, the statement regarding *sexual orientation* was seen by most in attendance as unnecessary and redundant. In the end, this statement was withdrawn from the final document.

What are the rights of gay and lesbian students in our public schools? And why should this small population of students be given special focus or attention? Take a few moments to fill out the **Gay/Lesbian Self-Survey** in Figure 8.1 to reflect upon your own beliefs regarding individuals who are gay, lesbian, bisexual, transgendered, and queer/questioning *(GLBTQ).*

In reality, gay and lesbian students are routinely and consistently denied the same educational opportunities that are afforded to their heterosexual peers. Teachers are often unwilling to allow discussions on GLBTQ issues, for fear of backlash from parents or their own administrators. The school environment is typically unsafe, both physically and emotionally. MacGillivray (2000) points out the following realities:

- Homophobic name-calling is commonplace in schools, and often ignored by teachers and administrators
- Gay and lesbian students are the most frequent victims of harassment, including attacks and physical injury
- Gay and lesbian students routinely face social exclusion at school, and rarely have opportunities to openly participate in GLBTQ clubs
- The school curriculum often excludes gay and lesbians, by reaffirming heterosexism and systematically ignoring homosexual role models and curricular materials; instead, the school curriculum more often perpetrates *homonegative* myths and stereotypes

In addition to challenges and even physical threats at school, gay and lesbian students also face other serious factors. For example, many are alienated from their families, and risk abandonment if they disclose their sexual orientation to their parents. Often, they are identified for being more at risk for truancy and dropping out of school. Gay and lesbian youth also face health risks, such as depression, drug and alcohol abuse, homelessness, HIV/AIDS, and suicide (Taylor, 2000). And while other minority groups have social systems to provide support and buffers against humiliation, such as families, churches, and schools, gay and lesbian students do not typically have these supports. As a result, they often are not exposed to or provided with a framework for building a positive sense of self.

What can teachers do to support gay and lesbian students? First, it is important to reflect upon our own biases and prejudices, so that these are not unintentionally reflected in our teaching or our interactions with students. Teachers also need to feel that they are genuinely supported by their administrators, so that they can adequately address the needs of this important group of students. Taylor (2000) suggests the following strategies for addressing gay and lesbian issues in the middle school, which is the time in which most young people begin to recognize and discover their sexual orientation. These strategies are organized according to the National Middle School Association's three essential elements of a middle school:

- **Educators are knowledgeable and committed to young adolescents**
  - Teachers need to begin by learning more about the realities of gay and lesbian history, and of the persistence of homophobia in our country today.

**Figure 8.1   ↓ Gay/Lesbian Self-Survey**

*Directions:* Reflect upon your own beliefs regarding the rights of GLBTQ youth and teachers, and write your responses in the spaces below.

1.  Is homosexuality a lifestyle choice, or an innate characteristic of an individual?

2.  Should an openly gay teacher be allowed to teach kindergarten?

3.  Should an openly lesbian teacher be allowed to teach middle school?

4.  Should GLBTQ students be allowed to form a club at your middle school? High School?

5.  Should you read a book aloud to your second grade students that portrays a same-sex parental couple?

6.  Should same-sex couples be allowed to attend the school prom together?

7.  Should you encourage students to read books on gay rights, even though you know that some of the school's parents will object?

8.  Should your school allow a club to meet at your school, even when its policies discriminate against gays (e.g., Boy Scouts)?

9.  Should you be required to support and respect openly gay students in your classroom, when your religious beliefs hold a very contradictory view of homosexuality?

- **The school curriculum is based on the needs of young adolescents**
  - Integrate information about gays and lesbians who have made significant contributions to society.
  - Discuss the experiences of gays and lesbians when teaching about discrimination.
  - Request books for the library that include those with gay and lesbian themes or written by GLBTQ authors.
- **The school climate fosters warmth, care, and respect**
  - Teachers need to use language that is inclusive of gay and lesbian possibilities (e.g., use "spouse" instead of husband or wife).
  - Teachers and school administrators must exhibit a zero tolerance policy for name-calling, harassment, or use of homonegative phrases.
  - Teachers should work to have "sexual orientation" added to the school's nondiscrimination and harassment policies.
  - Teachers should request staff development to develop sensitivity to gay and lesbian students' needs, address teachers' personal prejudices, and disseminate basic (and factual) information on sexual orientation.

As a public and democratic social institution, schools and their teachers have the legal and moral responsibility to educate all students to be responsible and tolerant citizens. Regardless of your own personal or religious views, it is imperative as a public school teacher that you support, respect, and protect *all* the students in your school—and that you demand that other teachers and administrators do the same.

## GLBTQ Rights in Schools

After you have finished reading the section of this chapter on Homonegativity in Schools, revisit your reflections in Figure 8.1. **Gay/Lesbian Self-Survey.** Have any of your views changed? If so, indicate those changes on the survey at this time.

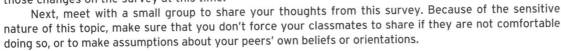

Next, meet with a small group to share your thoughts from this survey. Because of the sensitive nature of this topic, make sure that you don't force your classmates to share if they are not comfortable doing so, or to make assumptions about your peers' own beliefs or orientations.

1.  Which of the questions presented in the survey did your group have the most agreement on?

2.  Which had the least agreement? Why?

3.  Have any of the group members observed events of discrimination against GLBTQ students in the P-12 schools in your community? In your college or university?

4.  What incidences of discrimination have you or your peers faced? How did you handle those incidences?

5.  What advice would you give novice teachers who are confronted with discrimination against GLBTQ in their schools?

# Religion in Schools

Religion's roots in our national public education system are undeniable, as we have explored in previous chapters. In colonial times, we have learned that students were taught to read in large part so that they could have access to the words of the Bible—and therefore to gain personal salvation. Early forms of textbooks included biblical references and psalms, and even in our grandparents' day it was not unusual to say a prayer or read scripture as part of the daily classroom routine.

Today, religion and public education appear to be at uneasy odds. Courts are deciding whether the words "Under God" are to be taken out of the Pledge, whether religious symbols are allowed in public places such as school grounds, and even what can and cannot be included in the school curriculum.

If we are indeed a nation that emerged from a desire for religious freedom, why shouldn't religion be more accepted within the public education system today? While this is not the place to debate the politics of religion in American, one does need to remember that religious freedom also includes the right *not* to practice or believe. By imposing religion in a *public* institution, the community would be violating the basic precepts of our Constitution.

So where do we draw the line? If we are a religious person ourselves, are we required to deny that part of our identity when we walk into the classroom? Consider the following experience of a novice second-grade teacher, presented in the classroom vignette below.

**Think About It**

Where would you stand on this hotly contested political issue?

What would you have done, if you had been Bette? Do you think she violated public school policy by engaging students in a religious song? As luck would have it, the superintendent enjoyed the musical selection and simply joined in with the class. However, the consequences might have been quite disastrous under a different administrator.

**Religion in schools today**   The current battle over the role of religion in public schools has emerged from differing views regarding the free exchange of ideas in the classroom that includes topics such as religion, creationism, and sex education. Each community has very different views on how open and expansive this dialogue should be. Also at issue is how schools can maintain intellectual freedom while simultaneously guaranteeing the parents' and community's right to be heard (Fege, 1993/1994).

Also of concern is the issue of political pressure some communities may put on schools to insert—or delete—religious values from the educational process. Those who desire to sup-

## Classroom Glimpse

### Religion in the Classroom

Each November, Bette and her students studied a unit on "Old Fashioned Days," which introduced these second graders to concepts related to colonial America. This unit concluded with an "old fashioned" reenactment the day before the Thanksgiving break. Bette and her students would dress in simple clothes (skirts and dresses for the girls, and no sneakers!), and have a picnic of corn bread, cider, dried fruit, and homemade butter.

As part of the day's events, Bette developed lessons that were reflective of schooling in colonial America. Students wrote on paper hornbooks, recited poetry, and memorized math facts. Bette's students also enjoyed participating in musical activities, so she had songs ready to sing when the students were restless from their recitations.

On one such occasion, Bette and her students were singing a rather spirited version of "Michael Row Your Boat Ashore." Just as they were joining in a rather loud chorus of, "Alleluia!," the district superintendent walked into Bette's classroom. It then dawned on Bette that perhaps it wasn't such a wise choice to be singing what was clearly a religious song—but by then it was too late. ■

press certain materials or ideas that they find objectionable can easily exploit local control of education. In Chapter 2, we looked at the power that local school boards can have on the instructional practices that occur in the classroom. School boards may subtly restrict academic freedom by bypassing existing material selection in an effort to placate parents or special interest groups who wish to ban certain ideas from the classroom.

Parents, too, can find their views at odds with the school's mission or goals. There are certainly times when the interests of the school may not be compatible with the values of parents in some segments of the community. Problems will arise when parents try to deny the entire school community with access to targeted materials, programs, or educational opportunities based on their own belief that these materials will corrupt all students. Fege (1993/1994) urges educators to find that fine line between parents' rights to be involved with what occurs in schools, and the exploitation of that right by a few parents with very specific interests.

In short, who should decide which books and materials can be included as appropriate for all students, and which are to be banned? For example, should parents be permitted to pull the hotly popular *Harry Potter* series off school shelves because some object that the main characters are wizards? Or do you advocate to keep these books in the library because of their ability to motivate even reluctant students to read?

## Religion and School Standards

Despite the tensions that exist in many communities over issues of religion, there is an undisputed role of religion in the public school classroom. As was discussed in Chapter 7, academic standards provide the framework for a teacher's classroom instruction. Most states do incorporate religion into primary-level studies of communities and in historical issues related to world cultures and geography. These standards specify that students should know about the role of religion in our own history and contemporary life, and that students should also be able to describe the major world religious traditions as they impact history and culture.

For example, the following standards are part of Massachusetts' curriculum framework for social studies and history:

- Give examples of the major rights that immigrants have acquired as citizens of the United States (e.g., the right to vote, and freedom of religion, speech, assembly, and petition)
- Identify the language, major religion, and peoples of Mexico
- Identify the characteristics of civilizations, including the development of systems of religion, learning, art, and architecture
- Describe the polytheistic religion of ancient Egypt with respect to beliefs about death, the afterlife, mummification, and the roles of different deities
- Describe the monotheistic religion of the Israelites, including:
  1. the belief that there is one God
  2. the Ten Commandments
  3. the emphasis on individual worth and personal responsibility
  4. the belief that all people must adhere to the same moral obligations, whether ruler or ruled
- Describe significant aspects of Islamic belief, including the relationship between government and religion in Muslim societies
- Describe the religious and political origins of conflicts between Islam and Christianity, including the causes, course, and consequences of the European Crusades against Islam in the eleventh, twelfth, and thirteenth centuries

- Describe the indigenous religious practices observed by early Africans before contact with Islam and Christianity
- Explain the role of religion in the wars among European nations in the fifteenth and sixteenth centuries

How does religion impact the standards and curriculum in your state? Use the **Religion and Standards** chart (Figure 8.2) to record what you find about religion and your community.

| Figure 8.2    ↓ Religion and Standards |
|---|

**Religious Standards in My State**

*Use your state's academic standards to determine how religion is to be integrated into your curriculum.*

| Standard | Grade Level |
|---|---|
|  |  |
|  |  |
|  |  |
|  |  |
|  |  |
|  |  |
|  |  |
|  |  |

Why is the teaching of religion important in today's public schools? Douglass (2002) offers the following rationale:

- Teaching about religion helps prepare students for the global workplace. Workers will be more effective if they know the cultural preferences, habits, and taboos of diverse groups of people across the globe.

- We need to know about others and their beliefs so that we can unite in positive social conduct.

- Learning about history, culture, and belief systems of others makes our students more respectful and understanding of those views and beliefs that are different from our own.

- Knowing about the beliefs and practices of other people who share our world is vital to everyone's future.

## Acceptable Practices

While your state's standards may give you the "green light" to teach on religious topics in your classroom, it is important that educators clearly differentiate between the teaching *of* religion and teaching ***about*** religion. The teaching about religion is accepted, because it focuses on religion as a content topic. Further guidelines to teaching about religion in the public school classroom are provided in Figure 8.3. **Acceptable Teaching Practices.**

It is also important to remember what *not* to teach related to religion in the classroom. For example, the following practices are not acceptable in a public school setting:

## Unacceptable Practices

- Posting the Ten Commandments or other religious tracts on school walls or property
- Allowing teachers to read from the Bible during instructional silent reading
- Keeping books on Christianity (or other religions) in your classroom library
- Offering voluntary Bible classes during the school day
- Having materials that are published by your church or temple available in the classroom for students or their families
- Counseling students to receive assistance or mentoring from a religious leader in your community

Each of the practices above is not accepted because they promote a specific religious practice or belief. No matter how strong of a conviction you may have, it is not your place to promote that belief in your role as a public school teacher.

Just think how boring our world would be if we were all alike in our thoughts, cultural celebrations, and religious practices!

> *Teaching religious values in public schools is not only common practice, it is all but inescapable in our Judeo-Christian culture. The values taught command widespread, almost universal approval. Yet we witness today a vigorous controversy over the teaching of "religion" in public schools that often mounts to a bitterness and acrimony entirely out of keeping with the teachings of the great religious leaders.*
> (Bush, 1954, p. 226)

## Prayer in Schools

One particularly charged topic relating to religion in education is that of the role of prayer in schools. Isn't it natural, for example, for a teacher and his/her students to have a prayerful moment of silence when hearing of a national or global disaster? Or for a student to relieve tension before an exam by reciting a prayer or psalm? Could these honest expressions of faith be in violation of the separation of church and state?

---

**Figure 8.3** ⬇ **Acceptable Teaching Practices**

When is it acceptable to teach religion in the classroom? What are appropriate practices as they relate to lessons on religion? Douglass (2002) offers the following guidelines for appropriate classroom practices:

- ✓ Approach lessons on religion as an academic subject, not as a devotional issue
- ✓ Strive for your students' awareness of religions, but do not press for their acceptance of religion
- ✓ Expose students to a variety and diversity of religions and beliefs; never impose a singular belief or endorse a specific *doctrine*
- ✓ Educate students about religion, but don't promote—or denigrate—religion or religious practices
- ✓ Inform students about various beliefs and traditions, but don't ask that students conform to any particular belief
- ✓ Be sure to teach accurate terminology that is specific to the religions under study
- ✓ Embed the study of religion—where it is appropriate—into the curriculum
- ✓ Work out differences in religious beliefs through communication, rather than through confrontation

---

When determining policy, it is important to respect the rights of students to practice their faith. This includes the right of students to carry a Bible or other religious texts, wear clothing with religious messages, or to meet and discuss issues of faith with other students who share the same religious beliefs.

But what about prayer, either by individuals or in planned group meetings? Courts are tolerant of the use of school facilities for religious purposes—such as student prayer groups—when they are not part of the school curriculum or part of the typical school day. Student religious groups must be treated with the same acceptance as any other group's use of school facilities.

However, the courts have banned school-sponsored prayer or "moments of silence" that have the express purpose of fostering prayer in schools. The line is drawn when prayer is made a *required* part of the school day, such as broadcasting morning devotionals over the loudspeaker or offering prayers during school assemblies. In effect, schools (and their teachers) cannot sanction prayer as part of the school day.

A particularly complicated issue relates to the common practice of offering prayers during graduation. Graduation prayers are allowed under some circumstances, and are dependent on the intent of school officials in offering the prayer, who leads the prayer (e.g., student-led prayers are typically acceptable), and whether a full disclaimer is made regarding the schools' sponsorship of the prayer. An official invitation to a member of the clergy to offer a prayer at a high school graduation, however, is clearly not permissible. Okun (1996) suggests that, to avoid controversy, schools that wish to include prayer in their graduation celebrations should hold separate baccalaureate ceremonies off school property that are not sponsored or endorsed by school officials.

## Creationism and Religion

A final religious issue, that has become politically controversial in many communities, relates to the teaching of creationism (or *intelligent design*) as part of the science curriculum. Some would argue that it is not appropriate to teach students that something known to be true by the scientific community (i.e., evolution) is instead a false theory. Others contend that evolution is disputable, and therefore alternative theories—like creationism—have a place in classroom instruction. Some politicians are even pushing to add creationism into states' science standards.

## Religion in Schools

Your religious beliefs, while highly personal, will no doubt have an impact on how you teach and interact with students in your classroom. It is therefore important for you to clearly understand your own beliefs, and how they fit into the goals of public education.

Using the **Comparing Religious Views** chart (Figure 8.4), jot down what your beliefs are in the use of religious symbols on school property, teaching religion, school prayer, and creationism.

When you are finished, share your views with your group members. Keep in mind that this is a difficult topic for some people to share—so it is critical that your discussion is respectful and professional.

- Are there any issues where your group has consensus?
- Which issue is most hotly debated by your group? Why?
- How would you handle a student whose religious views are in stark contrast to your own?
- How would you work with a colleague whose religious views contradicted your own?

### Figure 8.4  ↓ Comparing Religious Views

**Where We Stand on Religious Issues**

|  | My Stand | Group's Stand |
|---|---|---|
| *Issue 1:* Religious Symbols in Public Spaces |  |  |
| *Issue 2:* Teaching Religion |  |  |
| *Issue 3:* Prayer in School |  |  |
| *Issue 4:* Creationism |  |  |

Legislation to teach creationism as a scientific theory in public schools has been found to be unconstitutional. Courts have also consistently ruled against anti-evolutionists' argument that science classes should present "alternative theories" to evolution, such as creationism. In these cases, creationism has been ruled as a religious view, not as a science, and therefore would be unconstitutional in a public school setting.

Pennock (2002) does find that it is appropriate to teach creationism in a comparative religion class, where an appreciation for American and global cultural diversity can be fostered and encouraged. However, the controversy surrounding the teaching of creationism arises when there is the insistence by some in the community to teach it as part of the science curriculum, where it is given the same weight as evolution.

The issues surrounding creationism and evolution have the potential of splitting members of the community into opposing factions. As a public school teacher, it is your responsibility to support the views of *all* of your students, while strictly adhering to the curriculum guidelines as they are established by your state's standards.

> *If freedom of worship is guaranteed by the Constitution, then, it is argued, we have no right to use the state's power of compulsory education to indoctrinate children with religious beliefs contrary to their parents' wishes . . .*
>
> *If we as educators are to be true to the spirit as well as the letter of our American heritage of religious freedom, we need to remember that no one may be compelled to adopt another's form of worship, and that each must be free to worship, or even not to worship, as he pleases.*
> (Bush, 1954, p. 227)

# School Choice

As explored in Chapter 7, new reforms surrounding No Child Left Behind (NCLB) legislation have had a profound impact on the choices that parents and community members have in regards to where their children will go to school. Providing more choices for parents is one of the specific pillars of the NCLB reform movement, which specifies that:

- Parents of children in low-performing schools are to be provided with increased options in where to send their child

- Parents are to be allowed to transfer their children to a better-performing public school, including a public **charter school,** within their district if their neighborhood school does not meet state standards for at least two consecutive years

In this new era of choice, parents and students are given more options in choosing a public school beyond their neighborhood boundaries. This has led to *open enrollment* policies, where parents have the ability to send their children to any district that has space available after the neighborhood children have enrolled.

Many community members—as well as educators—will argue that choice programs provide opportunities to disadvantaged students that were once only available to the middle class. Others claim that the school choice agenda makes education more like a business, in which an individual school will succeed or fail, based solely on how effective they are in attracting and retaining students.

Increasing choices has had a profound impact on public schools, and is specifically characterized by increases in *vouchers, charters,* and *home schooling.* We will explore each of these issues in this chapter. However, first consider the following brief vignettes, and consider how you would react to these situations if you were the teacher involved:

## School Choice

You have selected to teach in a school that serves underrepresented students, because you know that you will have the greatest impact with this population of students. However, your school has been labeled as "failing" for the past two years, and your students and their families now have the choice to transfer to another school. You also fear that you might lose your job, and consider taking a position in a district that serves an upper middle-class neighborhood. During conferences, several parents ask your advice regarding the decision whether or not to remove their students from your school. What do you tell them? ■

## Charter Schools

A leading politician in your community is a vocal advocate for charter schools, citing the district's inability to attain "performing" status for each of its schools on the state test. The politician argues that public schools are inept at reaching the needs of all learners, and that a strong charter presence will provide parents with the choices that they need to ensure that their students will succeed. It is also argued that charters will provide the competition that public schools need in order to have the impetus to improve. As a leading teacher at a public school in the community, you are approached by one of the charter school's governing board members to join the faculty at their new school. What do you do? ■

## Vouchers

Your state is considering a new law that would allow public tax money to be used as vouchers towards tuition at private schools, in those instances where students are attending a failing school. In effect, public funds would be used for private use—including faith-based schools. Your principal has asked you and your fellow teachers to write a letter to your state legislators that establishes your opposition to this use of vouchers. What do you do? ■

Classroom Glimpse

Classroom Glimpse

Classroom Glimpse

## Home-Schooling

You teach in a district that has a substantial number of home-schooled students, due to the presence of a very strong religious community that endorses this practice. You are approached by a parent of one of these students, who asks you to share materials on physics instruction from your high school curriculum. The parent explains that the student is gifted in the area of science, and that he/she is unable to provide instruction at the level that the student requires academically. What do you do? ■

### Figure 8.5  ↓ Choice Dilemmas

**Directions:** After reading the four vignettes on School Choice, fill in the chart below indicating what you would do in each of these situations. Also include the rationale for making this decision.

|  | Your Decision | Rationale |
|---|---|---|
| Vignette 1: School Choice |  |  |
| Vignette 2: Charters |  |  |
| Vignette 3: Vouchers |  |  |
| Vignette 4: Home Schooling |  |  |

As you consider what decisions you would make in each of these situations, fill out the **Choice Dilemmas** chart in Figure 8.5. Discuss your decisions with your classmates and instructor. On which issues is there most agreement? Most contention?

## Charter Schools

Charter schools represent the bulk of opportunities that are advanced under the banner of school choice (Viteritti, 2002). Definitions of *charter schools* differ from state to state. In most

Private charters are often affiliated with a religious faith, and are privately funded.

instances, however, charters refer to those schools that operate outside of the influence of public districts. Charter laws grant schools the autonomy to operate effectively and independently, free from the usual bureaucratic constraints that public districts are bound to enforce. Because of NCLB provisions, some districts are choosing to convert their low-performing schools to charters; some districts, however, are *forced* to make this decision.

Charters can be either public or private institutions. Typically speaking *public charters* follow much of the same state guidelines and requirements as regular public district schools, but might choose a certain "flavor" for their curriculum—such as a focus on the arts or sciences. Some advertise that their curriculum promotes "back to the basics" curriculum and discipline. Public charters receive tax-supported funding from the state and federal governments.

*Private charters* are typically those that charge student tuition, and therefore do not receive funding from the state. Because they are privately funded, they are typically not held to any of the state laws regarding testing and curriculum that public schools must follow. Private schools often are affiliated with a religious faith. The Catholic Church, for example, has supported private parochial schools for much of our nation's history.

Depending on where you live, many different organizations can receive a charter from the state to open a charter school. In some instances, even public school districts can open their own charters. Private tutoring companies, individual educators, and universities can, in some instances, also open charter schools.

Figure 8.6 provides an overview of **California's Charter Schools Act,** which includes specific rationale for implementing charters for their constituents. What is included in your state's chartering laws?

---

**Figure 8.6** ⇩ **Charters in California**

**Charter Schools Act of 1992**

It is the intent of the Legislature, in enacting this part, to provide opportunities for teachers, parents, pupils, and community members to establish and maintain schools that operate independently from the existing school district structure, as a method to accomplish all of the following:

(a) Improve pupil learning
(b) Increase learning opportunities for all pupils, with special emphasis on expanded learning experiences for pupils who are identified as academically low achieving
(c) Encourage the use of different and innovative teaching methods
(d) Create new professional opportunities for teachers, including the opportunity to be responsible for the learning program at the schoolsite
(e) Provide parents and pupils with expanded choices in the types of educational opportunities that are available within the public school system
(f) Hold the schools established under this part accountable for meeting measurable pupil outcomes, and provide the schools with a method to change from rule-based to performance-based accountability systems
(g) Provide vigorous competition within the public school system to stimulate continual improvements in all public schools

*http://www.leginfo.ca.gov/cgi-bin*

---

**Effects on Student Learning** Do charter schools really make a difference in the lives of their students? While the actual results on academic achievement are mixed, therefore not favoring either public district schools or charters, supporters of charter schools contend that this movement has had the following educational benefits (Howe, Eisenhart, & Betebenner, 2002; Viteritti, 2002):

- More rigorous standards for students
- Higher expectations for students
- Safer school environments
- More defined sense of community within the school
- Increased enthusiasm among teachers
- Higher satisfaction among parents
- Incentive for poorly performing schools to be forced to close if they don't improve
- Promotion of equity by allowing students in under-served and poor neighborhoods to leave failing schools
- More effective responses to students' diverse needs and interests

But what price is paid by communities that have a charter school presence? Is this the best choice for policymakers to improve the educational system for students and their families? Opponents of charter schools cite the following costs of the charter school movement:

- Increased competition between schools, often resulting in divided neighborhoods
- Potential for "skimming" the highest-achieving students from their neighborhood schools

- Potential for diverting schools' funds to market themselves in a competitive environment, to the expense of their educational mission
- Stratifying schools by race and economic status as White students choose schools outside of predominately minority neighborhoods (Howe et al., 2002)

Charter schools can provide students and their families with quality options. As an educator, you will need to decide whether the potential costs to public district schools is politically the best choice for you and your community's students.

## Vouchers and School Choice

The topic of vouchers is highly politicized, and debates regarding their implementation are often very contentious. In effect, *vouchers* are state-supported funds given to parents to use towards tuition at schools of their choice. Vouchers are part of some NCLB programs. When schools fail, parents may get vouchers to send their students elsewhere.

The use of vouchers to support students' enrollment specifically at private schools has gained increased momentum nation-wide. Supporters of vouchers claim that they have the right to take money that would be used to educate their students in public schools, and even apply taxpayers' money to the tuition at religious or private schools.

Viteritti (2002) argues that, in order to be effective, vouchers should be limited only to economically disadvantaged students who attend chronically failing schools. This educator also believes that private schools that accept public vouchers should be held accountable to a public authority. In effect, these schools should be required to demonstrate a level of academic proficiency that is comparable to those set by the states for regular public schools.

The use of vouchers in private schools opens up a very obvious legal issue—isn't providing students with *public* funding to attend *private religious* schools a violation of the First Amendment? While courts in many states have supported this view, others have upheld the use of vouchers regardless of the school setting.

Those who support vouchers suggest that this policy has the following benefits:

- Enhancing educational opportunity and equity
- Leveling the playing field, by allowing economically disadvantaged students with the chance to attend schools with more advantaged peers (Viteritti, 2002)
- Allowing families in sub-par neighborhoods to send their students to better schools in other areas

However, those who are opposed to vouchers believe that this practice could shift resources away from public education, particularly when they are used to fund private schools. Also of concern is whether the use of public funds for private schools does indeed violate the First Amendment, and whether the practice encourages fraud among those private schools that are competing for tax dollars (Viteritti, 2002).

# Home Schooling

The final issue of political debate in this chapter deals with the issues surrounding parents' choice to home school their students. Currently, approximately one percent of school-aged children are home schooled (Lines, 1996), and that number appears to be growing. Home schooling is often the choice of parents who are reacting to the perceived declining state of public education, and is one of the choices that is gaining prominence under current policies.

Home schooling is not a new phenomenon, and was in fact a mainstay of education in our nation's founding years (Duffey, 1998). However, until the 1970s, this practice was primarily limited to students in very remote areas and with those with chronic illness or physical disability.

The choice to home school often stems from the desire to be free to teach one's own values and to provide higher academic standards.

The most recent movement appears to have stemmed from a dissatisfaction with public education; religion is also a major factor in families' decisions to keep their children home for school. Families choosing home schooling are predominately White, evangelical, or fundamentalist Protestant Christians, who are relatively wealthy and well educated (Lubienski, 2000). The mother is typically the primary teacher in home school settings, and the use of technology is becoming more pervasive for these students.

The choice to home school today often stems from the desire to be free to teach one's own family or religious values and to provide higher academic standards. Safety also appears to be a key reason for choosing home schooling, as families are becoming increasingly concerned with the environment of their neighborhood public schools.

*No satisfactory substitute has ever been found for a good home. It is still the center of our social order.* (Gilliam, 1943, p. 98)

## Home Schooling and Accountability

With the implementation of rigorous state standards and accountability practices, there is increasing debate on how home schooling should be regulated—if at all. Although all states do require families to file basic information about the home schooling experience with either the state or local district, there are no uniform expectations across states. For example, some states do require the submission of a curriculum plan and regular testing of the students; others require education and/or testing for the parents themselves (Lines, 1996).

There are many community initiatives that are emerging to assist families who are making the choice to home school their students.

### Community Resources

- Parents share resources from other home-schooling families, which include both local and state support groups
- Community agencies, such as libraries, museums, parks, churches, and local businesses, provide families with educational resources
- Many private educational institutions offer curricular packages, books, and other materials to assist in instruction
- "Umbrella schools," which are incorporated under private school regulations, allow students to affiliate with these institutions without necessarily attending classes; this also provides home-schooled students with the opportunity to socialize with peers (Duffey, 1998)

Public neighborhood schools are also assisting home-schooled students in their communities. These unique partnerships can include:

1. Allowing families to use their facilities for activities
2. Providing specific services and personnel to assist students with special needs
3. Developing education centers for families, where they can access resources and support
4. Offering dual enrollment or other part-time school attendance, particularly with advanced subject matter
5. Allowing students to participate in sports, band, or other extracurricular activities

## The Choice to Home School

Does home schooling really work? What are the advantages and potential drawbacks for the students who receive their education at home?

Much of the research on the effectiveness of home schooling is mixed. For example, research has not determined whether the same students would perform better or worse in a public classroom or in a home school environment (Lines, 1998). And while virtually all data indicate that home-schooled students test above average, many home-schooled students are not tested at all.

Home-school advocates do point out that these students have significantly fewer behavior problems than their schooled peers, and do not lag behind conventionally schooled students in their social development (Duffey, 1998). Others point out the advantages of the home's safe environment, and the increased opportunity for students to interact with individuals of varied ages.

Many educators are vocally opposed to home schooling, however, and believe that this practice can have the following negative outcomes (Duffey, 1998; Lubienski, 2000):

- Disadvantaging home-schooled students because of a lack of social development, student diversity, classroom-provided stimulation of ideas, and academic competition
- Exposing home-schooled students to a lower quality educational experience and lower academic standards
- Undermining the ability of public education to improve and become more responsive as a democratic institution
- Intensifying inequities been advantaged and disadvantaged families
- Eroding the ability of the community to express its interests in the education of those who remain in public schools
- Undermining the public good by withdrawing students and social capital from public schools—to the determent of those who are left behind

Regardless of an individual's beliefs regarding home schooling, it is an increasingly common practice that will affect students in your community. How you respond to this phenomenon—

**Group Talk**

## Critical Issues

This chapter has dealt with a variety of sensitive and politically charged issues, including:

- Racism in schools
- Gender inequities
- Religion in the classroom
- School prayer
- Creationism vs. evolution
- School choice
- Charter schools
- Vouchers
- Home schooling

Where do you as a group stand on these critical national issues? For your Group Talk exercise, prepare a debate on one of the topics above. Using the following procedure, organize your debate and present it to the class:

1. Select one issue from the list above
2. Choose a moderator from your group to oversee the debate
3. Randomly split into two "teams" (pro and con)
4. Each team takes five minutes to brainstorm the pros or cons of the selected issue
5. The pro team begins by making its presentation on why it supports this issue
6. The con team has two minutes to rebut the pro team's presentation
7. The con team makes its presentation on why it opposes the issue
8. The pro team has two minutes to rebut the con team's presentation
9. The moderator provides a summary of the debate

After you have finished with the debate, spend a few minutes individually to reflect on what you have learned in this chapter. Look back on your responses on the **Choice Dilemma** chart (Figure 8.5). Have any of your beliefs changed on these issues?

---

both politically and educationally—will in turn impact the students whose families choose to school them at home.

## Looking Forward

This chapter has focused on a variety of issues that are sensitive both politically and individually. Some of these issues may anger you as a future teacher—and others you will embrace because they match your own philosophical or religious beliefs. Keep in mind that there are no absolutes in any of these issues, however. It is important that you respond to each of these issues with an open mind, and with acceptance to new ideas and to the students who are impacted by the decisions of others.

How political should you be in support or defiance of these issues? As political as you need to be to most effectively and appropriately advocate for your students!

As you conclude this chapter, read the "Talking to Teachers" vignette on Patty Phelps. How do you think Patty, or her previous teacher-mentors, would advocate for students in their classrooms? What political actions might they take in order to insure academic excellence?

 *In the final analysis, the classroom teacher is the key person in reaching our educational objectives.* (Shaftel, 1957, p. 298)

# Talking to Teachers—The Motivation to Teach

Why do individuals choose to become a teacher? Perhaps because the challenges of teaching are outnumbered only by the rewards that come from helping students realize their dreams. The following teacher shares her reasons for becoming an educator. Review her story and see if you understand and relate to her feelings and experiences

Patty Phelps is a professor of middle/secondary education and instructional technologies and faculty coordinator of the Instructional Development Center at the University of Central Arkansas. Her research interests include classroom management, middle-level teacher education, and professional development.

I became a teacher because of a teacher. No fan of school until the sixth grade, I had a teacher that year who seemed glad to be among children and who had a contagious enthusiasm for learning. This was the first teacher who inspired me to become a teacher. After this educational turning point, I had other teachers who loved learning and who enjoyed interacting with students. Their modeling was powerful because I decided that teaching was something that I wanted to do.

My high school Latin teacher greatly impacted my decision to become a Latin teacher myself. She was in her sixties and still had a zest for learning and helping young people. She was my teacher for three years. After she retired, I stayed in contact with her. She demonstrated the value of learning as a way to stay young. In her retirement years, she continued to take classes and to read—an inspiration to me.

Teaching is a wonderful profession. The many relationships that I have formed with students over the past twenty-seven years have provided me with great satisfaction. What other career choice is so different each day, so challenging, such a learning experience, and a positive chance to be around young people? I can't think of a better way to invest my life than to teach.

***Patty talks about building and maintaining a relationship with her favorite teacher. What do you want your former students to say about you? Why?***

## Research Citations

Au, K. (1998). Social constructivism and the school literacy learning of students of diverse backgrounds. *Journal of Literacy Research, 30*, 297–319.

Au, K. H., & Raphael, T. E. (2000). Equity and literacy in the next millennium. *Reading Research Quarterly, 35*, 170–188.

Blumer, I., & Tatum, B. D. (1999). Creating a community of allies: How one school system attempted to create an anti-racist environment. *International Journal of Leadership in Education, 2*(3), 255–267.

Bush, M. (1954). The common denominator in religious values. *Educational Leadership, 11*(4), 226–232.

Butler, D. (2004). Gender, girls, and computer technology: What's the status now? *Clearing House, 73*(4), 225–230.

Dawson, H. A. (1943). What we're up against. *Educational Leadership, 1*(1), 6–8.

Douglass, S. L. (2002). Teaching about religion. *Educational Leadership, 60*(2), 32–36.

Duffey, J. (1998). Home schooling: A controversial alternative. *Principal, 77*(5), 23–26.

Fege, A. F. (1993/1994). A tug-of-war over tolerance. *Educational Leadership, 51*(4), 22–23.

Gilliam, P. B. (1943). Youngsters in trouble. *Educational Leadership, 1*(2), 98–101.

Hammer, B. (2003). Reconsidering the status of Title IX. *Black Issues in Higher Education, 20*(4), 20–23.

Hanssen, E. (1998). A White teacher reflects on institutional racism. *Phi Delta Kappan, 79*(9), 694–699.

Howe, K., Eisenhart, M., & Betebenner, D. (2002). The price of public school choice. *Educational Leadership, 59*(7), 20–24.

Lines, P. M. (1996). Home schooling comes of age. *Educational Leadership, 54*(2), 63–67.

Lines, P. M. (1998). Educating a minority: How families, policymakers and public educators view home schooling. *The Journal of Early Education and Family Review, 5*(3), 25–28.

Lubienski, C. (2000). Whether the common good? A critique of home schooling. *Peabody Journal of Education, 75*(1/2), 207–232.

MacGillivray, I. K. (2000). Educational equity for gay, lesbian, bisexual, transgendered, and queer/questioning students: The demands of democracy and social justice for America's schools. *Education and Urban Society, 32*(3), 303–323.

McClure, L. J. (1999). Wimpy boys and macho girls: Gender equity at the crossroads. *English Journal, 88*(3), 78–82.

Mead, J. F. (2003). Single-gender "innovation": Can publicly funded single-gender school choice options be constitutionally justified? *Educational Administration Quarterly, 39*(2), 164–186.

Menchaca, V. D. (2001). Providing a culturally relevant curriculum for Hispanic children. *Multicultural Education, 8*(3), 18–20.

Newman, J. W. (1998). *America's teachers: An introduction to education.* New York, NY: Longman.

Nichols, W. D., Rupley, W. H., & Webb-Johnson, G. (2000). Teacher's role in providing culturally responsive literacy instruction. *Reading Horizons, 41,* 1–18.

Niemi, N. S. (2005). The emperor has no clothes: Examining the impossible relationship between gendered and academic identities in middle school students. *Gender and Education, 17*(5), 483–497.

Okun, S. J. (1996). Religion in public schools: What does the First Amendment allow? *NASSP Bulletin, 80*(581), 26–35.

Pennock, R. T. (2002). Should creationism be taught in the public schools? *Science and Education, 11*(2), 111–133.

Phuntsog, N. (1999). The magic of culturally responsive pedagogy: In search of the genie's lamp in multicultural education. *Teacher Education Quarterly, 26*(3), 97–111.

Pollard, D. S. (1996). Perspectives on gender and race. *Educational Leadership, 53*(8), 72–74.

Raby, R. (2004). 'There's no racism at my school, it's just joking around': Ramifications for anti-racist education. *Race Ethnicity and Education, 7*(4), 367–383.

Riordan, C. (2003). Failing in school? Yes; Victims of war? No. *Sociology of Education, 76,* 369–372.

Schniedewind, N. (2005). "There ain't no white people here!": The transforming impact of teachers' racial consciousness on students and schools. *Equity and Excellence in Education, 38,* 280–289.

Shaftel, F. R. (1957). Evaluation—for today and for the future. *Educational Leadership, 14*(5), 292–298.

Spencer, M. S. (1998). Reducing racism in schools: Moving beyond rhetoric. *Social Work in Education, 20*(1), 25–36.

State of the First Amendment: Freedom of religion. (1998). *Update on Law-Related Education, 22*(1), 10–16.

Taylor, H. E. (2000). Meeting the needs of lesbian and gay young adolescents. *Clearing House, 73*(4), 221–225.

Viteritti, J. (2002). Coming around on school choice. *Educational Leadership, 59*(7), 44–48.

# Teacher as Advocate

In the previous sections of this text, we explored the many facets of teaching as a profession, the politics of our profession, and how teachers fit into the broader community of schools. In Section 5, we'll examine just one "slice" of teaching—that of advocacy. As a teacher, you will of course be an advocate for your students. However, you will also be an advocate for your peers, your profession, your community, and yourself. How do you balance these responsibilities, and what legal rights guide your decisions?

What does the term "advocate" mean to you? Often, "advocate" is used as a term to describe someone who provides legal support and advice. Children who are victims of abuse, for example, might be assigned a child advocate from the court to insure that his/her rights are not taken advantage of by other adults. An advocate is also used more simply to describe someone who is a friend, and who will provide you with unconditional support. We generally consider advocates as those who are very passionate about their beliefs, and their strong convictions enable them to defend their views even when they might not be popular with the general consensus.

Our definition of "advocacy" combines each of these elements—legal guidance, unconditional support, and strong convictions. In this section will explore advocacy from two distinct angles:

## Chapter 9: Advocacy in the Profession

- Introduction to Advocacy
- Teacher Testing
- Professional Associations
- Merit Pay
- Legal Obligations
- Liability

## Chapter 10: Advocacy in the Classroom

- Inclusion
- Bilingual Education
- Ability Grouping
- Retention

As you read through and discuss each of these chapters, also consider other areas where you will defend your beliefs, and how you shape your emerging definition of "advocate."

# Advocacy in the Profession

I ssues of advocacy, whether related to education or societal beliefs in general, are not uncommon, as you are probably aware in reading your own local news or listening to classroom teachers in your community. There are many forms of advocacy, and always many sides to every story. How do you know which is right?

Often, your "gut" or instinct will guide you correctly, but that will not always be the case. It is important that you are fully aware of your legal rights and responsibilities, and how you can best advocate for quality educational experiences for all of your students' unique and varied needs.

**Definition**

**Ad-vo-cate** -n **1.** A person who argues for a cause; supporter or defender. **2.** A person who pleads in another's behalf; an intercessor.
*The American Heritage Dictionary of the English Language*

**Definitions**

**Collective Bargaining**   the negotiation process through which a school or district's contracts are developed. In some states, this process is done with the participation of professional associations or unions.

**Consensus Agreements**   extensive documents negotiated with unions and school districts that outline the very specific duties of school personnel, and which integrate pertinent state and federal law. Consensus agreements could include contracts, work assignments, policies for school discipline, and a variety of other important areas related to the daily operation of schools.

**Copyright**   the sole right to reproduce original works such as literature or art; teachers need to be aware of copyright laws when reproducing materials for instructional use in the classroom.

**In Loco Parentis**   a legal term related to being responsible for the health and safety of children in the place of the children's parents.

**Mediation**   the process of coming to a compromise when two or more sides disagree on an issue.

**Pilot**   to try out an idea or product; educators may pilot new curriculum materials to evaluate their future use in instruction.

## As you read, think about...

★ What are your own political beliefs, and how might these impact your effectiveness as a teacher?

★ What strategies are most effective—and most appropriate—for teachers to use when advocating for political positions supportive of student and teacher rights?

## Focus Questions

★ What roles to professional associations or unions play in your state (if any)? What issues do they advocate for?

★ What are the benefits and challenges of merit pay?

★ What laws are most pertinent to teaching and teachers?

★ What are the requirements for reporting suspected child abuse?

★ When is a teacher legally liable for student injuries or accidents?

★ What legal rights do teachers have?

# Introduction to Advocacy

What is advocacy, and how does it relate to a teacher's experiences and responsibilities? Consider the following brief scenarios, all of which could happen during the tenure of your career as a teacher:

1. *Teacher strike.* You have been working with an exceptional master teacher for three semesters, and look forward to completing your teacher preparation program by student teaching in her classroom. However, a week before beginning your student teaching semester, the teachers in her district go on strike over issues related to alleged unsafe working conditions. Do you advocate for appropriate working conditions by joining your cooperating teacher in the strike, or do you take the superintendent up on her offer to work through the strike as an emergency substitute?

2. *Association membership.* As a first-year teacher, you are encouraged by your peers to join one of the state's largest professional associations. Your mentor teacher, in particular, pressures you to join in order to show solidarity as a faculty and to provide you with liability insurance. You are not comfortable with some of the political stands of this particular association, but you know that your mentor teacher will be evaluating you at the end of your first year. Do you advocate for your own beliefs, or for those of your peers?

3. *Academic Freedom.* You are a middle school English teacher. During your unit on persuasive writing, you find that your students are not grasping this concept as well as you had anticipated. In order to make this experience more authentic, you divide your class into two debate teams. One team is to write a persuasive piece in support of the president's initiative on educational testing, and the other team is to present the opposing view. One of your school board members learns of this assignment, accuses you of inappropriately inciting students against the president, and asks that you immediately cease this activity and apologize to the community. In the meantime, your students are writing very effective persuasive pieces that clearly indicate their understanding of this concept. What do you do—follow the board member's advice or continue working with your students on what appears to be an effective and motivating lesson?

4. *Civil Liability.* One of your second grade students breaks his arm during recess while sliding down a snowy hill on a cafeteria tray. The student undoubtedly broke the school rules that prohibit such behavior. The teacher on duty fears that she will be liable for this accident and sued by the student's parents, even though she attempted to intervene in his misbehavior. Do you advocate for your student, or for your fellow teacher?

Before continuing with this chapter, consider what you would do in each of the cases above. Fill in your responses on the **Decision Chart** in Figure 9.1. Your decisions as a teacher will be critical to your success as an effective advocate for you and for your students.

# Teacher Testing

One of the very first professional issues you will encounter in your career will be your state's requirements for *certification* or *licensure* (these terms are most often used interchangeably). All states have some requirements for certification. Usually, this involves the completion of at least a four-year college degree, coursework in defined areas (such as the academic content that you'll be teaching and methods of teaching), and a felony clearance. The felony clearance is most often completed through a fingerprint screen (fingerprinting will be discussed in more detail later in the chapter).

Most states now also require candidates to pass a teaching exam or series of tests that measure your *content knowledge* (e.g., how well you do in math and reading) and your *professional knowledge* (e.g., how well you understand various methods and strategies of teaching, learning, and assessment). You may even have to take a basic skills exam **before** you are accepted into your college's teacher preparation program.

A decade ago, teacher tests were not as common as they are today. States would simply certify candidates after they had successfully completed their college teacher preparation program.

**Think About It**

What testing requirements are there in your state, and/or for the teacher education program that you're pursuing? Are there other admissions requirements that you must meet before entering the teacher preparation program? Knowing the answers to these questions will help you in selecting the most appropriate courses. Use the **Program and Testing** chart in Figure 9.2 to report your findings.

| **Figure 9.1**   ↓ **Professional Advocacy Chart** | |
|---|---|
| **Decision Chart—What Would You Do?** | |
| 1. Teacher Strike | **My decision:**<br><br><br>**Why I made this decision:** |
| 2. Association Membership | **My decision:**<br><br><br>**Why I made this decision:** |
| 3. Academic Freedom | **My decision:**<br><br><br>**Why I made this decision:** |
| 4. Civil Liability | **My decision:**<br><br><br>**Why I made this decision:** |

However, with recent movements in the area of *accountability* or professional responsibility (something we explored in depth in Chapter 7), teacher testing has become mandatory in nearly every state. Teacher preparation programs are required to report how well their students do on these tests to the state and federal government in annual "report cards."

Large testing companies create most of the teaching exams, and they are almost always short answer (e.g., multiple choice) with perhaps a few short essay questions. In the best of scenarios, the teacher tests are created with the input of other professionals in the field of teaching—such as classroom teachers, administrators, and college professors. Expert teams work with the testing company to create sample questions, which are *piloted* with teacher candidates in order to determine if they cover the content intended and are worded in a clear manner. If tests are developed correctly, they address two very basic questions: what should teachers *know* and be able *to do?*

**Figure 9.2   ↓ Program and Testing Requirements**

|  | Test(s) Required | Content Covered | Date to be Completed | Other Requirements |
|---|---|---|---|---|
| **Before Entrance to Teacher Education Program** |  |  |  |  |
| **During Teacher Education** |  |  |  |  |
| **Prior to Student Teaching** |  |  |  |  |
| **Initial Licensure Requirements** |  |  |  |  |
| **Standard Licensure Requirements** |  |  |  |  |

*In order to be successful in preparing for the required exams in my state and/or program, I should take the following courses and/or participate in the following experiences:*

## Why Tests?

Some argue that tests raise the professionalism of teaching by insuring that the most qualified candidates are certified; others will contend that such tests are unfair and unnecessary because they don't measure how well you might teach or interact with students in an actual classroom setting.

This is an interesting and important debate that is occurring today between educators and politicians throughout the country.

While very few people actually enjoy taking a high-stakes test such as a teaching exam, it can be argued that such tests support the profession by (Danielson, 2001; Newman, 1998):

- Insuring that the teaching force is academically competent
- Assuring consistency in the quality of classroom teachers
- Raising the standard for those entering the teaching profession
- Keeping teacher education programs focused on content outcomes that are supported by the state

**Think About It**

Is **what you know** (content) most important, or **how you use that knowledge** (pedagogy) when you're in the classroom with your students?

In most states, novice teachers receive a probationary or initial provisional license first, which is valid for one to three years.

However, teacher advocates also speak out against such tests, claiming that they (e.g., Newman, 1998):

- Decrease the number of qualified minority candidates because such tests are often culturally biased
- Contribute to a worsening teacher shortage by limiting the pool of teacher candidates
- Are irrelevant to the actual work that teachers do, because they can't measure actual teaching performance in the classroom
- Add an unnecessary cost to teacher candidates

Where do you stand on teacher testing? Are they necessary tools to insure that only the most qualified teachers enter the classroom, or do they exclude individuals who could have been exceptional teachers?

## What Comes Next?

Teacher evaluation does not end when you pass the teacher exam and get your first classroom position. In most states, novice teachers receive a *probationary* or *initial provisional* license first, which is generally only valid for one to three years. During that time, his/her administrator evaluates the novice. Quite often, an assigned mentor also observes the novice, several times a year. These evaluations generally take place in the classroom, as you are observed actually teaching a lesson to your students. Conferences are held with the observer before and after the lesson, to provide background information for the lesson and performance feedback about the quality of instruction. These formal evaluations occur on an annual basis, until a *standard* or *professional* license is issued.

Once you have a professional license, you can expect a formal evaluation from your school or district, ranging from once a year to every four years. You will also be expected to engage in self-directed professional growth activities such as participating in committees, attending workshops, and even hosting college students! Evaluations of veteran teachers can be combined with many different sources, including:

- Parent surveys
- Student surveys
- Observations from colleagues or peers
- Student achievement data (specifically test scores on standardized exams)
- Documentation of professional activities (such as committee work or participation in conferences)
- Administrators' reports
- Self-analysis of a videoed lesson

Why are experienced teachers evaluated? Primarily, this process provides helpful feedback so that teachers can continue to become more proficient in meeting the needs of their students. We all can improve our practice, regardless of the number of years we're in the classroom. Evaluations can also be tied to extra merit pay, as will be explored later in this section, and to your school's goals for accountability. Evaluation can also be used in a very positive manner, by acknowledging the achievements of your peers and highlighting the best practices to be emulated by other teachers. Evaluations used in this manner certainly provide teachers with advocacy for best practices and for supporting their peers in their professional journey.

# Professional Associations

One of the most visible advocates for teachers and educational issues is the presence of professional associations, or unions. There are two major associations in this country: the National Education Association (NEA) and the American Federation of Teachers (AFT). Professional organizations such as these use negotiation or *collective bargaining* and political action in an effort to upgrade teaching as a profession.

As some of us become keenly aware during each election season, unions can be very actively involved with political campaigns and in advocating for (or opposing) proposed legislation related to education and workers' rights. Unions that are associated with education take stands on issues ranging from curriculum and assessment, to teacher preparation and federal budgets. One of the goals of the professional teaching association is to make teaching more of a "profession" in the eyes of the public that is equal in status to other professionals such as lawyers and doctors. These organizations are also very active in increasing the economic security of teachers and improving their working conditions.

Figure 9.3 provides a summary of the missions of the NEA and AFT. How are these missions similar? What parts of their missions could you support—and which might you disagree with? What political actions do you think that these associations would most likely support?

## Negotiation and Collective Bargaining

One very specific way that professional organizations advocate for teachers is through negotiation or *collective bargaining,* through which a school or district's teaching contracts are developed. The primary focus in collective bargaining is on improving teachers' salaries, benefits, and working conditions.

Not all states use the collective bargaining process. However, in those that do, the process is very similar. Typically, the teachers in a school system choose one union to represent

**Figure 9.3** ↓ **Missions of the AFT and NEA**

"The mission of the *American Federation of Teachers,* AFL-CIO, is to improve the lives of our members and their families, to give voice to their legitimate professional, economic and social aspirations, to strengthen the institutions in which we work, to improve the quality of the services we provide, to bring together all members to assist and support one another and to promote democracy, human rights and freedom in our union, in our nation and throughout the world."

*http://www.aft.org/about/mission.htm*

"To fulfill the promise of a democratic society, the **National Education Association** shall promote the cause of quality public education and advance the profession of education; expand the rights and further the interest of educational employees; and advocate human, civil, and economic rights for all."

*http://www.nea.org/aboutnea/mission.html*

them. This is usually done through a secret ballot. The union that has the most support becomes the exclusive bargaining agent for all of the teachers in the system, whether the individual voted for that association or not. Most often, all teachers are required to pay a fee for the involvement of this association, which is usually equal to the cost of union dues. The union and the school board choose bargaining teams, who consider all sides of the issues that are up for revision or debate. This process is usually very slow and, once a new contract is drafted, does not end until all board members and teachers have the opportunity to review the new document.

In some districts where this is a very strong union presence, *consensus agreements* are negotiated that are very specific, and which cover every imaginable area of school functions including contracts. Federal and state laws are consulted and abided by when drawing up these documents, which are always evolving through annual negotiations between the district and the union. The agreement becomes the guiding document for school administrators, and they must conduct business with the content of these documents in mind. Specific areas included in these documents could cover the following:

- Contracts
- Academic freedom
- Association rights
- Calendar
- Class size
- Student discipline
- Extra duty pay
- Facilities, equipment, and materials
- Fringe benefits
- Health examinations
- Involuntary assignments or relocation
- Leaves of absence
- Professional improvement
- Safe working conditions
- Salary scales

- Substitutes
- Teacher assistants
- Committee appointments
- Report cards
- In-service credit
- Pay for performance
- Professional days
- Retirement incentives
- Student teacher policies
- Use of student test data

**Teacher Strikes—A Controversial Issue of Advocacy**   If the union and school board teams cannot agree to a contract, steps for *mediation* are implemented. Mediation typically involves outside participants, and their decisions are often binding (i.e., can't be changed). However, in a worst-case scenario, the teachers and school board do not agree—resulting in a strike.

In about half of our states, strikes by teachers are against the law. Illegal strikers can lose their jobs, face heavy fines, or even spend time in jail. Whether strikes are legal or not, they can also alienate teachers from parents and community members, who don't want their children spending critical school time with unqualified substitutes.

There are instances when parents do support teacher strikes, however, particularly when it is obvious to the public that the district's school board is treating teachers unfairly. When working conditions or insufficient salaries are truly intolerable, for example, teachers may have the full support of their community if they do decide to strike.

Even when strikes appear to be the only way for teachers to have an opportunity to assert their concerns to the governing board, and to rectify what might truly be unworkable conditions or inadequate pay, there is also an ethical question to consider—**is it right to leave your students without an opportunity to learn? Do you advocate for your profession first, or for your students?** This is not an easy decision for any teacher to make!

Professional associations do advocate for teachers in many very specific ways. For example, some believe that these organizations:

- Represent the best hope for improving public schools, by supporting teaching as a profession
- Strengthen the voice of teachers in making sound educational decisions that lead to improved schools
- Provide teachers with valued professional resources, such as journals, web sites, and professional development
- Offer teachers liability insurance to protect them in the event of any lawsuits arising from a job-related activity (Newman, 1998)

Professional associations for teachers are not without their detractors, however. Critics argue that unions hurt the teaching profession by:

- Putting bureaucracy in the way of quality education
- Serving their own goals, instead of those of individual teachers
- Supporting controversial stands they may not reflect the interests of your own community
- Using collective bargaining as a means to force union participation of all teachers (Newman, 1998)

Will your regional professional organization, or union, be the best advocate for you and your school? That is one of the many important decisions that you will need to consider as you continue to explore your career.

**Think About It**

**Where do you stand?** As a new teacher, you might be pressured to join a professional association that is most widely supported by your peers. However, simple peer pressure is not a valid enough reason to join a professional organization. How do you know what is the right decision for you?

# Merit Pay

An issue that is closely tied to teacher evaluation and contract negotiations is that of *merit pay*. Merit pay programs are intended to give teachers monetary reward, above their contracted base salary, for exceptional work (Ramirez, 2001). Some states have specialized taxes targeted at merit or performance pay for teachers. Sometimes, professional associations may negotiate for extra teacher pay for a district's most qualified teachers.

Extra pay for quality work—that certainly seems like an issue for teachers to advocate for! However, like many educational issues, merit pay comes with controversy. Most specifically, merit pay issues are complicated when states or districts connect teacher compensation with how well their students perform on state standardized tests. Is this a fair way to evaluate or pay teachers? Does it encourage teachers to try harder to improve their own performance in the classroom? Or, when the expectation mounts to insure that all students perform well, does it increase teachers' pressure to "adjust" student scores or teach to the test rather than to focus instruction on students' educational and individual needs?

Advocates of merit pay point to three advantages of these programs. These supporters would suggest that merit pay programs:

- Improve the quality of students' educational experiences (Newman, 1998)
- Provide teachers with the incentive to improve their practice (Morice & Murray, 2003)
- Provide effective incentives for overall school improvement (McCollum, 2001)

However, critics will argue that merit pay has very distinct disadvantages. Their arguments would contend that merit pay incentives (Morice & Murray, 2003; Newman, 1998):

- Are opposed by unions
- Cost too much money to effectively and fairly implement
- Make it difficult to objectively evaluate teachers
- Decrease morale amongst school staff
- May lead to staff dissension

## Making Merit Pay Work

Not all merit pay systems are inherently bad. Like any program, the success of merit pay depends on how the system is created and what purposes it will serve. If an administrator's primary purpose for merit pay is to "weed out" ineffective teachers, then it may not be very productive. However, if the school staff—including teachers—works directly in creating a program that has as its goal the improvement of student learning, then the program will have a much better chance of success.

As you talk with teachers in your community, find out what merit pay systems might be in place. Do these programs support quality teaching and learning, or have some other agenda? Figure 9.4 provides a **Merit Pay Checklist** to assist you as you discover more about merit pay in your own community. As you read about and discuss merit pay with others, you can also add additional components of a successful program to this checklist!

# Legal Obligations

We have looked at three distinct issues related to teacher advocacy—particularly as these relate to advocacy within the profession. There are many additional issues that are relevant to this topic, especially when considering how teaching and teachers are impacted by specific laws. In fact, you will probably take a class in educational law during your teacher preparation program. (If it's not required, we would strongly suggest that you take an educational law class, anyway!)

**Figure 9.4   ↓ Merit Pay Checklist**

School District: _____

Criteria for earning merit pay:

1.

2.

3.

4.

5.

The following is a list of quality indicators for effective merit pay programs. Which of these indicators does your district's program include?

This merit pay program:

❑ Involves teachers in its design, revision, and monitoring

❑ Is *not* linked to student achievement on standardized tests

❑ Is linked to overall school improvement and restructuring

❑ Does *not* lead to competition between teachers

❑ Does *not* penalize teachers for things that are out of their control, such as working conditions

❑ Accurately measures teaching effectiveness

❑ Focuses on described teacher behaviors such as planning, knowledge of curriculum, classroom environment, and accommodations

❑ Encourages a collaborative environment between the teacher and evaluator

❑ Leads to growth plans that are clear, specific, and attainable

❑ Offers meaningful rewards

❑

❑

❑

❑

*Sources:*

McCollum, S. (2001).

Morice, L. C., & Murray, J. E. (2003).

**Li·a·bil·i·ty**   *-n* **1.** Something for which one is liable; an obligation or debt.

**Li·a·ble**   *-adj* **1.** Legally obligated; responsible.

*The American Heritage Dictionary of the English Language*

**Definitions**

Exactly what are you responsible or *liable* for as a teacher? What laws are most likely to impact you? What are your limits as a professional? Although every state has laws that are slightly different, some of the precepts are essentially the same. In this section, we'll take a quick look at some of those issues related to teaching and the law.

## Licensure

One of the first legal issues that you will encounter will be that of state licensure or certification. This has been addressed previously, as it relates to teacher testing. Every state has requirements related to licensure, particularly for teaching within public schools (most private schools also require certified teachers, but in some cases are not held to the same requirements as public schools). You will not be able to legally teach in a public school without first meeting your state's licensure requirements.

Most often, licensure requires the following:

- Completion of a bachelor's degree
- Passing a state teaching exam
- Coursework in the academic content area that you'll be teaching
- Coursework in methods of teaching
- Freedom from convictions of any felonies (typically through fingerprinting; see Figure 9.5)

It is important that you become very familiar with the licensure requirements in your own state, so that you can carefully plan your course of study. By being prepared for what is expected of you upon graduation, you can be your own best advocate!

## Professional Contracts

As discussed earlier in this section, collective bargaining or negotiated contracts are typically settled between the local school board and a bargaining unit selected by a professional teaching association. This type of contract defines salary and conditions of employment for all teachers in the district. You may also have an individual contract from the governing board that offers you a position. Be aware that both types of contracts are legally binding; read any contract very carefully before signing it!

The school board must also comply with any specific conditions that are outlined in the contract. If your district does not honor your contract, you may seek a legal remedy to recover what you believe that you have lost (such as lost wages). However, laws also can work in favor of districts, in the event that you are the one who breaks the contract!

## Non-Discrimination and Civil Rights Laws

School districts are subject to federal civil rights laws, which ban discrimination on the basis of individual characteristics that are unrelated to qualifications like race, ethnicity, national origin, age, religion, gender, and disability, unless the disability renders an applicant unable to perform the responsibilities of the position. School boards must agree in their contracts to comply with all state and federal laws that prohibit discrimination. For example, a school board can't choose a male teacher for chemistry over an equally qualified woman simply because its president believes the erroneous stereotype that "men are better in science." Likewise, a board cannot purposely choose someone of a certain religion because they believe the individual teacher's beliefs are most like their community's. Employment decisions must be based on who has the best **professional qualifications** for the job that is advertised.

You are also subject to anti-discrimination laws as an employee of the district and cannot make judgments or take actions toward students or parents based on the same personal characteristics (like gender, ethnicity, and disability) that are unrelated to student learning and achievement.

**Figure 9.5  ↓ Fingerprinting 101**

### Fingerprinting 101: The Facts Behind the Felonies

What is all this fuss about fingerprinting? What's its purpose? Do you have to be fingerprinted, even if you're just a college student? What's the scoop behind the fingerprinting facts?

In order to become certified to teach in your state's public schools, you will have to prove that you are not a convicted felon (specifically for offenses related to drugs, child abuse, burglary, battery, assault, etc.). This proof is obtained through a fingerprint clearance.

In order to get this clearance, you first must get your fingerprints taken by an authorized agent. For example, some campus police officers may have an agreement with your College of Education to assist students in fingerprinting. Some campuses arrange with a private company to come directly to your school to process fingerprinting with large groups. In some instances, you'll need to go directly to your community's police station to complete the fingerprinting process.

Each state determines what step is taken next. Your fingerprints (and a fee, of course!) will need to be sent either to a state or federal agency—it will depend on the level of clearance that your state requires. Once the agency has checked your fingerprints against those of convicted felons, you will receive a clearance card. The card is usually valid for three years. You will need to renew your clearance card for as long as you are in the teaching profession.

So, what are the facts?
- Most schools require fingerprint clearances for anyone working in that school—including volunteers and student interns (like you!). So, you should get your fingerprint clearance as soon as possible.
- Some teacher preparation programs will require that you have your clearance before you are formally admitted. Do you know what your program requires?
- You will not be able to get a teaching job without a fingerprint clearance.
- Clearances are only valid for three to five years, so you will need to renew your fingerprint clearance as needed. Failure to do so will likely result in the termination of your position.
- If you have been convicted of felony drug or weapons offenses, assault, child abuse, or any similar crime, you will not be able to teach in public schools in this country.

Think carefully about your actions now, as they can (and will) affect your ability to teach in the future!

## Complying with Copyright Laws

Another legal area that you have probably encountered in your college classes involves the issue of *copyright* laws. Copyright protects the creative works of others, including musical, dramatic, pictorial, and printed material (such as this book!). Copyright laws require that individuals receive permission from the individual or company who holds the copyright before copies are made and distributed. The copyright holder generally is the publisher in the case of published work, and the creator of the original materials if the work is unpublished. Copyright law limits the amount of material from copyrighted work that you may copy or use without the holder's permission, subject to the exception for *Fair Use* discussed below.

As a teacher, you will want to share materials with your students—such as newspaper articles, poems, or clips from television shows—to keep your courses current and interesting. But how do you decide what can be shared, and what might violate copyright laws?

There are *Fair Use* exceptions in copyright law, which permit reasonable use of copyrighted material without first gaining permission. Typically, four criteria are used to determine fair use:

- The **purpose** of the use; why are you going to use it?
- The **nature** of the work; what is it that you want to use?
- The **amount** used in relation to the entire piece; how much are you planning to use?
- The **effect** of the use on the potential market or on the value of the work; how do your actions impact others?

Under fair use policies, some general rules of thumb for teachers include the following:

1. **Print material (teacher use):** teachers can typically make single copies for their own use of such works as book chapters, articles, short stories, poems, charts, cartoons, or pictures.
2. **Print material (student use):** multiple copies of some works can be made for classroom use, but only if:
   a. The number of copies made doesn't exceed more than one per student
   b. The material is brief *(brevity)*
   c. You don't have sufficient time to get permission prior to its planned use in the classroom *(spontaneity)*
   d. There is no negative impact on the use of the material to the work's creator or whoever holds the copyright *(cumulative effect)*
3. **Television clips:** televised programs can be videotaped and used by teachers, but the tape must be destroyed after 45 days.
4. **Software:** only one copy can be made of software for the purpose of backing up this material.
5. **Internet:** the laws are still evolving in regards to electronic materials. It is always best to cite any material that you download from the Internet!

## Reporting Child Abuse

In the previous sections, we have looked at issues related to teachers' rights and responsibilities. One very critical legal responsibility—and an issue of student advocacy—relates to suspected child abuse. Very simply stated, the law requires that teachers report any suspected instance of child abuse. This is one of our profession's most important legal obligations.

When do you report your suspicions? And what if your instincts are wrong? The law does not expect that teachers be absolutely sure that abuse occurs before reporting suspected cases. Teachers must simply have reasonable grounds or cause to believe that abuse has occurred. These suspicions must then immediately be reported to your school nurse, school counselor, or administrator, who will report the abuse to the appropriate authorities. Be assured that states do provide protection for you if your report does not turn up any actual abuse. You cannot be held legally liable if you make a report in good faith.

Consider the two vignettes, below. In each case, what would you do as a classroom teacher? Report, or wait and see?

## Suspected Abuse

You are a first-grade teacher. One of your students arrives to school mid-year with a black eye. She is also wearing the same shirt she had worn the day before, and it appears that she hasn't recently bathed. When you ask her how she received her injury, the student simply shrugs and looks away. During the day, she plays and interacts with the other students as she normally has done, though it is obvious she is in some discomfort from her injury. Is this a result of an innocent accident, or has stress at home led to abuse? What do you do? ■

## Suspected Abuse

You are a high school chemistry teacher. Over the course of the semester, you have noticed subtle signs that one of your straight-A fifth period students has become increasingly obsessed with sex. You have seen images from pornographic magazines wedged in his notebook, and have caught him touching himself during study hall. When you approach him, he reacts violently when you put your hand on his shoulder. Is this simply the normal effects of 15-year-old hormones, or something else? What do you do? ■

Discuss the vignettes above with a classmate. What would each of you do in these situations?

What signs should you be looking for in child abuse cases? Black eyes? Repeated bruising? Sore limbs? Strange marks? Is poverty necessarily a factor in child abuse or does abuse cross family income levels? What about race or ethnicity? There are many sources available to teachers for signs to watch for in child abuse cases. With your peers, use the **Guidelines for Child Abuse Reporting** chart (Figure 9.6) to create a plan that you can use to assist you in this very important discussion.

Once you have completed the Child Abuse Reporting chart, look back at the two proposed vignettes. Have you changed your views about what you should do in each of these cases? Keep in mind, however, that you should **always report any suspicions** that you have to your school nurse, counselor, or administrator.

However, also be careful of any unintentional biases that might misguide your judgments. In the first vignette, for example, did you associate poverty with abuse? Or, in the second vignette, did you assume all would probably be okay with the student because of his academic success? Look again at these vignettes, and consider where your own biases might lie.

## Dealing with Corporal Punishment

When is it legally acceptable to hit a child? Ironically, when that child is in school! Despite what is known about the long-lasting, negative consequences of physical punishment, more than half of our states still have laws that protect a school's use of corporal punishment. Some

| Figure 9.6 ↓ Guidelines for Child Abuse Reporting | |
|---|---|
| Our state law regarding the reporting of child abuse: | |
| | **Signs of Abuse** |
| Physical Abuse | ■  ■  ■  ■ |
| Sexual Abuse | ■  ■  ■  ■ |
| Emotional Abuse | ■  ■  ■  ■  ■  ■ |
| Our sources: | |

states authorize the use of corporal punishment even without prior permission of a child's parents. Those who support corporal punishment believe that it is an effective last-resort method of curtailing inappropriate student behavior.

Does your state allow corporal punishment? If so, do your community's districts advocate its use? Under what conditions? These are critical questions to ask as you explore the range of working conditions and educational philosophies in the communities around you.

When *should* it be legally acceptable to hit a child? **Never!** We believe that championing for the elimination of corporal punishment laws is one of the most important ways that you can advocate for the physical and emotional safety of your community's children.

## Liability

You are in your classroom, in the middle of teaching a lesson on cell division, and one of your students trips and cuts his eye on the corner of a lab table. Or one of your first graders gets lost on field trip and ends up injuring herself. Are you legally responsible? Where do the laws draw the line between accidents and personal liability? Are the laws different for teachers than other citizens? Who legally advocates for teachers should something occur?

Teaching is a huge and serious responsibility. It is important to keep in mind that, when you are on duty in your role as a teacher, *you,* as teacher in the district, are responsible for the health and safety of the students who are under your care (this follows the legal principle called *in loco parentis*). Liability in this area applies to the legal concept of **negligence,** or careless conduct which results in injury or damage to persons or property. Negligence does not require malice or intentional misconduct.

As a teacher, you have a duty of care to your students. If you fail to exercise that duty of care, and your failure causes damage or injury, your action may be negligent. So, when a teacher fails to exercise adequate care to protect students from injury or harm, the teacher may be *liable,* or legally responsible for negligence. Legal questions raised in determining liability are:

- What is the probability that the injury could have been foreseen?

- Would another reasonable person with similar training have handled the situation differently?

In order to avoid putting yourself into a liability situation, the following guidelines are offered:

1. *Make a reasonable attempt to anticipate dangerous conditions.* If you are planning a field trip, for example, visit the site ahead of time to check to see if there are areas where students might hurt themselves.

2. *Take precautions, and establish rules and procedures to prevent injury.* If you know that there is a steep hill in the park where you're taking your students, for example, make sure that you

To avoid a liability suit, make sure students are aware of proper procedure, and wear safety glasses and other protective gear.

establish guidelines *before* your trip that prohibit students from going to that particular area. Create a map of the area to give to your students and any adults who might be accompanying you on the trip.

3. *Warn students of possible dangerous situations.* Before doing a science experiment that involves acid, for example, warn students of this danger and demonstrate proper procedure. Also make sure that your students follow all procedures in regards to safety glasses and any other relevant protective coverings!

## School District's Liability Insurance

Be aware that the school district must have liability insurance for the board and all employees of the district. Generally, the board's insurance will protect you and provide coverage and legal representation if your negligence occurred within the scope of your duties as a teacher.

You may also consider purchasing your own professional liability insurance. Most commonly, teachers choose this coverage through their professional associations—who will most often offer legal advocacy if you are involved with a civil lawsuit. However, you can also check with your homeowner's insurance agency to see if they offer additional professional insurance for teachers.

## Important Teacher's Rights

Teachers do have many rights—and responsibilities—related to their professional careers. What are the rights with which you need to be the most familiar?

**Rights on Dismissal**   How secure is your position as a teacher? What happens after your contract expires? Can you be fired? These are very important questions to consider as you begin your career. Be assured that you do have employment rights as an employee. However, a district's freedom to discontinue your employment will depend in part on the number of years you have taught in the district—or whether you have achieved *tenure* in your teaching position. In elementary and secondary school systems, state law often governs and requires a certain number of years of successful teaching in the district before becoming tenured.

**Tenure/Non-Tenure**   New teachers are generally hired on a one-year contract. Typically, districts aren't required to provide you with a reason for not continuing your contract the following year. Often, if a district does not continue your contract, it is due to a school's enrollment patterns. For example, if there is a decrease in the number of students anticipated at your grade level for the following school year, the newest teachers are those who would be the first to be let go. (Don't despair, however—enrollment projections are just estimated guesses, and often districts end up needing all their teachers, anyway!)

Tenured teachers, or those who have been in a district for about three years, depending on state law or district policy, have considerably more job protection than new or untenured teachers. Tenured teachers can still be dismissed, but the district must meet legal requirements before dismissal and removal from the payroll.

**Due Process**   The Fourteenth Amendment to the United States Constitution and court cases, also referred to as "common law", require *Due Process* before dismissal of a tenured teacher. Due Process requires:

1. Just cause
2. Notice
3. The right to a hearing before the school board

According to Newman (1998), a district's just cause for dismissal would fall under the following categories:

- **Incompetence**—a general category that includes a teacher's lack of knowledge, violation of school rules, inability to impart knowledge to the students, or lack of discipline in class.

- **Incapacity**—this includes any physical or mental condition that keeps a teacher from performing her/his duties.

- **Insubordination**—generally speaking, this includes the violation of school rules and policies, after a warning or instruction.

- **Unprofessional conduct**—included in this category would be teachers who insult their peers or administrators; take time off without permission or due cause; drink or use illegal drugs while on the job; demean or injure students; or communicate to others false, defamatory statements about students or employees that injure their reputations.

- **Immorality**—this category is more difficult to precisely define, and will depend on the community in which you teach. However, dismissal could occur for such behaviors as criminal activity, sexual misconduct, dishonesty, or theft of school or district property.

When the board moves to dismiss a tenured teacher, he or she has the right to notification of any chargers and a hearing. At the hearing, the teacher may present witness and documentation, and challenge or question the district's evidence and witnesses. The teacher also has the right to legal counsel, transcripts of the hearing, and to appeal the board's dismissal decision in court.

**Academic Freedom**    You may have discussed academic freedom as it relates to your college courses and faculty, but do you have this right as a classroom teacher? You certainly do! The courts have held that academic freedom is based on an individual's First Amendment rights and is fundamental to our democratic society. But what are your limitations—especially if you choose to teach in a public school?

Academic freedom protects your rights to teach, research, and publish within certain parameters. The courts have supported teachers' rights to speak freely about the subjects that they teach, to experiment with new ideas, select materials to use in their instruction, and make decisions regarding their teaching methods. Courts have ruled in teachers' favor when school officials try to prescribe and limit *how* teachers teach.

However, this is an issue of balance. As was explored in Chapter 2, school boards have the responsibility and obligation to make sure that the district's adopted curriculum is actually taught in the classroom. Therefore, the courts generally do uphold the power of school boards to select or eliminate textbooks, as they are often the primary vehicles for covering the required curriculum. As a teacher, you must make sure that you effectively and adequately cover the content that is assigned to you. The material and methods that you select must also be *relevant* to your teaching assignment and *appropriate* for both the age and maturity of your students.

**Teachers and the Law**    In this chapter, we have overviewed many rights and responsibilities of teachers. What court cases, and resulting laws, are the most pertinent for you to know? As we have suggested previously, we would advise any future teacher to take a courses specific to educational law. However, as a means for initiating discussion and future dialogue on this important topic, we've provided a summary of important court cases in Figure 9.7. This summary was developed through a survey of school administrators, school attorneys, and law professors who selected court cases that they believed to be the most important for educators to understand (Grady, McKay, Krumm, & Peery, 1998). We encourage you to investigate other related cases, and to determine why they are important to you as a future educator.

**Figure 9.7** ↓ **Summary of Educational Court Cases**

### Due Process

*Goss v. Lopez, 419 U.S. 565 (1975)*
In this case, the U.S. Supreme Court affirmed the constitutional rights of students who have been suspended to the protection of due process through notice and hearing.

### Search and Seizure

*New Jersey v. T.L.O., 469 U.S. 325 (1985)*
This case focuses on student rights related to search and seizure of property on school grounds. It was found that the Fourteenth Amendment is not violated if the search is justified by a reasonable suspicion, the scope and conduct of the search is reasonable, and school officials take into account the students' age and nature of the offense. [Related case: *People v. Overton, 20 N.Y.2d 360 (1967)*]

### Student Attendance

*Plyer v. Doe, 457 U.S. 202 (1982)*
The Supreme Court held that, once a state establishes that it offers free education for students, it may not deny education to a group of students whether they are citizens or they are illegal aliens. [Related case: *Wisconsin v. Yoder, 406, U.S. 205 (1972)*]

### Education of Students with Disabilities

*Honig v. Doe, 484 U.S. 305 (1988)*
The Supreme Court upheld that regulation under the Education for All Handicapped Children Act that, when a student's misbehavior is caused by his or her disability, any attempt to expel the student from school will be overturned by the courts.

### School Curriculum

*Board of Education, Island Trees Union Free District #26 v. Pico, 457 U.S. 853 (1982)*
The Supreme Court held that, although School Boards have broad discretion in school affairs, that discretion must comply with the First Amendment. Therefore, they cannot remove books from a school library that board members find personally objectionable based on political or moral beliefs. [Related case: *Keefe v. Geanakos, 418 F2d 359 (1969)*]

### Church and State

*Lemon v. Kurtzman, 403 U.S. 602 (1971)*
The case determined the "lemon test" regarding the appropriate use of state money to finance parochial schools, and whether related statutes are in compliance with the First Amendment. The test requires that the statute have a secular purpose, does not advance or prohibit religion, and does not foster excessive government entanglement in religion.

### Desegregation of Schools

*Brown v. Board of Education of Topeka, 347 U.S. 483 (1954)*
In this historic case, the Supreme Court ruled that the Equal Protection Clause of the Fourteen Amendment requires that public schools cannot be operated by the state on a racially segregated basis.

### Teachers' Rights

*Pickering v. Board of Education, 391 U.S. 563 (1968)*
In this important case, the Supreme Court held that teachers do have a First Amendment right to publicly air their views on matters of public concern.

Source: Grady, McKay, Krumm, & Peery, 1998

## Advocacy in the Profession

Four brief vignettes were provided at the beginning of this section. Reread the vignettes, and your initial reactions.

Based on what you have read in this chapter, have you changed your mind? What do you now believe is the best course of action to be taken? Use the **Advocacy Decision Table** to record your perceptions.

Next, in your group, discuss what decisions each person made individually.

■ On which issues was there the most consensus amongst your group members?

■ On which issues was there the most disagreement? Why?

■ What further information does your group need in order to come to agreement on each of the issues?

■ Where can that information be found?

### Advocacy Discussion Table

**Advocacy Vignettes**

|  | Your Decision | Group's Decision | Additional Resources |
|---|---|---|---|
| *Vignette #1:* Teacher Strike |  |  |  |
| *Vignette #2:* Association Membership |  |  |  |
| *Vignette #3:* Academic Freedom |  |  |  |
| *Vignette #4:* Civil Liability |  |  |  |

We also encourage you to meet in peer groups to discuss your reactions to professional advocacy issues raised in this chapter. Review the vignettes from earlier in this chapter, and complete the **Advocacy Discussion Table** in Figure 9.8. How do your views differ from those of your group? Where is there consensus?

Understanding these issues, and the precepts of educational law, will help better prepare you for your career as a teacher!

# Looking Forward

We have explored a variety of critical legal and professional advocacy issues in this chapter. Teaching is a serious profession that demands a keen sense of responsibility and appropriate action. How well you understand and implement the legal obligations related to teaching, and advocate for your professional rights and responsibilities, will determine how successful you will be as a public PreK-12 teacher.

What can you do now to prepare you for success? We've provided some tips on **Action for Professional Advocacy** in Figure 9.8. The decisions and actions that you make now will impact the success that you will encounter in your future career!

---

**Figure 9.8** ↓ **Action for Professional Advocacy**

**What can you do?**

We have explored a variety of issues in this chapter. In order to help you sort through some of these issues of teacher advocacy, we recommend the following:

**During Teacher Preparation**

✓ Find out what exams you are required to pass for certification or licensure in your state. What is the content of those tests? Are there study guides or courses that are available to you? Are you taking the correct courses to insure that you will be successful?

✓ Become familiar with the websites for both the AFT and NEA. What resources are available to teacher education students? Do their political views reflect your own beliefs and convictions regarding teaching and learning?

✓ Research the laws in your state regarding unions and collective bargaining. The more knowledgeable you are, the better decisions you will be able to make.

✓ Does your state, or local school districts, have a merit pay system? How are these rewards determined? Are the requirements different across school districts? Answers to these important questions will help you as you make decisions regarding in which districts you might want to work.

✓ Become very familiar with the laws in your state regarding the protection of children against abuse, and teacher's legal responsibilities to protect children.

**As a Teacher**

One of the best ways to protect your rights, and to document your professional advocacy, is to keep organized records in a professional file. Some of the items that you might want to keep in your file would include:

✓ Your contract
✓ Your teaching certificate
✓ College transcripts
✓ Results from professional exams
✓ Performance reviews or evaluations (related to your classroom position)
✓ Personal growth plan
✓ Faculty Handbook and District Handbook (or consensus document)
✓ Information on district benefits
✓ Any correspondences with the district
✓ Any correspondences with parents

# Research Citations

Danielson, C. (2001). New trends in teacher evaluation. *Educational Leadership, 58*(5), 12–15.

Grady, M. L., McKay, J., Krumm, B. L., & Peery, K. L. (1998). School law for rural school administrators. *Rural Educator, 20*(1), 20–24.

McCollum, S. (2001). How merit pay improves education. *Educational Leadership, 58*(5), 21–24.

Morice, L. C., & Murray, J. E. (2003). Compensation and teacher retention: A success story. *Educational Leadership, 60*(8), 40–43.

Newman, J. W. (1998). *American's teachers: An introduction to education* (3rd ed.). New York, NY: Longman.

Ramirez, A. (2001). How merit pay undermines education. *Educational Leadership, 58*(5), 16–20.

The authors wish to thank Mary C. Stevens and Conrado Gomez for their assistance with this chapter.

# Advocacy in the Classroom

# 10

In Chapter 9, we explored a variety of issues related to a teacher's legal responsibilities and advocacy at the professional level. In this section, we'll examine some of the most current issues related to students.

Advocating for students is one of the most critical roles of the profession. However, this role is not always as easy as it may sound. In every issue that affects the learning lives of students, there are always "two sides of the coin." How do you know which side to support? Is there always one "correct" side, when advocating for students and their rights?

**Definitions**

**Contextual Clues**   the clues or cues found within the context of the situation that will assist in acquiring new knowledge. For example, a reader can use information about the context of a story to help figure out unfamiliar vocabulary in the text.

**Inclusion**   the practice of "including" students with special needs or disabilities into the regular classroom.

**Least Restrictive Environment**   a legal term that relates to the placement of a student with special needs. By law, schools are required to place students into a classroom setting that is the least restrictive for the student.

**Modeling**   demonstrating a skill or strategy before students practice the skill independently.

**Monolingual**   a person that only speaks one language.

**Native Language**   a person's first language; a person's native language is typically the one spoken in the home.

**Tracking**   the practice of grouping students by academic ability. At one time it was a common practice to group students in high school into college-bound or vocational "tracks."

## As you read, think about...

★ When you were in school, what were the educational experiences afforded to students with special needs? How effective or appropriate do you think these experiences were?

★ How were English-language learners supported when you were in school? How are these learners supported in schools today?

★ Have you, or any of your colleagues, been retained or held back in school? What were the experiences of these students, and how did they impact the students' future academic success?

★ What issues of student advocacy are currently most often discussed or debated in your state or community?

★ When talking with teachers in your community, what concerns do they have regarding the challenges of meeting the needs of all learners in their classrooms?

★ What are the needs of your future students, and how can you best advocate to support these needs?

## Focus Questions

★ What is the role of the classroom teacher in meeting the needs of students with disabilities? Of students who speak a language other than English?

★ What is the most effective way to teach students English within a school setting?

★ What labels do teachers and/or schools inadvertently put on students?

★ What effects to labels have on students' learning and expectations over time?

While there are a variety of relevant advocacy issues that confront teachers and schools today, those that we'll examine in this chapter will include:

- Inclusion
- Bilingual education
- Grouping
- Retention

## Inclusion

When you were a K-12 student, how did your school respond to students with special needs? Where these children kept in your classroom? Did they have aides to assist them and your teacher? Or was it more common that students with needs were pulled out of the classroom

**Think About It**

Before you begin reading this chapter, use the **Exploring Student Issues** chart in Figure 10.1 to jot down your perceptions on these issues. What do these terms mean to you? How do these impact students? And teachers?

**Figure 10.1   ⇓ Exploring Student Issues: Initial Perceptions**

*Directions:* Consider the terms below. Fill in how you define these terms, and what effects that you believe these practices have on students and teachers.

| | Your Definition | Effects on Students | Effects on Teachers |
|---|---|---|---|
| Inclusion | | | |
| Bilingual Education | | | |
| Grouping | | | |
| Retention | | | |

Responding effectively to a student with special needs will be one of the most critical strategies to learn as a classroom teacher.

into their own resource room for most of the day? How effective do you think your school's system was for those students? For your peers in the regular classroom?

Responding effectively to the needs of students with special needs will be one of the most critical strategies for you to learn as a classroom teacher. And one of the most important related student advocacy issues will be that of *inclusion.* Simply stated, inclusion is the practice of placing children with disabilities and learning challenges into a regular classroom. These students are supposed to also receive special services so that they can participate in the classroom both academically and socially. This special help is also intended to insure that the learning of other students in class is not disrupted.

Inclusion results from the 1975 Individuals with Disabilities Act. This federal law states that children with disabilities have the right to an education in the *least restrictive environment.* Removing students from their regular classrooms should only occur when that student is not able to achieve even when provided with supplemental support, aides, and services. Inclusion encourages an education system to bring support services **into** the regular classroom, rather than pulling students **out** for special services.

## What Are "Special Needs"?

You will be taking at least one course in your teacher preparation program that specifically outlines a variety of categories of special needs, and how to best accommodate for these students in your classroom. Briefly, the special needs that you might encounter in your classroom could be classified as:

- Learning disabilities
- Emotional difficulties
- Attention deficit disorders

### Inclusion

Casey is a vivacious seventh grader who loves her friends and socializing in class. Although she has severe cerebral palsy, which affects and restricts her physical movement, she is able to keep up with the academic lessons of her peers. Because she is academically capable, Casey is included in the "regular" classroom for most of the school day. She is assigned an instructional aide, who assists her with physical tasks while in the classroom; however, her peers are also anxious to help Casey out at any time during the day. Casey also has access to a specialized laptop, which she uses for any writing assignments. Casey does participate in all of the academic lessons of her classmates and moves with them as they change classes for each content area. However, she does leave lunch early each day for targeted physical therapy. She also works with a speech therapist twice a week while her classmates are at gym. ■

- Hearing impairments
- Visual impairments
- Physical disabilities
- Mental retardation
- Giftedness

Not all of these classifications will affect a student's academic potential in your classroom. Students with physical disabilities or hearing/visual impairments, for example, are likely to be some of the most academically capable students in your class! In order to meet their potential, however, some of these students may need a bit of extra help from you or a specially trained instructional aide. Students with more severe learning challenges may need some time in a resource or "special education" room in order to receive focused instruction at their academic level.

However, it is important that you not let labels or disabilities affect your impressions of any students in your class! All students have special gifts—and special talents—despite their labels! And we guarantee that you will have students with special needs in your classroom— whether you end up teaching preschool or twelfth grade biology!

## Implementing Inclusion

How does inclusion really work in the classroom? Consider the "Inclusion" vignette from a seventh grade class.

Although federal and state laws are very clear on protecting the rights of students with special needs, the ways in which inclusion is interpreted and implemented across districts does vary. In order for inclusion to really work, for example, students such as Casey in the vignette above, who are more severely disabled, should have a full-time special education aide. How else are Casey's experiences reflected of effective inclusionary practices?

Complete inclusion, when implemented properly, is very expensive. As a result, some school boards and administrators may treat "full inclusion" as a way to cut back on special education services (and save money). By simply placing all children in the regular classroom under one teacher's care, these boards feel that they don't need to hire as many special education teachers. In turn, this practice saves the district a great deal of money in salaries and benefits.

But what about the students themselves? How are they best served, given the expectation for inclusion? And what about the "regular" learners who are also in the classroom? Don't they get ignored when a teacher must spend so much of his/her time with the students with the most needs?

It is not surprising that there are both advantages and disadvantages to full inclusion. Some of these pros and cons are listed below. It will also be helpful to use the **Teacher Interview** in Figure 10.2 to learn what teachers in your community believe to be the benefits and challenges of inclusion.

Some of the advantages of inclusion include (Barry, 1994/1995; Shanker, 1994/1995):

- *Making education more equitable for all students;* when students with disabilities are included with their peers, they are given the chance to develop the social and academic skills necessary to function in society.

- *Eliminating problems associated with labeling;* children who are separated from their peers are often given a variety of labels (e.g., "slow learner," "retarded," "low functioning") that follow with them through their schooling experience. These labels can inadvertently keep them from fully realizing their academic potential.

- *Increasing "regular" students' awareness of human differences;* when they have a chance to work with students with special needs in a supportive setting, peers do have the opportunity to develop an understanding of a variety of academic and social differences that will help these students become more appreciative and understanding as adults.

- *Increasing the academic success of students with special needs;* when given the opportunity to learn in a supportive environment, which includes the assistance of trained aides as necessary, these children will perform at much higher levels academically than if they are only exposed to lower functioning students in segregated pull-out programs.

While inclusion may make sense intuitively, there are also some very strong critics. Potential problems associated with this practice include (e.g., Shanker, 1994/1995):

- *Limiting the range of services available;* some parents of children with special needs feel that inclusion may prohibit their child from receiving some of the special services that more traditional pull-out programs could offer.

- *Distracting teachers' attention away from the class as a whole;* when they are not provided with the assistance and resources they need to fully support the students with special needs, some teachers may find themselves spending an unbalanced amount of time dealing with the day-to-day challenges of their most demanding students.

- *Lowering the academic expectations of the class;* often, teachers teach "to the middle" of the class. If there are students with academic disabilities in the classroom, some might argue that the teachers would "dumb down" the curriculum so that these students could keep up with the rest of the class.

**Inclusion that works**   While inclusion will have its critics, most educators believe that this policy is best for both the students with special needs as well as their traditional peers. Whether or not inclusion works depends on a variety of factors, however. Some of these factors are provided below. As you read through this list, consider other solutions to the inclusion dilemma.

1. *Don't rush into inclusion.* Gradually introduce students with special needs into the regular classroom, once their academic and social skills approach a level consistent with their peers (Barry, 1994/1994).

2. *Collaboration is the key.* Classroom teachers and special educators need to work side-by side to best support those students with special needs. Classroom teachers can't think and act in isolated ways, but must instead integrate their planning with specialists (Villa & Thousand, 2003).

3. *Quality teacher preparation is critical.* Classroom teachers need to have adequate training so that they can appropriately handle a range of abilities in their classrooms.

**Figure 10.2  ↓ Teacher Interview: Inclusion Advocacy**

*Directions:* What do teachers in your community believe in terms of the most appropriate practices related to inclusion? What are the best learning environments for students with varying needs and abilities?

Teacher's name

Teacher's level

How long has the teacher been teaching?                How long at this level?

How does this teacher define "inclusion"?


What experiences has this teacher had with inclusion?


What is the school's policy regarding inclusion?


Are students currently included in this teacher's classroom? What special needs have been identified?


What are the benefits of inclusion?


What are the challenges to inclusion?


How does this teacher determine the most appropriate learning environment for students with disabilities?


What specific training or professional development has this teacher had to learn about effective inclusion practices?


What advice would this teacher give to novices regarding best practices for children with special needs?

4. *Also critical is visionary leadership.* School and district administrative leaders need to insist that all stakeholders are actively involved in decisions and policies regarding inclusion. These leaders also need to provide training and technical assistance, as well as the time needed for classroom teachers and special educators to meet and plan (Villa & Thousand, 2003).

5. *Implement cooperative learning in the classroom.* Planning guided group work between students and their peers with special needs is perhaps one of the most important and effective methods that classroom teachers can implement.

6. *Incorporate effective instructional strategies.* Instructional strategies that support inclusion include making subject matter more relevant to the students, using authentic "real-world" assessments, incorporating themes or units of instruction, using technology for communication and access, and building choices and variety into the daily instructional routine.

7. *One size doesn't fit all.* Districts need a continuum of placements that are based on the nature and severity of each individual student's disability or needs (Shanker, 1994/1995). Just as mandatory pullout programs won't work with all students, neither will full inclusion be appropriate for every individual. A balance of options and programs is key to success in accommodating for students with special needs.

How will you best meet the needs of your future students? We've provided some tips in Figure 10.3. **Action for Inclusion.** As you learn more about inclusion and accommodating for special learners throughout your preparation program, be sure to add to this list of strategies!

# Bilingual Education

Another very important—and controversial—advocacy issue relates to bilingual education. How do teachers best support language learning of students who are not yet proficient in English? What have we learned regarding the most effective strategies for this important and growing population of students? How do we as educators respond to this controversial issue? Or rather, the bottom line—how do we best advocate for our students who are ELLs?

As the number of non-native English speakers continues to grow in this country, the issue of how best to educate language minority students needs to be seriously addressed by anyone who considers a career in classroom teaching. The decisions you make regarding your advocacy for language minority students will impact your instruction every day.

Supporters of bilingual education programs believe that a child's *native language* should be valued, and through support and development of both the child's native language and English, language minority students will experience sociocultural benefits as well as cognitive advantages. Critics argue that English is the only language that should be taught in our nation's public schools, and that bilingual programs only delay students' English language development. In Box 10.1, ELL advocate Kate Mahoney shares her view of appropriate and effective practices in the instruction of students who are English-Language learners.

## Figure 10.3  ↓ Action for Inclusion

### What can you do?

Effectively implemented, inclusion is one of the most appropriate strategies that schools can use to advocate for all students—particularly those with special needs. What can you do to prepare yourself for this very important advocacy? We've listed some suggestions below:

### During Teacher Preparation

✓ Make sure that you are prepared to teach students who have a variety of learning needs. For example, you might want to consider getting an endorsement in special education, even if you don't plan to be a specialist. The experiences will greatly benefit you as a classroom teacher.

✓ Learn about a variety of effective classroom practices. The more classroom strategies that you know, the bigger your instructional "toolbox" will be once you are in your own classroom.

✓ Talk to current classroom teachers about any challenges they have faced with students who have special needs, and how they have found solutions that benefit all of their students.

✓ Talk to parents who have children with special needs. What are their thoughts on appropriate instructional settings for their children? What have their experiences been dealing with teachers and school administrators? What experiences have been the most positive?

✓ Volunteer to work with children who have special needs. Many teachers are uncomfortable having students with special needs in their classrooms simply because they are unfamiliar (and perhaps uncomfortable) with students who are "different." As you work with a variety of children, you will discover that all students have needs as well as talents—whether they have a "special" label or not!

### In the Classroom

✓ When you are in the classroom, practice good teaching techniques. These will include *modeling* (or demonstrating lessons before students practice them independently), explaining expectations clearly, interacting with students, and practicing a variety of strategies.

✓ Spend time meeting with other teachers or professionals at the school who also share these students (e.g., with other subject area teachers). Discuss those strategies that have worked positively, and brainstorm solutions to mutual challenges.

### Additional Strategies:

## Box 10.1   ↓ Bilingual Education (BLE) vs. English Only (EO)

### Special Feature by Kate Mahoney

One of the most hotly debated educational issues in our country concerns language minority students, and how best to provide opportunities for success to students who are *English Language Learners (ELLs)*. An ELL is a student whose first language is not English and who is not yet proficient in English. The Bilingual Education Act of 1968 began the federal government's involvement in ELL education. The 1968 act was a federal law mandating that ELLs be provided special language services in public schools, but it did not specify what program or methodology was to be used; this decision was left up to local communities. Over the years, this has sparked an intense debate over whether the meaning behind this federal law was intended to speed the transition to English or to promote bilingualism. Because the education of immigrant students is closely tied to issues of nationalism, immigration, and the politics of multilingualism, the debate over how best to serve ELL students has often been clouded by politics (Petrovic, 1997).

At the federal level, the Bilingual Education Act of 1968, which had been repeatedly reauthorized, was repealed concurrently with the passage of the No Child Left Behind Act, and replaced with the English Acquisition Act (more information on NCLB was provided in Chapter 7). As its name implies, the English Acquisition Act emphasizes the acquisition of English over dual-language instruction, and it imposes new accountability measures on schools. Those measures pressure schools to emphasize rapid transition to English-only instruction, a typical focus of mandated English-only instructional programs (Crawford, 2004). Recently, several states, including California (Proposition 227), Arizona (Proposition 203), and Massachusetts (Initiative 01-11), have passed ballot initiatives that restrict the types of educational methods and programs that may be used to instruct ELLs.

**Defining programs and labels.** Part of the controversy surrounding bilingual education stems from the general public's misunderstanding of the dizzying array of acronyms that attempt to describe the labels and programs for ELLs (see Figure B1.1 **Common Terms**). Generally speaking, *bilingual education* utilizes the native language to deliver instruction while these students become proficient in English. An effective approach to bilingual education is through *dual language immersion*, which occurs when students develop literacy in both their native language and in English. The most common in the United States are programs that teach Spanish to English background students and English to Spanish background students, while developing the native language skills of each group. The goal of bilingual education is for students to become proficient in *both* English and another language.

Also common are English Only program models such as *Structured English Immersion (SEI)*. While English Only and Bilingual Education programs may seem similar on the surface, the goals of English Only instruction are quite different from Bilingual Education. In SEI instruction, the goal is to encourage students to become proficient in English *only*, which often results in the abandonment of their first language. This can occur through pullout programs or structured immersion, and programs generally last for no more than three years (Thomas & Collier, 2002).

**Finding the right program.** What program and instruction is best for students whose first language is not English? Is it best to teach them both in their native language and in English—especially in content areas such as math and science (Bilingual Education)? Or is it better to focus only on learning English as quickly as possible, which might lead to students falling behind academically (English Only)? Should we focus on one national language (English Only), or on preparing students for a multilingual, global economy (Bilingual Education)?

Public opinion and research about whether Bilingual Education is more effective than English Only programs for ELLs appear to tell two stories. There is more evidence, however, that supports the effectiveness of Bilingual Education programs over English Only programs (Willig, 1985; Ramirez, et al. 1991; Greene 1998). Although highly criticized for methodology flaws, there are also a number of studies supporting English Only programs

**Figure B1.1 ↓ Common Terms in Language Minority Education**

**What Does it Mean?**

| | |
|---|---|
| ELL (English Language Learner) | Student who is not yet proficient in English and whose native language is not English. |
| LEP (Limited English Proficiency) | An outdated term for students who are learning English; ELL is now a more accepted term. |
| BLE (Bilingual Education) Programs | Programs that utilize the native language as a way to help English Language Learners succeed in school. There are different types of BLE program models. This became a federal policy in 1968, and is designed to help Spanish-speaking students who were seen as failing in the school system. |
| TBE (Transitional Bilingual Education) | A type of BLE program where a portion of instruction is in the native language to help children keep up in academic areas while they learn English. Typically, the duration of the TBE program is one to three years. |
| DBE (Developmental Bilingual Education) | A type of BLE program that focuses on learning English and developing the native language with biliteracy as the goal. There is less emphasis on exiting students from the program quickly. Typically, DBE programs continue through sixth grade. |
| Dual Language Immersion | A type of BLE program where speakers of two languages are placed together in a bilingual classroom to learn each other's language. The primary goal includes continued development in two languages (sometimes referred to as *two-way immersion* or *bilingual immersion*). |
| EO (English Only) Programs | Programs that utilize English as the only language of instruction. The goal is to learn English as quickly as possible with no attempt to develop the native language. |
| English as a Second Language (ESL) Pullout | A type of EO program where students are pulled out of the regular classroom to study English. Traditionally, these programs focus more on grammar and less on communicative skills. |
| Structured English Immersion (SEI) | A type of EO immersion program that focuses on teaching English through subject-matter instruction in English. Lessons are geared toward a student's level of competence (also referred to as Sheltered Instruction). |
| SIOP (Sheltered English Observation Protocol) | Model for making content more comprehensible for ELLs. SIOP uses specific strategies to teach content while promoting English language development. Can be used in either BLE or EO programs. |
| SDAIE (Specially Designed Academic Instruction in English) | Model for making content more comprehensible for ELLs; SDAIE uses specific strategies to teach content while promoting English language development. Can be used in either BLE or EO programs. |

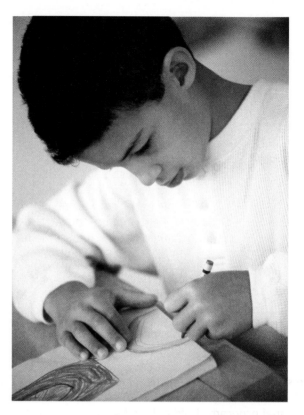

There is considerable debate on whether Bilingual Education or English Only is the best program for English Language Learners.

over Bilingual Education programs (Baker & De Kanter, 1981; Rossell & Baker, 1996). However, we cannot expect a simple answer to the question of whether or not bilingual education is more or less effective than English Only education because there are so many factors and variables involved in this seemingly simple question.

Supporters of *bilingual education* will argue that bilingual education programs have the following benefits:

- ELLs won't fall behind academically. They will have the opportunity to make faster progress in their grade-level content instruction, taught in their own native language, in which the curriculum is not watered down.

- Learning multiple languages stimulates students' cognitive growth, which in turn leads to enhanced creativity and analytical thinking.

- Although it may take up to six years for individual students, bilingual education programs can close the achievement gap that now exists between English Language Learners (ELLs) and native English speakers (Thomas & Collier, 2002).

- Bilingual skills will enable students to respond to the increasing demands of their communities and the expanding global economy.

Within bilingual programs, there are also benefits for language majority students—or native English speakers—who enroll in these programs. English-speaking students often learn a second language quickly, and become more fluent, than if they wait until high school to begin second-language instruction. If a child learns a new language early, he/she often will not have an accent and consequently will sound very much like a native speaker. Native English speakers, who are already on grade level, often exceed the academic achievement of their **monolingual** (e.g., English-only) peers when they also participate in a bilingual program (Thomas & Collier, 2003).

Despite the support of many educators for bilingual education, there are also educators that instead favor English Only approaches. Supporters of *English Only instruction* over Bilingual programs cite the following:

- ELLs in English Immersion programs learn English rapidly, and quickly use English in their content area classes.
- English Only programs level the playing field by removing language barriers (Porter, 1999/2000). When students are proficient in English, for example, they can fully participate with their peers in the educational experience.
- Although highly controversial, supporters of English Only Instruction say that academic outcomes of dismantling transitional bilingual education will increase achievement test scores (Rossell, 2005).

Although immersion in English Only programs may sound like the most sensible approach to teaching English, some educators will caution that many English Only programs are simply too brief to allow students to reach their full academic potential. If ELLs enter the mainstream classroom too soon, they are unprepared for the level of academic language and will fall behind their native English-speaking peers. There is also the concern that teachers lack the training needed to effectively teach ELLs, who are often placed into the regular classroom too soon. This practice places the primary responsibility for the education of language minority students on monolingual classroom teachers who lack the adequate preparation to be effective.

**Why not implement bilingual education?** If there are so many benefits for both ELLs and native English speakers, what criticisms could there be for bilingual education?

For many, criticism of bilingual education is a political or ideologically-driven decision. Some critics of bilingual programs hold a deficit view of students whose native language is not English and programs that utilize the native language. These individuals believe that the sooner children stop speaking their native language and learn English, the sooner they will be able to succeed in school. Some proponents will even go as far as to suggest that it is un-American to speak any language but English. These deficit views are exactly what led to laws in the states of California, Arizona, and Massachusetts—laws that actually ban bilingual education in public schools.

What do the bilingual education bans really mean? In California, for example, schools are required to offer Structured English Immersion (SEI) programs to all students who are ELLs. Immersion refers to putting students into classrooms where English is the only language of instruction, even when that student may not yet know the language (i.e., *"immersing"* students in English). The primary goal of this instruction is to develop English proficiency as early and as quickly as possible. Students are provided with all instruction in English with an emphasis on **contextual clues.** Students are included into mainstream classrooms as soon as possible, for maximum exposure to native English speakers.

Are bilingual programs still possible in states that ban such programs? In those states with bilingual bans, public schools can implement these programs only if enough parents request this option and certain restrictions are met.

**How can teachers best support ELLs?** Figure B1.2. **Comparing Program Models** provides an overview of the two most prominent approaches for teaching students who are not native English speakers: Bilingual Programs and English Only programs. In answering the question—What is best for ELLs?—you first must decide what your programmatic goal is. Then you can better select the program that meets these specific outcomes.

**Figure B1.2** ↓ **Comparing Program Models**

**What Program is Best?**

|  | Bilingual Programs | English Only Programs |
| --- | --- | --- |
| *Goal* | Proficiency in English and the native language | Proficiency in English |
| *Method* | Instruction is designed to learn English and native language while teaching content classes in both English and native language | Structured instruction to learn English while mainstreaming students in content classes taught only in English |
| *Duration* | Up to six years | Up to three years |
| *Student View* | Additive–bilingual skills are an asset to the individual cognitively, academically, socially, and economically | Subtractive–students whose native language is not English are at a disadvantage when entering school |
| *Long-term Result* | Student becomes biliterate–Globally competitive individual | Student becomes monolingual–Universal American language |

## Effective Strategies for English Language Learners (ELL)

Regardless of what you may believe about the use—or the ban—of bilingual education in public schools, there are some best practices that can be used to help support the language learning of all of the students in your classroom:

1. *Value students for who they are, and the experiences that they bring into the classroom.* One of the first characteristics of an effective program is a supportive school-wide climate that values the linguistic and cultural background of students who are ELLs (Mora, 2000). It is also important to encourage families to maintain their home language and culture.

2. *Encourage talk and collaboration between students.* The "student talk" that occurs in your classroom gives students access to many kinds of social and linguistic interactions that they need in order to make sense of demanding assignments, particularly in reading and writing.

3. *Don't wait to teach reading and writing until after students have mastered basic oral language skills.* Language development is not linear; the development of oral language occurs simultaneously with reading and writing. The process of listening, speaking, reading, and writing in one's first and second language is highly interrelated and interdependent (Gebhard, 2002/2003). Therefore, it doesn't make sense to wait until a student is fluent in oral language *before* introducing him/her to words in print.

4. *Use assessment to guide instruction.* Regularly planned (or systematic) student assessment can inform ongoing efforts to improve student achievement and to measure how successful the school's language program is in reaching its desired outcomes. Assessment of students' language skills should always be ongoing and occur in context.

5. *Insist on training.* Ongoing staff development that is relevant to students' needs and which reflects the goals of the programs adopted by your district will help you be more effective in teaching students of varied English proficiency.

6. *Involve the community.* Schools that gain a high level of support from parents, and which actively involve the community, are more successful in implementing whatever language program

> **Figure 10.4 ⬇ Action for Supporting ELLs**
>
> **What can you do?**
>
> It is guaranteed that you will also have students whose native language is not English. What can you do now, and as a novice teacher, to prepare to most effectively teach your students so that you can best advocate for their needs?
>
> **During Teacher Preparation**
>
> ✓ Enroll in as many classes as you can to learn the foundations, instruction, and theories surrounding language development for ELLs.
> ✓ Become an endorsed or certified ELL teacher in your state.
> ✓ Become familiar with the laws and policies regarding bilingual education in your community and state. Are there certain programs that are banned? What are the most common programs that are used? Be sure to investigate many perspectives about how the law is being interpreted.
> ✓ Become familiar with the cultures in your surrounding neighborhoods. Interning in classrooms that have diverse student populations or volunteering for social organizations in communities different from your own can perhaps best achieve this goal.
>
> **In the Classroom**
>
> ✓ Seek out the proper training to learn how to integrate a language focus into your curriculum. ELLs need to be explicitly learning all areas of language (speaking, comprehending, reading, and writing) in each and every activity in order to learn English well enough to compete with their English-speaking peers.
> ✓ As a classroom teacher, get to know your students as individuals. What are their personal academic strengths and learning styles? What languages are used in the home? What are the most prevalent cultural beliefs and practices? Integrate this information into your lessons.
> ✓ Encourage students to use their native language in your classroom. Language can be used as a cognitive tool, and it allows students to more quickly grasp concepts and clarify directions.
> ✓ Use visual clues as much as possible. Students who are learning English will be able to grasp concepts more easily if you provide visual aids and supports.
> ✓ Assign peer mentors. When you have a new student in your classroom that is not yet proficient in English, make sure you match that student with a peer who is language proficient. It is most helpful when that peer mentor also speaks the new students' native language.
> ✓ Reach out to language minority parents and welcome them into your classroom. Take advantage of their expertise and experiences by inviting them to be volunteer assistants or guest speakers.

they have adopted. When creating policies, schools need to take the wishes of local parents of bilingual children into account.

In Figure 10.4, we have provided a list of action strategies for supporting English-Language learners in your classroom. What other strategies can you implement to advocate for the needs of students who are learning English?

# Ability Grouping

How do you best advocate for the needs of individual students? Is it through inclusion, in which students of varied academic, cognitive, and language abilities are immersed in your classroom? Or is it best to separate students into specific learning groups (or even into separate programs)? The answers to these questions are not as easy as they may seem!

The practice of *ability grouping*, or **tracking** students by expected academic ability, has long been used in the American public school system. Elementary students, for example, are often grouped by ability for reading instruction. For those schools that do not fully implement inclusion programs, students are sometimes sorted by achievement level ability and grouped with others with similar academic needs. Students who show the most potential for success in post-secondary experiences are often tracked into "college bound" courses in high school.

The use of grouping does have an impact on the experiences of students. Under the right circumstances, these experiences can be very positive. Unfortunately, however, grouping or tracking can also lead to negative labeling that might remain with students throughout their academic career. Those first-grade students labeled as "blackbirds" in reading, for example, may keep that distinction—and corresponding low expectations for success—through high school.

**Think About It**

What encounters have you had with grouping or tracking in your own P-12 experiences? Were these experiences positive for you? If not, why not?

## What Should Teachers Do?

As a teacher, you will have a wide range of abilities in your classroom, whether you teach second grade or high school algebra. Grouping students by ability is one way to manage the instruction of students, particularly with large class sizes. But is this the best course of action for your students?

Advocates of grouping would acknowledge the following benefits of this practice (e.g., Atkins & Ellsesser, 2003):

- As opposed to "teaching to the middle," in which the needs of neither the highest nor the lowest performing students in your class are not fully met, grouping helps teachers instruct at each students' ability level.

- Through effective grouping, the potential exists to better address the individual needs and learning styles of each student.

- When students are placed with peers of similar ability, students are more confident and will participate more fully in the learning process.

This practice also has its critics, however. Some of the primary concerns regarding grouping relate to the observation that minority students and those who are ELLs are often disproportionately tracked into lower groups than their White peers. This, in turn, decreases the expectation for these students to succeed at high levels within the educational system. Other criticisms include the following:

- Grouping or tracking can be used as an excuse to keep poor and/or minority students "in their place," therefore denying them access to the best quality education (Atkins & Ellsesser, 2003).

- Tracking practices can lower the expectations for some groups of students. In contrast, it is recognized that all students should be held to high expectations in order to fully reach their learning potential.

- Tracking assumes that students have the same instructional needs within all content areas. However, this is rarely found to be true. A student who struggles in reading, for example, may excel in mathematics. By labeling students through ability grouping, however, those students may come to believe that they are less capable in *all* academic areas.

- Students in lower tracks are often exposed to instruction that is very literal and skills-based. As a consequence, higher-level communication and thinking skills may not be fully addressed or developed.

- Students need models and opportunities to interact with many different types of people. Collaborative work with a range of abilities and experiences develops critical communication and life skills for all students. Grouping only by ability denies students these valuable collaborative experiences.

- Labels remain with students for a very long time. When students are labeled as less able, even some teachers come to believe that those students are not expected to succeed at the same level of their peers. Unfortunately, expectations and perceptions often shape reality, and these students become stuck in a cycle of expected failure.

Keep in mind that diversity strengthens classroom learning. By putting high academic achievers with peers of varied ability, those students who are struggling are provided with a model and challenge to achieve themselves.

## Effective Grouping Strategies

While we have just learned about the advantages and criticisms of ability grouping, eliminating any form of student grouping altogether seems like an impractical strategy. Effective grouping can greatly enhance instruction for all learners. But how can this be done?

How is grouping effectively and appropriately handled in a classroom setting? Consider the following vignette of a fourth grade literacy block. While this is an elementary classroom example, how could the grouping strategies be used with younger or older learners?

### Grouping Practices

*8:30*—Mr. Ingle and his students are gathered in the classroom's reading corner, where he is introducing a chapter on the new topic of habitats based out of the class science series. He first previews the chapter, generating predictions from his students. He then reads the chapter out loud, pausing to discuss the class predictions.

*8:45*—The students return to their desks to independently complete a reflection paper on the text that has been read aloud. During this time, Mr. Ingle pulls one student aside that was assigned to his classroom the previous week. This student is not yet proficient in English. Mr. Ingle reviews the key vocabulary from the new chapter, and gives the student independent key word cards to take home.

*9:00*—Mr. Ingle introduces four new texts to the class that are related to the topic of habitats. The books range in reading level and text complexity. After briefly previewing each of the books, Mr. Ingle invites the students to choose the one that they are most interested in reading. The students rearrange themselves into four groups, where they each have copies of their selected text. The students are instructed to silently read the books first, and then work together to create a concept map based on the text.

*9:30*—The students are instructed to take out their independent writing journals, and continue with their self-selected topics. Mr. Ingle pulls five students aside who are struggling with the concept of sentence structure. He models appropriate structure, and guides these students through a mini-lesson. He then instructs the students to first individually edit their own journals for sentence structure, and then to peer edit with a buddy.

During this time, a parent volunteers comes into the classroom to work with another group on the computer. These students have finished their story drafts and editing, and are ready to "publish" their piece for the class magazine. The parent volunteer introduces them to a new graphic program, which they integrate into their final copies.

*10:00*—During the final portion of their literacy block, Mr. Ingle's students gather with the third and fifth grade classes in the common area. Students join their cross-grade reading teams to review a story in the district's adopted literature series. Mr. Ingle facilitates the discussion with the students who are reading from the grade 5 series. Together, they generate a list of new terms to add to their individual dictionaries. They also identify five key words to be used for the week's spelling test. ■

**Classroom Glimpse**

**Figure 10.5** ↓ **Grouping Strategies**

| | How Used | Advantages | Disadvantages |
|---|---|---|---|
| Whole Group | | | |
| Ability Group | | | |
| Interest Group | | | |
| Multi-Age Group | | | |
| Peer Partners | | | |
| One-On-One | | | |
| Other: | | | |

What grouping strategies did you note in Mr. Ingle's classroom? Use the **Grouping Strategies** chart in Figure 10.5 to identify the types of groups used, and what advantages (and disadvantages) each might have. Also consider what additional grouping strategies could have been incorporated into this particular literacy sequence. Then use the Group Talk activity to share ideas regarding the effective uses of student grouping. We also encourage you to refer to Figure 10.6. **Grouping in Action** for a list of strategies you can implement to make this practice effective in your future classroom.

**Figure 10.6  ↓ Grouping in Action**

**What can you do?**

So much in teaching demands a delicate balancing act. As decisions are made for what is "best" for students, teachers need to be very flexible in recognizing that there are not "black and white" answers to teachings' challenges. This holds very true for decisions regarding tracking or grouping. How do you know what is best for your students, to balance between individualized instruction and appropriate management? How do you avoid labels, while insuring that students are taught at their instructional level?

Some of the hints that we've gathered for appropriate tracking and grouping practices include the following:

**In the Classroom**

✓ Regardless of the grouping system that you use, make sure that you have *high and consistent expectations* for **every** student.

✓ When grouping is used, make sure that your groups are flexible. When grouping is flexible, students change their peer groupings periodically, therefore allowing opportunities for collaboration with a more diverse range of classmates.

✓ Avoid the use of labels that may have negative connotations for students.

✓ Insure that your course material is rigorous, no matter what group of students you're instructing.

✓ Never compare students with each other, or one group to another.

✓ Get to know your students as individuals, and vary your instruction accordingly.

✓ Keep parents informed. Regular communication with parents will assist you not only in mutually defining strategies that work with a particular child, but will also be of great benefit if the time should come to make a decision to retain a child.

**Grouping Practices**

What are the most effective grouping strategies that teachers can use in their classrooms? Before completing this discussion activity, individually fill out the **Grouping Strategies** chart in Figure 10.5. Then discuss the questions below with your group members.

**Group Talk**

■ Compare your charts. Were there any grouping strategies that were not illustrated in the vignette? If so, discuss an example of this strategy.

■ Which strategy does the group feel is most effective?

■ Which strategy does the group feel is least effective? Why?

■ Which strategies would be most beneficial with younger children? Adolescents? Students in high school?

■ What grouping strategies do your college instructors use? Which are most effective for you?

# Retention

A final area of student advocacy is that of *retention*, or requiring that a student repeat a grade level. Retention is often contrasted with *social promotion*, or the advancement of a student to a higher grade level before the student has mastered the skills or content of the current grade level.

If students don't pass the material of one grade level, it makes sense to hold them back until that material is covered. Or does it? Consider the following vignette from Bette's experiences as a second grade teacher.

### Retention

As a novice teacher, Bette encountered a rather unique experience regarding her school's retention policies. Mark, a student in Bette's class, was a tall and robust boy who struggled a bit with reading but was very willing and persistent with his schoolwork. Although a bit shy with his peers, Mark was very eager to please others and to work very hard in school. At the end the year, Mark had passed all of the second-grade curriculum with average grades, and was promoted with his peers to third grade.

Approximately three weeks into the next school year, the third-grade teacher, who was concerned with Mark's lack of progress, approached Bette. Bette reiterated her belief that Mark had successfully passed all of the content criteria in second grade. The third-grade teacher pressed the issue, however, and called a meeting with Mark's parents, the reading specialist, the school counselor, and Bette.

Mark's parents were hard working low-income adults who themselves had not pursued education beyond high school. At the meeting, they offered little to the conversation, except to reiterate their desire to do what was right for their only son. Both the specialist and third-grade teacher, who were veteran teachers, emphasized their belief that Mark would not be successful with the content in third grade and should be returned to Bette's class. Bette, herself a two-year novice, concluded that these tenured teachers knew more than she about such matters and conceded to their decision.

Mark, who was now at least a head taller than any of his peers, returned to second grade. Because he had already mastered the content, Bette attempted to rebuild Mark's self-esteem by assigning him as a peer tutor for math and science—areas where he excelled. She also attempted to change her content units so that Mark would not become bored with the curriculum. At the end of the year, Mark once again met the second-grade proficiencies.

Was retention the right decision for Mark? ∎

## Advantages of Retention

In this age of *accountability* and *standards* (issues we have explored in Chapter 7), the practice of retention has many supporters in education and within our society. Many educators will suggest that schools do a disservice to students when they are promoted to another grade when they haven't yet mastered the basic concepts. This issue is compounded by the increasing use of standardized tests. How can teachers justify placing students in the next grade when they can't pass the required tests at the appropriate level?

Advocates for retention will also suggest that social promotion allows students to arrive in higher grades being under-prepared for the content and instructional level that they are expected to learn. In turn, the teachers who receive these students are under-prepared to meet their instructional needs. In sum, social promotion becomes a vehicle for educational mediocrity (Potter, 1996).

## Retention's Negative Side

Undoubtedly, there are also many educators who are opposed to practices related to retention. Critics have cited the following disadvantages of this increasingly common practice (e.g., Amrein & Berliner, 2003; Doyle, 2004; Potter, 1996):

- Retention is an inappropriate strategy used by some educators in a failed attempt to cure academic failure.

- Students from ethnic minorities and/or economically disadvantaged backgrounds are disproportionately retained; therefore, retention as a policy can increase our nation's White/minority achievement gap.

- Because of the pressure to show performance on standardized tests, some teachers opt to retain students that they think might fail those tests that are tied to promotion to the next grade level.

## Retention and Student Advocacy

What is best for students—retention or social promotion? How do you best advocate for your students, while following the policies and curricular expectations of your district? Reread the vignette about Mark at the beginning of this section. As a group, discuss the following:

**Group Talk**

- Do you think that the best decision was made for Mark? Why or why not?
- On what data was the decision for retention made?
- As a teacher, what other information would you need to make the decision whether or not to retain Mark?
- When making retention decisions in general, what do you think are the most important criteria when deciding whether or not to keep a student from moving on to the next grade?

Use the **Retention Discussion Table** to record questions that *should* have been asked during the conference. Also record your group's conclusion regarding what would have been the best solution to Mark's dilemma.

## Retention Discussion Table

Critical Questions Table

| | Questions that should have been asked: |
|---|---|
| Bette (Grade 2 teacher) | |
| Grade 3 teacher | |
| Mark's parents | |
| Reading Specialist | |
| Counselor | |

*As a group, we believe the best solution for Mark would have been:*

### Figure 10.7 ↓ Solutions to Retention

**What can you do? Solutions to retention**

There are many ways that you can advocate for students. One way is to work with your educational peers to craft solutions to those issues that lead to a decision of whether or not to retain a student. The best solution is to address instructional issues *as they occur* so that you don't need to resort to retention!

The following suggestions provide different ways to consider the retention issue. Some of these can be accomplished within your classroom; others require the restructuring of a school or district's grade level organization.

**In the Classroom**

✓ As a teacher, you can retool your instructional strategies so that instruction leads to student success. Using a variety of strategies on a regular basis increases your chances of finding just the right method for reaching even the most reluctant learners.

✓ Devise methods of working with students *before* they fail. This could include tutoring, mentoring, after school, summer, and Saturday programs that provide developmentally appropriate and critically challenging experiences.

✓ Seek out an administrator who supports a positive vision, in which the school as a whole believes that all children can learn at a high level. A supportive administrator can be the best advocate for your success, as well as that of your students.

**Restructuring Schools**

✓ Educators must abandon the mindset that, when children fail, it is the fault of the child. Instead, the instructional processes and structure of learning must be critically considered and changed, when necessary (Potter, 1996).

✓ Instead of grouping students by age (i.e., by grade level based on age), group students by accomplishment. Age is only a rough indicator of content mastery, and is likely to mask students' actual developmental differences (Doyle, 2004). Multi-age classrooms would be one way to attain this goal.

✓ Because all students learn and develop differently, advance students in grade level as they master concrete standards over time. This sets a pace consistent with their own developmental "clocks."

**Think About It**

What are your beliefs regarding retention? When is this an appropriate practice for students? Use the Group Talk activity to share your thoughts and experiences with your peers. We've also included some **Solutions to Retention** in Figure 10.7.

- Much in the educational literature suggests that retention is harmful to students in terms of their achievement and personal adjustment.

- Retention is often tied to higher dropout rates and, in fact, is often cited as the **single most consistent predictor** for dropping out.

- There are no gains in holding students back; they just repeat a failed experience and are socially dismissed by their peers.

- Retention as a practice is both cruel and ineffective.

# Looking Forward

What does it mean to be an "advocate?" In this section, we have explored advocacy from a variety of different angles, including advocacy for your own professional views and beliefs, for your students, and for your profession. We have looked at advocacy as a professional issue, which impacts such areas as teacher testing, decisions whether or not to join professional associations, issues of equity and merit pay, and legal issues that affect what you can and can not do within the classroom. We also explored advocacy as it relates to classroom decisions

# Talking to Teachers—The Motivation to Teach

Why to individuals choose to become a teacher? Perhaps because the challenges of teaching are outnumbered only by the rewards that come from helping students realize their dreams. The following teacher shares her reasons for becoming an educator. Review her story and see if you understand and relate to her feelings and experiences

Theresa Ann Knipstein Meyer is an advocate for special needs students at Sunnyside Elementary School in Indianapolis. She was instrumental in the development and evolution of a reverse integration program in which regular students work with special education students. Theresa was presented with the Milken National Educator Award in 2002.

"Teaching is the chance to lead others into knowledge and discover through their eyes the new things of this world" (Knipstein, 1985). I wrote this quote in my senior year of high school. That is the main reason I became a teacher. I wanted to be a part of the journey that supports and assists young children in discovering the world.

In the last eight years, I have had a great deal of interest in helping teachers stay in the field of education and supporting them in their professional development. I see it as a continuation of "leading others into knowledge and the new things of the world." I became a teacher to become a team member in the field of education and learn from others in the field. I always wanted to strive to help students and teachers be their very best.

Teaching interested me because I could make a difference and impact lives. The field of education also provided me diversity in what I did every day. It gave me opportunities to learn about educational law issues and see that impact on families. I was able to get experience on current research on brain development and that influenced me greatly in staying in the field of education. I was motivated to see how research worked within a classroom and school setting. I also saw opportunities to grow and work as a team. I liked the people in education and wanted to surround myself with people who valued making a difference in the next generation. Over the years, these are the things that have interested me the most in becoming a teacher and remaining in the field of education.

I started babysitting in the sixth grade and especially enjoyed working with children with disabilities and their families. I continued working the next eight summers until I decided to become a teacher of students with disabilities. I always had a heart for special education and teaching. I was just not sure I would choose this as a career. As a high school senior, I made the decision to become a teacher and I have never regretted that path.

I became a very involved and giving teacher. I am a strong voice for kids with disabilities. When working with teachers and students, I really build on all my experiences in life and education. I became a teacher leader who did her personal best to give back to the profession. I found that teaching is a very complex job. It requires a person to wear many different hats in a day and also demands a great deal of knowledge. Teaching can consume your life and burn a person out unless one stays balanced. These are just some of the things that have surprised me about being a teacher in the last fifteen years.

**Theresa Ann clearly has a strong commitment to students with special needs. How do you feel about working with students that have learning challenges?**

that directly impact students, such as inclusion, bilingual education, ability grouping, and retention. As we have seen, each of these issues has both "pros" and "cons" that can complicate our daily decisions as professional educators.

Being an effective advocate is one of the most complex—and critical—aspects of your role as a teacher. Often, you will find it difficult to balance your own beliefs with the rights and responsibilities of your students and your colleagues. Advocacy issues are also often controversial, which demands that you know as much as possible about multiple sides of the issues so that you can make the most equitable decisions for your students. A teacher as advocate is a professional who can look at many different angles to the most complex and highly charged issues—and make the best educational decisions for each student in the classroom.

In the Talking to Teachers vignette, Theresa Meyer shares her passion for working with and advocating for students who have disabilities. What issues will you advocate for as you emerge as a professional educator?

## Research Citations

Amrein, A. L., & Berliner, D. C. (2003). The effects of high-stakes testing on student motivation and learning. *Educational Leadership, 60*(5), 32–38.

Atkins, J. T., & Ellsesser. (2003). Tracking: The good, the bad, the questions. *Educational Leadership, 61*(2), 44–47.

Baker, K., & de Kanter, A. A. (1981). *Effectiveness of Bilingual Education: A Review of the Literature. Final Draft Report.* Washington, DC: Department of Education Office of Planning, Budget, and Evaluation.

Barry, A. L. (1994/1995). Easing into inclusion classrooms. *Educational Leadership, 52*(4), 4–6.

Crawford, J. (2004). *Educating English Learners: Language Diversity in the Classroom,* 5th Ed. Los Angeles, CA: Bilingual Education Services, Inc.

Doyle, D. P. (2004). Letter from Washington: Does social promotion work? *Educational Leadership, 61*(8), 96.

Gebhard, M. (2002/2003). Getting past "see spot run". *Educational Leadership, 60*(4), 35–39.

Greene, J. P. (1998). *A meta-analysis of the effectiveness of bilingual education.* Claremont, CA: Thomas Rivera Policy Institute.

Mora, J. K. (2000). Policy shifts in language-minority education: A mismatch between policies and pedagogy. *The Educational Forum, 64*(3), 204–214.

Petrovic, J. E. (1997). Balkanization, bilingualism, and comparisons of language situations at home and abroad. *Bilingual Research Journal, 21*(2–3), 233–254.

Porter, R. P. (1999/2000). The benefits of English immersion. *Educational Leadership, 57*(4), 52–56.

Potter, L. (1996). Examining the negative effects of retention in our schools. *Education, 117,* 268–270.

Ramirez, J. D., Yuen, S. D., Ramey, D. R., Pasta, D. J. & Billings, D. (1991). Final report: Longitudinal study of immersion strategy, early-exit and late-exit transitional bilingual education programs for language-minority children. San Mateo, CA: Aguirre International. *(ERIC Document Reproduction Service No. ED330216)*

Rossell, C. (2005). Teaching English through English. *Educational Leadership, 62*(4), 32–36.

Rossell, C. H., & Baker, K. (1996). The educational effectiveness of bilingual education. *Research in the Teaching of English, 30*(1), 7–74.

Shanker, A. (1994/1995). Full inclusion is neither free nor appropriate. *Educational Leadership, 52*(4), 18–21.

Thomas, W. P., & Collier, V. P. (2003). The multiple benefits of dual language. *Educational Leadership, 61*(2), 61–64.

Thomas, W. & Collier, V. (2002). A national study of school effectiveness for language minority students' long-term academic achievement. *(ERIC Document Reproduction Service No. ED475048)*

Villa, R. A., & Thousand, J. S. (2003). Making inclusive education work. *Educational Leadership, 61*(2), 19–23.

Willig, A. C. (1985). A meta-analysis of selected studies on the effectiveness of bilingual education. *Review of Educational Research, 55*(3), 269–318.

# Teacher as Artist

Research confirms what parents already know. What teachers do makes the most difference in what students learn. Research consistently demonstrates that it is the quality of the teacher that makes the greatest difference in a student's school career. If a student has highly qualified and competent teachers throughout his/her schooling, that student will most likely be academically successful. Unfortunately, the converse is also true. Students who have poorly prepared and/or incompetent teachers for a majority of their schooling tend to have extremely poor academic performance (Laczko-Kerr & Berliner, 2004; Elmore, 1995).

In fact, when all the issues that contribute to student achievement are compared, teacher expertise is the most responsible for this success. As much as forty-two percent of the variation in student achievement is attributable to teacher expertise. This is almost double the next closest factor, which is the level of parental education (twenty-four percent). Other background factors such as poverty, language, and family characteristics combine for twenty-six percent of the variation. Put simply, good teaching overcomes a variety of socioeconomic challenges to student academic success (Darling-Hammond & Ball, 1997; Darling-Hammond, 2003).

How do we ensure that all students have access to expert teachers? First, we need to understand that expert teachers develop over time (Sternberg & Horvath, 1995). This section examines phases of teacher development, appropriate professional development, and the development of "teacher as artist." The following definition describes this person's commitment and skill.

In this section, we will be exploring the following issues surrounding teacher development as they relate to the growing professional:

## Chapter Eleven: How Do Teachers Grow Professionally?

- Phases in a Teacher's Career
- Growth Cycle
- Induction Programs

## Chapter Twelve: Enhancing the "Art" of Teaching

- National Board for Professional Teaching Standards
- Case Studies: National Board Certified Teachers Examine their Practice
  - Building Community—Looking into a Primary Classroom
  - Student by Student—Looking into a Secondary Classroom
- Professional Development
- Professional Organizations

# How Do Teachers Grow Professionally?

# 11

Becoming an effective teacher requires deliberate effort, knowledge, experience, and practice. But that is not all. It takes reflection, which is defined as careful thought, especially the process of reconsidering previous actions, events, or decisions (Steffy, Wolfe, Pasche, & Enz, 2000). Teachers make virtually hundreds of decisions a day and take thousands of actions. Reflection produces new ideas that, in turn, further actions and decisions (Feiman-Nemser, 2001; Norlander-Case, Reagan, & Case, 1999). It is through the process of reflection that teachers grow and develop the knowledge, skills, and dispositions that enable them to become highly effective. A teacher's skills and knowledge grow through a process of continuous reflection in the growth, renewal, and reflection cycle.

**Definition**

**Artist** -n. **1.** Expert who practices craft or profession. Artists are often described as passionate about their craft or profession. Artists are always searching for ways to challenge themselves and improve their performance.

**Definitions**

**Amateur**   someone who has only limited skill and knowledge.

**Apprentice**   one who is learning by practical experience under skilled workers in a trade, art, or calling.

**Coach**   someone who is a trained mentor, particularly for a novice (new) professional. A coach provides specific support and advice so that the novice can grow professionally.

**Community**   a group of people with a common background or with shared interests and concerns.

**Emeritus**   one retired from professional life but permitted to retain the rank of the last office held as an honorary title. Many retired professors remain on the faculty of a college as emeritus professors.

**Expert**   having, involving, or displaying special skill or knowledge derived from training or experience.

**Induction**   an initial experience. An educator's induction into the profession typically occurs during the first one to three years of teaching.

**On-Site**   something that occurs at a specific site or location. In the case of education, on-site typically refers to a classroom or school (e.g., field experience practicums are on-site experiences).

**Practicum**   a practice experience related to a person's profession. In education, field experiences that are conducted in P—12 classrooms are often referred to as practicums.

**Reflection**   careful thought, especially the process of reconsidering previous actions, events, and decisions.

**Renewal**   the quality or state of being renewed; to return to doing something, revitalized.

**Retention**   the state of being retained; in this case, staying in the field of education.

**Sabbatical**   a leave of absence, typically paid, that allows an individual the opportunity to pursue prolonged professional development. Teachers who have been in the classroom for a number of years may take a sabbatical to pursue a research project or complete an advanced degree.

## As you read, think about...

★ Think about a time when you reflected upon your actions and decisions.

★ What changes did you make?

## Focus Questions

★ Since expert teachers are the key to successful students, how do we ensure that every student has access to qualified teachers?

★ What is being done to help prepare and support teachers so that they can provide the kind of education that all students deserve?

Often teachers in the Emeritus phase serve as mentors for younger teachers.

# Phases in a Teacher's Career

Teachers, like doctors and lawyers, develop over time. As their skills and knowledge develop, teachers move through distinct phases that help us to understand and support their current place in the career cycle (Steffy, et al., 1999).

- *The Novice phase* begins when pre-service students first encounter **practicum** experiences as part of their teacher education program and continues through student teaching. You are currently in the Novice phase of teaching.

- *The **Apprentice** phase* begins when teachers receive responsibility for planning and delivering instruction on their own (i.e., when they have their first job as a classroom teacher). This phase continues until integration and synthesis of knowledge, pedagogy, and confidence emerges.

- *The Professional phase* emerges as teachers grow in their self-confidence as educators. Student feedback plays a critical role in this process. Students' respect for teachers and teachers' respect for students form the foundation upon which this stage is built.

- *The **Expert** phase* symbolizes achievement of the highest standards. Even if they do not formally seek it, these teachers meet the expectations required for National Board Certification (discussed later in Chapter 12).

- *The Distinguished phase* is reserved for teachers truly gifted, the "pied pipers" of the profession. Distinguished teachers impact education-related decisions at city, state, and national levels. The title of Expert-Distinguished Teacher is another name for teacher as artist. These teachers are truly gifted in their field. They consistently exceed expectations for what teachers are expected to do.

- *The **Emeritus** phase* marks a lifetime of achievement in education. Teachers who retire after a lifetime of teaching deserve society's recognition and praise. Often they continue to serve the profession as tutors or mentors, or even as field supervisors or faculty for your teacher education program!

# Growth Cycle

Teaching is a highly complex profession. Teachers, like doctors and lawyers, improve with practice over time. The *Life Cycle of the Career Teacher* model (Steffy, et al., 1999) is based on the premise *that given the appropriate learning environment,* all teachers will continue to grow and develop throughout their professional lifetime.

## Phases in a Teacher's Growth

As in any professional career, teachers develop over time. As their skills and knowledge develop, teachers move through distinct phases that help us to understand and support their current place in the career cycle (Steffy, et al., 1999).

But how does a novice teacher proceed from one level to the next? Researchers (e.g., Steffy, et al., 1999) suggest that teachers' ability and willingness to reflect upon their practice, and to consider new information as they plan lessons and work with students, are at the heart of teacher development. If every student is to have a competent teacher, then virtually all their teachers must be learning virtually all the time (see Figure 11.1. **Reflection Cycle Model of Growth**).

Observe how one new teacher, Ms. Redendo, uses *reflection* about her day to reconsider her instruction and classroom organization.

*After spending an hour putting away the materials from a science project her fifth-grade students completed today, a frustrated Ms. Redendo realized she had once again underestimated the amount of time the students would need to explore and experiment. The students had been working right up to the minute the bell rang. Nearly all of her students rode the bus so they would have to leave immediately; the other students had younger siblings they needed to pick up.*

*Her first thoughts this afternoon led her to consider cutting back on her hands-on science approach. This was the third time she had done a rather messy science activity and the third time she was cleaning up. Moreover, the students didn't have a chance to summarize the findings from their experiments. A few minutes later, she realized she needed to reorganize her time in the afternoons that they did science experiments. Ms. Redendo realized that if she only did science on the afternoons without Music and PE, it would give her an extra forty minutes for experiments, recording data, and clean up. As she was driving home that night, Ms. Redendo stopped at the drugstore to pick up a timer. She realized her plan would work even better if she set the timer at fifteen-minute intervals.*

This type of self-reflection, though simple, was critical to help Ms. Redendo figure out a technical issue of time management and relations to instruction and student learning. However, many times professional growth and becoming more efficient and effective requires more than just self-reflection—it requires more knowledge. This is called *professional develop-*

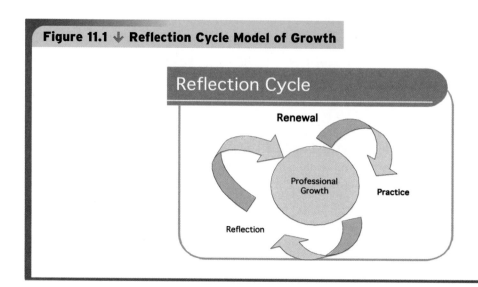

**Figure 11.1 ↓ Reflection Cycle Model of Growth**

Reflection Cycle

Renewal

Professional Growth

Practice

Reflection

*ment.* Professional development serves as the bridge between where a teacher is now, and where he/she wants to be.

Never before has there been a greater recognition of the importance of professional development for teachers. Professional development provides opportunities for teachers to explore new roles, develop new instructional techniques, refine their practice, and broaden themselves both as educators and as individuals (Blase & Kirby, 1992; DuFour & Eaker, 1998). Effective professional development should also reflect teachers' needs, interests, and readiness, because what a new teacher wants to learn about may be different than an experienced veteran.

# Appropriate Professional Development Experiences by Phases

Teachers progress from one phase to another when they reflect upon daily practice; when they attend master's courses, district workshops, professional conferences, and meetings; and when they work with their colleagues (Hargreaves, 1994; Little & McLaughlin, 1993; Rosenholtz, 1989). However, at each point along their career path, certain types of professional development opportunities appear to be more effective as teachers deal with the issues and concerns typically associated with their developmental phase. The following section presents the major concerns and suggestions for growth throughout the life cycle phases of a teacher's development (see Chapter 12 for more information about professional development options and opportunities).

## Novice Teacher Phase

The Novice phase is likely the one you are currently experiencing. As you read the "typical" concerns for novices, below, think about your own concerns about becoming a teacher. Are your concerns the same as those that we've listed?

Concern—*Developing instructional skills & behavior management strategies*

Suggestion—In your courses, seek out instructors that model reflective practices and guide you and your peers through this process. For example:

- Connect prior experiences and beliefs to new knowledge
- Reflect on how theory is translated to practice
- Seek out activities that allow you to practice reflective processes (e.g., case studies, autobiography, journals)

Concern—*Coping with the realities of classroom life*

Suggestion—When in the classroom, observe teachers that provide explicit instruction and model the basics of managing a classroom. For instance, look to see how teachers:

- Organize instructional content
- Implement and maintain classroom routines
- Assess and share student performance (e.g., report cards, portfolios, written narratives)

Suggestion—Develop your own observation techniques. This will help you:

- Build professional vocabulary
- Determine cause and effect regarding teacher actions and student behavior/achievement
- Evaluate other teachers' instructional planning and delivery
- Assess your own instructional performance

**Classroom Glimpse**

Vanessa was worried. The class she was observing was very challenging. Though the students behaved well for their teacher, Ms. Lopez, she had seen how terribly they had misbehaved for the substitute teacher last week. Vanessa was planning on teaching this class a lesson in two weeks, but now her planning was being complicated by her growing worries about how she was going to manage these students. ∎

*Questions:* As you review the concerns and professional development suggestions for the Novice teacher, please identify professional development opportunities that would be most helpful to Vanessa.

*Research support:* Kortman & Honaker (2002); Veenman, S. (1985)

## Apprentice Teacher Phase

The Apprentice phase is the one that typically marks your first years in the classroom. What concerns do you think you will have as a first-year teacher? How will you address these concerns?

Concern—*Overwhelmed by full-time responsibilities*

Suggestion—As an Apprentice teacher, seek out developmentally sequenced workshops that:

• Provide tips on managing instructional demands
• Are explicit and include models and specific examples
• Accommodate individual needs

Concern—*Need to be competent and accepted within their school site*

Suggestion—Find a peer mentor to offer context-specific information, such as:

• Reviewing district curriculum and offering successful methods
• Identifying and locating appropriate instructional resources and materials
• Responding to emerging needs on a daily basis

Concern—*Questioning career choice*

Suggestion—Seek out other apprentice teachers or cohort groups to provide psychological support by:

• Discussing common concerns and needs
• Problem-solving and determining appropriate solutions
• Building *community* within school and across district
• Sharing ideas, materials, and strategies

Marianne was exhausted. Each night, for the last month, she had been working from 7 AM to 8 PM. "I knew my first year would be tough but I didn't expect thirteen-hour days. I'm always behind on my grading because I'm spending so much time developing my lessons and trying to find instructional resources." ■

**Classroom Glimpse**

Concern—*School or district disregard of apprentice teachers*

Suggestion—Seek out "new teacher-friendly" schools. Effective school systems need to provide Apprentices with:

- Optimum teaching loads
- Realistic class/student assignments
- Comprehensive *induction* programs
- Time to confer/observe other teachers

*Questions:* As you review the concerns and professional development suggestions for the Apprentice teacher, please identify professional development opportunities that would be most helpful to Marianne.

*Research Support:* Gilbert (2005)

## Professional Teacher Phase

In the Professional phase, teachers are "on a roll" as a classroom teacher. Though more confident in their abilities, new concerns will arise. What do you think those concerns might be? What resources would you use to overcome these new concerns?

Concern—*Boredom with profession, lack of professional growth*

Suggestion—As a Professional teacher, you will need to expand and refine your instructional practices. You will need professional development opportunities that:

- Support personal reflection, (e.g., the process endorsed by the National Board)
- Provide you and your colleagues time and opportunity to learn from each other
- Emerge from your own professional goals and interests
- Are grounded in current research and best practices

Concern—*Professional isolation*

Suggestion—Administrators need to recognize the ongoing contributions Professional teachers make, and need to deliberately design and allow time for teachers to interact. This could include:

- Weekly, half-day group planning time
- Time for peer observations
- Financial support to attend professional conferences
- Internet-networking with colleagues

**Classroom Glimpse**

In his fifth year of teaching, Joe was becoming somewhat restless. This feeling had surprised him since he had tried several new math strategies last year with his eighth graders. The new strategies had proved highly successful, both in terms of student achievement and test scores. ■

Concern—*Lack of career growth opportunities*

Suggestion—In most professions, there is an ascending ladder of job responsibilities that recognizes experience with promotions in title and pay. This is not typically the case with the teaching profession. However, as a Professional teacher you will need some recognition of your expanding knowledge and skill. This may be accomplished by engaging in:

- Peer coaching teams
- Leading **on-site,** in-service workshops
- Developing units of study for school or district
- *Coaching* pre-service teachers in early internships

*Questions:* As you review the concerns and professional development suggestions for the Professional teacher, please identify professional development opportunities that would be most helpful to Joe.

*Research Support:* Barth, R. S. (1990)

## Expert Teacher Phase

An expert teacher is one who has excelled in the classroom, with colleagues, and in maximizing personal reflection to improve practice. Even at this phase, however, new concerns emerge. Are the concerns below those that you anticipate once you attain this phase in your development?

Concern—*Time for professional growth*

Suggestion—As an Expert teacher, you will need time and district support to continue your professional growth. Expert teachers may need:

- Time to attend professional conferences
- Encouragement to present at national conferences
- *Sabbatical* leaves to continue education

Concern—*Need to share professional talents*

Suggestion—Find ways to become involved in pre-service instruction and induction programs. This could include:

- Support to create videos of exemplar lessons
- Opportunities to co-instruct methods courses, and/or in-service workshops
- Serving as a mentor to Novice and/or Apprentice teachers
- Writing for professional journals

Tara had just earned her master's degree in literacy. Though the course work had been challenging and time consuming, it was also a weekly opportunity for her to talk to colleagues who shared the same interests and teaching passions. After a couple of months, Tara found herself wanting to try to professional challenges. "What good is my master's degree if I can't do something more?" ■

**Classroom Glimpse**

Concern—*Lack of career growth opportunities*

Suggestion—As with their "Professional" colleagues, Expert teachers need recognition of their exceptional knowledge and skill. This may be accomplished by:

- Coordinating peer coaching teams
- Determining and delivering district in-service workshops
- Developing units of study for district
- Offering input into administrative decisions

*Questions:* As you review the concerns and professional development suggestions for the Expert teacher, please identify professional development opportunities that would be most helpful to Tara.

*Research Support:* Berliner, (1988); Schlechty, (2001)

## Distinguished Teacher Phase

Will you someday become a "Distinguished" teacher? For those of you who will exceed professional expectations, what possible concerns might you encounter at this professional stage?

Concern—*Time to reflect and opportunities to learn*

Suggestion—As a Distinguished teacher, you will need time and district support to continue your professional growth. In addition to attending conferences, Distinguished teachers may also need:

- Support to become leaders in national organizations
- Encouragement to present at national conferences
- Sabbatical leaves to continue education

Concern—*Need to share professional talents*

Suggestion—Become involved in the development and delivery of:

- Course work for Novice and Apprentice teachers,
- Master's level work for Professional teachers,
- Support to create videos of exemplar lessons,
- Opportunities to instruct methods courses and/or in-service workshops,
- Mentoring for Novice and/or Apprentice teachers, and
- Writing for professional journals.

**Classroom Glimpse**

Reynaldo was finishing his twenty-fifth year of teaching at a private school. The award-winning teacher was seeking new challenges. His history-political courses were exciting and many of his students had become politicians and lawyers. As he reflected upon his career, he wondered about his sphere of influence while he had been devoted to helping very bright but also very privileged students prepare for college, he thought about doing more. ■

Concern—*Professional challenges*

Suggestion—Distinguished teachers need new challenges to fuel their reflection and *renewal* cycle. This may be accomplished by encouraging these teachers to:

• Teach at a new level

• Teach a high-risk population

• Review national curriculum

• Serve as consultant to legislative bodies

*Questions:* As you review the concerns and professional development suggestions for the Distinguished teacher, please identify professional development opportunities that would be most helpful to Reynaldo.

*Research Support:* Shulman, (1987); Sternberg & Horvath, (1995)

## Emeritus Teacher Phase

Will you remain in the teaching profession for the lifetime of your career? If so, you may be recognized someday as an "Emeritus" teacher!

Concern—*Opportunities to contribute*

Suggestion—As an Emeritus teacher, you may be offered numerous ways to contribute to the public school system, including:

• Tutoring children in a one-to-one relationship

• Mentoring Apprentice teachers

• Serving as substitute teachers

Concern—*New roles and responsibilities*

Suggestion—Emeritus teachers can assume new and rewarding responsibilities by becoming actively engaged in the profession through:

• Development and delivery of course work for Novice and Apprentice teachers

• Delivery of master's level work for Professional teachers

• Supervision of Novice teachers

• Opportunities to offer in-service workshops

• Service as a mentor to Apprentice teachers

After a thirty-three-year career, Don was now retired. The first few months he traveled to Egypt, painted the house, relandscaped the yard, and reorganized the den. All these travels and tasks brought Don a sense of completion, he had been waiting years to travel and the time to really get into a big project. However, after repainting the bedroom for the third time, he realized he was bored. Longing to feel needed again, Don wondered what he should consider next. ■

Concern—*Professional challenges*

Suggestion—Emeritus teachers are in a position to advocate for the teaching profession; they may wish to:

- Lobby state and national legislators
- Serve on advisory councils
- Serve as officers on state and national educational associations
- Serve as consultants to legislators bodies

*Questions:* As you review the concerns and professional development suggestions for the Emeritus teacher, please identify professional development opportunities that would be most helpful to Don.

*Research Support:* Steffy, Wolfe, Pasche, & Enz, (2000)

# Induction Programs

In Chapter 5 we introduced the INTASC standards, which describe what new teachers should know and be able to do. Novice teachers learn about these standards in their teacher preparation courses and begin to practice these skills during student teaching. However, since the practice of teaching is so complex, apprentice teachers must continue to refine these skills through the first years in their own classroom. Tragically, in the past, too many new teachers try to practice these skills in isolation. This led to many teachers becoming overwhelmed with the responsibilities of teaching, and unfortunately without enough help to become competent at instruction. The isolation, combined with feelings of inadequacy and failure, caused many new teachers to abandon their careers. Research conducted by The National Commission on Teaching and America's Future reveals that nearly one-third of all new teachers leave the profession before their fifth of year of teaching (NCTAF, 1996).

Some costs and consequences of teacher career flight (called turnover or attrition) are more obvious and more easily measured than others. One type of cost that is less easily quantified includes the negative consequences of high turnover for organizational stability and productivity, defined in education as student achievement (Darling-Hammond, 2003). Decades of educational research have documented that the presence of a sense of personal and professional community and cohesion among families, teachers, and students is important for the success of schools (e.g., Ingersoll, 2001). High rates of teacher turnover can inhibit the development and maintenance of a learning community. In turn, a lack of community in a school may have a negative effect on teacher **retention,** thus creating a vicious cycle. Beginning teachers'

Teacher induction programs support a teacher's skill development and increase their success in teaching and learning.

perpetual turnover leaves us with a workforce of *amateurs*. This problem is further exacerbated in low-socioeconomic urban schools, where the turnover rate is fifty percent higher. High rates of beginning teacher turnover are of concern not only because they contribute to school staffing problems and perennial shortages, but more importantly because teacher attrition leads to lower student achievement.

Fortunately, in the past two decades, a number of induction programs have developed within the United States in an effort to stem the tide of teacher dropouts and respond to the need for quality teaching. Teacher induction is the process of socialization to the teaching profession, adjustment to the procedures and "cultures" of a school site and school system, and development of effective instructional and classroom management skills. The availability of formal induction programs and their structures varies among states and local school districts (Feiman-Nemser, 2001; Hargreaves, 1994; Ingersoll & Kralik, 2003). Numerous studies document the value of teacher induction programs and describe multiple prototypes for implementation. The benefits of the programs include not only reduced attrition rates among new teachers, but also improved teaching capabilities.

Keeping good teachers is essential for the educational futures of our children, as research has consistently demonstrated that capable teachers have the largest impact on student learning (Wilson et al., 2001; Laczko-Kerr & Berliner, 2003). Research has also demonstrated that teacher effectiveness greatly increases through the first few years of teaching. Supporting teachers' skill development and reflective practice is critical from the onset of their career, as it sets the stage for ongoing professional development, and success in teaching and learning. Box 11.1 **Offering the BEST,** provides an example of the components of a comprehensive induction program.

## Box 11.1   ↓ Offering the BEST

**Special Feature by Sharon Kortman**

The effective structure and context of a quality induction program can positively impact teacher retention. Teacher induction programs are those designed to help provide support and encouragement for new teachers. Teacher induction programs have been increasing in number in quality since the early 1990s. Unfortunately, induction programs vary greatly in intensity and consistency of support from state to state and district to district. However, research (Feiman-Nemser, 2001; Gilbert, 2005; Kortman & Enz, 2005) over the past decade suggests that the most effective induction programs have consistent features, including:

- **Daily support** provided by an on-site mentor who is matched as closely as possible to grade level and/or subject matter. This person is prepared to provide immediate guidance to building-level information on a constant basis.

- **Frequent in-service** that targets the new teachers' changing needs. Since teachers develop at different rates, their professional development should be both developmental (relating to what most new teachers need), and individual and specific.

- **Instructional coaching** that identifies both pedagogical strengths and areas of need. The coach, in addition to already being an outstanding teacher, has received preparation in working with new teachers and providing instructional tutoring on a one-to-one basis.

These three features are present in effective induction programs (Kortman & Honaker, 2002). The BEST Program (Beginning Educator Support Team) provides an example of how this induction program works.

*BEST for Beginning Educators*—Support is provided to beginning teachers by developmentally-aligned seminars throughout the school year, one-to-one coaching, and on-site mentoring. Inservice is both developmental, and individual and specific. This is accomplished through the use of monthly developmental workshops and individually selected choice activities that relate to the context of their teaching and school community. Developmental seminars include:

Fall
- Beginning the year successfully
- Creating positive interactions with students and parents
- Balancing teacher stress
- Developing corrective discipline strategies

Spring
- Accommodating student differences
- Understanding standards for teachers
- Celebrating best practices in teaching
- Closing down the school year

Within each of these major units, the new teacher identifies specific concerns they have as part of their choice to develop and improve. Most of the choice activities include working with their on-site mentor and other colleagues, which helps them to build a sense of professional and personal community. In addition, the beginning teacher is offered support by both his/her on-site mentor and visitation coach.

*BEST for Mentor Teachers*—Support and preparation is provided for mentors by developmentally—aligned seminars throughout the school year, one-to-one beginning teacher interactions, and choice activities that relate to the context of their mentoring and school community. Mentors engage in applied research projects in mentoring, measuring the affects of support to beginning teachers in relationship to factors such as reflective questioning and collaboration. The training seminars include the following:

- Establishing a mentoring relationship
- Encouraging teachers through mentoring
- Developing teaching skills and support through mentoring
- Analyzing and planning for professional growth through mentoring
- Strengthening teacher practices through mentoring
- Reflecting on the mentoring relationship

*BEST Visitation Coaching*—The visitation coaching relationship fosters tailored individual teacher growth based on specific areas of teacher expectations. The visitation coach, being a master teacher, brings expertise to what defines effective teaching practice. This leadership role is time-devoted to allow for specific direction in content areas, curriculum, instruction, management, and assessments. The coach provides drop-in visits, classroom observations, individualized standards-based coaching, personalized needs assessments, conferences, model lessons, co-teaching opportunities, reflection processes, data collection, and professional growth goal-setting.

Within these program components, elements are aligned to research-based criteria for quality induction, mentoring, and professional development. These include developmentally appropriate content, collaboration with colleagues, standards-based professional development, reflective processes, assessments, reinforcements of teacher strengths, process of teacher refinement, and impacts to student achievement.

Research conducted throughout the United States has begun to demonstrate that induction programs help to retain new teachers by providing opportunities to interact with professionals (Hargreaves, 1994; Ingersoll, 2001).

## Teacher Stages

Teachers within the same community, and within the same school, represent a wide range of teaching stages. As you and your group members interviewed local teachers, what did you find were the most common stages that were observed?

Use the information from your Teacher Interviews (Figure 11.2) to collaboratively complete the **Interview Data Chart.** Then, discuss the following with your group:

- What was the most common teacher stage? Why do you think it was most commonly observed?
- What were the most common characteristics of:
    - Novice teachers?
    - Apprentice?
    - Professional?
    - Expert?
    - Distinguished?
- What were the most common concerns expressed by these teachers? How are they overcoming these challenges?
- What were the most common goals expressed by these teachers? How do these goals relate to the teachers' stages?

## Interview Data Chart

Teacher Stages (Interview Data)

|  | Stage | Evidence for Decision | Teacher's Concerns | Teacher's Goals |
|---|---|---|---|---|
| Teacher 1 |  |  |  |  |
| Teacher 2 |  |  |  |  |
| Teacher 3 |  |  |  |  |
| Teacher 4 |  |  |  |  |

**Figure 11.2  ↓ Teacher Interview Activity**

*Directions:* What teacher phase is most prevalent in the classroom you observe? Use the questions below to guide you in determining what teacher phase best matches the experiences and expertise of your host teacher.

Teacher's name

Teacher's level

How long has the teacher been teaching?                   How long at this level?

How does this teacher use student feedback in his/her instructional planning?


What kind of professional development does this teacher engage in?


How does this teacher support other colleagues?


What professional concerns does this teacher express?


How does this teacher describe his/her classroom management?


How does this teacher impact change in his/her school or community?


How does this teacher use reflection to guide instructional decisions?


Is this teacher engaged in research or committees at the national level? In what way?


What professional goals does this teacher have for him/herself?


I believe this teacher demonstrates the _____ phase because:

# Looking Forward

As you have learned from this chapter's discussions, becoming an effective teacher takes time, practice, support, and a lot of personal and professional determination. Fortunately, you are one of the millions of lucky beneficiaries of the millions of many caring, concerned teachers who felt that you and your peers were worth their professional efforts and energy.

What do exceptional teachers do to become excellent? The following chapter provides two illustrations of the art of teaching. When the skills of teaching are automatic, the craft is elevated to what appears to be a seamless interaction of knowledge and mutual growth between teacher and student.

## Research Citations

Barth, R. S. (1990). *Improving schools from within: Teachers, parents, and principals can make the difference.* San Francisco, CA: Jossey-Bass.

Berliner, D. (1988, February). *The development of expertise in pedagogy.* Paper presented at the meeting of the American Association of Colleges for Teacher Education, New Orleans, LA.

Blase, J. & Kirby, P. C. (1992). *Bringing out the best in teachers: What effective principals do.* Newbury Park, CA: Corwin.

Darling-Hammond, L. (2003). Keeping good teachers: Why it matters, what leaders can do. *Educational Leadership, 60*(8), 7–13.

Darling-Hammond, L., & Ball (1997). *The right to learn: a blueprint for creating schools that work.* San Francisco, CA: Jossey-Bass.

DuFour, R. & Eaker, R. (1998). *Professional learning communities at work: Best practices for enhancing student achievement.* Alexandria, VA: Association for Supervision and Curriculum Development.

Elmore, R. (1995). Structural reform and educational practice. *Educational Researcher, 24*(9), 23–26.

Feiman-Nemser, S. (2001). From preparation to practice: Designing a continuum to strengthen and sustain teaching. *Teachers College Record, 103*(6), 1013–1055.

Gilbert, L. (2005). What Helps Beginning Teachers? *Educational Leadership, 62*(8), 36–39.

Hargreaves, A. (1994). *Changing teachers, changing times: Teachers' work and culture in the postmodern age.* New York, NY: Teachers College.

Ingersoll, R. M. (2001). Teacher turnover and teacher shortages: An organizational analysis. *American Educational Research Journal, 38*(3), 499–534.

Ingersoll, R., & Kralik, J. (2003). *A review of empirical research on the effects of teacher mentoring programs in elementary and secondary schools.* Denver, CO: The Education Commission of the States.

Kortman, S. & Enz, B. J. (2005). *Induction as a context for development: Support to competence and accountability.* Paper presented at the Annual conference of American Education Research Association, Montreal, CN.

Kortman, S., & Honaker, C. (2002). *The BEST beginning teacher experience: A framework for professional development.* Dubuque, IA: Kendall/Hunt.

Laczko-Kerr, I, & Berliner, D. C. (2003). In harm's way: How undercertified teachers hurt their students. *Educational Leadership, 60*(8), 34–39.

Little, J. W., & McLaughlin, M. (Eds.). (1993). *Teachers' work: Individuals, colleagues and contexts.* New York, NY: Teachers College.

National Commission on Teaching and America's Future (NCTAF) (1996). *What matters most: Teaching for America's future.* New York, NY: NCTAF.

Norlander-Case, K. A., Reagan, T. G., & Case, C. W. (1999). *The professional teacher: The preparation and nurturance of the reflective practitioner.* San Francisco: Jossey-Bass.

Rosenholtz, S. (1989). *Teachers' workplace: The social organization of schools.* New York, NY: Longman.

Schlechty, P. C. (2001). *Shaking up the school house: How to support and sustain educational innovation.* San Francisco, CA: Jossey-Bass.

Shulman, L. (1987). Knowledge and teaching: Foundations of the new reform. *Harvard Educational Review, 57*(1), 1–22.

Steffy, B., Wolfe, M., Pasche, S., & Enz, B. 2000. *The Life Cycle of the Career Teacher* Thousand Oaks, CA: Corwin.

Sternberg, R. J., & Horvath, J. A. (1995). A prototype view of expert teaching. *Educational Researcher, 24*(6), 9–17.

Veenman, S. (1985). Perceived problems of beginning teachers. *Review of Educational Research, 54*(2), 143–178.

Wilson, S., Floden, R., & Ferrini-Mundy, J. (2001). *Teacher preparation research: Current knowledge, gaps, and recommendations.* Seattle, WA: Center for the Study of Teaching and Policy, University of Washington.

# Enhancing the "Art" of Teaching 12

While experience is an excellent teacher, experience alone is insufficient to cause a new teacher to develop into a highly skilled and competent professional. The National Commission on Teaching and America's Future (NCTAF, 1996) states that what must be done to help teachers is a threefold approach to professional development:

1. Teachers need *content* knowledge—a deep understanding of their disciplines, typical of advanced study of the discipline.
2. Teachers need *pedagogical* knowledge—knowledge about how to teach.
3. Teachers need *pedagogical-content* knowledge—knowledge of subject-specific teaching strategies.

**Definitions**

**Cognition** the act or process of knowing, including both awareness and judgment.

**Disciplinary** of or relating to a discipline, such as a subject or branch of learning. In education, science, art, mathematics, music, social studies, history, and languages are examples of disciplines.

**Expository** a term used in writing to describe pieces that are factual and informational. An expository essay might be written to provide facts on a current issue.

**Proposition** something offered for consideration or acceptance.

**Repertoire** the complete list or supply of skills, devices, or ingredients used in a particular field, occupation, or practice. Teachers, for example, have a repertoire of instructional strategies that they use when planning their lessons.

## As you read, think about...

Your own professional teaching program.

★ In what courses or experiences will you learn your content?

★ Methods of teaching (often called pedagogy)?

★ Your subject-specific teaching strategies?

## Focus Questions

★ What will you do to address any gaps to insure that you will have the professional development that you need in order to be successful in the classroom?

★ How do teachers develop their knowledge?

# National Board for Professional Teaching Standards (NBPTS)

The NBPTS answers the needs of teachers' professional development by providing a way for teachers to deeply examine and strengthen their practice. The NBPTS is the home for National Board Certified Teachers (NBCT). National Board Certification (NBC) is a growing part of the national effort to strengthen standards for the teaching profession. Developed by teachers, with teachers, and for teachers, NBC is a symbol of professional teaching excellence. NBC is a voluntary, advanced teaching credential that goes beyond state licensure by creating national standards for what accomplished teachers should know and be able to do. The National Board certifies teachers who successfully complete its rigorous certification process.

While you would not pursue National Board certification as a novice teacher, its ideals and mission are important to understand as they do define quality teaching. Becoming Nationally Board certified is certainly a laudable—and obtainable—goal for any teacher serious about his/her "art"! The National Board's mission is to advance the quality of teaching and learning by:

- Maintaining high and rigorous standards for what accomplished teachers should know and be able to do
- Providing a national voluntary system certifying teachers who meet these standards
- Advocating for related education reforms to integrate National Board Certification in American education and to capitalize on the expertise of National Board Certified Teachers

At the time the National Board was founded in 1987, it was understood that a critical first task was the development of a policy that would spell out the National Board's vision of accomplished practice. In 1989, it issued its policy statement, *What Teachers Should Know and Be Able To Do,* which has served as a basis for all of the standards development work NBPTS has conducted. To this day, it remains the cornerstone of the system of National Board Certification and has served as a guide to school districts, states, colleges, and universities with a strong interest in strengthening the initial and ongoing education of America's teachers. It also holds the promise of being a stimulus to self-reflection on the part of teachers at all levels of accomplishment, as well as a catalyst for healthy debate and the forging of a new professional consensus on accomplished practice in each field of teaching.

## What Teachers Should Know and Be Able to Do—The Five Core Propositions

The National Board has led the effort to develop professional standards for elementary and secondary school teaching. The National Board stands for professionalism in the schools. The National Board's responsibility is not only to ensure that teachers who become Nationally Board Certified meet its professional standards of commitment and competence, but also to maintain standards and assessments that are so well regarded that America's most accomplished teachers will voluntarily decide to seek National Board Certification.

Teachers report that National Board assessments provide a unique form of professional development that improves their teaching practice. Because candidates internalize the National Board standards, analyze their teaching in relation to them, and provide reflective commentaries about the impact of teaching strategies on student learning, many teachers have characterized National Board Certification as the most valuable professional development that they ever have ever experienced.

The National Board for Professional Teaching Standards seeks to identify and recognize teachers who effectively enhance student learning and demonstrate a high level of knowledge,

Proposition 1 in the National Board of Professional Teaching Standards states that accomplished teachers are dedicated to making knowledge accessible to all children.

skills, abilities, and commitments reflected in the following five core *propositions* (www.nbpts.org/about/coreprops.cfm):

- Commitment to students and learning
- Knowledge of subject matter and pedagogy
- Management and monitoring of student learning
- Systematic use of experience to enhance the practice of teaching
- Engagement in learning communities

Each of these propositions is explored in depth on the following pages.

**Proposition 1   Teachers are committed to students and their learning.** Accomplished teachers are dedicated to making knowledge accessible to all students. They act on the belief that all students can learn. They treat students equitably, recognizing the individual differences that distinguish one student from another and taking account of these differences in their practice. They adjust their practice based on observation and knowledge of their students' interests, abilities, skills, knowledge, family circumstances, and peer relationships.

Accomplished teachers understand how students develop and learn. They incorporate the prevailing theories of *cognition* and intelligence in their practice. They are aware of the influence of context and culture on behavior. They develop students' cognitive capacity and their respect for learning. Equally important, they foster students' self-esteem, motivation, character, civic responsibility, and respect for individual student's, cultural, religious, and racial differences.

**Proposition 2    Teachers know the subjects they teach and how to teach those subjects to students.** Accomplished teachers have a rich understanding of the subject(s) they teach and appreciate how knowledge in their subject is created, organized, linked to other disciplines, and applied to real-world settings. While faithfully representing the collective wisdom of our culture and upholding the value of *disciplinary* knowledge, they also develop the critical and analytical capacities of their students.

Accomplished teachers command specialized knowledge of how to convey and reveal subject matter to students. They are aware of the preconceptions and background knowledge that students typically bring to each subject, and of strategies and instructional materials that can be of assistance. They understand where difficulties are likely to arise and modify their practice accordingly. Their instructional *repertoire* allows them to create multiple paths to the subjects they teach, and they are adept at teaching students how to pose and solve their own problems.

**Proposition 3    Teachers are responsible for managing and monitoring student learning.** Accomplished teachers create, enrich, maintain, and alter instructional settings to capture and sustain the interest of their students and to make the most effective use of time. They also are adept at engaging students and adults to assist their teaching, and at enlisting their colleagues' knowledge and expertise to complement their own. Accomplished teachers command a range of generic instructional techniques, know when each is appropriate, and can implement them as needed. They are as aware of ineffectual or damaging practice as they are devoted to "elegant" practice.

They know how to engage groups of students to ensure a disciplined learning environment, and how to organize instruction to allow the schools' goals for students to be met. They are adept at setting norms for social interaction among students and between students and teachers. They understand how to motivate students to learn and how to maintain their interest even in the face of temporary failure.

Accomplished teachers can assess the progress of individual students as well as that of the class as a whole. They employ multiple methods for measuring student growth and understanding, and can clearly explain student performance to parents.

**Proposition 4    Teachers think systematically about their practice and learn from experience.** Accomplished teachers are models of educated persons, exemplifying the virtues they seek to inspire in students—curiosity, tolerance, honesty, fairness, respect for diversity, and appreciation of cultural differences. They are also models for the capacities that are prerequisites for intellectual growth—the ability to reason and take multiple perspectives, to be creative and take risks, and to adopt an experimental and problem-solving orientation.

Accomplished teachers draw on their knowledge of human development, subject matter, and instruction, and their understanding of their students to make principled judgments about sound practice. Their decisions are not only grounded in the literature, but also in their experience. They engage in lifelong learning that they seek to encourage in their students. Striving to strengthen their teaching, accomplished teachers critically examine their practice, seek to expand their repertoire, deepen their knowledge, sharpen their judgment, and adapt their teaching to new findings, ideas, and theories.

**Proposition 5    Teachers are members of learning communities.** Accomplished teachers contribute to the effectiveness of the school by working collaboratively with other professionals on instructional policy, curriculum development, and staff development. They can evaluate school progress and the allocation of school resources in light of their understanding of state and local educational objectives. They are knowledgeable about specialized school and community resources that can be engaged for their students' benefit, and are skilled at employing such resources as needed.

**Figure 12.1  ↓ NBCT Teacher Interview Activity**

**Directions:** Nationally Board Certified Teachers are truly a gift for any community. Find a NBCT educator in the area in which you live, and use the following questions to guide your interview. Focus on how this teacher has incorporated the five propositions of the National Boards.

Teacher's name

Teacher's level

How long has the teacher been teaching?          How long at this level?

Describe the process of National Board Certification. What was the most difficult part of this process? What was the most surprising?

How does this teacher adjust his/her practices to make sure that every student can be successful?

How does this teacher use students' own personal experiences to guide instruction?

How does this teacher set up his/her classroom to maximize student learning?

How does this teacher engage in "life-long learning"?

How does this teacher collaborate with others in his/her school or district?

What challenges does this teacher still face professionally?

What advice would this teacher give to novice teachers?

Is this educator still teaching in the classroom? Why or why not?

# Case Study 12.1

Dr. Rebecca Stahlman

Teacher researchers argue that highly competent, artistic teachers develop because they use reflective practices of as a mechanism for growth and renewal (Steffy, et al, 2000; Louis, Marks, & Kruse, 1996). The following vignette was written by Dr. Rebecca Stahlman, a National Board Certified Teacher who also challenged herself to earn a doctorate in early childhood education. Notice how her reflections on her students, practice, and the children's learning parallel the five core propositions. Her reflections are also filled with the deepening knowledge of student learning.

## Building Community: Looking into a Primary Classroom

In 1993 I began my career as a classroom teacher and embarked on a journey filled with many challenges. Building a community of learners with my young students and their families was an honor and privilege. As a National Board Certified Teacher, I embrace strongly held beliefs about best practices for young children. I endeavor to remain true to this commitment through careful examination of my own practice, collaboration with like–minded educators, and continuing professional growth. In my new role as a teacher-educator I am privileged to have the opportunity to guide a new generation of teachers. In the following narrative I describe and illustrate how I create and sustain a climate in my classroom that supports children's development and appreciates the diversity represented among my young students.

**Instructional Context**—A glimpse into our learning community finds two students in the *peace corner* sharing viewpoints as they try to resolve a conflict, four students playing a game to enhance multiplication skills, and one student "lost" in a book. A few are gathered on the floor—solving the daily math problem by helping each other use varied strategies, several are engaged in self-paced computer programs, and I can be found sitting on the floor guiding a book talk. A parent is assisting students edit their writing, while three students build an intricate design with wooden blocks. Welcome to our classroom, where twenty-four students, seven to nine years old, and one much older learner, grow together every day.

A multi-grade class, fourteen children are third graders and ten are second graders. There are eleven girls and thirteen boys. The strategies I use to help us create and maintain our community recognize the wide range of developmental needs of my students. As we model respect for each other, we learn to resolve conflicts. We work together for our common good, and appreciate the strengths each brings to our community. Our reading abilities span several years so I provide a wide variety of books for literature study by small groups. Groups are based on interest or need, and are flexible. Flexible groups promote respect and self-esteem so students never see themselves as either better or less capable than another, but as able members of our learning community. Some struggle to write simple sentences with high frequency words spelled correctly, while others write complex paragraphs. Writing activities address the wide range of abilities by suggesting a basic structure and by being open-ended. Peer editing allows students to help each other with conventions as well as ideas and content. As mathematicians, some students can perform single digit addition, while others are adept at multi-digit addition and subtraction, multiplication, and division. Sharing our thinking is important during daily math activities because we learn by hearing and seeing multiple strategies for problem solving. Three students receive tutoring in reading or math, several receive counseling for self-esteem/ behavioral issues, and one student receives speech therapy. I know that learning cannot occur when a child's emotional well-being is in doubt; therefore I enlist the help of our counselor and others who are available to meet student needs.

Classroom Glimpse

**Classroom Glimpse**

**Organization of Space and Materials**—Our classroom resembles a scientist's laboratory, a writer's studio, an artist's workshop—a structure that is predictable, where complex and changing interactions occur naturally (Calkins, 1994). We work together to make sense of our experiences and participate in all that interests us through meaningful inquiries that promote cognitive growth as well as social, physical, and emotional growth. Students meet at tables of four but have the flexibility to find spaces for more, or less, collaboration. Our classroom houses nearly 2000 books of wide ranging levels that include fiction, non-fiction, poetry, and student-authored stories. A reading corner is complete with pillows and a beanbag chair as well as a tape player for listening to stories. Math games proliferate and are used as a powerful means to develop logico-mathematical knowledge. When students play these games, rules are negotiated, intellectual and social skills are enhanced, and students of differing abilities learn from each other. A writing center holds tools needed for daily writing, and a bookcase contains writing resources such as a variety of dictionaries, thesauri, spell checkers, and writing/illustrating ideas. Games that promote language skills are available. An art center holds supplies needed to design cards, create illustrations, and plan projects. Four computers are used for word processing or skill enhancement, and games related to thematic studies. Tools for scientific exploration abound. Throughout the room, student-generated posters provide a recap of mini lessons. A *peace corner* provides students with a quiet place filled with symbols and words of peace, where they go to resolve disagreements. Classical music can be heard while students are engaged in writing activities, or the hum of voices heard as we collaborate or read with buddies. When we enjoy silent reading, known as DEAR: **D**rop **E**verything **A**nd **R**ead, the sound of pages turning is heard.

Our use of space and materials changes over the course of the year because our curriculum is organized through a year-long theme, with several units of study that require a wide variety of resources for study and exploration. This year's theme is *Under Construction*, with an organizing concept that form follows function. It is comprised of three major components: *Builders of Community, Builders of Art,* and *Builders of Structures.* The study of quilting transformed our classroom into an art gallery of family history as children brought old and new quilts, each with a story to tell. These were displayed along with many books about quilting, charts of vocabulary related to quilting, books about slavery, the Underground Railroad, and pioneer days. The resources and displays changed to provide a new frame of reference for research and study. My students are involved in determining the course of our studies as we discuss what we want to learn.

The children and I make decisions related to space and materials as we change our focus throughout the year, but they revisit previous studies as they weave connections within all that they learn. This is a powerful tool to promote learning, so I encourage students to make those connections and revisit resources, materials, ideas, and activities. As it became clear that many students were interested in the Underground Railroad, for example, we added books and activities to our quilt study. Through class meetings, we talk about a new unit of study and suggest resources that we will need. Students sometimes notice a resource already on hand that will be useful in a new way. Shape blocks used to make quilting designs may be used next to build homes like those made by Native Americans. Students may suggest changes in the location of materials to facilitate their use. They create spaces that allow them to write, read, collaborate, play, observe and record, build and display those things that are important to them.

Miles and Brad sometimes leave their tables to find a place to write, free from distraction, when they are experiencing "writer's block." Max finds that the *peace corner* is where he can do his best thinking. When Terri brought her rock collection, she decided where and how to display it, as well as the rules needed for exploration of her treasured items. Peter brought a crystal making kit to school after receiving it as a gift, because he wanted his classmates to observe and enjoy this science project. Each member of our class has a job: to take care of our books, computers, recycling or writing center, check tables and floors, or dust. Jobs are assigned on a rotating basis, so everyone can do each job throughout the year. Through brainstorming sessions, class meetings and reaching consensus, we discuss our needs, thereby fostering social autonomy. New jobs may result while others are eliminated as we share responsibility for our classroom.

**Norms and Routines**—Our classroom community establishes norms and routines for living and working in a crowded place. Students remain in our classroom for two years and new, younger students arrive each fall. The older students embrace our new students with care, explaining the norms and routines, they established the year before. The younger students are accustomed to shared decision making in their previous classes and soon feel comfortable discussing their ideas. This can lead to a new norm or routine and therefore norms and routines may change over time. It is one of the most powerful benefits of our multiage class that older students guide and direct the younger students into full membership in our community. Another important benefit of such a classroom as ours is that, as students get to know each other, special gifts and needs become evident. For example, Max is very quiet and shy but he became the class expert when stitching quilt blocks by hand was difficult for everyone else. His friend Bobby often helps him correct spelling errors by reminding him of word families he knows.

The creation of a community of learners who are supportive of each other is essential for learning to thrive. A school-wide program known as *Lifelong Guidelines and Lifeskills* was established by the founding teachers of our school several years ago. These are values that guide our personal and group responsibilities and provide us with a common language, but are subject to interpretation by each learning community as we share what they mean to us in the context of our classroom. In the absence of competition in our classroom, it is each student's responsibility to do his or her personal best in all endeavors, to listen attentively, be truthful and trustworthy, and to avoid any actions or words that are "putdowns" to others. The emotional health of my students is of utmost importance because I know that when a student is hurt, learning cannot occur. Such *lifeskills* as courage, organization, perseverance, curiosity, caring, respect, flexibility, and initiative are illustrated through literature and demonstrated through our daily interactions with each other. Within our classroom, we consider these when making decisions about our daily schedule and the roles each of us plays in our community. From the opening recitation of the pledge, to the focus on the daily agenda to help organize our work, to our weekly inquiries, everything we do has a frame of reference in the *Lifelong Guidelines and Lifeskills*.

To establish or change our norms and routines we value personal responsibility and collaboration. Each child has a vital role to play in the development and nourishment of our learning community. My older students and I have a special role to play at the beginning of the school year to make our new students aware of and comfortable with their new environment. Free exploration of materials and resources is essential. The older students, who jump right in where they left off in the spring, patiently explain and demonstrate when necessary. We collectively discuss the *why* and *how* of our norms and routines while expecting the older students to be effective role models. Soon the younger students feel comfortable sharing new ideas that often replace old routines. Literature is a vehicle that helps us welcome our newest community members. *The Rag Coat, Chrysanthemum,* and *The Secret of the Peaceful Warrior* remind us why some of us feel we don't belong, while *Amos and Boris* and *Peach and Blue* show us the importance of friendship among those who are different.

**I encourage family participation** from the beginning of the school year, when I host Parent Orientation, I suggest ways they can participate in their children's learning and provide a snapshot of our classroom routines. I answer their questions and concerns and provide information about the range of normal development throughout early childhood. Diversity in its many forms is celebrated when I talk about learning styles and rates of growth. I am grateful to have two years to nurture these relationships with families, and it is important to me to help parents grow in their knowledge and understanding of how children learn. Parents participate in our classroom in various ways. Rick gives spelling pretests, Lorna plays math games, and Paula guides students in a sewing project, to name a few examples. Every Friday morning, parents spend time in our classroom for Family DEAR—reading silently alongside their children and sharing what they read. We invite families for learning celebrations such as our poetry tea party, when students read favorite poems and we enjoy an elegant tea. Regular and enthusiastic support from parents is important to our learning community in richly abundant ways. ∎

Certainly, Dr. Stahlman is a master teacher who embodies the characteristics of a Nationally Board Certified teacher. She did not develop into these characteristics overnight, however. Dr. Stahlman was once a novice teacher, as you will soon be, who developed her "art" over time, with persistence and mentoring, and with the philosophy that learning to teach well is a life-long process.

## Stahlman's Classroom

After you have read Dr. Stahlman's reflections on her students, class, and practice, talk with each other and determine how Dr. Stahlman demonstrates the National Board's five core propositions.

*1.* Teachers are committed to students and their learning:

2. Teachers know the subjects they teach and how to teach those subjects to students:

*3.* Teachers are responsible for managing and monitoring student learning:

*4.* Teachers think systematically about their practice and learn from experience:

*5.* Teachers are members of learning communities:

How does Dr. Stahlman challenge herself as a learner?

# Case Study 12.2

Anne Hanson

Anne Hanson is a National Board Certified Teacher in Early Adolescence/English Language Arts. She has lectured and written extensively on writing and the brain and is the author of *Write Brain Write*, brain-friendly strategies for teachers, *Visual Writing*, strategies for students writing under "demand writing" high-stakes test pressure, and *Thin Veils*, a young adult novel, about teens caught up in deadly dieting. As you read through Ms. Hanson's vignette below, consider how her beliefs and practices are different than Dr. Stahlman's experiences. As a National Board Certified Teacher, how does Ms. Hanson define her "art" of teaching?

## Student by Student: Looking into a High School Classroom

**Students**—The majority of my seventh hour class is intelligent and affluent. Today's five absentees are at the US Open golf tournament. There are five Spanish children in the class, among them, Duvelsa, at poverty level, and Maria L. mainstreamed from the ESL program. Maria has asked me not to call on her unless she raises her hand, and I have obliged her, because I see that she works hard to read, write, and listen, and I want her to feel comfortable within her new class. In the beginning of the year I had grouped students based on information I'd gathered from my interest survey responses. The compiled information helped me form groups that reflected the learning styles plus diverse interests. I reorganized students for the second half of the school year by creating groups that combined students who represented performance differences: leaders versus followers; speakers versus (shy) listeners; high achievers versus low. Students had grown very comfortable with the original seating arrangement, so I was pleased with the maturity they displayed when I regrouped them.

**Planning and Teaching**—Today the language arts curriculum objective was: "Students will write an opinion essay based on a specific prompt." The biggest weakness in last year's responses was the students' inability to support their opinions with effective reasoning. My comment in my last year's plan book was: *"Take more time! Students are jumping from opinions to facts. Ugh."* I reviewed sample essays and noted that students who had written poor essays, had typically jumped from stating their opinions to stating facts without expressing the reasoning they had used: i.e., what conclusions had they drawn from the facts to form their opinions?

I decided to demonstrate to students that people draw "small" conclusions from facts through reasoning, and that it is these "mini-conclusions" that form the ultimate conclusions: opinions. This lesson was critical. To be effective communicators, my students must be able to express themselves in a clear, organized manner and demonstrate the reasoning behind any thesis or opinion statements they make. The fourth quarter assesses oral and written persuasion. I wanted my students to demonstrate skill in supporting their written opinions, so that they would be able to effectively *persuade* others to *accept* their opinions. I prepared a lesson with structured activities that intentionally provided students time—necessary to think and to reason. With their notes as their tools and my modeling as their guide, students were to build their understanding of how that often "missed step"—reasoning—occurs.

Materials used in this lesson were varied. Students looked and listened as I shared photographs of my visit to Mount Saint Helens and my story of fear and awe as I drove up thousands of feet to witness stark, lifeless terrain, once beautiful. Students viewed a video on the eruption of Mount Saint Helens and completed a quiz, which I handed out before each day's viewing. To further ensure their attention to details they might later wish to use, students were encouraged to take notes, "stats that astound." I invited students to "surf the net" for information on Mount Saint Helens. Each group had at least one printout of information, distributed from a general pool.

To create an atmosphere conducive to the third quarter's focus on report and **expository** writing, I had redefined my classroom as a media center. As such, we became newspaper and (eventually for oral presentations) television writers. Students first learned the language of advertisements. They had created ads that required them to sell "hard-to-sell" products like, for example, half a car. After viewing the video, students created an advertisement that answered the question: "Should there be tourism at Mount Saint Helens?" Students needed to effectively "sell" their opinions through effective use of copy, layout, and slogan.

Having experienced the challenge of selling their opinion, I shifted them from the advertising department to the editorial department of a newspaper. They read an excerpt from the book, *MOUNT SAINT HELENS*, "A Long Sleep Comes to an End," to gather more facts—as competent newspaper columnists would. I used the article to review with students how to identify and record critical facts and ideas. I set up lines to the right of each paragraph, which I numbered. I modeled for them by telling them I had summarized the last paragraph in six words. I challenged them to silently read it and guess my words. Students were able to interpret the figurative "sleep," identify my six words, "Mount Saint Helens might erupt again," and outstripped me with five: "The mountain might erupt again." Having transformed the task into a game, students eagerly summarized each paragraph, thereby creating another resource of facts regarding the eruption. I shifted my students' attention to the main objective: writing an opinion essay. I used the framework of an editorial page of a fictitious newspaper, *The Hanson Haven Gazette.*

To prepare for this lesson, the following homework was assigned: "Think about the facts of the eruption and the meaning of Voltaire's quote from the video: 'Men may argue, but nature acts.'" Specific procedures included a demonstration of the logical evolution of forming an opinion. The goal on the board (which is read each day by a student) stated: "Today we *review* our facts, *draw* conclusions and *form* opinions for our editorials." Students were directed to produce all their resources on the eruption and to share responses to the first part of their homework assignment, within their groups first, and then aloud. Together as co-learners, we discussed the facts about the eruption that seemed to be most important. After reaching consensus regarding a fact's essential value, I wrote those chosen on the board for all to copy.

My next step was to elicit responses to the second, challenging part of their homework assignment: "What did Voltaire's quote mean?" As for facts, I invited students to share their ideas in small groups first; this time, because I know that even if they intuitively understand the meaning, students might not be able to express it without first hearing the language from peers. My students uniformly attempt to explain the meaning, using responses that are repetitive, basic, yet admirable. Very young people are willingly tackling a formidable challenge, and they are doing a commendable job creating "broad, global" explanations.

Having compiled our facts about the eruption and our list of conclusions regarding the meaning of Voltaire's quote, I ask students to place a star next to one of the conclusions they might draw from the facts on the board. I do this to provide students time to reflect on which makes most sense to each of them. Later on, I invite students to make explicit connections between the conclusions and the facts on the board: "I see a real connection . . . Who can explain how I made that connection?" Having suggested they connect, students realize they *do* connect. Ultimately Alex T. and Alex S. state that all the conclusions created for the quote apply to the facts. I am comfortable with their demonstrated awareness that facts and conclusions "connect" and decide to show them the essay prompt that I hid under the partially lowered screen. I had not revealed it prior to this moment, because I know that, upon hearing a prompt's task, students often dive into its directive—without listening to important suggestions tied to successful completion of the task.

I am extremely satisfied when, upon revealing the prompt, students acknowledge that there are, indeed, three possible responses—i.e., the winner is man, nature, or no one. I model how facts plus reasoning (through small, drawn conclusions) form an opinion. I use a source I know they will relate to: "The Simpsons." Students listen, engage, and giggle as I explain how facts from the show help me draw small conclusions that I ultimately use to form my opinion that: "TV, as seen in 'The Simpsons,' does not support family values."

Next, I asked students to recognize that while our conclusions on the board "fit" the facts about Mount Saint Helen, they fit out of coincidence. They were really statements on our interpretations of a quote's meaning. I challenged them to examine the facts and draw more conclusions that, now, relate to their opinions about the winner in the figurative battle between man and nature. This class offered several, among them: "Nature destroys what man creates. Nature destroys, but man can rebuild. Man suffers when nature acts." These excellent, relevant statements were written on the board below the original conclusions.

For homework, students were asked to map out their opinions, draw conclusions, and facts regarding the prompt. This assignment would help me assess how well this lesson worked, inclusive of modeling. The lesson had challenged students to *read* through resources and *speak* and *listen* to each other for the purpose of gathering and selecting data. The final proof would be in how well the lesson influenced student ability to synthesize data to write opinion essays.

Results from this lesson exceeded my expectations. The next day, using their mapped brainstorms, students worked on rough drafts for 20 minutes. At that point I facilitated a peer-conference activity. Peer-teams were directed to read each other's drafts-in-progress, draw straight lines under opinion statements, wavy lines under statements representing drawn conclusions (which by now I interchangeably referred to as "reasons"), and circles around at least two facts. They returned drafts to the owners only after signing their name and writing a (required) comment that identified which, if any, components were still missing. This written comment emphasized missing components that were already identified by lines or circles—conspicuous by their absence. Students revised and continued drafts, completing the writing process to final copy. Last year, students had written rough drafts, which I took home to examine, addressing weaknesses in whole group instruction the next day. My decision to model the process of forming opinions *first*, gave me better drafts from the outset. Further, as I walked around observing drafts *annotated with lines and circles*, I easily identified which students had used all the elements, and which peer partners had correctly identified and distinguished one element from another. Each draft provided information about two students. I doubled my understanding of all my students, their strengths and weaknesses, and was better able to identify who required direct intervention via teacher conferencing during the process. I do not believe these stronger drafts would have been written had I not planned the whole group instruction lesson that invited my students to think for themselves—and to think along with me—about important questions about facts, about nature and man, about making connections. I had no idea what the results would be. My students might have struggled and come up with little. Believing as I do that teachers are researchers, I was prepared to lead them to possible answers, offering possible interpretations of the quote, if necessary.

**Reflection**—This entire lesson immersed students in language arts. Students were able to *read* from resources to gather pertinent information. They were able to *listen* and *speak* to each other and me: examining and evaluating facts about the eruption; deciding through consensus which were most important; creating their plans for success. Students impressively analyzed and interpreted Voltaire's quote, developing responses that gradually helped them discover how to draw their own conclusions from facts. Thus prepared, the lesson empowered students to *write* outstanding opinion essays.

I am particularly proud of how diligently my students worked to draw meaning from Voltaire's quote, a challenge worthy of high school students. I believe that it was the very fact that the challenge was so high that students worked so diligently. Students love challenges. If they are wrapped in a package of appropriately engaging materials, students rise to the occasion.

Could I have started the assignment with: "Summarize the main ideas in the excerpt, 'A Long Sleep Comes to an End'"? No. The sequence in which the materials were used was every bit as important as the selection of materials themselves. And what could be more engaging to seventh graders than a monster volcano eruption? I packaged the ultimate objective within the framework of a newspaper—students first learned how to sell ideas through advertisements, then their opinions through the editorial page. I gained their interest, and they gained important skills. Whether called a package, a gimmick, a framework, or schema, when teachers invest the time to design "it" to teach an objective, "it" becomes meaningful. The lesson influenced success beyond third quarter's focus on exposition to the fourth quarter's focus on persuasion. It armed students with the tool of reasoning so necessary to express and effectively argue opinions.

**Classroom Glimpse**

**Think About It**

The art of teaching is a complex craft, illustrated through the two vignettes that you have just read. Consider what components of quality instruction you hope to integrate into your own future classroom. Will you have "what it takes" to be Nationally Board-certified?

**Classroom Glimpse**

A big teaching moment was when I modeled the three elements of forming an opinion, showing it as a cycle to defend at any point. Students were totally engaged. They followed my logic and reasoning and they "got it." At the rough draft, lines, and circles stage, I saw notable success from all students. Those who missed a step had a written comment and graphic indicators from peers to help them correct their oversights *before* they moved on to future drafts.

Uniform, required note-taking seldom occurs in my classes; when it does, students know: This is important. I do not prepare notes in advance, presenting them on transparencies for all classes to copy. Notes generate within each class as my students and I discover together what is important. Our discussions, rich with open-ended questions, produce our authentic notes. After analyzing this segment I felt as if I had played the role of a coach leading her team to a big game. My students knew I was part of their team, learned the key plays, and when the whistle blew, they executed brilliantly. ∎

**Group Talk**

### Hanson's Classroom

After you have read Ms. Hanson's reflections on her students, class and practice talk with each other and determine how Ms. Hanson demonstrates the National Boards five core propositions.

*1.* Teachers are committed to students and their learning:

*2.* Teachers know the subjects they teach and how to teach those subjects to students:

*3.* Teachers are responsible for managing and monitoring student learning:

*4.* Teachers think systematically about their practice and learn from experience:

*5.* Teachers are members of learning communities:

How does Ms. Hanson challenge herself as a learner?

How is her instruction and learning climate different—and the same—as that of Dr. Stahlman?

# Professional Development

As you have read, National Board certification embodies what is the very best in the "art" of teaching. But how will you, as a novice, develop the skills needed to become a master teacher yourself? Much of this journey will depend on your openness to reflect honestly on your practice, and your involvement with appropriate and high quality professional development. Depending on your state's requirements, active participation in professional development opportunities may also provide one avenue for your recertification as a teacher.

Research, insights from practice, and common sense converge around the understanding that skilled teachers have a significant impact on student learning. Helping teachers develop the knowledge and skills they need begins with rigorous teacher training programs. Subsequently, effective professional development helps teachers continue enhancing their knowledge and skills throughout their careers (Little & McLaughlin, 1993; Louis, et al., 1996). Effective professional development opportunities:

1. Focus on the intersection of content and pedagogy
   - Focus on improving students' achievement and understanding
   - Include opportunities for practice, research, and reflection
   - Provide time for teachers to observe other's practice
2. Are embedded in educators' jobs and take place during the school hours
3. Are sustained over time (at minimum for a least one year)
4. Include and foster elements of collegiality and collaboration among teachers and principals

Raising student achievement requires even our best teachers to reflect deeply on their current teaching, refining what works and abandoning or changing what does not. Professional development programs that support continuous reflection and improvement are critical to increasing student success. These programs also have another benefit to the teacher— that of becoming a member of a professional community. This in turn, increases the likelihood that teachers will not only strengthen their practice but also stay in their profession.

The following promising professional development practices have been described by NCTAF (1996). These examples reflect the features that are described above. Which one of these practices would be most appealing to you?

- **Teacher Networks**—Networks provide teachers with a supportive professional community beyond the school building. They typically are organized around specific subject matter, and seek to deepen teachers' understanding of content as well as their facility with new teaching strategies. Some networks are national in scope, while others cover only one state or region. Members stay in touch via electronic bulletin boards.

- **Joint Work**—Joint work refers to shared responsibility for tasks such as team teaching, curriculum writing, assessment development, or other jobs that create interdependence and cooperation among teachers. Joint work promotes on-the-job learning because it facilitates productive exchanges among teachers and reflection about practice.

- **Collaborations Between Schools and Colleges**—A number of organizations such as the Carnegie Corporation and the Pew Charitable Trusts are actively promoting partnerships between colleges and K-12 schools. These cooperative programs not only help teachers to gain access to new knowledge, they enable college professors to develop new understandings of how to teach their students.

- **Professional Development Schools**—These schools, which are roughly analogous to teaching hospitals, are a special form of collaboration between K-12 schools and higher education. While much attention has been given to their role in pre-service education, they also are playing an important role in ongoing professional development, bringing both novice and experienced teachers together with university faculty to improve practice.

- **Teacher Research Projects**—Increasing numbers of teachers are conducting research in their classrooms and schools in cooperation with their colleagues and university faculty. While some of these research projects are defined by academic interests, many are directed at problems identified by teachers themselves. The major activity in teacher research is the collection and analysis of data for the purpose of understanding and improving practice.

- **Mentor/Induction Programs**—Through mentoring programs, highly experienced teachers play a leadership role in guiding the activities of other teachers. Mentoring programs often match beginning teachers with veterans, enabling the veterans to share their knowledge and expertise.

- **Peer Coaching**—Like mentoring, peer coaching allows teachers to build more collegial relationships, share their experiences, and assume more responsibility for the quality of teaching. Coaching programs usually involve teachers on the same professional level. Teachers observe each other's classrooms and offer feedback on practices and behaviors.

What kinds of professional development opportunities do teachers in your area have access to? Figure 12.2. **Professional Development Interview** provides you with the opportunity to determine what types of professional learning are available within your own community.

## Professional Organizations

**Think About It**

Which organization might be the most appropriate for you? Use the activity in Figure 12.4. **Exploring Professional Organizations** to determine some potential groups that could provide you with invaluable resources as you develop professionally.

In their research of craftspeople, Lave and Wenger (1991) use the phrase "community of practice" to describe the behavior of groups of people who share a common craft. Professional organizations provide this opportunity for teachers. They contain structures that allow members to participate in the professional dialogue and build new craft. Professional organizations nurture newcomers and provide structures for emerging leaders to shape new directions. Professional organizations collect the wisdom of the community and influence practice through publications, conferences, and training in specialized areas within teaching.

Professional organizations reflect the changing needs of the teaching force. Professional organizations enable all phases of teachers to find new ideas and energy and collegial affiliation. In short, professional organizations provide a way for the species of modern educators to flourish.

Figure 12.3. **Professional Teaching Organizations** provides a list as a resource for new professionals to consider. Whether you are an early childhood education or a biology teacher, there is an organization that will help you develop as a professional educator.

**Figure 12.2 ↓ Professional Development Interview**

*Directions:* Teachers have access to a variety of professional development opportunities, most of which is coordinated by their schools or districts. What professional development opportunities are available in your communities? Which are most effective—and least useful for teachers?

Teacher's name

Teacher's level

How long has the teacher been teaching?                    How long at this level?

What professional development requirements does this teacher's school or district expect? Are these opportunities tied to recertification?


What types of professional development has the teacher participated in most recently? What were some of the topics?


What was the most useful professional development opportunity that this teacher has participated in? What made it so beneficial?


What was the least useful professional development? Why was it less helpful to this teacher?


According to this teacher, what is the most effective format for professional development?


What kinds of professional development does the district or school provide for novice teachers?


What *should* the school or district provide to teachers to enable them to develop professionally?

## Figure 12.3 ↓ Professional Teaching Organizations

- ❑ American Alliances for Health, Physical Education, Recreation, and Dance
  *www.aahperd.org/*
- ❑ American Council on the Teaching of Foreign Languages
  *www.actfl.org*
- ❑ Association for Childhood Education International
  *www.acei.org*
- ❑ Association for Computer in Mathematics and Science Teaching
  *www.aace.org*
- ❑ Association for Education Communications and Technology
  *www.aect.org/default.asp*
- ❑ Association for Supervision and Curriculum Development
  *www.ascd.org/portal/site/ascd*
- ❑ Council for Exceptional Children
  *www.cec.sped.org/*
- ❑ International Reading Association
  *www.reading.org/*
- ❑ Kappa Delta Pi
  *www.kdp.org/*
- ❑ National Art Education Association
  *www.naea-reston.org/*
- ❑ National Association for Music Education
  *www.menc.org/*
- ❑ National Association for the Education of Young Children
  *www.naeyc.org/*
- ❑ National Association of Biology Teachers
  *www.nabt.org*
- ❑ National Association of Geoscience Teachers
  *www.nagt.org/nagt/index.html*
- ❑ National Board for Professional Teaching Standards
  *www.nbpts.org/*
- ❑ National Council for the Social Studies
  *www.ncss.org/*
- ❑ National Council of Teachers of English
  *www.ncte.org/*
- ❑ National Council of Teachers of Mathematics
  *www.nctm.org/*
- ❑ National Reading Conference
  *www.nrconline.org/*
- ❑ National Science Teachers Association
  *www.nsta.org/*
- ❑ Teachers of English to Speakers of Other Languages
  *www.tesol.org/s_tesol/index.asp*

*Other Organizations:*

**Figure 12.4  ↓ Exploring Professional Organizations**

*Directions:* Professional organizations offer teachers excellent opportunities for growth and collegial interactions. Please select one of the organizations listed on the **Professional Teaching Organizations** chart and do an in-depth examination of the benefits the organization provides.

Name of the organization:

Reason you chose this organization to examine.


What is the organization's mission?


What benefits are available to members?


What resources does the organization provide?


Does this organization offer professional development to teachers?


Does the organization have any journals? If so, what are they?


List three other publications produced by the organization.


Does the organization create policy papers? If so, give examples of two recent topics.


Are there standards for teachers and/or students associated with this organization? Give an example of the standards.


What is the cost of joining this organization? Is there a student membership?


Is there a regional or state affiliate for your area of the country? If so, what activities or conferences does this affiliate offer?

### Professional Development

All teachers engage in some form of professional development, particularly that which is provided by the school or district. Based on your interviews with teachers, decide as a group which kinds of professional development were beneficial to teachers in your community.

First, collate information from your interviews to complete the **Development Comparison Chart.** Then, discuss the following with your group:

- What were the most common topics for professional development in your community? Why do you think that these topics were so popular with schools?
- Why specific opportunities were made available to novice teachers?
- What topics did teachers find the most useful? The least useful?
- What format for professional development did teachers find to be the most effective?
- What format was the least effective? Why?

Based on your findings, create a draft policy for effective professional development in your future school.

### Development Comparison Chart

**Professional Development Consensus**

| Common Topics | Effective Professional Development | Ineffective Professional Development |
|---|---|---|
|  |  |  |
|  |  |  |
|  |  |  |
|  |  |  |

From this information, what types of professional development opportunities are *most* appreciated by teachers?

_____

From this information, what types of professional development opportunities are *least* appreciated by teachers?

# Looking Forward

Becoming a teacher is a major life choice. Very few professions demand so much of a person's skill, time, energy and creativity. While this multifaceted career offers only modest monetary compensation, the impact one has on human lives is priceless.

As a *scientist* and a *scholar,* teachers must understand the theories and philosophies that underlie their profession as a whole and their practice in particular. They must be ever mindful about the growing knowledge base in child development and student learning. They must be able to articulate their beliefs and practices on many audiences.

As *craftsman,* teachers must acquire and employ a repertoire of instructional methods and strategies, yet remain critical and reflective about their own practice. Professional teachers continue to refine and strengthen their practice on a daily basis.

As an *advocate,* accomplished teachers often make difficult and principled choices. Every day teachers must exercise careful judgments—for the choices and decisions affect their students' lives in small and profound ways. Every day a teacher goes to work, he or she honors the complex nature of the educational mission to influence students' lives, to build student confidence, to provide a role model for the passion of learning. While teachers employ technical knowledge and skill, they must be ever mindful of teaching's ethical dimensions. Teachers care! They care about their students as individuals and as part of an ever-evolving complex community. Our primary mission is to foster the development of skills, dispositions, and understanding, while responding thoughtfully to a wide range of human needs and conditions

As *politician,* the professional teacher has the responsibility to question long-held traditional structures and practices. They must redefine, invent, and test new approaches. As agents of the public interest in a democracy, teachers through their work contribute to the dialogue about preserving and improving society, and they initiate future citizens into this ongoing public discourse.

As *artist,* teachers' professional responsibilities focus on instructing the unique students in their care, while they also participate in wider activities within the school and in partnership with parents and the community.

On the following pages, a teacher shares his motivation to teach, and the impact that a great teachers has had on his own professional decisions. Would you describe this teacher as a scientist, craftsman, or artist? Or perhaps a combination of all?

## Talking to Teachers—The Motivation to Teach

It's hard to find any American who isn't touched in some way by public schools, whether that person is a student, parent, taxpayer, employer, or any combination of the above. Why do individuals choose to become a teacher? Perhaps because of the rewards that come from helping students realize their dreams.

Larry Hurt is the 1999 Indiana Teacher of the Year. He teaches at Ben Davis High School in Indianapolis, Indiana. What rewards does Larry gain by teaching?

I entered Mrs. Burton's class one day excited about a television program on optical art that I had seen the night before. After hearing all the details, she very gently said, "Why don't you tell the rest of the class about this?" After an initial wave of panic, I agreed. Everyone gathered around, and I very carefully described the exciting new method of painting I had seen. I then demonstrated a small version of the process involved. Whether they were inspired or bored by this mini-lesson, I do not know. I do know that it stayed with me for years as an anchor moment—a defining experience that received a great deal of thought and reflection.

Virginia Burton taught me about great teaching by *being* a great teacher. What made her great? She was passionate about learning, about kids, about school, and about life. Whether we were discussing a new drawing technique or the debut of a new song, she was present, totally engaged, and always excited about learning. She was not our buddy or peer, she was our teacher. Mrs. Burton taught us about art, about standing up for things that matter, about taking risks, and about imagining our futures. I felt empowered in her class to try, to succeed, to occasionally fail, and to try again. She taught us about the importance of craft, the power of good questions, and the joy of community. When a member of our class was killed in an auto accident, she taught us about grieving and going on, challenging areas of discussion for adolescents who believed they were indestructible.

I did not become a teacher because I love kids, though I do love kids and I enjoy being a part of their growth to young adulthood. I did not become a teacher because I love art, though I do love art, a subject that still excites me and enriches my life. I became a teacher because I am irrationally passionate about learning! When presented with a new or intriguing topic, I begin to search for information. Books or web sites lead to links, links lead to more articles, and articles lead to discussions! If I discover something new or interesting, I want to discuss it with everyone I know. Units of instruction are not times to deliver facts; they are opportunities for sharing amazing things. Teaching is my vocation and art is my vehicle for learning. I am always "becoming" an educator; it is a journey, not a destination. I have spent thirty years becoming a teacher, and each year I invent, reinvent, and reorganize my thoughts and processes. As students and their world change, I change.

Mrs. Burton's unwritten curriculum broke through all of the chaos and turmoil of high school life. After transcripts, tests, interpersonal struggles, and insecurities had passed, her core message to her students remained: you are loved, you can achieve great things, and you must NEVER stop learning. Her enthusiasm was infectious and her belief in lifelong learning was authentic. She taught me well, and I learned. For thirty years, my philosophy of teaching has been grounded in one word: PASSION. My passion for teaching and learning drives everything I do. Whether I am working on a standards writing team, leading a discussion, participating in a student critique, speaking to a community organization, or working with a student whose world is falling apart, there is no room for a disconnected or dispassionate approach.

Quality teaching is a story that is handed down from generation to generation. Within every classroom like Mrs. Burton's, there are students like me who are paying attention to every word. The style, the love of learning, the excitement, and the depth of the vocation are communicated and clearly received. Most great teachers I know have an inspiring ever-present mentor like Mrs. Burton in their past. These inspiring guides help us discover the potential teachers within ourselves. Thanks to Mrs. Burton, I decided when I was 17 years old that I would be a teacher. My decision was as clear then as it is now. I love teaching, and I will be an educator until the day I die. I continue to teach because there is so much more to learn and so many stories to be told!

**Think About It**

A magical mentor inspired many of the teachers who have shared their stories. Think about those teachers who inspired you. What qualities did they possess that you want to emulate?

## Research Citations

Calkins, L. M. (1994). *The art of teaching writing.* Portsmouth, NH: Heinemann.

Lave, J., & Wenger E. (1991). *Situated learning: Legitimate peripheral participation.* Cambridge, NY: Cambridge University.

Little, J. W., & McLaughlin, M. (Eds.). (1993). *Teachers' work: Individuals, colleagues and contexts.* New York, NY: Teachers College.

Louis, K., Marks, H., & Kruse, S. (1996). Teacher's professional community and restructuring schools. *American Educational Research Journal, 33*(4), 757–798.

*National Board for Professional Teaching Standards (1987).* www.nbpts.org/about/coreprops.cfm).

National Commission on Teaching and America's Future (NCTAF) (1996). *What matters most: Teaching for America's future.* New York, NY: NCTAF.

Steffy, B., Wolfe, M., Pasche, S., & Enz, B. 2000. *The life cycle of the Career Teacher.* Thousand Oaks, CA: Corwin.

# Index